THE COLOR OF SCHOOL REFORM

THE COLOR OF SCHOOL REFORM

RACE, POLITICS, AND THE CHALLENGE OF URBAN EDUCATION

Jeffrey R. Henig

Richard C. Hula

Marion Orr

Desiree S. Pedescleaux

PRINCETON UNIVERSITY PRESS   PRINCETON AND OXFORD

Third printing, and first paperback printing, 2001
Paperback ISBN 0-691-08897-7

*The Library of Congress has cataloged the cloth edition
of this book as follows*

The color of school reform : race, politics,
and the challenge of urban education / Jeffrey R. Henig . . . [et al.].
p.   cm.
ISBN 0-691-01634-8 (cloth : alk. paper)
1. Education, Urban—Social aspects—United States.
2. Education, Urban—Political aspects—United States.
3. Children of minorities—Education—United States.
4. Educational change—United States.
I. Henig, Jeffrey R., 1951–   .
LC5131.C586   1999
370'.9173'2—dc21   99-11258

This book has been composed in Caledonia

Printed on acid-free paper. ∞

www.pup.princeton.edu

Printed in the United States of America

3   5   7   9   10   8   6   4

To Clarence N. Stone

MENTOR, COLLEAGUE, FRIEND, AND, MOST OF ALL,

TRAILBLAZER IN THE STUDY OF URBAN POLITICS

Contents

Figures

Tables

Acknowledgments

MORE THAN MOST, this work is a collaboration involving many more people than those whose names appear on its cover. The book grew out of a larger research project, Civic Capacity and Urban Education, examining the politics of urban education reform in eleven cities, including Atlanta, Baltimore, Boston, Denver, Detroit, Houston, Los Angeles, Pittsburgh, St. Louis, San Francisco, and Washington, D.C. We thank the National Science Foundation for its generous support of this project. The research team was a wild and wooley group held in loose check only by the steady hand of Clarence N. Stone. Some were in it from beginning to end; some joined us along the way, and some dropped by the wayside, but all contributed to a rich and sometimes frenzied intellectual environment that certainly helped to shape our thinking. They include: Susan Clarke, Mara Cohen, Al DiGaetano, Kathryn Doherty, Bari Anhalt Erlichson, Barbara Ferman, Luis Fraga, Whitney Grace, Fernando Guerra, Rodney Hero, Connie Hill, John Hutcheson, Jr., Byran Jackson, Richard Jelier, Valerie Johnson, Bryan Jones, Cheryl Jones, Robin Jones, Stephen Kidd, Mark Kugler, Tom Longoria, John Portz, Carol Pierannunzi, Timothy Ross, Mark Schauer, Lana Stein, Heather Strickland, Mara Sydney, Marta Tellado, and Jorge Ruiz de la Vasco. Others who gave helpful feedback at various stages of the process are Christopher Foreman, Marilyn Gittell, Jennifer Hochschild, Katharine McFate, Michael Mintrom, Carol Pierannunzi, Wilbur Rich, Hanes Walton, Jr., Fred Wirt, and John Witte. Although these individuals were invaluable assets, responsibility for the writing of this book rests entirely with the authors.

Finally, we wish to thank our spouses—Robin, Catherine, Ramona, and Dwight—and families. We owe debts to them that cannot be repaid. They have endured the disruptions of family that the writing of a book inevitably demands. Without their encouragement, reassurance, and, most important, love, this book would not have been possible.

THE COLOR OF SCHOOL REFORM

CHAPTER ONE

Civic Capacity, Race, and Education in
Black-Led Cities

BLUNT ATTACKS on the quality of American public education mask a more pernicious problem. While many schools are delivering a mediocre product that sells their students short, for some children, especially those living in large central cities with high minority populations and heavy concentrations of the poor, the tale is much more tragic. Broad economic changes are putting a higher and higher premium on educational attainment, yet these students languish in decrepit school buildings where many of the teachers lack the skills and training they should have, the resources to meet their special challenges, and/or the enthusiasm and faith that might once have led them to consider education their mission and not simply their job. Urban school districts are twice as likely as nonurban districts to hire uncertified teachers, and more than three out of four students in high-poverty schools within urban districts fail to score at even "basic" reading levels on national tests.[1]

Schools and teachers are not responsible for the economic and family problems that are the sources of the deepest indignities afflicting many inner-city children. Yet schools, historically, are the public institution that we have most relied upon to heal the wounds imposed by inequalities in more private spheres. Sensitive portrayals, such as those by Jonathan Kozol and Jean Anyon, make palpable the human costs when our schools succumb to those same inequalities.[2] If the measure of a society is how well it takes care of its neediest,[3] the condition and performance of our inner-city schools are unlikely to earn us a passing grade.

The continued erosion of inner-city education is more troubling and perplexing in the context of the expectation, which some have held, that political and demographic changes well under way would set the stage for positive reforms. From the mid-1960s through the mid-1970s, rapid racial change

---

[1] "Quality Counts '98," *Education Week* special report (January 1998).

[2] Jonathan Kozol, *Savage Inequalities* (New York: Crown, 1991); Jean Anyon, *Ghetto Schooling: A Political Economy of Urban Educational Reform* (New York: Teachers College Press, 1997).

[3] The allusion is to Pearl S. Buck, who put it this way: "The test of a civilization is in the way it cares for its helpless members" *In My Several Worlds* (New York: Day, 1954).

and the political mobilization of black Americans created turmoil,[4] uncertainty, and anxiety in many large central cities, but at the same time it raised expectations among analysts, activists, and citizens who believed that racial turnover in positions of power and authority would unlock the last door to genuine opportunity and advancement.[5] According to Karnig and Welch, "some believed that [black elected officials] would be 'supermen and superwomen' who could cure the ills of three centuries overnight."[6]

Schools, traditionally seen in American culture as the "great equalizer," were a special focus of attention. Research showing that teachers' low expectations preordained some children to become poor students gave a sharper edge to the demand by some black activists that white teachers were a part of the problem facing inner-city schools.[7] In the vitriolic battles over community control of schools in New York City, for example, leaflets demanded "that only black and Puerto Rican teachers are employed in Our (sic) school. . . . All outsiders-teachers (baby sitters) must be released as soon as Negro or Puerto Rican educators are available."[8] An Urban League Director in Atlanta proclaimed, "I have always believed that if you could ever achieve equity in the administration of the school system, then it would improve the chances of black kids getting a better education."[9]

Carmichael and Hamilton, in a controversial and widely read articulation of the goals of the black power movement, were wary of the notion that changing the color of urban bureaucrats would make much difference unless it was accompanied by racial turnover at even higher levels of political power. Yet they, too, identified racial transition in the levers of control over public schools as a critical prerequisite to progressive reform.

---

[4] One result of the civil rights struggle of the 1960s was the replacement of the term "Negro" by "black." By the late 1980s, the term "African American" began to appear more frequently. Good arguments have been made for the use of both "black" and "African American," as each suggests different emphases in regards to racial and global identity and the American experience. In addition, the black/African-American community in the United States remains divided over its own preference. On balance, then, we have chosen to use the two terms interchangeably. For a discussion of racial nonmenclature, see Ruth W. Grant and Marion Orr, "Language, Race and Politics: From 'Black' to 'African-American,'" *Politics & Society* 24 (June 1996): 137–53; Ben Martin, "From Negro to Black to African American: The Power of Names and Naming," *Political Science Quarterly* 106 (1991): 83–107; and Robert C. Smith, *Racism in the Post-Civil Rights Era* (Albany: State University of New York Press, 1995), 100–104.

[5] See, for example, Mervyn Dymally, ed., *The Black Politician: His Struggle for Power* (Belmont, CA: Wadsworth, 1971).

[6] Albert K. Karnig and Susan Welch, *Black Representation and Urban Policy* (Chicago: University of Chicago, 1980), 13.

[7] William Ryan, *Blaming the Victim* (New York: Vintage, 1976).

[8] Excerpted in *Confrontation at Ocean-Hill Brownsville*, Maurice R. Berube and Marilyn Gittell, eds. (New York: Praeger 1969), 165–66.

[9] Gary Orfield and Carol Ashkinaze, *The Closing Door* (Chicago: University of Chicago Press, 1991), 110.

There can be no doubt that in today's world a thorough and comprehensive education is an absolute necessity. Yet it is obvious from the data that a not even minimum education is being received in most ghetto schools. White decision-makers have been running those schools with injustice, indifference and inadequacy for too long; the result has been an educationally crippled black child turned out into the labor market equipped to do little more than stand in welfare lines to receive his miserable dole.[10]

Survey research undertaken during that turbulent era suggests that the average black citizen shared this expectation that putting blacks in positions of political authority would lead to policies and practices more beneficial to black neighborhoods and families.[11]

Much of the existing literature on racial politics reflects the national political context in which African Americans' status as a racial minority has normally coincided with their status as a political minority. By the middle 1970s, however, a new black governing elite, presenting itself as a harbinger of fundamental change, had taken over the formal machinery of governance in several big cities. Attention was focused largely on general electoral offices—gains in city councils seats and the capturing of the mayoralty in some cities—but these shifts were also translated into administrative changes and staffing patterns within the schools and other key bureaucracies. Meier, Stewart, and England have shown that the presence of African-Americans on school boards was associated with the hiring of black administrators and teachers, and that their presence, in turn, was associated with policy consequences, such as less discriminatory assignment of minority students to dead-end vocational tracks.[12]

We believe that the dynamics and implications of racial politics may be quite different in black-led cities than in the nation, states, or other cities in which blacks remain minorities in the true sense of the word—where they constitute less than half of the politically mobilized electorate and where they have not yet gained full access to the levers of local governmental power. Where racial minorities lack formal political power, the absence of such formal power easily becomes the dominating focus. What happens when they finally hurdle across the barrier of formal power? This terrain has only recently been inhabited in American cities, and empirical research into its consequences is in its relative infancy.[13]

---

[10] Stokely Carmichael and Charles V. Hamilton, *Black Power* (New York: Vintage, 1967), 59.

[11] E.g., David O. Sears, "Black Attitudes Toward the Political System in the Aftermath of the Watts Insurrection," *Midwest Journal of Political Science* 13 (November 1969): 515–44.

[12] Kenneth J. Meier, Robert E. England, and Joseph Stewart, Jr., *Race, Class, and Education* (Madison: University of Wisconsin Press, 1989).

[13] One notable exception is Wilbur Rich, *Black Mayors and School Politics* (New York: Garland, 1996).

Central to our interest is the apparent anomaly that—in spite of hopes and expectations to the contrary—dramatic successes in the movement to put African Americans into the most important positions of formal local power and authority have not sufficed to bring about progressive educational reform on anywhere near as dramatic a scale. Indeed, by most accounts the situation is bleaker than ever. Nor is disappointment with the fruits of racial transition limited to the educational arena. Despite dramatic gains in access to government, Browning, Marshall, and Tabb note that "the value of the benefits gained is questioned by some; the momentum of the effort has greatly slowed, its successes have been uneven over time and from city to city, and its gains are subject to attack and reversal."[14]

Why—in spite of early optimism that racial transition among teachers, administrators, and policymakers would set the stage for urban education reform truly responsive to the needs of inner-city minorities—is there so little evidence of broad, sustained school reform in black-led cities? In this book, we trace the relationships among demographic change, political change, and education in four cities[15]—Atlanta, Baltimore, Detroit, and the District of Columbia—where the levers of the formal institutions of local governance have passed into the hands of African-American officials. Blacks became a majority of the population during the 1950s in the District of Columbia and by the 1970s in the other three cities. By the mid-1970s, black mayors had been elected in Atlanta, Detroit, and the District. Baltimore, the most recent of the four to turn into a predominantly black city, elected its first black mayor, Kurt Schmoke, in 1987. All four cities have African-American school superintendents, faculty and school administration are largely African Americans.

Our approach involves focusing on the governance regimes that have evolved in these cities, especially on the ways in which race has complicated or facilitated the development of civic capacity to undertake and sustain educational reforms that will help low-income and minority children. Although each city is different and has experienced spurts of enthusiasm for school reform, our four cities are all dealing with objective indicators of educational failure: high drop-out rates, poor performance on standardized tests, and employer dissatisfaction with graduates' basic skills.

In focusing on the role of race, we join others who have argued that Americans have been either too quick to declare that racial problems are an historical artifact of rapidly diminishing relevance to contemporary life or too timid to address openly an issue they realize to be potent, painful, and potentially

---

[14] Rufus P. Browning, Dale Rogers Marshall, and David H. Tabb, eds., *Racial Politics in American Cities*, 2d ed. (New York: Longman, 1997), 5.

[15] And their associated school districts.

divisive.[16] In our research, we have encountered numerous instances in which the behavior of local stakeholders has been affected by fears, suspicions, expectations, loyalties, tactics, and habits related to race.

Our analysis puts us at odds with much contemporary rhetoric about school reform, which systematically downplays the significance of race. Even if they do not ignore the issue of race entirely, some advocates of educational reform argue either that race has been displaced by class as a key variable in social behavior or that concerns about educational equity needlessly distract us from more pressing problems of educational quality.[17] While recognizing that the central problems facing black-led cities in many important ways parallel those in other urban school districts, which are typically overseen by whites, we argue that race plays an important confounding factor in the development of civic capacity; it would be foolish and counterproductive to overlook it. In the vivid, if not completely coherent, words of one Baltimore business executive with whom we spoke: "Everywhere you look there's some type of myriad aspect of race that creeps in. It's almost like the smoke sandwich is worse than the actual flame of the fire and it just gets into the heat so many ways."

While focusing on race and black-led cities, we also are interested in a broader question that transcends particular groups and settings: Why is meaningful school reform so elusive? Americans claim to care deeply about the quality of education their children receive, and the need for systemic school reform has had a prominent place on the agendas of elected leaders at least since the publication of *A Nation at Risk* in 1983. Why have we failed to make more progress?[18] Our research on racial politics within black-led cities developed in the context of a larger project on Civic Capacity and

[16] Most notably President Clinton, who in 1997 declared his intention to stimulate a national dialogue on race.

[17] The error of omission is more typical of articles written by and for educators; racial differences are recognized as a challenge facing teachers in the classroom, but there is a seeming reluctance to deal with race as it relates to interactions among major stake-holders such as superintendents, school boards, state legislators, and the business community. Among political analysts, the demotion of race to a peripheral status is sometimes more self-conscious. This was the basic position adopted by some radical critiques of education in capitalist societies (e.g., Samuel Bowles and Herbert Gintis, *Schooling in Capitalist America* (New York: Basic Books, 1976), who saw attention to race as deliberate distraction from more serious interests rooted in economic inequalities. Today's debates are more likely to be framed by neoconservatives who see concentration on racial inequalities and race-based politics as a deliberate distraction used by liberals, civil rights advocates, and professional educators to deflect attention into channels unlikely to generate meaningful change, e.g., Charles Murray, *Losing Ground* (New York: Basic Books, 1984); Chester E. Finn, *We Must Take Charge* (New York: Free Press, 1991).

[18] As elaborated upon below, we do not subscribe to the position that there has been no progress at all.

Urban Education in eleven central-city school districts.[19] These districts, which we will use for comparative purposes throughout, vary in demographic patterns, population trends, formal institutions, and informal political style. Four of these districts (Pittsburgh, Denver, Boston, and St. Louis) were predominantly white in population at the last U.S. census. Four (Los Angeles, San Francisco, Houston, and Denver) had large proportions of Hispanic and Asian residents (25% or higher). But in spite of their differences, these eleven districts share many similar problems in undertaking school reform. Moreover, the tendency to produce sporadic, ephemeral, and disjointed efforts is observable even in some wealthy, suburban communities.[20] Although some findings that we emphasize are particular to black-led cities and the African-American experience, others relate to general problems of coalition building across racial, ethnic, and economic lines, problems endemic to pluralistic societies like the United States.

The answer we craft to the broad question of why school reform is so elusive also puts us at odds with much of the commentary offered within the education community. Just as it overly de-emphasizes race, we argue that the contemporary school reform literature tends to de-emphasize the importance of politics and coalition building in determining the viability of reform endeavors. The de-emphasis of politics is manifested in an overfascination with educational ideas and organizational form. Many proponents of broad structural reforms seem to believe that the solution involves little more than bringing into town an entrepreneurial superintendent full of hot new concepts and a gunslinger's readiness to face down recalcitrant bureaucrats.[21] Similarly, the market metaphor that animates many proposals for systemic reform dismisses the importance of collective action in favor of a narrow

---

[19] Clarence Stone was the principal investigator, funded by the Education and Human Resources Directorate of the National Science Foundation (Grant Number RED 9350139). Bryan Jones and Jeffrey Henig were the co–principal investigators. Richard C. Hula, Marion Orr, and Desiree Pedescleaux were members of a large team of political scientists who carried out the field research in the eleven cities. The cities are Atlanta, Baltimore, Boston, Denver, Detroit, Houston, Los Angeles, Pittsburgh, St. Louis, San Francisco, and Washington, D.C. For a broad overview of the project, see Clarence N. Stone, "The Politics of Urban School Reform: Civic Capacity, Social Context, and the Intergroup Context" (paper presented at the annual meetings of the American Political Science Association, San Francisco, August 1996). Elements of the research design are described later in this chapter.

[20] Cheryl Jones and Connie Hill, "Strategy and Tactics in Subsystem Protection: The Politics of Education Reform in Montgomery County, Maryland," in *Changing Urban Education*, ed., Clarence Stone (Lawrence: University Press of Kansas, 1998).

[21] One manifestation of this viewpoint is the extraordinarily high turnover among urban school superintendents, whose average tenure lasts only about three years. More recently, this notion that reform can be readily imposed by a tough-minded outsider has been reflected in attempts by some states (and, in the case of Washington, D.C., the U.S. Congress) to disempower local school boards and superintendents in favor of externally imposed intervention teams.

focus on the behavior of individual households acting as rational consumers.[22] We argue, however, that there is no route *around* politics. To the contrary, the concept of "civic capacity," which lies at the core of our framework, suggests that the prospect for meaningful and sustainable reform depends upon lines of conflict and cooperation among a wide array of actors, both inside and outside the educational arena. Building civic capacity—the capacity collectively to set goals and effectively pursue them—calls for exercising political leadership and mastering political skills.

It is a premise of our analysis that locally crafted initiatives *can* make a difference. But local decision making takes place in the context of legal, political, and economic forces that generate real and powerful constraints. Recent analyses have underscored the limits of local governments, especially when they are expected to fashion policies targeted at their least advantaged residents.[23] We believe these limitations are substantial; indeed, we argue that they are in several ways *especially* substantial when overlaid with racial differences between cities and their surrounding jurisdictions. While suggesting that citizens and leaders in black-led cities can do more to meet the educational needs of their children, we also strongly believe that state and national officials and their constituencies continue to bear substantial responsibility for the poor condition of education in American cities. Indeed, the purpose of building coalitions for meaningful and sustainable school reform includes the need to assert and exercise influence in these larger jurisdictions.

THE CHALLENGE OF URBAN EDUCATION

American schools are widely regarded to be in serious need of reform. Since the National Commission on Excellence in Education warned that "the educational foundations of our society are presently being eroded by a rising tide of mediocrity that threatens our very survival as a nation and a people," numerous reports, articles, speeches, and campaign platforms have declared

[22] Jeffrey R. Henig, *Rethinking School Choice* (Princeton, NJ: Princeton University Press, 1994).

[23] Douglas Yates, *The Ungovernable City* (Cambridge, MA: MIT, 1977); Paul Peterson, *City Limits* (Chicago: University of Chicago, 1981); Paul Kantor, *The Dependent City* (Glenview, IL: Scott, Foresman & Company, 1988). Peterson emphasizes the limits on cities' capacity to undertake redistributive policies. In *City Limits*, he acknowledges that cities may differ in their treatment of education, so that it may be primarily redistributive or primarily developmental, depending upon the specifics of the case. But in his more recent work, he emphasizes that education is primarily a developmental policy. See his *The Price of Federalism* (Washington, D.C.: Brookings Institution, 1995), 65.

that the existing educational crisis requires dramatic action.[24] Much of that concern is expressed as a relatively undifferentiated lack of confidence in the performance of public schools. This portrayal of a broad systemic failure—Lieberman goes so far as to conjure an "autopsy" of public education—is linked to calls for radical structural change, including state takeovers, privatization, and school vouchers.[25] According to another influential analysis, the problem *is* the system; Chubb and Moe argue that the most fundamental causes of poor educational performance "are, in fact, the very institutions that are supposed to be solving the problem: the institutions of direct democratic control."[26]

Such broad-brushed critiques of American education, and such dismissals of all recent reform initiatives as symbolic or pitifully incremental, are convenient to conservative analysts because they bolster their claim that only a radical introduction of market forces can save education from the stifling confines of public bureaucracy, professional domination, and political manipulation. Yet, the same data that Chubb and Moe rely upon make it clear that many American public schools are doing a good job at providing the conditions generally conducive to high performance.[27] Since the release of

[24] Besides *A Nation At Risk: The Imperative for Educational Reform*, released by the National Commission on Excellence in Education in 1983 (Washington, D.C.: U.S. Government Printing Office, 1983), some of the other commission, foundation, and public interest group reports include: Ernest Boyer, *High School: A Report on Secondary Education in America, The Carnegie Foundation for the Advancement of Teaching* (New York: Harper & Row, 1983); Education Commission of the States Task Force on Education for Growth, *Action for Excellence* (Denver: Education Commission of the States, 1983); National Governor's Association, *Time for Results: The Governors' 1991 Report on Education* (Washington, D.C.: National Governors' Association, 1987); Research and Policy Committee of the Committee for Economic Development, *Investing in Our Children: Business and the Public Schools* (New York: Committee for Economic Development, 1985); Twentieth-Century Fund, *Making the Grade* (New York: Twentieth-Century Fund, 1983). Some of the important analyses by education scholars are: Mortimer J. Adler, *The Paideia Proposal* (New York: Collier Books, 1982); John I. Goodlad, *A Place Called School* (New York: McGraw-Hill, 1984); Theodore R. Sizer, *Horace's Compromise: The Dilemma of the American High School* (Boston: Houghton Mifflin, 1984). For a good overview of many of the reform proposals, see Philip G. Altbach, Gail P. Kelly, and Lois Weis, eds., *Excellence in Education: Perspectives on Policy and Practice* (Buffalo, NY: Prometheus, 1985).

[25] Myron Lieberman, *Public Education: An Autopsy* (Cambridge: Harvard University Press, 1993).

[26] John E. Chubb and Terry M. Moe, *Politics, Markets and America's Schools* (Washington, D.C.: Brookings Institution, 1990), 2.

[27] Chubb and Moe argue that constraints imposed by higher-level administrators are the critical factors leading to ineffective school performance. While private schools are much less likely than public schools to experience such administrative constraints (the point that Chubb and Moe emphasize), their own analysis shows that almost half of the schools with low constraint are publicly controlled and that suburban public schools, in particular, often combine low levels of bureaucratic control and high performance. Ibid., 170–71. Valerie E. Lee, Julia B. Smith, and Robert G. Croninger, "Another Look at School Restructuring," *Issues in Restructuring Schools*, Issue Report, no. 9 (fall 1997): 10, using much of the same data, make a much more emphatic case that public schools can undertake reforms that will improve achievement.

A Nation At Risk, American public schools have made substantial progress in exposing American students to more demanding course requirements; moreover, accumulating evidence shows improved performance on standardized national and international examinations.[28] We believe it is both possible and important to acknowledge such progress without settling into complacency or losing sight of the significant problems that remain.

Although some public school systems are providing rigorous academic programs and recording acheivement gains that rival private schools, others clearly are not; those that fall short are disproportionately concentrated in large urban areas with racially and ethnically more heterogeneous populations. Children in urban school districts perform much more poorly than others on standardized tests designed to measure educational achievement, and within those urban districts minority children and children in high-poverty schools perform more poorly still. About two-thirds of nonurban students scored at the "basic" level or higher on the National Assessment of Educational Progress reading, math, and science tests. In contrast, only about 40 percent of all urban students, and fewer than one-third of those in high-poverty schools, met this minimal standard.[29] This uneven performance is reflected in public assessments of education, which finds that blacks are more likely than whites to say that the *nation's* schools are doing a good to excellent job, but are less likely than whites to say that about *their local school*.[30] Two out of three blacks and one out of two whites believe that limited access to good education is an important reason for persistent racial gaps in jobs, income, and housing.[31]

This problem of poor school performance in predominantly black and Hispanic school districts presents troubling portents. Black and Hispanic youth are a growing proportion of our population. Between the years 2000 and 2020, the white population from ages 5 to 13 is expected to decline by about 11.2 percent, while the number of blacks of that age is expected to increase 15.4 percent, and the number of Hispanics by 47 percent.[32] While the nation's economy is growing and many Americans are faring well, large segments of the minority population are in danger of being left behind because

[28] Henig, *Rethinking School Choice*, chap. 2; David C. Berliner and Bruce J. Biddle, *The Manufactured Crisis* (Reading, MA: Addison-Wesley, 1995); Division of Research, Evaluation, and Communication, Directorate for Education and Human Resources, *Indicators of Science and Mathematics Education, 1995* (Arlington, VA: National Science Foundation, 1996).

[29] Lynn Olson and Craig D. Jerald, "The Achievement Gap," *Education Week*, special issue on "Quality Counts '98: The Urban Challenge," 17 (8 January 1998): 12.

[30] Stanley M. Elam, Lowell C. Rose, and Alec M. Gallup, "The 28th Annual Phi Delta Kappa/Gallup Poll of the Public's Attitudes Toward Public Schools," *Phi Delta Kappa* 78 (September 1996): 41–59.

[31] Lee Sigelman and Susan Welch, *Black Americans' Views of Racial Inequality* (New York: Cambridge University Press, 1991), table 5.3.

[32] U.S. Department of Education, *National Center for Education Statistics, Youth Indicators 1996*, indicator 2.

negative changes in the economy fall disproportionately on those who lack
high school diplomas and basic employment skills. As Blank observes, "Fundamentally, the demand for less-skilled workers appears to be declining
faster than the number of less-skilled workers, and their wages are therefore
drawn downward. This trend is related to the increasing internationalization
of the U.S. economy, which places less-skilled U.S. workers in competition
with less-skilled (and typically lower-paid) foreign workers, and to technological changes that have accelerated the demand for more-skilled workers."[33] Research on student performance makes it clear that an important
factor in student performance is the socioeconomic background of the other
children in the school. Nearly two out of every three (65 percent) black
children in the United States attend a high-poverty school, compared to 27
percent of white children; thus, the odds are stacked against African-American educational success.[34] Although poor schools do not provide the sole
reason that urban minority youth may lack requisite skills and this lack of
requisite skills does not supply the sole reason that minority youth might
have difficulty finding decent jobs, Blank, after reviewing the evidence, concludes that "the best long-term response to the declining demand for less-
skilled workers is policy that promotes skill training and effective schooling
for today's children."[35]

REFORMS THAT GO NOWHERE

Claims to the contrary notwithstanding, a growing body of evidence suggests
the problems in America's schools are *not* attributable to a lack of energy, a
lack of ideas, or even a lack of willingness to change. Rather, the problem
involves both an inability to build small school-based efforts into citywide
programs and an incapacity to sustain existing initiatives in the face of competing priorities or hot new ideas. In spite of frequent charges that the educational community is reflexively resistant to innovation and reform, we find
that the school systems in Atlanta, Baltimore, Detroit, and D.C. are virtually
overrun with reform initiatives. Some of these efforts may represent political
posturing or efforts to substitute the *appearance* of reform for the genuine
article, but we find many signs of sincere efforts in which committed educators and parents are investing time, energy, and emotional capital. The problem, we suggest, is less an unwillingness to try something new—in this

---

[33] Rebecca M. Blank, "The Employment Strategy: Public Policies to Increase Work and
Earnings," in *Confronting Poverty*, ed. Sheldon H. Danziger, Gary D. Sandefur, and Daniel H.
Weinberg (Cambridge: Harvard University Press, 1994), 173.

[34] National Center for Education Statistics, *The Social Context of Education* (U.S. Department of Education, 1997), 15.

[35] Ibid., 200.

respect school professionals seem more like gullible consumers than complacent bureaucrats—than a fragmented, episodic effort.

Farkas refers to this tendency as the "reform du jour" and notes how it
can contribute to a "legacy of skepticism."[36] Bryk, Easton, Kerbow, Rollow,
and Sebring similarly note that some Chicago schools have become "Christ-
mas tree" schools, bedecked with a myriad of programs ranging widely in
content, purpose, and methods: "A natural concomitant to the multiplicity
of the programs, however, is that they are often uncoordinated and may
even be counterproductive in terms of student learning. The addition of new
programs on top of old ones may result in a disjointed and fragmented set
of experiences for students. . . . Much of school life seems to follow an end-
less cycle of soliciting funds, implementing new initiatives, and then going
out to solicit more funds for even newer initiatives to replace current ones."[37]

Lee and Smith also have found evidence that, when it comes to school
reform, one can have too much of a good thing. Their analysis of the National
Educational Longitudinal Study data indicates that students in "restructured" public schools (those that have in place at least three out of twelve
practices deemed "significant departures" from convention) do better than
children of similar background who attend more traditional public schools.
They find evidence, as well, that these restructured public schools manage
to close the gap a bit between students from the lowest and highest socioeconomic groups. But they also find some evidence that public schools that try
to do too much restructuring showed less of an advantage than those that
had implemented just a few of the reform practices.[38] Similarly, in an analysis
of school reform in fifty-seven urban schools districts, Hess found considerable evidence of what he labels "policy churn": "Not only is a great deal of
reform proposed, but . . . about 90 percent of these proposals were reportedly enacted. Reforms are proposed at a rapid rate, and almost never rejected."[39] Like Bryk, and like Lee and Smith, Hess concludes that reforms
are more likely to succeed when districts try only a few new ideas: "Districts
which did less did it much, much better."[40]

This pattern of piecemeal and ephemeral reform suggests that the challenge of improving urban schools calls for a different orientation than is

[36] Steve Farkas, *Educational Reform: The Players and the Politics* (New York: The Public
Agenda Foundation for the Charles F. Kettering Foundation, 1992), 4.

[37] Anthony S. Bryk, et al. *A View From the Elementary Schools: The State of Reform in
Chicago* (Chicago: Consortium on Chicago School Research, August 1993), 26.

[38] Valerie E. Lee and Julia B. Smith, "Effects of High School Restructuring and Size on
Gains in Achievement and Engagement for Early Secondary School Students" (Madison: Wisconsin Center for Education Research, 1994).

[39] Frederick M. Hess, "Initiation Without Implementation: Policy Churn and the Plight of
Urban School Reform" (presented at the annual meetings of the American Political Science
Association, Washington, D.C., August 1997), 12.

[40] Ibid., 18.

typically provided in the education reform literature. The challenge may be less one of gaining attention and commitment than of sustaining attention and commitment, less one of reorganizing educational bureaucracies than of organizing whole communities so that the education enterprise keeps moving in the right direction even when attention and commitment flag. Successful school reform requires selectivity, institutional capacity, and sufficient political support to maintain positive momentum in the face of various forces that can block, contain, or gradually erode promising initiatives. Rather than create a self-sustaining cycle of progressive reform, many of the highly touted reform initiatives may themselves require that there already be in place certain political, social, and institutional preconditions that make it possible for a community collectively to define goals, assess needs, mobilize resources, and act purposefully and in a sustained manner. Such preconditions are problematic in large urban areas marked by racial and ethnic divisions, budgetary constraints, and the threat that key interests will choose the exit option over the costly and uncertain option of tackling problems head on. Absent such preconditions, the constant public call for new reforms and innovations may exacerbate problems; limited energies and resources further dissipate in a frenetic search for the combination that will take root and flourish.

CIVIC CAPACITY: ORGANIZING COMMUNITIES TO GET THINGS DONE

Why are some communities able to undertake and sustain systemic educational initiatives while others settle for shallow or symbolic efforts or deplete their energies in brief spasms of reform that do not take root? We have settled on the term "civic capacity" to refer to the extent to which various sectors of a community have developed formal and informal means to define common objectives and pursue common goals. "If we think of the usual state of affairs as one in which participants are focused only on their immediate connections and their particular occupational roles," Clarence Stone has written, "then civic capacity is marked by a move beyond this stage toward embracing a *community* role and accepting a *civic* obligation."[41]

Our interest in civic capacity points us away from thinking about education as solely the province of a discrete school bureaucracy and leads us toward both assessing the web of alliances and interactions that potentially support human capital initiatives and identifying the obstacles to such alliances where they do not exist. To explore this empirically, we approached the issue of school reform from both the outside-in and the inside-out. In each city we made it a point to interview general influentials (city council members, business leaders, and the like) and community advocates who,

---

[41] Stone, "The Politics of Urban School Reform," 4; emphasis in the original.

either as individuals or as organizational representatives, played an important leadership role outside the education arena. Before we zeroed in on questions about education and school politics, we asked these respondents broadly framed questions about the nature of their community's problems and the patterns of conflict and cooperation among key interest groups. When we interviewed education specialists, we did not restrict ourselves to asking about the internal workings of the system; many of our questions probed their relations with external actors (the research design is discussed more fully below).

The American education system historically and deliberately has been somewhat buffered from political influence. During the Progressive Era, reformers were convinced that the parochialism and patronage concerns of local politicians threatened the independence and expertise of education professionals, who were best equipped to articulate the public's interest and employ the techniques to pursue that interest.[42] Although some institutional buffers remain, we find that the education system has multiple points of contact with outside actors. Like the reforms that they produce, however, these contacts are fragmented, partial, and episodic. The shortcomings of these efforts contrast starkly with the relatively coherent and comprehensive plans, sustained by relatively broad public-private partnerships, that these same cities have produced to meet downtown economic development needs.

The concept of civic capacity, in and of itself, has little to say about the role of race. We believe (and present evidence to support the fact) that race is an extremely potent factor in determining how localities respond to the challenges they face. Yet, we also believe that it is both possible and desirable to incorporate race as a central variable in a broader theoretical framework, rather than to give it primacy. Understanding race *helps* to explain the nature of local school-reform politics; it does not *serve* as an explanation on its own terms.

A TOUGH TASK: WHY HUMAN DEVELOPMENT MAY BE MORE DIFFICULT THAN ECONOMIC DEVELOPMENT

Douglas Yates, in an influential book, characterized the contemporary American city as being "ungovernable."[43] Extreme decentralization, institutional fragmentation, and a readily mobilizable public, he argued, contribute to an environment of "street-fighting pluralism . . . a political free-for-all, a pattern of unstructured, multilateral conflict in which many different com-

---

[42] Lawrence A. Cremin, *The Transformation of the School: Progressivism in American Education, 1876–1957* (New York: Alfred A. Knopf, 1961); David B. Tyack, *The One Best System: A History of American Urban Education* (Cambridge: Harvard University Press, 1974).

[43] Yates, *The Ungovernable City.*

batants fight continuously in a very great number of permutations and combinations."[44] Public officials are left in a reactive mode; rather than setting goals and pursuing them rationally, they hop from crisis to crisis: "Relying on reflexes rather than on any considered plan of action."[45]

Yet, in spite of such obstacles, some cities manage to get things accomplished on a reliable basis and with good results. That they can do so in spite of centrifugal forces and limited formal powers appears attributable to their success in weaving together formal and informal sources of power by establishing viable working relationships between city hall and other powerful sectors within and outside the community. Urban scholars have adopted the term "regime" to characterize such relationships; a nascent body of research has explored the forms such regimes may take and the conditions under which they are likely to either strengthen or erode.[46]

Most studies of successful urban regimes have focused on public-private collaboration in pursuit of economic development objectives. Moreover, the range of development strategies explored has been relatively narrow; most commonly cited success stories involve *downtown* development, usually with a strong reliance on the *physical* infrastructure, including projects oriented around the construction of convention centers, sports facilities, mixed-use developments, and the like.

Developing the civic capacity to address the educational needs of low-income and minority youths means moving into more problematic territory. Compared to rebuilding the urban downtowns, reformulating educational systems involves different types of interests, actors, and institutional environments. As Peterson argues, groups that might otherwise compete can coalesce around issues that clearly promote local economic growth; education has some attributes of a development issue, but it also may be perceived in redistributive terms.[47] Peterson argues that redistributive policies present formidable obstacles to local governments, which must be wary about pursuing initiatives that are seen to benefit lower-income residents at the expense of wealthier citizens and businesses that not only provide more tax revenue but can also exercise the option to relocate.

Many major costs and benefits of a downtown development project are material, relatively near-term, and likely to accrue to a small and identifiable set of actors; however, systemic initiatives to develop *social capital* often presume that the benefits may be quite diffuse, slow to materialize, and more likely to mobilize grassroots involvement that exposes existing fault lines

---

[44] Ibid., 34.

[45] Ibid., .91.

[46] Clarence N. Stone, *Regime Politics: Governing Atlanta, 1946–1988* (Lawrence: University Press of Kansas, 1989); Gerry Stoker, "Regime Theory and Urban Politics," in *Theories of Urban Politics*, ed. D. Judge, G. Stoker, and H. Wolman (Thousand Oaks, CA: Sage Publications, 1995); M. Lauria, *Reconstructing Regime Theory* (Thousand Oaks, CA: Sage Publications, 1997).

[47] Peterson, *City Limits*, 94.

based on race and class.[48] Moreover, since the products of a local educational system—better informed and more capable young women and men—are free to take their skills in pursuit of opportunities in other jurisdictions, the parties to any original agreement cannot be confident that they will be able to capture the benefits even if the initiative succeeds.

In addition to engaging a broader range of actors in competition over more amorphous goals in a less predictable environment, education policy takes place in an institutional context that may make generating public-private partnerships a more problematic arena than downtown development. Urban agencies charged with promoting economic development tend to be relatively new, relatively small, led by persons drawn from the local business community—people infused with the belief that creating a "business friendly" climate is an integral part of its mission and accepting of the notion that outside actors in the business community possess at least equal expertise in the central issues. In contrast, agencies charged with providing public education have long traditions of bureaucratic autonomy and norms of professionalism that between them can create an institutional and ideological buffer zone that holds private actors at arm's length. Jones, Portz, and Stein suggest that successful school reform requires both "an *inside strand* of changes and innovations within schools and an *outside strand* of community support and resources."[49] The bureaucratic norms and traditions that evolved over time to enable the education profession to pursue the inside strand with professionalism and expertise may pose an obstacle when it comes to building the broader coalitions that the outside strand demands.

COMPETING VIEWS OF RACE AND SCHOOL POLITICS

Important theories about urban politics and education generate competing predictions about the prospects for meaningful school reform in black-led cities. One key dimension on which these theories differ involves the relative optimism embedded in the theories' assumptions about the prospects that public and private leaders will discover and act upon shared interests in investing in the education of local residents. Theories that assume actors are motivated by personal, material, and relatively short-term interests see collective action problems as looming obstacles; the incentive to free-ride, the option to use exit as an alternative to political involvement, and the uncertainty of payoffs generate pessimistic predictions. Theories that assume actors are motivated by a sense of responsibility and community, as well as

[48] Stone, "The Politics of Urban School Reform," appendix B.

[49] Robin R. Jones, John Portz, and Lana Stein, "The Nature of Civic Involvement and Educational Change in Pittsburgh, Boston, and St. Louis," *Urban Affairs Review*, 32, no. 6 (July 1977): 872.

	Fragmentation	Cohesion
Racialized Politics	Racial Cleavage Symbolic and emotive conflict	Progressive Race-Based Regime Black official and community based redistribution
Deracialized Politics	Politics as Usual Bargaining and patronage	Deracialized Development Regime Economic interest overrides race

Figure 1.1 Competing view of race and school politics

personal material gain, generate more optimistic scenarios. Even some of those hewing to the more cynical view of human nature believe that changes in the international economy will make more real and apparent to local actors their shared stake in making the transition from street-fighting pluralism to a human capital regime.

A second dimension on which these theoretical perspectives differ involves the relative importance that they place on race as a motivator for human behavior. Some theories hold that race is a fundamental component of personal identity and perception; at least in the contemporary American context, these theories hold that distinct histories and experiences lead whites and blacks to view the world through different lenses; they read different risks and opportunities, feel different bonds of loyalty and trust, and harbor different types of fear and mistrust. Others see race more as a vestigial and spurious variable. Socioeconomic class is seen as the stronger force. Where race and class overlap, patterns of behavior may appear to have racial roots, but as blacks are moving into the middle and upper classes and into positions of social status and political power the significance of race can be expected to decline.

Figure 1.1 highlights four competing predictions about the possible intersection between race and politics in a post-transition city. The four predictions are distinguished on the basis of their assumptions about both the extent to which local interests related to education will remain fragmented or begin to coalesce and the continued salience of race as opposed to its gradual irrelevance as an influence on political perceptions and behavior.

Racial Transition as the Solution: A Progressive, Race-Based Regime

As already noted, during the 1950s and 1960s, the transition to strong black majorities and the election of black leadership were seen by many as the potential solution to the conflict and inequality that then characterized large central cities undergoing the early waves of racial change. According to this perspective, years of discrimination and inequality have forged strong bonds among African Americans. Some of these bonds, cognitive in nature, comprise similar understandings of the nature of power, the role of government, the meaning of fairness. Some of the more communal bonds consist of feelings of trust and solidarity, loyalty and responsibility.[50] Such shared ideas and values, it was hoped, would mitigate the divisive effects of crosscutting interests born of class, status, power, and material well-being. *Descriptive* representation, accordingly, would result in *substantive* representation. Black elected officials would be more committed than their white predecessors to the goal of aiding minorities and the economically disadvantaged; other important groups in the community would be more inclined to lend support and resources to that effort.

If accurate, this perspective would lead us to look for signs of an emergent human capital regime in which black elected officials join forces with other groups traditionally supportive of redistributive, human investment, and community-oriented programs—including advocacy groups, nonprofit social service providers, religious leaders, and progressive foundations—and the growing population of African-American business owners and African-American corporate executives.

Race As a Resilient Cleavage

Rather than a bridge to shared goals, collective effort, and enhanced civic capacity, racial transition might exacerbate existing racial fissures, continuing to define conflicts inside the city and even more sharply to define the orientation of the city versus the suburbs and the state. Race can remain a potent cleavage within black-led cities if, for example, the white minority retains important economic leverage in its roles as property owners, tax payers, and employers. Historians and sociologists have noted that groups suffering erosion of their social or political status often mobilize energetically to retain or regain their position;[51] if so, remaining white residents and invest-

---

[50] Colbert I. King, a black editorialist for the *Washington Post*, writes, "This is a city in which much is made of African-American kinship. It is the basis on which we are told to vote, shop, make friends, party, and do business. . . . We are told that loyalty to community, brotherhood and sisterhood should dictate our actions. We are asked to think about race when choosing a career, to think about race in deciding whom to trust, and—for a few of us—to rely on race when the going gets tough. When we reach lofty positions and find ourselves teetering on the edge because of something we've done—or failed to do—we hope to God that judges, juries, journalists and other folks out there will be guided by race in their thinking too." "Betrayals of Kinship," *Washington Post*, 12 July 1997, A21.

[51] E.g., Joseph Gusfield, *Symbolic Crusade: Status Politics and the American Temperance Movement* (Urbana: University of Illinois Press, 1963); Samuel P. Hayes, "The Politics of Re-

ors in black-led cities might become a more cohesive and active force. By the same token, if control of formal positions of power does *not* lead to clear improvements in their quality of life, black residents might conclude that their interests deliberately are being undermined by white elites employing hidden and informal means. In these ways, racial transition could raise the level of resentment on all sides and increase the likelihood that political alignments will polarize along racial lines.

Less predictably, race may remain a cleavage even *within* the black community.[52] The historical centrality of racial issues in the evolution of political consciousness among African Americans has fused certain policy stances, personal styles, and political symbols into a "black identity" that is compelling—but not universally so—within the black community. Appeals to racial identity and racial symbolism can be used to both rally and divide the black community. It is not uncommon, as we shall see, for some black political and educational leaders to be labeled "less black" than others. Race-based politics, as a result, is not tied just to skin color but to socioeconomic class and political ideology as well.

Finally, race may become a defining aspect of the relationship between black-led cities and important external actors. Large central cities are limited in their capacity to undertake meaningful school reform without the support or, at the least, the acquiescence of suburban neighbors, state legislatures, governor, courts, and the national government. These limitations are financial legal, and political. While blacks control the local levers of formal governmental authority in each of our cities, in each case the key external actors are white. Conflicting priorities and interests, whether rooted in race or something else entirely, may easily come to be *interpreted* in racial terms and to engender a more emotionally intense and combustible politics as a result.

The Declining Significance of Race

Two alternative perspectives are based on the premise that race is becoming less significant in American society. Over the last several decades, there has emerged a larger and somewhat more secure black professional and economic elite. Between 1950 and 1990, the proportion of blacks employed as

---

form in Municipal Government in the Progressive Era," *Pacific Northwest Quarterly* 55 (October 1964): 157–89.

[52] Rufus P. Browning, Dale Rogers Marshall, and David H. Tabb, eds., *Racial Politics in American Cities*, 2d ed. (New York: Longman, 1997), observe that "open conflict within and between minority groups now represented in city governments has sometimes replaced the unity that was once attained when the city and its white, established power holders were the common enemy" (p. 4).

professionals or managers increased from five percent to twenty percent.[53] There is at least some evidence that this expanding black elite holds priorities and perceptions that mirror those of their white counterparts in important ways.[54] No reasonable observer would go so far as to proclaim that race is no longer an important part of self-identity within the emerging black middle class, but the claim that it is being *relatively* less important is worthy of attention.

One perspective compatible with a declining role for race is optimistic about the prospects for building civic capacity in black-led cities. As black public officials move from the challenge of building *electoral* coalitions to the challenge of building *governance* coalitions, this view holds, they increasingly will find that their interests overlap those of others—often white—who emphasize the importance of economic development as a focus for city efforts. Similarly, predominantly white business leaders, who may have feared that the racial transition in political power would leave them marginalized, increasingly will realize that they have a stake in allying with the new black leadership to gain a competitive advantage in other areas in the battle for private investment, national status, tourism, and state and federal support. Without gainsaying the tension and mutual adjustments that may have to be worked through, this perspective foresees a natural alliance between black officials and white business leaders. While such an alliance might be expected to emerge first and most aggressively in issues related to physical renewal and downtown redevelopment, some foresee a further and equally natural progression to school reform—at least to the extent that school reform is conceived of in developmental rather than redistributive terms.

A diminishing role for racial cleavages, however, does not necessarily bode well for the prospect of school reform. The fourth cell in Figure 1.1 reflects the fact that "politics as usual" in American cities often has consisted of political conflict, hyper-pluralism, and inefficacious governance and predicts that if race becomes less potent as a motivating force, black-led cities will refragment along other lines. Rather than mounting a cohesive assault on educational problems, black leaders, according to this perspective, will square off against other black leaders by substituting neighborhood, class,

---

[53] Jennifer Hochschild, *Facing Up to the American Dream* (Princeton: Princeton University Press, 1995), 43.

[54] Although middle-class blacks express opinions similar to middle-class whites on some types of issues, the weight of the empirical evidence indicates that *both* race and class have influence on black attitudes. See, e.g., Sigelman and Welch, *Black Americans' Views of Racial Inequality*. Middle-class blacks retain a greater allegiance than similarly situated white Americans to the notion that government can and should address social problems. The presumption that middle-class blacks will see the environment as less racially biased gets a sharp challenge from Hochschild, *Facing Up to the American Dream*.

and old-fashioned patronage for racial identity as the currency on which they build their political bases.

We should not expect to find that all black-led cities fit neatly in one cell or another. Indeed, we should not expect to find that any single city is unambiguously or permanently fixed in a particular style of racial politics. Rather, we argue that a gradient of difficulty incorporated into our typology provides a kernel of a dynamic theory of the politics of educational reform. Our thesis is that collective purposive action to address social problems is, in general, difficult to mount and to sustain especially when formal authority is fragmented (as it is in the American system of federalism, checks and balances, and individual rights) and where the combination of concentrated poverty and the pull of the exit option (as it is in central cities, that face suburbanization and white flight) exacerbate problems and sap resources. Race is potent, in this context, because race not only amplifies some structural problems faced by cities but also presents a powerful perceptual filter, rooted in personal and historical experiences, that affects the bonds of trust and loyalty upon which collaborative political endeavors depend.

For these kinds of reasons, there is likely to be a "natural state" tendency for cities like those we focus on to resort to less demanding and problematic modes of action: settling for immediate material incentives (i.e., politics as usual), focusing on straightforward, more technical tasks (i.e., downtown development projects), and substituting solidarity and symbol for tangible gain (i.e., the politics of racial divisiveness). Thus, a gradient of difficulty is implicit in our typology. We can expect that a progressive human capital regime will be the hardest to sustain, that a development regime will be easier although still a challenge, and that patronage and racial polarization are the equilibrium states toward which we can expect cities to gravitate *unless* they can build the kind of civic capacity we describe.

RESEARCH DESIGN

Using a common field research guide, teams in each of eleven cities collected a wide range of documentary evidence regarding demographic change, enrollment patterns, governmental expenditures, and school policies. In each city, the teams interviewed three types of respondents. *General influentials* were individuals who by position or reputation were likely to be important actors in local decision making across a range of policy issues, not limited to education.[55] *Community-based representatives* were individuals active in

---

[55] Researchers were instructed to attempt interviews with the following individuals or their representatives: the mayor; two city council members (if mixed at-large/district one from each category); city manager or chief administrative officer; two school board members; president or executive director of the chamber of commerce or other major business organization; CEO or

TABLE 1.1

Interviews Completed, By Type of City and Respondent

	Type of City		
	Black-Led	Other Cities	Total
Type of Respondents			
General Influentials	97	157	254
Program Specialists	69	85	174
Community Activists	47	69	116

children's advocacy groups, minority organizations, neighborhood organizations, religious organizations, and PTAs.[56] *Education specialists* were persons especially knowledgeable about the implementation of school system policies and programs.[57] Table 1.1 summarizes basic information about the distribution of respondents in our black-led and comparison cities.

Researchers employed an interview template comprised mostly of open-ended questions; the sets of questions differed somewhat for the three broad types of respondents, although most questions were common across the

---

personnel director of one of large private employers or officer of a local bank or utility; minority business executive; Private Industry Council (PIC) chair; head of education committee of chamber of commerce or counterpart in another business organization; member of city future commission or strategic planning body; head of teachers union/organization; executive director of United Way; board chair of Black United Fund or other minority charity; board chair or executive director of local foundation; editor/publisher of local newspaper or reporter who covers city hall or education; state legislator from city, preferably on education committee; judge or attorney on desegregation case/issue. Here, as elsewhere, each research team was given considerable discretion in adapting its research quota to the idiosyncrasies of its city.

[56] Researchers were instructed to attempt interviews with the following individuals or their representatives: head of community-based organization with some concern in area of education and children's issues, preferably from an umbrella organization; two influential religious leaders, at least one of whom should be from a coalition or alliance of religious groups; systemwide PTA officer; head of another parent advocacy group or, if there is no such group, a second PTA officer; education committee chair or other specialist from a good government group (such as the League of Women Voters); three minority organization representatives, spread as appropriate to the city's demographic base, and should include at least one non-mainline organization; two heads of children's advocacy organization or day care advocacy groups.

[57] Researchers were instructed to attempt interviews with the following individuals or their representatives: the superintendent; two assistant school superintendents or equivalents; Head-start administrator; Chapter One administrator; police department official with responsibility to address school violence; social services individual who liaisons with schools (e.g., JOBS or preschool); two principals in innovative school or heads of innovative education programs; economic development administrator with education portfolio; school board staff member, preferably someone with institutional memory; education compact administrator or counterpart for school/business partnerships; PIC staff member with education responsibilities; United Way or similar staff member (with preschool or youth development responsibilities); lobbyist for school district in city hall or state capitol.

groups.[58] In both D.C. and Detroit, the interviewers were white; in Atlanta, some interviews were conducted by white researchers, some by a black member of the team. The Baltimore interviews were all conducted by a black member of the research team.[59] We designed questions to elicit information about the broad political context, the way that education issues are conceptualized by central actors, lines of conflict and cooperation, and the kinds of program initiatives and reform efforts underway. Interviews were taped, transcribed, and coded.[60] Unless otherwise indicated, direct quotations throughout the book are drawn from the transcripts of those interviews.

A strength of the research design is that it enables us to combine some advantages of in-depth case studies with the critical leverage by making comparisons. Each team was headed by at least one professional political scientist already familiar with the history and context of political life within the city.[61]

---

[58] As noted earlier, the interview schedules used for the three types of respondents differed in some respects. Overlap of questions was greatest for the general influentials and community advocates. Interviews with program specialists were intended to get detailed information on decision making and policies *within* the education community; the interview schedule employed for the specialists, as a result, did not include as many questions about the broader political and policy environment. All the quantitative analyses of survey results presented in this book draw from questions to questions that overlapped in the general influential and community advocate interviews, but not all of questions were asked of program specialists. This is the major explanation for the different number of responses from question to question. In addition, while interviewers tried to make certain that they covered the core material in each interview, the need to follow lines of inquiry and the fact that they were dealing with strong-minded individuals who often had their own sense of what needed to be said, inevitably resulted in some questions not being asked of some respondents.

[59] The interaction between the race of the interviewer and that of the respondent undoubtedly affected the dynamics and content of the exchanges in some instances. In some cases, we sensed a wariness on the part of respondents that may have been race-based. Yet, because of their status as significant actors, most of our respondents operate in settings that entail regular crossrace interaction. In most cases there was little sign of racial sensitivity; reticence, where it was apparent, seemed more commonly linked to the respondents' position (elected officials and bureaucrats being more wary, in general, than community advocates or business leaders) than to racial differences between the respondents and interviewers.

[60] Whitney Grace and Heather Strickland carried out the coding, under the supervision of Bryan Jones. A handful of respondents requested that the interviews not be taped. In those cases, interviewers took as detailed a set of notes as possible, and coding was carried out using those notes.

[61] The team leaders were: Atlanta: John Hutcheson (Georgia State University), Carol Pirannunzi (Kennesaw State College), and Desiree Pedescleaux (Spelman College); Baltimore: Marion Orr (Duke University); Boston: John Portz (Northeastern University); Denver: Susan Clarke and Rodney Hero (University of Colorado); Detroit: Richard Hula (Michigan State University) and Alan DiGaetano (Baruch College–CUNY); Houston: Thomas Longoria (University of Wisconsin–Milwaukee); Los Angeles: Fernando Guerra (Loyola Marymount University); Pittsburgh: Robin Jones (University of Pittsburgh); St. Louis: Lana Stein (University of Missouri–St. Louis); San Francisco: Luis Fraga (Stanford University); Washington, D.C.: Jeffrey Henig (George Washington University).

During the formative stages of the project, the team members met several times to help design the study and to discuss its implementation; this helped ensure team members' common understanding of the objectives, key concepts, and data instruments.

Each of the eleven cities presents an interesting and important set of stories that we could tell. For the most part, however, our analysis focuses on two broad types of comparisons. The most important involves comparisons between the four black-led cities and the remaining seven cities, which we will refer to as the "comparison" cities. By using these comparison cities as a backdrop, we provide some basis for distinguishing patterns that are linked to racial change and the transition to black leadership from patterns that might be common to large central cities regardless of their demography.

A second type of comparison involves distinctions across the four black-led cities. The strong correlation between race and class in the United States has tended to obscure the substantial variation that does exist within the African-American community. While sharing many attributes, Atlanta, Baltimore, Detroit, and Washington, D.C., are not cut from a single cloth. The variation in black education and income levels across the four case cities provides us with a great opportunity to consider the consequences of class differences within the black community.

By juxtaposing D.C. and Atlanta to Baltimore and Detroit, we are able to disentangle the threads of race and class, at least to some degree. It is reasonable to hypothesize that the stronger socioeconomic base of the black community in D.C. and Atlanta would translate into stronger civic capacity to undertake educational initiatives. A strong black middle class presumably values education and could become a potent source of leadership for a black constituency that would demand school improvement for its children. The presence of a sizable black middle class also increases the potential for a coalition between middle-class black leaders and the middle-class white families still living in the city. Although reasonable, we find such a hypothesis does not carry us very far in understanding variation among the four cities.

The four cities also differ in other ways, including their traditions of political action and their place in the federal system. Detroit, and to a lesser extent Baltimore, have traditions of strong unionism that, while identified primarily with their white populations, may have affected the ways that the black working class and its leaders have come to evaluate political tactics. In Atlanta and D.C., the civil rights movement is the more vibrant paradigm. Detroit and Baltimore are located in states that have been national leaders in the movement to assess and hold responsible local school districts; Michigan's initiatives have been identified with a Republican governor and a more conservative agenda, while Maryland is a heavily Democratic state. Georgia does not have the same history of aggressive state action. D.C., of course, has a unique relationship vis-à-vis the federal government. Do such varia-

tions among black-led cities in fact *make* a difference as far as their capacity
to mount school reform efforts and the extent to which race emerges as a
complicating factor? Although no research design can isolate race as a pure
variable for analysis, our ability to compare black-led cities to other cities as
well as to one another gives us a vantage point that would not be available
in a study of any single city, and our ability to delve deeply into these cities
gives us a better chance to identify subtle and sometimes deliberately
masked consequences of racial politics than might be available in a study
of many more cities that was limited to secondary analysis of quantitative
indicators.

THE PLAN OF THE BOOK

In chapter 2, we trace the demographic changes and subsequent political
changes that culminated in black control of the local levers of public power
over education policy. Although racial change in the cities and their schools
built up over decades, the transition in formal political power, once it began,
was remarkably rapid. The transition was especially rapid in public schools;
key white elites proved willing to cede schools to black control while they
concentrated their political efforts on maintaining influence over decisions
more directly related to economic development, taxation, and policing. Ironically, the fact that the racial transition in power over schools occurred so
rapidly and, at the end, with relatively little resistance, may have contributed
to some of the cities' subsequent problems in generating civic capacity. During the years of political subordination, black leaders primarily focused on
the issues of representation and power as necessary and perhaps even sufficient conditions for improving the educational performance of minority
youth; they had little need or incentive to develop a more comprehensive or
specific agenda for education reform. Suddenly finding themselves in power,
these same leaders lacked a blueprint for action. In the vacuum, intramural
battles over political control became distinguishing characteristics of educational decision making.

In chapter 3, we examine the state-of-school performance in the four
cities. Making meaningful comparisons across school districts is challenging
for two main reasons: reliable and consistent measures of student performance are limited; and existing measures do not readily allow one to assess
the "value added" by the schools once the differing characteristics of school
populations are taken into account. The weight of the evidence, nonetheless,
convinces us that these four school districts are performing poorly; certainly,
they have failed to deliver on the promise that replacing white teachers and
administrators with black teachers and administrators automatically trans-
lates into higher expectations, a more supportive environment, and break-

throughs in academic achievement. Many critics of central-city public school systems charge that poor performance is evidence of complacency and bureaucratic unresponsiveness, but we argue that each city has initiated sincere efforts at systemic reform. Citizens and businesses have mobilized to raise the issue on the public agenda, to unseat ineffective school board members, and to insist upon new superintendents with strong credentials and a willingness to shake things up. That reform has proven elusive nevertheless indicates a realization that the task of undertaking sustained and effective school reform requires much more than acknowledging a problem's existence. A key element to moving beyond good intentions is developing civic capacity: the ability to draw together and hold together a viable coalition of public and private stakeholders linked not necessarily by coincident interests, shared visions, or altruistic motives, but by habits of collaboration, a requisite level of trust, and a pragmatic orientation toward making things work.

Chapters 4 through 7 sequentially focus on some key stakeholder groups and consider the obstacles that have complicated coalition building around school reform and the specific complications introduced by the politics of race. Much of the literature on urban schools spotlights the educational bureaucracy—teachers, principals, and administrators—as the fundamental stumbling block: a powerful and self-interested clique with an effective veto power. In chapter 4, we examine the role of educators and their unions, but we do so through a wider lens that considers the roles that schools play in the local political economy as sources of citywide economic development, community identity and stability, and upward mobility for individuals and groups. The politics of jobs can be—and often is—an impediment to systemic school reform, but the power of education professionals rests on more than the votes and campaign contributions they can muster from within their own ranks. African-American educators in black-led cities share perceptual, ideological, and communal bonds with elected officials, parents, and other important community actors, including the black churches that play a pivotal role in shaping the political life in many inner-city areas. These bonds help to account for the fact that community mobilization around school issues often takes the shape of protecting jobs and their incumbents instead of demanding higher levels of performance and structural change.

Chapter 5 examines more closely the role of parent and community participation. We suggest that much that has been written about parent participation in education is irrelevant to the particular context and challenges of inner-city school reform. That literature frames participation in terms of individual families and presumes a natural collaborative relationship among parents, educators, and other stakeholders. Instituting systemic school reform, we believe, calls for collective rather than individualistic mobilization and often requires confronting conflicting values and interests in a political environment where the rhetoric of consensus masks historical cleavages. In spite of the challenges to mobilizing parents and communities in low-income inner cities, we find that each of our cities has areas in which participation is well established, and each has witnessed significant efforts to mobilize the community on a broader scale. The problem, we argue, is less one of sparking participation than it is one of sustaining systemwide participation. Ironically, we suggest that some of the very tools advocated by proponents of school reform—encouraging parental choice, focusing on school-based decision making—may be contributing to the diffuse and episodic character of community participation in these cities. Race plays a special role, moreover, in dampening potential reform leadership within both white and black communities.

In chapter 6 we turn our attention to another sector that figures prominently in many observers' ideas about who can and should serve a leadership role in the reform of central-city schools. The corporate sector has material and in-kind resources to bring to bear, and presumably holds a key stake in the health of the public school systems that produce their future employees. Many business leaders, in these cities and others, have indeed become outspoken advocates for school reform, and some have devoted personal energies and corporate support to the cause. Many, many examples in our four cities show partnerships linking individual businesses with individual schools. Each city, to varying degrees, has experienced efforts by the corporate community to take on a broader role as part of a citywide reform coalition or in a formal "compact" through which business and education leaders set common goals and accept specific responsibilities. Based on our respondents' assessments, business is a major player in education decision making in black-led cities. Nonetheless, as we demonstrate, the business role is more shallow, selective, and ephemeral than the celebrants of public-private partnerships might lead one to expect. We argue that enthusiastic and optimistic proponents for reform may have misgauged the extent to which business feels bound to central-city public schools and underestimated the personal and corporate risks that make business leaders wary about adopting a public role in addressing complex social problems in a racially charged environment.

Local school districts are not autonomous and independent. They function within a broader federal system in which most formal power ultimately rests with the states (or, in the case of D.C., in Congress). Traditions of local control and the predominance of local funding, among other factors, for many decades sufficed to dissuade external actors from undertaking aggressive efforts to intervene. But the ground has shifted substantially. Many states have begun to involve themselves directly in local school districts, and Michigan and Maryland are among the leaders in those respects. Congress, which adopted a relatively hands-off stance for a little over two decades after establishing a locally elected school board in D.C., in recent years has intervened directly, mandating specific policies and replacing the local school board and superintendent with a board of trustees and chief executive officer responsible to Congress rather than the local electorate. In chapter 7 we review the evolution of external intervention in our four cities and argue that some— but not all—of that involvement must be considered in racial terms. Although sharp and authoritative intervention by higher levels of government can play a productive role in mobilizing the process of reform, we suggest that external efforts ultimately require a broad local constituency if they are to be sustained. When predominantly white external institutions partner with predominantly white internal constituencies to impose reform on local black decision makers, the prospects for long-term success are undermined.

In chapter 8 we summarize our major themes and findings and reflect on their implications for the general understanding of local civic capacity. Reforming urban public education is a daunting challenge made even more complex and uncertain by the persistent influence of race. Solving the problems of central-city schools requires more than an intense flurry of interest, improved management, or organizational restructuring. These may be necessary, but they are not sufficient. Improving urban schools ultimately requires forging and maintaining political constituencies to support and sustain such initiatives over time and in the face of competing demands. Race complicates this process of coalition building because of the ways in which it is tied to differences in political experience, perception, and trust. Racial transition in power does not provide the solution because cross-race alliances are necessary even in cities in which the levers of local authority are firmly in the hands of black leaders. Daunting though it may be, the challenge of improving education in America's central cities is too important to sidestep, and we finish with some guidance about how those who care about the quality of urban education can better take into account both politics and race in their efforts to bring about sustainable school reform.

Racial Change and the Politics of Transition

"We have a school system that is more than 80
percent African-American. GBC [Greater
Baltimore Committee], I suspect will be for the
next 50 years perceived as a white organization.
And so there is at least a tension that will always
be there of: is whitey trying to tell us what to do. Is
whitey trying to take over our school system."
(Baltimore business executive)

POLITICAL scientists often write about how politics and policy slow the processes of change. Political elites, they note, can often use their privileged position to defeat or preempt challenges from newly mobilizing interests.[1] Countervailing interests, formal checks and balances, division of authority among levels of government, cozy and self-protective relationships between regulators and the interests they regulate, and the problematics of bureaucratic implementation sometimes combine to make incrementalism, even rigidity, appear to be defining traits of the American political system.[2]

Rapid demographic change is one force powerful enough to overwhelm these forces of inertia. This is especially true at the local level, where inflow and outflow of population can occasionally be highly concentrated and selective.

A defining characteristic of every American black-led city is its transition through a period of rapid demographic change. In the years between 1910 and 1970, more than 6.5 million African Americans migrated to urban areas. This migration continues even today as the overall population of cities declines. In 1990, approximately 83 percent of the African-American population lived in metropolitan centers, with 56 percent living in central cities. As

---

[1] Robert S. Lynd and Helen M. Lynd, *Middletown. in Transition* (New York: Harcourt, Brace and Company, 1937), and Floyd Hunter, *Community Power Structure* (Chapel Hill: University of North Carolina Press, 1953) offer two classic presentations of this perspective. Later, more nuanced, analyses include Peter Bachrach and Morton Baratz, "Two Faces of Power," *American Political Science Review* 56 (September 1963): 947–52; Clarence N. Stone, *Regime Politics* (Lawrence: University Press of Kansas, 1989).

[2] Charles Lindblom, "The Science of Muddling Through," *Public Administration Review* 19 (1958): 78–88; Martha Derthick, *New Towns In-Town* (Washington, D.C.: Brookings Institu-

a result, 40 percent of all African Americans are concentrated in only eleven central cities, including the four that are the focus of this book. Before about 1950, there were no major U.S. cities with more than half of the population black; by 1992, there were nine. In almost every instance, racial change was rapid, and, in probably every case, turnover in the student population outpaced that within the overall population. While some cities and school districts elected blacks to positions of importance before blacks became an absolute majority of the population, the full transition to black leadership did not occur until a black majority was entrenched.

In this chapter, we set the stage for our contemporary analysis by taking an historical perspective on race, politics, and schools in our four cities. But we are not interested in history for its own sake. By drawing on literature on urban regimes and theories about civic capacity that we have been developing as part of the broader project, we advance the thesis that coalition building takes place in a context that is strongly influenced by key actors' perceptions about the reliability and strength of potential partners, the feasibility of specific political tactics, and the capacity of government to bring about intended results.

As we demonstrate in subsequent chapters, many urban education problems black-led cities face are similar to those in other central cities, but race sometimes seriously complicates efforts to build coalitions for significant, sustained educational reform. In spite of theoretical arguments that black leaders, local corporations, and concerned parents share strong objective interests that should be propelling them toward a shared agenda, our research in Atlanta, Baltimore, Detroit, and Washington, D.C., reveals repeated instances in which the prospects for collaboration unravel in the face of mutual suspicion, loaded rhetoric, and political symbolism, all weighted by race. These patterns—seemingly anomalous from the perspective of theories of rational, interest-based behavior—are less surprising if we recognize that key actors filter their perceptions of opportunities and threats through different lenses and that these lenses, in turn, are strongly influenced by a legacy of political experiences shared and developed over time.

PATTERNS OF RACIAL TURNOVER IN ATLANTA, BALTIMORE, DETROIT, AND D.C.

Figure 2.1 shows the dimensions of the racial transition in our four cities. It presents changes in the absolute numbers of black and white residents from 1950 to 1990. There are both similarities and differences worthy of noting.

tion, 1972); Jeffrey L. Pressman and Aaron B. Wildavsky, *Implementation* (Berkeley: University of California Press, 1973).

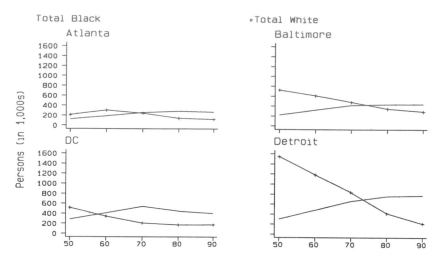

Figure 2.1 Racial change, 1950–1990. *Source*: U.S. Bureau of Census, Census of Population and Housing, various years.

First, *all four are "mature" cities as far as this racial transition is concerned*; all had become predominantly black before the 1980 census, and the period of rapid increase in the black population has passed. Second, in all four cities the *change involved both an out-movement of white residents as well as an in-movement of blacks*. The phenomenon of white suburbanization has received a tremendous amount of attention, and, in a later section, we study the tie between racial turnover, especially its combination with school desegregation, and the white flight with which it appears to be linked. In the early years, however, racial change in these cities was driven as much by the in-movement of blacks as the out-movement of whites; to aspiring black families in the mid-twentieth century, large cities served as beacons for economic and political advance and offered the significant prospect of better education for their children.[3]

The cities differ somewhat in the timing and extent of the changes they have undergone. The District was the earliest to become predominantly black; indeed, its period of transition was essentially complete by 1970. Atlanta was slightly behind the District, but otherwise its pattern of change looks quite similar. In both cases, the pace of racial change has slowed substantially; *compared to Baltimore and Detroit, D.C. and Atlanta have had*

[3] See, for example, Nicholas Lemann, *The Promised Land: The Great Black Migration and How it Changed America* (New York: Knopf, 1991).

more time to "digest" the racial changeover. Both reveal that *racial turnover does not necessarily accelerate endlessly*; in both cities the pace of white flight leveled off, leaving a relatively small but by no means insignificant white population. Most markedly in D.C., but in Atlanta as well, there is *evidence of a growing out-movement of blacks.* In Baltimore and Detroit racial turnover came somewhat later. In both absolute and relative terms, Detroit has undergone the greatest shift over this thirty-year period. Compared to D.C. and Atlanta, Baltimore and especially Detroit, appear to be in a more volatile period with dynamics of turnover still underway as of 1990.

RACIAL TRANSITION AND POLITICAL CHANGE: THE RISE OF BLACK POLITICAL POWER

The demographic transformation that occurred from the 1950s through the 1970s had political ramifications in our four cities. The out-movement of white residents and the in-movement of blacks gave rise to increased black demands for a bigger share in the local decision-making processes. As African-Americans reached a majority or near majority of the population, a heightened effort to capture political offices commenced. Broad, powerful national forces—the civil rights movement, federal civil rights and voting rights legislation, and urban riots—affected developments in all four cities. As a result, the timing and style of change across the cities was more synchronized than might have been the case if events had unfolded in response to local rhythms alone.

As data in Table 2.1 indicated, while the cycles of population turnover differ across the four cities by as much as twenty years, the period of political transition is relatively compressed, with many of the key milestones occurring between 1968 and 1974. Nonetheless, local idiosyncrasies tied to personalities, tactics, balance of power among various interest groups, parochial norms, and indigenous institutions also affected the form and timing of the translation of demographic change into political transformation. In this section we sketch the outlines of the transformation as manifested in the general offices of local power—the mayoralty and council. Subsequently, we focus on changes specifically related to the schools.

While Washington, D.C., had a predominantly black student population by 1950 and a predominantly black residential population by 1960, its unique political status as the nation's capital artificially delayed the translation of demographic change into local political power. It was not until 1967 that Walter Washington, the city's first black mayor, was appointed by President Lyndon B. Johnson. The mayor, however, had very limited powers. D.C. government operated like an agency of the federal government with Congress serving as its direct legislative body. Prior to home rule, the House

TABLE 2.1

Key Dates in the Transformation to Black Political Regimes in
Atlanta, Baltimore, Detroit, and Washington

	Atlanta	Baltimore	Detroit	Washington
Black Majority of Population	1970	1980	1980	1960
Black Majority of School Enrollment	1963	1960	1962	1950
Black Representation on School Board	1953	1944	1955	1969
Black Representation on City Council	1965	1955[a]	1957	1974
Black School Superintendent	1973	1971	1974	1970
Black-elected Mayor	1973	1987	1973	1974
Black Majority School Board	1973	1973	1977	1969
Black Majority City Council	1973	1995	1977	1974

[a] Baltimore had black Republicans on the city council from 1890 to 1931.

and Senate committees that overlooked D.C. affairs were controlled by white segregationists from the Deep South. Influential congressional leaders, like South Carolina's John McMillan, who chaired the House D.C. Committee, displayed no sympathy for the desires of the District's black residents. According to Charles W. Harris, "McMillan ruled the city as a kind of czar. He was viewed as the holder of ultimate authority over almost every aspect of life in the city."[4] Leaders in D.C.'s black community accused the Congress of racism and lacking an ability to appreciate the needs of a large urban black population. Hence, as the black power movement swept the nation in the 1960s, D.C.'s African-American leaders broadly resented Congress.

Moreover, African Americans in D.C., like blacks in other major cities, were galvanized by the civil rights movement and mobilized by the civil disturbances that occurred in D.C. in 1968 and engulfed hundreds of communities from Gary, Indiana, to Los Angeles, California. Not satisfied with their "colonial" status, black leaders demanded more authority in running D.C. government. In other cities, local black politicians learned over time how to play the game of electoral politics—how to balance the need to mobilize supporters with clear goals and big promises against the practical need to broker deals and make compromises with other powerful actors. Lacking both local electoral channels and formal representation in Congress, black leaders in D.C. had a different type of training ground. Those who sought to build local support could champion idealistic positions and paint Congress as the enemy. Because they had no real power to get things done, their supporters were unlikely to hold them responsible if these strategies failed to garner tangible gains. Other local leaders, interested in near-term, albeit incremental, gains, learned the art of directly lobbying those who, unchecked

[4] Charles Wesley Harris, *Congress and the Governance of the Nation's Capital* (Washington, D.C.: Georgetown University Press, 1995).

by the need to submit their performance to a public electoral test, did hold the reins of formal power.

The institution of home rule removed the lid from a long-simmering pressure cooker, and the transition to black control of local offices was immediate. In 1968, D.C. residents were allowed for the first time in the twentieth century to elect representatives to a local governing body, the school board. Since then, the school board has been composed almost entirely of African Americans. After Congress passed the first home-rule charter in 1974, D.C. voters elected the sitting mayor, Walter Washington, and he took office as the first *elected* black mayor in 1975; since then, every mayor has been black. The pattern in the city council is the same; all but two of the thirteen members elected to the first council in November 1974 were African Americans, and blacks held the majority until 1999.

The dominant figure in local elected politics has been Marion Barry, who was first elected mayor in 1978 and reelected in 1982, 1986, and 1994. He was a prominent civil rights leader who played a role in the effort to wrest power from Congress. After winning a seat on the elected school board, Barry began his transition from street activist to big-city politician. Supported by some white business leaders who viewed him as a calming antidote to the racial strife manifested in the 1968 riots and by many liberal white residents who saw him as a fresh and progressive voice, Barry used his position on the school board to launch a campaign for an at-large seat on the D.C. city council. After Barry won a tight three-way race for the Democratic mayoral nomination in 1978, he was supported in the general election by a broad spectrum of blacks, liberal whites, the *Washington Post*, and D.C.'s business elite. For much of his tenure, Barry focused on economic development issues. He worked closely with corporate leaders who were willing to invest in D.C.'s economic development projects. A select group of black businessmen benefited as Barry required developers to hire minority firms as a prerequisite for engaging in downtown projects. Barry also worked hard to expand his support within the black religious community, which had eyed him warily during his first mayoral campaign. "During his first term he wooed the city's black clergy by funding church-sponsored programs in housing, nutrition, drug and youth-counseling, and aid to the elderly," one biography notes. "The churchmen . . . would stand behind Barry in future elections."[5]

Accused of corruption and incompetence, Barry gradually lost much of his support in the white community. Black Washingtonians, however, have been reluctant to abandon Barry. Many of his policies—such as his popular summer youth employment efforts, affirmative action program, and mea-

---

[5] Jonathan I. Z. Agronsky, *Marion Barry: The Politics of Race* (Latham, NY: British American Publishing, 1991), 185.

sures to help senior citizens—have affected the lives of thousands of blacks. Whites, however, view Barry as a polarizing figure and question his integrity. After serving a short prison term for misdemeanor drug possession, Barry launched a political comeback. First, he captured a city council seat by defeating a long-time incumbent in the city's poorest ward. In 1994, to the chagrin of many white voters, Barry was triumphantly returned to the mayor's office largely on the strength of D.C.'s majority black voters. Given the racial composition of the nation's capital, blacks are likely to control many key positions in local government.

Blacks in Atlanta captured the local levers of power at about the same time as those in D.C., but the path they took was different: during a long period in waiting, a complicated relationship evolved between the white business community and the educated black elite. For decades Atlanta's white business leaders worked with the black community, forging a formidable coalition that kept the southern "rednecks" from gaining control of city government. They sought to avoid having Atlanta seen as "another Birmingham," where open resistance to the civil rights movement had tagged the city with a reputation as parochial and racist. White business leaders in Atlanta may not have been dramatically more progressive in their racial views than those elsewhere in the South, but they did learn early that they had an economic interest in avoiding open confrontation. By the spring of 1960, after a series of boycotts and demonstrations organized around civil rights issues, "the Atlanta Chamber of Commerce had learned an important lesson: black protests were bad for business."[6] Also helping to shape the evolution of racial politics in the city was the existence of an older, respected core of leadership within the black civil rights community; less rash and more pragmatic than the student leaders who often dominated in other settings, this core was more willing to strike bargains with white power-holders, accept partial victories, and solidify gains without necessarily losing track of longer term objectives for more radical change.[7]

In 1973, Maynard Jackson, who had served as the first black deputy mayor, defeated a white opponent in a campaign that divided Atlanta's voters along racial lines. Jackson had definite plans to bring blacks into an equal place in the city's power structure.[8] On one level, his strategy initially included delivery of more services to low-income black neighborhoods, appointments of blacks to boards and commissions, and more minority hiring and promotions. The other strategy was to expand minority participation in economic development. Maynard Jackson fashioned a minority set-aside program that called

---

[6] Gary M. Pomerantz, *Where Peachtree Meets Sweet Auburn*, (New York: Scribner, 1996), 257.

[7] Ibid., 266–68.

[8] Peter K. Eisinger, *The Politics of Displacement: Racial and Ethnic Transition in Three American Cities* (New York: Academic Press, 1980).

for nonminority contractors to form limited joint-venture partnerships with minority-owned firms in order to receive special consideration in the competitive bidding process for a new Atlanta airport. Jackson's effort provoked a heated response from Atlanta's white business community.

Now, with the ascendancy of black political control, white business and civic leaders lost their upper hand. Even many of those who had favored voluntarily accommodating the movement toward civil rights resented this loss of control. "What had occurred was a racial shift of political power that brought blacks to a position of equality. White business and political leaders resisted and complained about this shift and saw it as antiwhite."[9] Eventually, as Stone has noted, Mayor Jackson had to moderate his progressive stance and reconcile with Atlanta's business and civic leaders. Andrew Young, the civil rights leader and former congressman, succeeded Jackson in 1981. Once in office Young made it clear that he wanted to govern with the cooperation of Atlanta's business elite. Maynard Jackson was returned to the mayor's office in 1989. In 1993, Jackson retired. In 1993, Bill Campbell became the third African-American elected mayor of Atlanta. Black political empowerment, at least electorally, is strong in Atlanta.

Detroit's transition to black political control owes as much to the influence of industrial unionism as the massive demographic changes that occurred after World War II. In the 1940s and 1950s, black Detroiters forged an alliance with the leaders of the United Auto Workers (UAW). UAW emerged as the one influential force in the Motor City willing to support black leaders' position on such issues as housing and public education.[10] The labor movement had a profound influence on black Detroiters. It became an important political socializer and training ground for black civic and political leaders in the Motor City. Unionism helped shape black political thought in Detroit. "Union organizers were not content to organize for better conditions and higher pay; they were actually attempting to build a whole new political force in America. Political ideas that were debated within the labor movement helped to educate blacks in the various *isms* of the world. The labor movement was as much a place for the exchange of ideas as the black church."[11]

A number of scholars attributed the "radical activity" of Detroit's black leaders that began in the late 1950s to their growing involvement in the labor movement. The growth in black radicalism was in part a response to usual tensions between workers and owners and the more bitter polarization be-

---

[9] Ronald H. Bayor, *Race and the Shaping of Twentieth-Century Atlanta* (Chapel Hill: University of North Carolina Press, 1996), 51.

[10] August Meier and Elliott Rudwick, *Black Detroit and the Rise of the UAW* (New York: Oxford University Press, 1979).

[11] Wilbur C. Rich, *Coleman Young and Detroit Politics* (Detroit: Wayne State University Press, 1989), 63.

tween black and white rank-and-file workers over housing, job discrimination, police/community relations, and other issues of concern to African
Americans.[12] By the late 1950s black labor organizers began to operate much
more independently of the UAW. For example, in 1957 a number of "angry"
black labor activists formed the Trade Union Leadership Conference
(TULC). TULC grew out of a need in the black labor movement to attack
racism within the auto industry.[13] The growing independence of the black
unionists was especially evident when TULC helped elect William Patrick
the first black on the Detroit City Council in 1957. In 1961, when the UAW
endorsed the reelection of conservative Mayor Louis Miriani, TULC threw
its support behind a political novice, the more liberal Jerome P. Cavanagh.
Cavanagh won.

The middle to late 1960s witnessed the formation of a number of radical
black worker organizations. Founded under of the auspices of the League of
Revolutionary Black Workers, these militant organizations (Eldon Avenue
Revolutionary Union Movement, Dodge Revolutionary Union Movement,
and Ford Revolutionary Union Movement) "organized black workers, conducted demonstrations, held wildcat strikes, participated in union electoral
politics, and generally fought to improve the lot of black workers as part of
the process of transforming American society."[14] Sociologist James Geschwender maintains that poor social and economic conditions of black Detroit facilitated the development of "black pride, black militancy, and black
activism" and what he called "black worker insurgency."[15] In Detroit, black
participation in the labor movement allowed the black working class more
of a role in local politics than in Atlanta or Washington, D.C. It also provided
a window of opportunity for black activists with ties to the labor movement
to enter the political arena.

In 1974, Coleman A. Young, a former union organizer, became Detroit's
first black mayor. Detroit experienced a deadly and costly civil disturbance
in 1967.[16] The racial polarization engendered by school integration changed
the racial character of the city. Young came into office during a period of
heightened racial polarization. Young's election was a direct result of the
white exodus that accelerated in the years after the riot. Nevertheless, Young
came into office with one main goal: to bring substantial changes to the De-

---

[12] Thomas J. Sugrue, "Crabgrass-Roots Politics: Race, Rights, and the Reaction against Lib-
eralism in the Urban North, 1940–1964," *Journal of American History* 82 (September 1995):
551–78.

[13] Dan Georgakas and Marvin Surkin, *Detroit: I Do Mind Dying* (New York: St. Martin's
Press, 1975), 43.

[14] James A. Geschwender, *Class, Race, and Worker Insurgency: The League of Revolutionary
Black Workers* (New York: Cambridge University Press, 1977), 189.

[15] Ibid.

[16] Sidney Fine, *Violence in the Model City* (Ann Arbor: University of Michigan Press, 1989).

troit police department. Police-community relations, which had inflamed race relations before, during, and after the riot, took a decided turn for the better as a result of Young's election. Young's combative style and willingness to stand up to whites brought a sense of pride to Detroit's black community.[17] Young's electoral base was firm. He became the city's longest-serving mayor.

Despite his continuing electoral success, Mayor Young's relationship with private corporate interests and investors was less solid in nature.[18] Mayor Young and his supporters were not slow to attack the white business community for abandoning the city. As a group, corporate leaders—especially during Young's last two terms in office—were often made to feel uncomfortable by Young's criticism of their suburban investment strategies and lifestyles and were fearful of racist accusations. According to Widick, Young not only "earned the grudging respect of the white power structure that runs business and industry in Michigan" but also "has been criticized frequently by whites for being resentful and belligerent."[19] Nevertheless, by the late 1970s, the chief of police, the superintendent of schools, five of the nine city council members, and eight of the thirteen members of the Detroit Board of Education were African Americans. When Coleman Young retired in 1993, Dennis Archer, a former state supreme court judge, became Detroit's second African-American mayor. Archer was elected with the strong backing of Detroit's corporate community. As a mayoral candidate, Archer portrayed a conciliatory posture. He talked about reaching out to the largely white suburban communities and strengthening ties between city hall and the corporate sector. In Detroit, political power is securely lodged in the hands of blacks; economic power continues to be in white hands.

During the middle 1970s through the middle 1980s, when Atlanta, Detroit, D.C., and other big cities with huge black populations elected their first black mayors, Baltimore, despite its huge black population, was unable to elect a black chief executive. The powerful and popular Mayor William Donald Schaefer was able to retain the mayor's office for several years after Baltimore reached a black majority. In addition, whites maintained a majority of the nineteen city council seats until 1995—more than fifteen years after blacks reached a numerical majority of the population. Baltimore's tradition of machine-style politics weakened and divided Baltimore's growing African-American population.[20] Machine politics created considerable

[17] Rich, *Coleman Young.*

[18] Marion Orr and Gerry Stoker, "Urban Regimes and Leadership in Detroit," *Urban Affairs Quarterly* 30 (September 1994): 48–73.

[19] B. J. Widick, *Detroit: City of Race and Class Violence* (Detroit: Wayne State University Press, 1989), 239.

[20] Marion Orr, "The Struggle for Black Empowerment in Baltimore: Electoral Control and Governing Coalitions," in *Racial Politics in American Cities*, ed. Rufus P. Browning, Dale Rogers Marshall, and David H. Tabb, 2d ed. (New York: Longman Press, 1997), 201–19, and Marion

distrust and jealousy between black voters and black politicians and among political leaders themselves. For example, Baltimore's failure to elect a black mayor in 1971 was the result of division in the black community. In the 1971 Democratic primary, then-city council president William D. Schaefer defeated two prominent black candidates by capturing much of the white vote while the two black candidates divided the black vote.[21]

Schaefer concentrated on downtown redevelopment, especially the Inner Harbor redevelopment project. Working closely with the business community, Schaefer led the effort that eventually transformed Baltimore into a "renaissance" city. Baltimore's large African-American community, however, benefited least from Baltimore's redevelopment. In November 1981 the U.S. Commission on Civil Rights held hearings in Baltimore to gauge the extent of minority business involvement in Baltimore's economic development projects. The Commission concluded that civic and political leaders had not done enough to include minority businesses.[22] In addition, Baltimore's black neighborhoods continued to experience high unemployment, a scarcity in affordable housing, and disintegration of their public schools. Levine comments: "The evidence . . . clearly suggests that residents of Baltimore's neighborhoods, particularly its black neighborhoods, derived little benefit from the downtown boom. For most Baltimore neighborhoods, the 1970s were years of increasing poverty, deteriorating housing, and shrinking economic opportunities."[23]

Schaefer, however, held on to the mayor's office by rewarding his black supporters with patronage appointments in city government. In particular, he used his formal authority over the city's public school system—and the access to jobs and patronage it provided—in order to maintain black support.[24] In 1986, Schaefer resigned to become governor of Maryland.

Today, black political incorporation is strong in Baltimore. In 1987, Kurt L. Schmoke became the first African American to be elected mayor of Baltimore.[25] Schmoke, who was reelected in 1991 and 1995, has focused much of

Orr, *Dilemmas of Black Social Capitol: School Reform in Baltimore, 1986–1998* (Lawrence: University Press of Kansas, forthcoming).

[21] G. James Fleming, *Baltimore's Failure to Elect a Black Mayor in 1971* (Washington, D.C.: Joint Center for Political Studies, 1972).

[22] United States Commission on Civil Rights, *Greater Baltimore Commitment: A Study of Urban Minority Economic Development* (Washington, D.C.: U.S. Printing Office, 1983), 1.

[23] Marc V. Levine, "Downtown Redevelopment as an Urban Growth Strategy," *Journal of Urban Affairs* 8 (1987): 113.

[24] Kenneth Wong, *City Choices: Education and Housing* (Albany, NY: State University of New York Press, 1990).

[25] The distinction of being Baltimore's "first" African-American mayor belongs to Clarence "Du" Burns. As city council president, Burns automatically ascended to the mayor's office in December 1986 after Schaefer resigned to become governor. Schmoke defeated Burns in late 1987.

his energy and leadership in reforming the city's public school system. In the late 1990s, African-Americans, with a majority of the nineteen seats on the city council, hold the seat of city council president, and the position of comptroller, both citywide posts. The administrative leadership of the city is also predominantly African-American.

African Americans' ascension to power in general city politics in our four cities was similar to what occurred in other major cities with large black populations. In Atlanta and Detroit, black mayors came to power on the strength of the black vote and in an atmosphere of heightened racial polarization. Both Coleman Young and Maynard Jackson defeated popular white candidates who were supported by Detroit's and Atlanta's white political and civic establishment. Baltimore and D.C., however, were different. In D.C., the broad resentment of Congress temporarily muted differences between locally oriented blacks and whites. Marion Barry, for example, depended on white support to win victory in his initial race for mayor. However, in his 1986 election the situation had changed. Dogged by skepticism about his integrity and effectiveness, Barry's support among white voters dropped considerably. Over the course of his long tenure as mayor, Barry lost much of the support of white supporters.[26] Blacks' ascension to power in Baltimore politics carried very little racial overtones. This was partly due to fact that many of city's white political and civic elites were prepared for the racial transition.

MANAGING SCHOOL DESEGREGATION

So far, our story about demographic change and political transition has had little to say about the schools. But changes in education were inextricably intertwined with changes in population and power. Although precisely disentangling issues of cause and effect is complex, it is clear that changes in the schools were not simply consequences or accompaniments to these broader changes. At key instances, events in the education arena dominated the local agenda and defined in the minds of leaders and the public what desegregation meant and what was at stake. Rather than just reflecting population shifts, changes in the racial composition of schools almost certainly had some independent effect upon population shifts. And, rather than just reflecting racial changes in the control of general offices of local power, such as the mayor's office and city council, racial changes in the control of school boards and school administrations often predated—and served as a foundation for— extending of black power to those higher offices.

[26] Dennis Gale, *Washington, D.C.: Inner City Revitalization and Minority Suburbanization* (Philadelphia: Temple University Press, 1987), 160–83; Jeffrey R. Henig, "Race and Voting:

Managing the process of school desegregation was a major challenge in each of our cities, and the way the process unfolded has had lasting consequences for local institutions and local attitudes. In this section we review the history of school desegregation in the four cities in order to highlight its role in shaping three important aspects of the contemporary political landscape: (1) the special symbolic status and material role of public schools in the black community; (2) the mismatch between needs and resources created by suburbanization and white flight in the wake of school desegregation; and (3) the emergence of exit as a powerful alternative to politics and coalition building as a vehicle for addressing educational needs.

Desegregation and the Special Status of Public Schools in Black Political Consciousness and Political Life

Over the course of history, race has been the single most important factor in determining the quality of education received by schoolchildren in Atlanta, Baltimore, Detroit, and D.C. The intersection of racial attitudes and segregation policy forged—in each city, albeit with varying degrees of formality—an inadequate system of education for African Americans. White citizens' desire to avoid racial mixing created two educational systems: one black, one white, separate and unequal. The subordinate position of African Americans steered black children into lower quality schools.

In Atlanta, Baltimore, and Washington, D.C., dual systems were formally constituted by law in the nineteenth century.[27] Each system had its own separate staff and its own separate school buildings. Detroit had no official policy on racial segregation. By the middle 1930s, however, segregation had developed. Mirel attributes Detroit's trend toward racially segregated schools to the changing composition of its neighborhoods and the manipulation of school attendance boundaries by school officials.[28]

Continuity and Change in The District of Columbia," *Urban Affairs Quarterly* 28, no. 4 (June 1993): 544–70.

[27] The history of school segregation in the four cities is discussed in Paul E. Peterson, *The Politics of School Reform, 1870–1940* (Chicago: University of Chicago Press, 1985); Bayor, *Race and the Shaping of Twentieth-Century Atlanta*, 197–251; David N. Plank and Marcia Turner, "Changing Patterns in Black School Politics: Atlanta, 1872–1973," *American Journal of Education* 95, no. 4 (August 1987): 584–608; Sherry H. Olson, *Baltimore: The Building of an American City* (Baltimore: The Johns Hopkins University Press, 1985); Lillian G. Dabney, *The History of Schools for Negroes in the District of Columbia, 1807–1904* (Washington, D.C.: The Catholic University Press of America, 1949); and Constance M. Green, *The Secret City* (Princeton: Princeton University Press, 1967).

[28] Jeffrey Mirel, *The Rise and Fall of an Urban School System: Detroit, 1907–81* (Ann Arbor: University of Michigan Press, 1993).

No matter how they were institutionalized, white schools and black schools never approached genuine equality. In Atlanta, for example, black schools had high teacher-pupil ratios, were forced to hold double sessions, and received secondhand supplies and textbooks. Per pupil expenditures were never equal: as late as 1945, $139 was spent on the education of each white child, while only $58 was spent on each black child.[29] Atlantans "not only were educated separately from whites, they also were relegated to markedly inferior schools."[30] In Baltimore, schools officials refused to build new schools for blacks. School policy was to turn over schools deemed unfit for whites for use in the black community. Schools for black children were "dangerously overcrowded."[31] African-American schools in D.C. were also underfunded compared to white schools; in 1947 per pupil expenditures for white children were $160.21 compared to $120.52 in black schools.[32] Black parents and leaders complained that black students were forced to attend overcrowded schools while many white schools had thousands of unused spaces. In 1953, pupil-teacher ratios in the District of Columbia, were much higher in black schools than white schools: 26 percent in high schools, 19 percent in junior high, 11 percent in elementary, and a whopping 52 percent in kindergarten.[33] Black students in Detroit were warehoused into the academically deficient general curriculum at twice the rate of whites.[34] Because blacks lived in the oldest section of Detroit, the schools their children attended were often in terrible physical condition, and their supplies and equipment fell far below standard. Black parents in Detroit also complained about the small number of African-American teachers, while white teachers were accused of publicly degrading black students and having low expectations of them.

The separate school systems—de facto and de jure—left important legacies. First, they strengthened the special symbolic role that public education plays within the African-American political consciousness. Early black leaders embraced the notion that public education and democratic society were inextricable. The dual school systems reinforced the contradiction of American democracy. As we shall see, this symbolic role continues to influence education politics in black-led cities. Reform initiatives that appear to undermine control of public education often spark a forceful and intense resistance and a tendency—sometimes mystifying to white residents, outsiders, and

[29] Plank and Turner, "Changing Patterns in Black School Politics," 589.
[30] Paul E. Peterson, The Politics of School Reform, 96.
[31] Olson, Baltimore, 115.
[32] David L. Lewis and Joanne Engel, Washington, DC: The Flight for Freedom at Home and Abroad, 1940–1953 (Washington, D.C.: D.C. Public Schools, 1979), 44.
[33] Martha Shollenberger Swaim, "Desegregation in the District of Columbia Public Schools" (master's thesis, Department of History, Howard University, 1971), 158.
[34] Mirel, The Rise and Fall, 186–96.

others unfamiliar with the historical legacy—to portray such initiatives in starkly racial tones.

Second, the separate school systems in Atlanta, Baltimore, and D.C. helped produce and nurture an important segment of the African-American community—elementary and secondary school educators. By the second half of the twentieth century, black teachers and principals were important role models and respected leaders in their communities. They also comprised a significant proportion of the African-American community's middle-class.[35] While their special status has somewhat eroded as other avenues of advancement have been opened for educated and ambitious black youth, black educators continue to hold a somewhat privileged place in the status hierarchy within the African-American community; this may somewhat shield them from criticism by dissatisfied citizens and may better enable them to rally supporters when they feel that their own interests are threatened.

Third, although the implementation of desegregation in the post-*Brown* era was sometimes manipulated in ways that protected white teachers and administrators while blacks lost their jobs,[36] in growing central-city school systems many black teachers and administrators were absorbed into the unified systems. This means that the education bureaucracy was much more quickly integrated than was the case, for example, in police and fire departments. In Washington, D.C., in 1955, the teaching force was already 55.8 percent black, and the staff members in administrative and supervisory positions were 47.9 percent black.[37] In Baltimore in 1954, 37 percent of elementary school teachers and 27 percent of secondary school teachers were African American by contrast, in 1965, 55 percent of the elementary teachers were black, as were 45 percent of the high school teachers.[38] Atlanta's numbers were similar; in 1963 blacks constituted 49.6 percent of elementary level teachers and 42.9 percent of high school teachers.[39] Among professional personnel, blacks grew from 3.9 percent of Detroit schools' staff in 1946 to 21.6 percent in 1961, but they did not account for a majority until 1975.[40] As black residents looked to the public sector as a potential avenue for jobs and personal advancement, the public school system presented itself as a hospitable target. This rapid integration of the public schools bureaucracy

[35] Bart Landry, *The New Black Middle Class* (Berkeley: University of California Press, 1987).

[36] John Smith and Bette M. Smith, "Desegregation in the South and the Demise of the Black Educator," *Journal of Social and Behavioral Sciences* 20 (Winter 1974): 28–40.

[37] Carl F. Hanson, *Addendum: A Five-Year Report on Desegregation in the Washington, D.C. Schools* (Washington, D.C.: Anti-Defamation League of B'nai B'rith, 1960), 8–9.

[38] Maryland Commission on Interracial Problems and Relations, *A City in Transition: The Baltimore Community Self-Survey of Inter-Group Relations* (Baltimore: Baltimore Commission on Human Relations, 1955); and Marilyn Gittell and T. Edward Hollander, *Six Urban School Districts* (New York: Praeger, 1967), 234.

[39] Bayor, *Race and the Shaping of Twentieth-Century Atlanta*, 230.

[40] Mirel, *The Rise and Fall*, Table 5.

also meant that black educators were in position to develop more readily and effectively as an organized interest.

Finally, the dual systems galvanized and unified the black community behind the goal of obtaining full-citizenship rights. In all four cities, the black community exhibited considerable unity under the leadership of the black clergy and other representatives of the black middle class to bring education equity to the black community. In Baltimore, for example, the National Association for the Advancement of Colored People (NAACP), the black clergy, and the influential publisher of the *Baltimore Afro-American* rallied behind black public school teachers for equal pay, more equitable resources for black schools, and African-American representation on the city school board.[41] In Detroit, the battle over desegregation forced the black community simultaneously to build outside alliances and to develop internal cohesion. According to Lewis and Nakagawa, "resistance to public school desegregation forced liberal whites, labor unions, and black activists into potent coalitions. . . . At the same time, black communities identified their own community leaders, which resulted in an important new force in city politics."[42]

Demographic and Economic Correlates to Racial Change: White Flight and Concentrated Need

The nature of the relationship between school desegregation and white flight into the suburbs and private schools has been the focus of considerable controversy. Some analysts have argued that mandatory school desegregation efforts played an important role in accelerating the process of white flight,[43] while others argue that suburbanization was just as evident in cities that did not undergo massive desegregation, that flight in the immediate wake of desegregation initiatives, attributable to short-term panic, subsequently abated, or that white flight could have been prevented if desegregation policies were less timid and incremental.[44]

---

[41] George H. Callcott, *Maryland and America: 1940 to 1980* (Baltimore: The Johns Hopkins University Press, 1985), 147–49.

[42] Dan A. Lewis and Kathryn Nakagawa, *Race and Educational Reform in the American Metropolis* (Albany: SUNY Press, 1995), 40.

[43] James S. Coleman, Sara D. Kelly, and John A. Moore, *Trends in School Desegregation* (Washington, D.C.: Urban Institute, 1975); Christine H. Rossell, *The Carrot or the Stick for Desegregation Policy* (Philadelphia: Temple University Press, 1990); David J. Armor, *Forced Justice: School Desegregation and the Law* (New York: Oxford University Press, 1995).

[44] Thomas F. Pettigrew and Robert L. Green, "School Desegregation in Large Cities: A Critique of the Coleman 'White Flight' Thesis," *Harvard Educational Review* 46 (1976): 1–53; Gary Orfield, *Must We Bus?* (Washington, D.C.: Brookings Institution, 1978).

This debate about the causal connection between desegregation and white flight is of more than academic interest. Many conservative opponents of government intervention in general have used the example of desegregation to build a case that well-intentioned public-sector intervention usually makes things worse. And some leaders within the black community have used the example of white flight to legitimate their claims that white racism is pervasive, that the promise of genuine integration is illusory, and that a separatist approach, rooted in Afrocentrism and self-help, is the only realistic route to power and independence.

However, one does not need to fully disentangle these causal threads to decipher some ways in which the shape and concomitants of racial change left lasting legacies. Determining the ultimate cause of white flight is immaterial: its aftermath is the more salient factor in this discussion. White flight has left a structural legacy of high need; black-led school districts have a disproportionate share of those children who are most challenging and costly to educate because of the disadvantages that poverty imposes upon them. Racial turnover has been closely linked to economic changes that have had long-term consequences for governance of the schools. As the cities became increasingly black, they also lost economic ground to their surrounding suburbs. This general relationship between racial turnover and relative economic decline is hardly surprising to those who have even a passing familiarity with the history of urban and metropolitan development in the United States, but the sharpness of the pattern and its particular consequence for the schools are important to keep in mind.

Figure 2.2 juxtaposes two indicators of the cities' status relative to their suburbs. The scale on the right, which corresponds to the downwardly sloping lines, indicates the ratio of median household income in the city to that of the metropolitan area. Entering the 1970s, the four cities had median household incomes about 74 percent to 83 percent of those for the metropolitan area; by 1990 the range was lower—from 55 percent to 67 percent. The scale on the left, which corresponds to the upwardly sloping lines, compares the cities' share of poor children to their share of the total metropolitan population; a ratio above 1.00 indicates a disproportionate share of children living in poverty. In 1970, this ratio ranged from 1.44 in Baltimore to about 2.07 in D.C.; by 1990 it ranged from 2.31 in Baltimore to 2.88 in Atlanta.

Poor children, for a variety of reasons, present special challenges for schools, and this measure of the disproportionate share of poor children, therefore, can indicate the burden that central-city schools encounter. Figure 2.3 presents the same indicator for all eleven cities in the larger project and relates it to the racial composition of the city population. As should be apparent, there is a strong relationship, at least across these eleven cities, between racial composition and the concentration of poor children. This is a reminder that—quite apart from the vigor and capacity that black-led cities

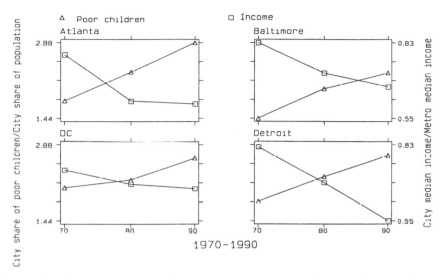

Figure 2.2 Cities' proportion of metropolitan income and share of poor children.
Source: U.S. Bureau of Census, Census of Population and Housing, various years.

may or may not muster in promoting education—the local politics of urban education is enmeshed in broader forces that make it much less likely that black-led cities will succeed.

Exit, Trust, and the Prospects for Interracial Coalitions

Broad changes in the metropolitanwide distribution of needs and resources occurred gradually and at a macrolevel not directly perceptible to the average citizen. At the level of individual schools and neighborhoods, however, the impacts of desegregation were often more immediate and intense. Although some schools remained buffered from racial change for decades, in others the temporal juxtaposition between desegregation and white flight was so close that citizens at the time would be hard-pressed to avoid the conclusion that the two went hand in hand.

D.C. is an interesting case to consider because not only was it the first among our cases to go through the process of racial change but also its experience with school desegregation was played out on a national canvas and was cited by many as a model for others to emulate.[45] Only eight days after the

---

[45] A version of the presentation in this section appeared as Jeffrey R. Henig, "Patterns of School-Level Racial Change in D.C. in the Wake of *Brown*: Perceptual Legacies of Desegregation," *PS: Political Science and Politics* 30, no. 3 (September 1997): 448–53.

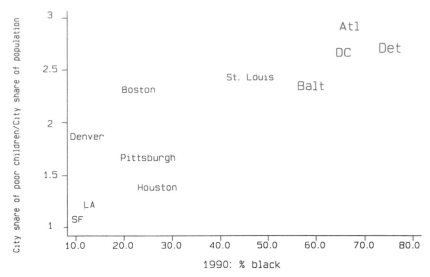

Figure 2.3 Cities' share of poor children by percentage black. *Source*: U.S. Bureau of Census, Census of Population and Housing, various years.

Brown decision, the appointed school board adopted a desegregation policy. "The press celebrated 'massive compliance' when, on 13 September 1954, the Washington public schools opened with mixed classes and faculties throughout the District."[46]

Although called a "miracle" by those impressed with the relative speed and calm with which desegregation took place at the level of individual schools, at the level where most D.C. parents and children directly experienced the changes the story was more complex. Incredibly rapid change in some parts of the system was combined with surprising stability in others. In 1953, the year before the *Brown* decision, just under half of D.C. schools (47.2 percent), containing about 56 percent of those enrolled, were in Division 2, which meant that they were legally restricted to black students. *None of these schools experienced more than minor integration during the rest of the decade.* As a group they continued to average over 97 percent black each year from 1954 through 1960 and averaged fewer than fourteen white students per school during each of those years. The pattern for the Division 1 schools—the schools legally restricted to white students before 1954—is more complicated. *Nearly two-thirds of formerly all-white schools experi-*

[46] Raymond Wolters, *The Burden of Brown* (Knoxville: University of Tennessee Press, 1984), 12.

enced abrupt and dramatic rapid racial turnover;[47] all of these schools had become predominantly black by 1960, and more than half of them did so within just two years. At the same time, *one-third of the previously all-white schools remained primarily white through the rest of the decade.* This latter group, comprising thirty schools, still averaged less than 5 percent black in 1956 and just under 12 percent black in 1960. About ten of these schools had begun a clear trend toward racial turnover by the end of the decade, but twenty still had fewer than 5 percent black in 1960.[48]

In other words, within six short years after the *Brown* decision, many pieces of the current structure were already in place. A small number of schools, predominantly in the northwest sections of the District, had become sharply distinguished from the rest. The emergence of an elite subset of predominantly white, upper socioeconomic status schools, combined with the deterioration and unresponsiveness that characterized the broader system, provided parents with an incentive to pursue their children's needs at a microlevel. Parents—predominantly white—who lived in the regular attendance zones of these schools could devote their considerable energies and resources to fund-raising and politics oriented around their own school, rather than systemwide reform.[49] Thus, even for those who could not or would not opt for exit to the suburbs or private schools, an intramural alternative to political voice developed.[50] We discuss more thoroughly these dynamics and their counterparts in the other four cities in chapter 5.

In addition to steering parents toward school-level solutions, the post-*Brown* experience may have complicated contemporary coalition building for systemic reform initiatives in other ways. To those who hoped that judicially mandated desegregation would lead to relatively stable integrated schools, the rapidity with which schools once again became identified as white or black (albeit informally) must have been disappointing. To some

---

[47] Of the seventy-two Division I schools that remained in existence in 1960, forty-seven had become majority black by 1960; they averaged 84.3 percent black in that year.

[48] These schools that remained white in 1960 subsequently traveled different paths. One group quietly and steadily continued along path of racial transition. In others, small groups of parents, committed principals, and others mobilized. All support began with the stated intent of maintaining the quality of their programs: some proceeded with an explicit agenda of creating models of stable racial integration, and some were perhaps primarily motivated to keep the racial composition predominantly white. Some of these schools lost the battle to maintain a racially diverse student body. Others, though, still stand out among D.C. public schools, in terms of the racial and class composition of their student bodies and the test scores their students earn.

[49] Over time, many middle-class black parents came to regard these schools as superior as well; absent a clear or consistently reformed student transfer policy, principals were left with considerable discretion to selectively accept transfers of families and children that seemed most likely to support the school's academic missions (see chapter 5).

[50] Albert O. Hirschman, *Exit, Voice and Loyalty* (Cambridge: Harvard University Press, 1970).

black residents, seeing almost no whites attending formerly black schools and seeing most of those formerly white schools that attracted large numbers of black students (primarily those in predominantly black neighborhoods) rapidly turn over, it may have been tempting to draw the lesson that even white liberals who professed allegiance to the concept of integration were unreliable partners. Others, both white and black, may have been converted to a more wary orientation toward the feasibility of pulling off radical systemwide change, at least with the courts as a mechanism.[51] This wariness toward the courts, moreover, was occurring at the same time that African Americans in many large central cities were finding new strength in the vote. Tactics oriented around lawsuits made sense while blacks were outnumbered and outmaneuvered in the electoral arena, but as they became the new majority, African Americans discovered that they could sometimes parlay their numbers into political concessions quicker and with greater certainty through traditional politics.

POLITICAL COMPROMISE AND TRANSITION: THE EVOLUTION OF BLACK-LED SCHOOL DISTRICTS

Rather than occupying a separate political sphere, school politics in Atlanta, Baltimore, Detroit, and D.C. became intertwined with city politics writ large. Galvanized by the national civil rights movement, African Americans in Atlanta, Baltimore, Detroit, and D.C. began flexing their political muscles. The increasing size and electoral power of the African-American community led to increased demands for black access to positions of authority and influence in not only city hall but also school systems. Wilbur Rich, in his multicity study of school reform in Detroit, Gary, and Newark, indicates that

[51] Our interpretation of the evolution of attitudes toward the judicial system as a vehicle for change is more complicated than we can develop here. Lacking genuine political representation in the pre-home rule era, Black Washingtonians did not abandon the federal courts as an alternative channel for defending their interests. The 1967 Hobson case can be seen as a second major effort to use the courts to bring about equal opportunity in the schools, although it, too, had mixed results. Home Rule might have created the conditions through which black residents could use electoral power to drive systemwide reform, but that potential was never realized. Instead, throughout the 1980s and into the 1990s, the major parents advocacy group in the city was heavily oriented toward the courts as a vehicle for change. In adopting this orientation, the group may have passed up opportunities to develop a needed grassroots base. See Anna Speicher, "Community Involvement in Public Education: Parents United for the D.C. Public Schools," Center for Washington Area Studies, George Washington University, Occasional Paper 11; Jeffrey R. Henig, "Civic Capacity and Urban Education in Washington, D.C.: Second Year Report," August 1992. By early 1997, some leaders of this group were publicly expressing reservations about the course they had taken. See Michael Powell and Vernon Loeb, "For Reformers, Fire Code Lawsuit Brought Dismaying Side Effects," *The Washington Post*, 18 February 1997, A9.

"blacks achieved their first political successes in school politics."[52] By the early 1970s, it was clear that the public school systems in our four cities were quickly becoming the "black" agency of local government.

The 1973 Atlanta Compromise gave the black community administrative control of the city's public schools.[53] Business and civic leaders wanted to end the city's long struggle over school desegregation. They feared that enforced busing to achieve racial balance would result in more white flight. Local black leaders agreed to back away from their push for massive busing if given administrative control of the school system.[54] The Atlanta Compromise required the board of education to hire an African-American superintendent and reserved 50 percent of all administrative posts in the system for blacks. In 1973 Alonzo Crim became Atlanta's first black superintendent. In effect, the plan put African Americans in control of the school system in exchange for a plan that left many schools segregated. This control was valuable, both symbolically and practically: access to jobs and patronage came along with the plan.[55] But it also exacted a cost. The white business community, a potentially valuable ally in any effort to mobilize community resources toward the goal of strengthening the schools, psychologically disengaged from the public school system once it became perceived as the responsibility of the black elected elite.[56]

The arrangement and compromise that designated the Baltimore public school system as the black agency was less formal and explicit than the Atlanta Compromise. In the early 1970s, as African Americans began mobilizing politically, white civic and political leaders were forced to make them junior coalitional partners, thus eligible for a greater share of power and patronage. Roland N. Patterson became the first black superintendent in 1971. After defeating two prominent African Americans and winning the mayor's office, William Donald Schaefer moved quickly to consolidate his support in the black community. Schaefer's black supporters were appointed as school administrators and principals and hired in other school positions as rewards for their political support. The education department was one of the first departments of city government to be headed by a black. Baltimore's department of education—when compared to other city agencies—came

---

[52] Wilbur C. Rich, *Black Mayors and School Politics* (New York: Garland Publishing, Inc., 1996), 15.

[53] The Atlanta Compromise followed the pattern of "negotiated settlements" between Atlanta's white civic leaders and black middle-class community that has been a part of the city's politics since the 1940s. See Stone, *Regime Politics*.

[54] Gary Orfield and Carole Ashkinaze, *The Closing Door: Conservative Policy and Black Opportunity* (Chicago: University of Chicago Press, 1991), 107–12; Bayor, *Race and the Shaping of Twentieth-Century Atlanta*, 247–51; Plank and Turner, "Changing Patterns in Black School Politics," 599–602.

[55] See chapter 4.

[56] See chapter 6.

under the administrative control of African Americans especially early. For example, a black did not head the city's fire department until 1993; the first African American to head the planning department was appointed in 1991.

While Mayor Schaefer solidified African-American control of the city's schools, he began to put considerable distance between himself and the black-led school system. He typically left school policy to trusted associates on the school board and African-American administrators who owed him their appointments to city hall. Explaining Mayor Schaefer's apparent lack of concern for the public school system during the 1970s and 1980s, a member of the city council asserted: "The problem was that you had a white mayor and a black educational system. Mayor Schaefer and the school system couldn't get along. The school board was a battleground. I would go to the board meetings; they would put on a show each week. [Former Mayor] Tommy D'Alesandro really wanted justice for the school system. He wanted to help the system but couldn't because of the conflict. William Donald Schaefer understood this. He didn't want to mess with it."[57]

Similar to what happened in Atlanta, the advent of black administrative control corresponded with declining corporate-sector interest in Baltimore public schools. In the middle 1970s, although some adopt-a-school programs were launched, the business community's interest in school affairs continued to decline. Superintendent Patterson accused the city's civic leaders of "insensitivity to the school system."[58] As an official of the Greater Baltimore Committee (the city's largest business organization) conceded, the business community "abandoned the school system and gave it to a segment of the black community."[59] Community involvement in the schools dropped as many middle-class whites (and later the black middle class) moved and invested their time and money to help make their suburban schools superior.

In D.C., where racial change came early in the general population—student enrollment, teachers, principals—racial transition at the top rungs of the educational hierarchy was delayed due to the absence of local control. When it came, however, it came quickly. By 1950, the majority of school children in D.C. were black. By 1960, D.C. was officially the country's first majority black city (53 percent black). And by 1970, D.C. had become perhaps the nation's most important example of a predominantly black central city: its population was 71 percent African-American, and enrollment in D.C. schools was 95 percent African-American. Some residents proudly proclaimed Washington, D.C., as America's "Chocolate City," a slogan that even appeared on bumper stickers during the 1970s.[60]

---

[57] Quoted in Marion Orr, "Urban Regimes and Human Capital Policies: A Study of Baltimore," *Journal of Urban Affairs* 14, no. 2 (summer 1992): 173–87.

[58] Quoted in Wong, *City Choices*, 114.

[59] Quoted in Orr, "Urban Regimes and Human Capital Policies," 178.

[60] Gale, *Washington, D.C.*, 167.

Until the late 1960s, the D.C. school board was appointed by federal judges, who for many years maintained the racial balance of the board at six whites to three blacks. In 1962, the composition shifted to five whites and four blacks. With the student body already about 90 percent black and the teaching force about 75 percent black, "the presence of a white majority on the board angered black leaders."[61] In 1968, Congress established an elected school board. The city conducted its first independent school board election in 1969. For its entire existence as an elected body, the school board has been composed predominantly of African-American members. The new black-majority school board immediately clashed with the school administration.[62] The board accused white administrators of being insensitive to the needs of black students. Former superintendent Carl Hansen, who was forced to resign in 1968, acknowledged the role of race in D.C. school politics: "It is a rare happening in the Washington public schools that is free of racial consideration. This is hardly surprising, considering that at the last count nearly 93 percent of the schools' 150,000 pupils are Negroes, as are nearly 79 percent of its teachers and administrators. Five of the nine school board members, including the president and vice president, are Negroes."[63]

In 1970, Hugh Scott became the first African American to head D.C. public schools on a permanent basis. Hence, by the early 1970s the D.C. public school system was firmly under the control of the city's black majority. White civic and parental involvement in the D.C. schools dropped. Most links between the business community and the District's schools had been on an individual rather than a systemic level. Moreover, the out-migration from the District of middle-class whites lessened the involvement of white parents in school affairs. Many white parents pointed to the declining quality of education in the public schools as a major contributor to their limited activism in school affairs. During the 1970s D.C. school officials concentrated efforts on meeting the needs of the poor and black children. School curriculum stressed student mastery of certain "basic" skills. However, for many white parents—most of whom had attractive education credentials themselves—the common complaint was that the schools' curriculum was not challenging their children. Many of them enrolled their children in private schools, and thousands more moved to suburban Virginia or Maryland. Others have maintained a commitment to D.C. public schools. But, as we shall see in chapter 5, various factors, including racial sensitivity, have limited

[61] Steven Diner, "Crisis of Confidence," Occasional paper, Department of Urban Studies, University of the District of Columbia (May 1982), 33.

[62] Nancy L. Arnez, *The Besieged School Superintendent: A Case Study of School Superintendent-School Board Relations in Washington, D.C., 1973–1975* (Washington, D.C.: University Press of America, 1981).

[63] Quoted in Arnez, *Besieged School Superintendent*, 61.

their effectiveness as champions of systemwide school reform. Most of their energy and skills are centered on a small number of "enclave" schools.

Most of the city's whites work for the federal government or for related businesses, such as consulting and law firms, trade associations, and cultural and public interest organizations. Thousands, migrating from other communities to Washington, are thus not natives. Unlike whites in other cities, many whites in Washington pay less attention to local matters and more attention to national concerns associated with their careers and their political and personal viewpoints. Seen in this light, the local issues of everyday urban life are of secondary importance to many whites.[64]

Black administrative control of the Detroit public schools came in the midst of a long and racially polarized struggle over school desegregation. During the 1960s, a progressive school board and Superintendent Norman Dachler implemented a number of reforms that enhanced integration efforts. They hired black teachers, appointed black administrators, rescinded the system's liberal transfer policy, and established school boundaries that facilitated integration. However, further pursuit of integration goals aroused protest from both blacks and whites who wanted racially homogenous districts. Throughout the 1960s and 1970s, community control was favored over integration by some of the more vocal advocates. As Rich observed, "Black groups saw community control as a 'black power' goal."[65] The NAACP filed suit alleging that the school district was engaging in *de jure* segregation. Judge Stephen Roth agreed and ordered the district to implement a metropolitan busing plan—an order that the *Milliken* decision by the U.S. Supreme Court eventually over-ruled.

White flight out of the city, well underway following the 1967 riots, reached pandemic proportions. Jeffrey Mirel, in his comprehensive history of the Detroit schools, argues that whites conceded the schools to blacks in the middle 1960s and early 1970s, "primarily because this group opposed racial desegregation and higher taxes for the predominantly black school system."[66] By the middle 1970s, the racial balance of school board officials and key administrative posts began to shift in favor of black control. Detroit elected its first black mayor, Coleman Young, in 1973; the next year Arthur Jefferson was appointed the school district's first black superintendent, a post he held for the next fifteen years. Like the city at large, the school system in the 1960s and 1970s was punctuated by white disinvestment. As Mirel observed, "by 1968 . . . a variety of factors, including the Detroit riot, the King and Kennedy assassinations, the drop in white school enrollment, and controversy about integration, led many whites to withdraw their sup-

[64] Ibid., 176.
[65] Rich, *Black Mayors and School Politics*, 27.
[66] Mirel, *The Rise and Fall*, 400–401.

port from the schools entirely."[67] The Detroit public school system had evolved into a black-led school district.

Race and racial polarization permeated the political context that gave rise to black-led school districts. The dual school systems in Atlanta, Baltimore, and D.C., and *de facto* racial segregation in the Detroit schools, daily reminded blacks of all ages of their continued subordination. Throughout American history, black leaders considered education a key source of economic and social advancement. In our four cities, church leaders, educators, race-advancement organizations, and community-based groups allied to improve the quality of education available to black children. The accelerated exodus of white students after the *Brown* ruling dramatically changed the racial and socioeconomic composition of student enrollment. By the mid-1970s, black students comprised a supermajority in all four school systems. As the black population reached majority or near-majority in our four cities, increased political clout translated into influence in city politics. In Atlanta and Baltimore, white civic and political leaders sought to adjust to the changing political dynamics and incorporated blacks as junior partners in the governing regime. In exchange for their political support, African-American leaders were given administrative control over the public schools. In D.C., federal officials made the school board the first elected body in the nation's capital, where the city's black majority captured control of a majority of board positions. In Atlanta, through formal agreement blacks received control of the schools. A similar, yet less explicit, agreement was hatched in Baltimore during the same period. In Detroit, the massive exodus of whites to the suburbs assured the emergence of a black-led school system. In all four cases, it appears that the school systems became the first agency of local government in which blacks dominated.

The cumulative effect of these rapid racial, social, and political changes on our four school systems was enormous. The demographic, economic, and racial changes that had overtaken our four cities compounded the political and educational problems faced by school leaders.

THE POLITICAL LANDSCAPE IN BLACK-LED CITIES: FROM FORMAL TO INFORMAL POWER

By 1990, Atlanta, Baltimore, Detroit, and D.C. were firmly established as black-led cities with formal levers of local authority in the hands of African-Americans. But would control of local offices translate into policies more responsive to the needs of the cities' black children? According to the optimistic black-power scenario that saw racial transition as the solution

---

[67] Ibid., 325.

(see chapter 1), this might have been sufficient to usher in a new era of progressive urban policy oriented around redistribution as well as development, social capital as well as physical development. Yet, the record suggests much more complexity. Gaining control of the formal positions of local government authority has not had the hoped-for effect.[68] Descriptive representation has not been translated into straightforward and reliable substantive representation.

One reason that black control of local public offices might not make much difference is that civic capacity—the power to do things in the collective interest—may have less to do with formal structures than with informal arrangements. One strain of thought about urban politics has long held that the real power in cities rests with the control of private capital; in the words of Floyd Hunter: "The under-structure personnel [city officials] may be likened to a keyboard over which the top structure [corporate elites] personnel play."[69] The work of Stone and others in developing the concept of governing regimes, as discussed in chapter 1, has suggested a less stark vision. Formal power may be necessary but insufficient for civic capacity; local officials may depend upon alliances with other stakeholders—notably, but not exclusively, the business community—if they are to translate their campaign platforms into a viable governmental agenda.

How has this history of demographic and political change affected the relative prominence of key stakeholders and the alliances and cleavages that characterize black-led cities today? As discussed in chapter 1, some theoretical perspectives are more optimistic than others about the likelihood that racial transition will facilitate the kinds of broad-based coalitions that we believe are critical if school reform is to be systemic and sustained. One optimistic prediction is that racial transition could provide the foundation for a new race-based progressive movement that supports investment in human capital; race, in this sense, serves as an alternative to economic interest as the foundation for a governance regime. This perspective leads us to look for signs, in black-led cities, that black elected leaders have allied with predominately black grassroots, community-based organizations, with common interests in civil rights and social justice. A different, but also optimistic, view sees racial transition in power as the necessary, and perhaps sufficient, precursor to a broad transformation through which race itself will become a less significant and divisive social force. If accurate, this perspective leads us to look for signs of an emergent regime in which elected officials and business interests, regardless of race, are linked by a common set of interests in addressing the city's economic and development needs.

<hr>

[68] Rufus P. Browning, Dale Rogers Marshall, David H. Tabb, *Racial Politics in American Cities*, 2d ed. (White Plains, NY: Longman, 1997), 5.

[69] Floyd Hunter, *Community Power Structure: A Study of Decision Makers* (Chapel Hill: University of North Carolina Press, 1953), 94.

Two alternative perspectives anticipate that black-led cities will continue to be characterized by political conflict, hyper-pluralism, and inefficacious governance. The deracialized version predicts that black-led cities will re-fragment along other lines, that is, black leaders will square off against black leaders, using neighborhood, class, and old-fashioned patronage, in place of racial identity, as the currency on which they build their political bases. The racialized version envisions sharp racial cleavages continuing to define conflicts inside the city and even more sharply to define the orientation of the city versus the suburbs and the state.

Drawing upon the coded results of interviews conducted with general in-fluentials, community activists and education specialists in eleven cities, we present in this section some suggestive evidence about key stakeholders in general politics and common lines of cleavages. Among the early questions, before the interviews honed in on education issues, respondents were asked, "What are the major groups in the city, the active stakeholders . . . by that I mean those that play a major part in decision making?" Coders subsequently classified responses into twenty-three categories and recorded up to five stakeholders for each respondent.[70] Table 2.2 shows the percentage of re-spondents mentioning each type of actor, for our four black-led cities and for the comparison group of seven other cities as discussed in chapter 1.

As far as general stakeholders are concerned, the similarities between black-led and other large central cities are perhaps more pronounced than the differences. Business actors are the most likely to be mentioned as im-portant stakeholders, in both types of cities, with city government in general and the mayor more specifically the next most consistently mentioned.[71] The fact that business is so clearly and consistently seen as an active stake-holder—and mentioned even more frequently than locally elected officials—might be seen by some as encouraging evidence that business is not aban-doning central cities and by others as discouraging confirmation of the conventional elitist view about the disproportionate power of economic in-terests. We discuss the business role more thoroughly in chapter 6. Commu-nity groups and ethnic and race-based groups were also mentioned frequently.[72] Even though the question at this point in the interview was framed in terms of general decision making, many respondents, especially in the seven comparison cities, did mention school boards as important actors in local decisions.

[70] About half of all respondents mentioned as many as four stakeholders; only one-third men-tioned as many as five.

[71] Coders used this category for responses that mentioned specific businesses or corporations and for general mention of the business community. The category "Chamber of Commerce" was reserved for specific mentions of that organization.

[72] The category "community groups" was used only when that term was employed by a respondent with no elaboration or mention of specific groups that would permit a more precise categorization.

TABLE 2.2

Major City Stakeholders and Players in Education Politics (percent)

	Black-Led Cities		Other Cities	
	Stakeholders in City Politics	Players in Education Politics	Stakeholders in City Politics	Players in Education Politics
Mayors and County Executives	52.9	33.9	46.5	26.0
City Government	56.6	50.8	64.3	47.5
State Government	14.0	11.3	25.4	16.9
Federal Government	8.8	10.5	1.9	5.1
City Council	15.4	15.3	15.5	9.0
School Board	19.1	42.7	35.7	50.3
School Superintendent	14.0	22.6	9.4	20.3
Educators	13.2	10.5	15.5	29.4
Chamber of Commerce	16.9	5.6	16.0	9.0
Business Community	73.5	50.0	70.0	53.7
University Community	5.1	4.0	8.5	9.0
Community Groups	29.4	25.8	36.6	27.1
Nonprofit Community	19.9	18.5	10.3	10.2
Ethnic Groups	19.9	8.1	16.9	5.6
Neighborhood Citizen Groups	2.2		8.0	2.3
Parent Organization	14.0	16.9	10.3	21.5
Unions	9.6	9.7	4.2	3.4
Media	4.4	3.2	3.8	0.6
Church Groups or Church Leaders	18.4	11.3	6.6	2.8
State Courts	1.5			1.1
Labor	7.4	1.6	4.7	
Political Parties	2.2		1.4	
Everyone in General		2.4	0.9	5.6
None				0.6

Source: Reports the percentage of respondents agreeing that actors are either "key stakeholders" or "players" in education politics. Respondents were asked: "What are the key groups in the county. . . . By that I mean those that play a major part in decision making? Sometimes people talk about stakeholders. Who would they be in X?" Total adds to more than 100 percent because respondents were allowed to name up to five stakeholders. Respondents were then asked whether education was a specialized arena or had several important players. Those who felt that there were several players (68 percent in black-led cities, 58 percent in other cities) were asked "who they were." Again total responses add to more than 100 percent because each respondent was allowed to name up to five "players."

TABLE 2.3
The Character of Education Politics (percent)

	Black-Led City	Other Cities
Education politics is[a]		
Specialized	32.0	41.8
Several players involved	68.0	58.2
Education Politics Visibility[b]		
Highly visible	68.7	58.2
Out of public eye	9.6	14.8
Become more visible	3.5	3.8
Become less visible	3.5	0.5
Combination of more and less visible	14.8	22.5

[a]Respondents were asked, "Is community education a specialized arena or do general leaders play an important role in education?"

[b]Respondents were asked, "Are education decisions in City X highly visible and generate a lot of attention, or are they handled pretty routinely and out of the public eye?"

Some important differences emerge between the black-led and comparison cities, although many do not involve the most visible stakeholders. Although not listed among the very top actors, religious leaders,[73] unions,[74] foundations,[75] and the federal government are more prominent in the black-led cities than in our seven comparison cities. School boards, state government, and neighborhood citizens' organizations were less frequently mentioned in black-led cities than elsewhere.

Table 2.3 zeros in more closely on the issue of education decision making and questions specifically whether school politics in black-led cities is a pluralistic arena. We asked two questions that, although similar, seem to have tapped somewhat different dimensions of this issue.[76] First, we asked whether education in the community is an open arena in which general leaders play an important role or a specialized arena with a more limited scope of involvement. Later, we asked whether education decisions "are visible

[73] The important role of the black church as a social and political institution has been noted by others, and in our forthcoming book we suggest that its role in the politics of education in black-led cities is both significant and complex.

[74] Although teachers and unions appear to be more visible actors in the black-led cities, the relatively low proportion of respondents that mentions unions or teachers may be somewhat surprising in light of the frequent emphasis on unions as a powerful veto group.

[75] The greater involvement of foundations and the federal government may be a legacy of the War on Poverty and the various social programs that were targeted especially on large central cities with high minority populations during the 1960s and 1970s.

[76] Mark Kugler looks in greater depth at this issue of pluralism in his paper "Race and Perceptions of Pluralism in Urban Education" (presented at the annual meetings of the Urban Affairs Association, Toronto, April 16–19, 1997).

TABLE 2.4
Sources of Conflict in Education Politics (percent)

	Black-Led Cities	Other Cities
Local government versus business	3.6	3.3
State or federal government versus local government or school board	9.0	3.3
Citizen versus local government or school board	15.4	16.1
Intracity government versus school board	30.3	33.2
Citizens versus business	0.9	2.2
City versus suburbs	1.8	2.5
Ethnic conflicts	9.0	18.8
Inability of government to deal with education problems	2.7	2.5
Inability of government to deal with social problems		0.3
Lack of leadership/agenda setting process	1.8	0.6
Unions	2.7	1.1
Interest group versus interest groups	17.2	14.1
Conflict but no recurring lines	5.4	1.9

Source: Respondents were asked, "When is conflict (about education decisions), what is its source?" Table reports percentage of respondents identifying particular source. Because each respondent was allowed to list three sources, percentages add to more than 100.

and attract a lot of attention or are handled pretty routinely and out of the public eye." Given the key role that school politics has played in black-led cities and its historical interrelationship with electoral politics, we would expect black-led cities to show more signs of an open, pluralistic education regime, and the results provide some support for that view.[77] Respondents in the four black-led cities were not only more likely than those in the seven comparison cities to characterize education as an open arena ($p < 0.05$) but also more likely to characterize education decision making as highly visible (although this difference was not statistically significant).

Finally, Table 2.4 looks at the question of cleavage lines in black-led and other cities. Respondents were asked, "When there is conflict, what is its source?" Coders identified thirteen types of response and recorded up to three answers per respondent. At least as far as internal politics, racial and ethnic cleavages are not dominating factors in black-led cities. To the contrary, respondents from the comparison cities—where demographic trends are more volatile and where neither blacks, whites, nor Hispanics are a large

[77] City-by-city analysis shows that this is less true of Atlanta, where the school board and business community have been more involved and where the mayor and other general elected officials have sometimes shied away from direct involvement. It should be noted that there is quite a bit of variation among the nonblack-led cities on this indicator.

enough majority to dominate local politics—are more than twice as likely to indicate that these sorts of cleavages are important. As predicted by the "politics-as-usual" perspective, which sees racial transition as simply the emergence of a new group of actors engaging in the old battle over patronage, intramural competition between general elected officials and the school board as well as among special interest groups marks major lines of cleavage in black-led cities, just as they are in other cities. In spite of the racial and economic divide that distinguishes these black-led cities from their suburbs and separates black officials from the still predominantly white business sector, neither the city-vs.-suburbs, the government-vs.-business, nor the citizen-vs.-business cleavages emerge as especially notable. Nor have the combination of a predominantly black population and a predominantly black set of local officials generated a new regime cemented by racial identity. Conflict between citizens and government is still a major cleavage, mentioned only slightly less likely than in our comparison cities.

Not all of the findings run counter to the perspectives that see race as a factor of continued significance, however. The sharp cleavage between local predominantly black decision makers and external predominantly white decision makers fits the prediction of those who see race as a major defining variable. We say more about that in chapter 7. Moreover, as we illustrate in each remaining chapter, the role that race plays in black-led cities may be subtler than this type of analysis is likely to reveal. Key actors in black-led cities devote substantial energies toward keeping racial cleavages from opening, but they do so precisely because they see these cleavages as powerful and volatile. The effort to keep race a nonissue thus provides a critical background factor that insinuates its way into many political interactions and plays an important role in complicating the process of coalition building in black-led cities.

CONCLUSION: HISTORICAL LEGACIES AND RACIAL POLITICS

The 1950s and 1960s were turbulent times for Atlanta, Baltimore, Detroit, and D.C., but by the middle of the 1970s the demographic transition from white to black was relatively complete, and the hand-off of political power was well under way. Compared to many other school districts in the United States, so these four are now relatively stable and relatively homogenous. If racial change is a destabilizing force, then these districts enjoy the advantage of having had time to consolidate and digest their change. If racial and ethnic heterogeneity are potential sources of fragmentation and cleavage, then these cities appear to have the advantage of forming solid racial majorities within which agreements on collective goals and priorities might more easily be reached. If black power brings greater sensitivity to the needs of the disadvantaged, then these cities might be expected to be at the forefront in articulating and pursuing a progressive agenda of investment in the human capital of inner-city youth. Yet, as alluded to in chapter 1, and detailed in chapter 3, these ingredients have not been translated into systemic or sustained reform of inner-city schools.

Although the period of rapid change may be over, it has left complex institutional and perceptual legacies that still constrain educational policy options. These institutional legacies comprise (a) the distribution and structure of formal authority within local government, including the relative authority of the mayor and council versus the school board and the extent of centralization versus decentralization of decision making within the public school bureaucracy; (b) the distribution and structures of formal authority between local governments, states, and the national governments, including the degree of involvement by federal and state courts in local schools; (c) the level and access to financial resources funding locally defined educational initiatives; (d) the metropolitan distribution of social needs and disadvantaged youth. Perceptual legacies include: (a) the way different key actors tend to define problems and the solution-sets they are quickest to turn to; (b) the way stakeholders evaluate reliability of potential allies and strength of potential opponents; (c) habits and preferences in political tactics, including perceptions of the relative advantages of electoral, judicial, and protest-based strategies and the viability of exit as an alternative to political voice.

Along with relative racial stability and homogeneity, the citizens of Atlanta, Baltimore, Detroit, and D.C. have inherited a number of wide-ranging perspectives: a disproportionate share of their regions' poor children, a pluralistic local decision-making arena in which the dominant position of educational professionals has been eroded and the allocation of legitimate authority among various claimants remains unsettled; a protective stance toward public education and public-sector jobs linked to the special role these have played in black aspirations and upward mobility beyond that accountable for by narrow, individual self-interest alone; an especially early and well-developed black stronghold in the education sector (compared to other urban bureaucracies) tied to a history of dual segregation in which blacks had access to jobs as teachers and administrators in the black systems and schools; wariness of white elites as allies tied to the experience of white suburbanization and the perceived overeagerness of business to disengage in schools to focus on economic development; wariness about the limitations (and potential for backfire) of broad and dramatic efforts at social intervention, including that by the courts; and a tradition of "exit" as an alternative to voice through both suburbanization and the pursuit of school-based solutions and mobility within the public school system. These legacies make more understandable the elusiveness of educational reform in black-led cities.

CHAPTER THREE

The Elusiveness of Education Reform

We have lots of programs. I do not believe that
they are any more successful here than they've
proven to be any place else. In other words, there
are fad type programs that have never, that were
not clearly demonstrated to be successful when
they were initiated.
(Detroit teachers' union representative)

There are programs that spring up every day. You
see and hear about different projects and different
programs that just spring up that people think of
and try them out. . . . When you got so many
programs and projects everything is scattered and
difficult to measure success.
(Executive of a Baltimore charity)

THE ASSUMPTION of political power by African Americans in Atlanta, Baltimore, Detroit, and Washington was accompanied by the widespread expectation that schools in those jurisdictions would subsequently better serve the children in those cities. However, as we highlight in this chapter, the history of education reform in each city reveals that positive change is extraordinarily difficult. In spite of numerous efforts over the past decade, there is no evidence of substantial improvement in the quality of schools. Indeed, most evidence suggests that the quality of education in each city has declined, in some cases dramatically. Not only have reform efforts failed to provide significant improvement, but education authorities also seem unable even to marshal support for a sustained effort of implementing an overall reform plan. Rather, leaders turn first to one project, then another—sometimes with remarkable speed.

This dramatic failure of education reform presents an interesting puzzle. True, the tendency to substitute sporadic and small-scale initiatives for systemic reform is not unique to these cities, but one might reasonably have expected more. The "racial transition as solution" perspective, as we discussed in chapter 1, predicts that black-led cities will broadly support human capital investment and value schools as an institution through which to address important social and economic inequalities. Although we present some evidence that this is the case, we also show that in each city public consensus exists that the schools are not meeting the public charge of educating the city's youth.

To be sure, these school districts face daunting problems and limited resources. Nevertheless, there is a significant capacity for local action given the autonomy of local educational actors; moreover, each district operates with a substantial budgetary base. In fiscal year 1993, the four cities were able to spend, on average, $6,488 per student, fully one-third more than the average expenditure among the 100 largest districts in the United States.[1]

Why, then, has the record of school reform been so disappointing? Our challenge in this chapter is to eliminate some seductive, but overly simplistic, answers. The conventional literature on education reform offers a series of "solutions": improve leadership, adopt better curriculums and standards, institute organizational reforms, establish public-private partnerships, and the like. These proposals share a similar view of the existing school systems as impenetrable to new ideas. The current influentials in the local education arena are commonly portrayed as complacent, parochial, self-interested, reactionary, or belligerent. Although each of our four cities has its fair share of individuals and groups that put their own interests above the public good, we make the case in this chapter that school reform is *not* just a matter of breaking through walls of resistance. We demonstrate to the contrary: (1) key influentials in these cities think about education and school reform in terms very similar to those used by so-called reformers; (2) each city has experimented with a wide range of favored reform practices; and (3) in each there has been at least one serious effort to mobilize a broad coalition for systemic reform. Nonetheless, the typical pattern is for initially vibrant reform movements to sputter and run out of steam.

As we suggested in chapter 1, the challenge is more formidable than most school reform literature implies. Even after their introduction into the local environment, good reform ideas and practices prove to be neither self-replicating nor self-sustaining. Control over the local levers of formal authority is insufficient. Moving systemic school reform from "good idea" to "established practice" requires on-going support from actors outside both formal government and the education community as well as support from higher levels of government. Instituting and maintaining such broad coalitions are resource-intensive and politically risky enterprises, and the pay-offs to key actors, we argue, are more amorphous and uncertain than in many other activities that

---

[1] The per pupil expenditures and rankings (among the 100 largest districts) of the four were: D.C. ($8,382/ Rk #2), Atlanta ($6,401/ Rk #14); Detroit ($5,748/ Rk #19); Baltimore ($5,462/ Rk #24). National Center for Education Statistics, *Digest of Education Statistics, 1995* (Washington, D.C.: U.S. Department of Education, 1995).

compete for local attention. These challenges are not limited to black-led cities, and neither is the consequent pattern of intermittent and incomplete reform. For these reasons, as we suggest in chapter 1, the "natural state" tendency for cities is to fall back on less demanding and problematic modes of action such as patronage politics and downtown development. The transition to a predominantly black population and leadership had the potential to propel school reform higher on the local agenda; however, in subsequent chapters we show that race also complicates the political challenge of implementing comprehensive and sustained education reform.

THE CONDITION OF EDUCATION: POOR PERFORMANCE AND EVEN POORER CONDITIONS

Many factors make it extremely difficult to measure school performance fairly and reliably: Americans would like to see schools pursue so many goals, and no clear consensus emerges on which are the most important. The highly decentralized nature of education policy making in the United States, allows thousands of school districts the authority to select their own goals and employ their own means of testing performance. Standardized examinations of academic achievement serve as the most common proxy for assessing school performance, but overpowering evidence suggests that family and class background are much more important in shaping student performance than are measurable differences in what occurs in the classroom; we lack the data to control for this sufficiently.

Auxiliary goals may be important; however, academic achievement, the physical and mental well-being of children, and financial responsibility rank high on most people's list of a school system's primary obligations. Although we may not have uniform or completely reliable indicators that permit us systematically to compare Atlanta, Baltimore, Detroit, and D.C. to other districts on these conditions, most available, objective educational performance indicators raise serious questions about the capacity of these local systems to meet their education mission.

Observers have wryly commented on the "Lake Wobegone Effect," whereby almost all school districts report that their children are above average.[2] In spite of this tendency, all four of our cities report that significantly more than half of their students fall under the national norms for standard-

---

[2] The phenomenon, named after radio star Garrison Keillor's fictional hometown, where "all the children are above average," is driven by not only districts' tactical selection of testing mechanisms most likely to show them in good light but also the fact that percentile scores may be based on the performance of a first generation of test-takers who typically do not fare as well as subsequent cohorts whose teachers have learned to teach to the test.

ized testing in math and reading.[3] Performance levels sometimes seem shockingly poor. For example, Detroit reports that the average grade point average in the city's high school is 1.8 (with an A being 4). Less than 20 percent of Detroit's high school students who took the state proficiency test scored at the proficient level.[4] More than 64 percent of Atlanta's high school students scored as either "inadequate" or "minimal" on a state writing test. In the 1990–91 school year, 56 percent of Atlanta high school graduates who attended Georgia's public colleges were required to take remedial courses.[5] Test scores on the Maryland School Performance Program in 1993 show that fewer than 12 percent of Baltimore's fourth-grade students tested at the "satisfactory" level, and fewer than 5 percent of the city's eighth graders tested at the "satisfactory" level in science.[6]

A nationwide assessment of mathematical abilities of children in the fourth, eighth, and twelfth grades found that students in the District of Columbia ranked behind every state or territory except the Virgin Islands.[7] On 12 November 1996, the financial control board appointed by Congress to bring Washington, D.C., back from the brink of bankruptcy justified a take-over of the Washington schools because the district deserved "an absolute F."[8] In its report on *Children in Crisis: A Report on the Failure of D.C.'s Public Schools,* the control board declared: "In virtually every area, and for every grade level, the system has failed to provide our children with a quality education and a safe environment in which to learn. . . . This failure is not of the students—for all students can succeed—but with the educationally and managerially bankrupt school system."[9] For sixth graders, math scores on the Comprehensive Test of Basic Skill fell from the 67th to the 62nd

---

[3] Summary data is provided by Council of the Great City Schools (1994). It should be noted that the quality of these performance data is highly suspect. Testing inconsistencies across the cities make direct comparisons impossible. However, the fact that each city performs at a relatively low level is clear.

[4] Jennifer Juares Robles and Chris Christoff, "Archer may seek partnership to help schools," *Detroit Free Press*, 27 February 1997, 1A.

[5] Good Government Atlanta, "A Program of Financial Reform for the Atlanta Public Schools" (Atlanta: Good Government Atlanta, 1995), 1.

[6] While there is no doubt that Baltimore scored significantly below the state norms on the MSPP exams, these data probably understate the achievement levels in the Baltimore schools. The MSPP examinations were challenging even for high-achieving districts. For example, on average in 1993, 27 percent of third graders were seen as "satisfactory" in reading and 27 percent of eighth graders were seen as "satisfactory" in science.

[7] National Center for Educational Statistics, *The State of Mathematical Achievement* (Washington, D.C.: U.S. Department of Education, June 1991), 17–31.

[8] David A. Vise and Sari Horwitz, "Control Board Blasts System as it Readies Takeover Plan," *Washington Post*, 13 November 1995, A01.

[9] The District of Columbia Financial Responsibility and Management Assistance Authority, *Children in Crisis: A Report on the Failure of D.C.'s Public Schools* (Washington, D.C.: Financial Responsibility and Management Assistance Authority, November 1996).

percentile from 1991 to 1996, and reading scores fell from the 52nd to the 45th percentile. While more stable over time, test scores at the higher grade levels were even lower; in 1996, eleventh graders scored at the 41st percentile in math and 24th percentile in reading. The control board concluded, "the longer students stayed in the District's public school system, the less likely they are to succeed educationally."[10] Each city also reports other indicators of educational failure, including erratic attendance and high dropout rates.

The magnitude of challenges facing these urban districts seems nearly overwhelming. Indeed, the mass of statistical evidence on achievement seems almost irrelevant when observers in each school district cite the inability of school authorities to guarantee even the physical safety of students. Violence against students and staff is an important issue in each district. In redefining the agenda for the Detroit School District, Superintendent Snead identified "safe schools" as a major priority for the district. The D.C. control board, citing high levels of violence and disruptive behavior as a rationale for its intervention into the governance of the District schools, indicated that "nearly two-thirds (64%) of the District's teachers say that violent student behavior interferes with teaching. Nationally the percentage is half."[11] The *Washington Post* reports that public officials "appeared almost resigned." The vice president of the school board indicated "there is no way we've got the budget to have security at every door." "Are you going to put the whole Metropolitan Police Department in schools?" a former police chief asked rhetorically. "Then someone would get killed walking home from school."[12]

The physical facilities in these districts provide yet another measure of poor performance. Some schools are in such disrepair that they pose a threat to students and faculty who use them. Facilities issues have been particularly acute in the District of Columbia. According to a report of the General Accounting Office, about two-thirds of the District schools have faulty roofs, heating or air conditioning problems, and inadequate plumbing:[13] "Old boilers have steam leakages causing such infrastructure erosion that whole school wings have been closed and cordoned off, leaky roofs are causing ceilings to crumble on student and teachers desks; fire doors are warped and stick. . . . Some of the schools lack air-conditioning and are so poorly insulated that children must wear coats to keep warm in the winter time."[14]

---

[10] Ibid., 8.

[11] Ibid., 11.

[12] Sari Horwitz, "Measures to Make D.C. Schools Safer Fall Fatally Short," *Washington Post*, 7 March 1994.

[13] *School Facilities: Profiles of School Conditions By State; Conditions of American's Schools* (Washington, D.C.: General Accounting Office, 1996).

[14] Ibid., 38.

In both 1994 and 1996, many D.C. schools opened late when D.C. Superior Court Judge Kaye K. Christian issued orders blocking school openings until fire code violations were repaired. In spite of the controversy and confusion that had occurred because of the 1994 delay, and in spite of the fact that the city council subsequently allocated an extra $2.7 million for fiscal year 1996, school officials apparently failed to spend most of the available funds and improperly allocated $700,000 to other uses. According to Superintendent Smith, the focus on this unspent and misspent money missed the key point. "We're talking about 2.7 million, and I have 1.2 billion of deferred need. What can I do but patch when I have peanuts to fix major problems."[15] In 1997, Julius Becton, the chief executive officer appointed by the control board, made repairs of school roofs and the opening of school on time a top priority. When Judge Christian declared some schools still not ready to open, Becton decided to delay the opening of *all* schools for about three weeks.[16] The resulting disappointment and resentment greatly tarnished his reformer image.

Atlanta, Detroit, and Baltimore also have serious infrastructure needs. In 1992, only 38 of Baltimore's 178 schools were judged to be in "good" condition—the highest ranking—by the Baltimore City Public School's own experts. A total of 110 schools were rated "fair," and 27 were classified as being "poor" according to an annual report that evaluates roofs, wiring, plumbing, heating and cooling equipment, windows, and general cleanliness. In recognition of Detroit's infrastructure needs, voters in 1995 agreed to give the district authority to issue 1.5 billion dollars of bonds to help rebuild the system's physical plant.[17] In 1997 Atlanta voters approved a one-percent increase in the local sales tax to finance necessary renovations.[18]

Finally, considerable evidence indicates that administrative and financial controls are lacking in all four cities. For example, an independent manage-

---

[15] DeNeen L. Brown and Michael Powell, "DC Schools Failed to Use Fire Code Funding for Repairs" *Washington Post*, 8 August 1996, A01.

[16] Becton argued that a short delay for all schools would be less confusing and disruptive than would be a piecemeal plan to open some schools but not others. It is possible, too, that he thought the threat of a broad delay would entice Parents United or Judge Christian to reconsider their insistence that roof repair work be completed before school could get underway. In either case, he seriously miscalculated.

[17] Although there was general agreement that the Detroit Public School District did in fact have significant infrastructure needs, some opposition to the bond issue was based on a lack of clear documentation of that need and a well-articulated strategy on how the bond funds would be utilized.

[18] Renovations in Atlanta have been slowed by a dispute between the district and the state over affirmative action policy. The state attorney general ruled that the district's efforts to promote the use of minority construction firms was illegal and on that basis has refused to allow state construction funds released to the district. See Gail Towns, "Funds Ready, But School Projects Wait," *Atlanta Journal and Constitution*, 25 January 1997, D1.

ment study in Baltimore concluded that although the Baltimore City Public Schools had "a cadre of capable school and central office managers, many school-based and central office administrators were less competent." The report claimed that it was routine personnel policy to transfer "burned-out" classroom teachers from the school to noneducational positions in the central administration. Evidence was also cited that school-based administrators were assigned to the central office as a result of personnel problems.[19]

An external review in 1992 characterized the District of Columbia as having "an unstable and mismanaged school system with a relatively long history of poor performance."[20] The District of Columbia Public Schools (DCPS) policies on curriculum were judged "obsolete and incomplete," with few schools in compliance."[21] Auditors found "no method or means for systematic control of selecting, implementing or evaluating" ongoing programs, with special projects being *ad hoc* and "the result of site-based entrepreneurship rather than part of a district thrust." Among the most explosive of the findings was evidence of DCPS-payroll "ghosts"—persons presumably drawing salary, but without any apparent responsibilities.[22] Accounting procedures in the District are so poor that auditors are unable to track millions of dollars of funds. For example, much of the $180 million allocated to the district for capital improvement since 1985 seems to have been applied to other expenses.[23]

The leadership of the Detroit Public School System faces similar criticism of widespread mismanagement. School officials have been widely criticized for failing to provide basic supplies to classroom teachers, even though the supplies are available in district warehouses. Detroit's Superintendent Snead was explicitly rated as "unsatisfactory in fiscal management" in his 1996 annual review after he revealed to a shocked school board an unanticipated $25-million deficit in the school budget.[24]

In 1993 an Atlanta Chamber of Commerce issued a report that claimed that the Atlanta Public Schools handled public finances better than the "pub-

---

[19] Associated Black Charities, *A Report of a Management Study of the Baltimore City Public Schools* (Baltimore: Associated Black Charities, 1992).

[20] National Curriculum Audit Center, *A Curriculum Audit of the District of Columbia Public Schools, Washington D.C.* (Arlington, VA: American Association of School Administrators, 1992), 12.

[21] Ibid., 15.

[22] Ibid., 18.

[23] Stories abound about waste and administrative incompetence. For example, it has been widely reported that millions of dollars have been invested in buildings that were closed the following year or roofs were repaired by district workers only to be immediately replaced by a private contractor.

[24] John Hart, "Inside Detroit: Snead misses out on raise amid school fiscal woes," *Detroit News*, 27 November 1996, D3. Although Snead was denied a raise for the following year, his contract extended was as customary. In February 1997, Snead formally asked the board not to

lic perceives." However, the Chamber documented several areas that could be improved including salary and staffing structure. Although the student body had declined by 40 percent in twenty years, the number of school employees had declined only 15 percent. The report emphasized that staff numbers had actually increased between 1982 and 1992, while student population had declined by 14 percent; during this same period salaries had exceeded the rate of inflation by 30 percent. A 1996 report issued by Good Government Atlanta, a biracial public-interest lobby, expressed similar concerns about the size of staff and compensation. Results have been poor, in part, "because the APS has not hired the high quality of personnel it needed." The report notes that previous boards, unable or unwilling to dismiss non-performing employees, have continued such employees with full pay and benefits in meaningless or nonexistent jobs.

The presence of severe problems such as these does not mean these systems have broken down in all respects. Although average student performance is undeniably low, some students are quite successful. As noted in chapter 2, each system is charged with educating students who are often poorly prepared and whose academic performance is limited by a wide range of variables beyond the control of any school system.[25] Nationally, at least some evidence indicates that the test scores of low-income and minority youth would be even lower were it not for the success of American public schools in chipping away at the disadvantages associated with family educational background and socioeconomic class.[26] Moreover, a careful analysis of student achievement reveals that at least some schools in each system do perform at reasonable academic levels. For example, from 1986 through 1992, the D.C. elementary schools averaged percentile scores of 59 on third-grade math and 50.3 on third-grade reading as assessed by the Comprehensive Test of Basic Skills. There was, however, considerable variation around this mean. Six of the elementary schools had average reading scores above the 80th percentile nationally, and eight had average math scores above the 80th percentile. Between 1986 and 1992, scores declined an average 15 points on the third-grade reading scores and declined very slightly (less than 0.2 points) in math. But during that period twenty-seven schools saw their

---

consider renewing his contract. He later explained that he was not resigning and might ask for a renewal at a later date.

[25] It is widely recognized that economic status and educational achievement are positively related. This finding is obtained even within the more limited parameters of these cities. That is, schools that show on average a higher socioeconomic status tend on average to have higher student achievement. The implication here is that at least some of the relatively poor performance of urban school districts is a function of the nature of the student population, not solely a failure in the education system.

[26] David W. Grissmer, et al., *Student Achievement and the Changing American Family* (Santa Monica, CA: RAND Corporation, 1994).

scores rise by an average 9 points in reading and 18 points in math. Similar variation exists in Atlanta, Baltimore, and Detroit. In each city individual schools can claim relatively high levels of academic achievement.

While many teachers, administrators, and parents can be rightfully proud of such accomplishments against high odds, these modest victories are a far cry from the broad gains black leaders envisioned in the 1960s. Isolated successes are not enough to buck the downward spiral of confidence in these inner-city public schools. Local stakeholders in these cities recognize the need to do more.

LOCAL PROBLEM DEFINITIONS:
A FAVORABLE FOUNDATION FOR REFORM

Both the objective characteristics of problems and also the way problems are subjectively framed and interpreted determine whether and how they are carried onto the public agenda.[27] If key stakeholders do not believe that schools represent a problem, or if they conceptualize the nature of the education problem in very different terms from those relied upon by national school reformers, such differences in problem definition might account for the apparent failure of these cities to undertake more aggressive and successful reforms. As noted in chapter 1, many Americans do not believe that their own children's schools are performing all that badly. In addition, black parents may bring a different set of values to the task of evaluating schools. Some studies suggest they are more concerned with the role of schools in building student self-esteem, instilling discipline, providing basic job skills, or addressing other social problems than they are in academic performance per se.[28]

There is little evidence, however, that stakeholders in Atlanta, Baltimore, Detroit, or D.C. are complacent about school performance or resistant to the notion that schools should be held to higher standards of academic performance. Respondents in all four cities have serious concern for the future of their cities and their schools. Table 3.1 provides three ways to look at the problem definitions reigning among major stakeholders in our four cities. The table summarizes responses, coded from open-ended interviews, to three questions asked of general influentials, community activists, and education specialists in our four black-led cities and the comparison group of

[27] Bryan D. Jones, *Reconceiving Decision-Making in Democratic Politics* (Chicago: University of Chicago Press, 1994); David A. Rochefort and Roger W. Cobb, eds., *The Politics of Problem Definition* (Lawrence: University Press of Kansas, 1994).

[28] Mark Schneider, et al. "Shopping for School In the Land of the Blind, The One-Eyed Parent May be Enough" (paper presented at the annual meetings of the Midwest Political Science Association, Chicago, April 10–12, 1997).

TABLE 3.1

Problem Definition in Black-Led and Comparison Cities (percent)

What Are Schools in This City Doing? [a]

	City Type	
	Black-Led	Other
Everything that can be done	5.6	3.1
Fairly well	26.2	22.1
Falling short	55.1	56.4
Not well at all	13.1	18.4

What Are the Major Problems Facing the City? [b]

	City Type	
	Black-Led	Other
Inadequate government bureaucracy	9.6	15.7
Poverty and unemployment	69.6	70.4
Loss of tax base	20.7	7.4
Ineffective leaders	13.3	5.1
Social problems	26.7	39.8
Crime	43.0	38.4
Drugs	14.1	5.1
Inadequate schools	57.0	56.9
Race relations	23.7	31.9
Inadequate workforce	5.2	2.3
No problems	0.0	0.5

What Are the Major Challenges Facing the City? [c]

	City Type	
	Black-Led	Other
Workforce preparation	23.9	9.6
Low self-esteem	17.4	13.9
Health and social issues	34.8	29.4
Crime and drugs	20.1	22.4
City government	9.8	12.9
School board	4.9	8.9
Social service	4.9	5.9
Child care	1.1	1.7
Finances	34.8	36.6
Minority relations	8.7	18.8
Union conflicts	1.1	0.7
School resources	10.3	6.6
Teaching quality	33.2	43.9
No problems	0.0	0.0

[a] Percentage of respondents agreeing to statement.

[b] Percentage of respondents identifying specific problem. Respondents were asked up to five problems.

[c] Percentage of respondents identifying specific challenges. Respondents were asked to name up to three challenges.

seven other central cities.[29] As indicated in the first panel, the perception that local schools are not successful is pervasive. When asked to select among four alternatives, fully 68 percent of all respondents across the four cities indicate that the schools are at least "falling short," and slightly more than 12 percent indicate that the schools are simply not doing well at all. Early in each interview, before questions zeroed in on issues related to education and schools, respondents were asked a general question about the major problems facing their city. When asked to identify major problems in their city, not a single respondent replied that his or her city had none. For the most part, respondents in black-led cities painted pictures similar to those in other cities. Education problems were mentioned by more than half of respondents, second only to problems broadly related to poverty, unemployment, low wages, and the like. There is mild support for the possibility that other pressing issues may distract attention from education; compared to the seven other cities in our broader study, respondents in black-led cities were significantly more likely to mention loss of tax base, ineffective leadership, and drugs. But education still outstripped these concerns, and there is little evidence that the agendas of the comparison cities are less crowded overall.[30]

This view that urban schools are ineffective is strongly reflected in the comments of those familiar with the school systems. When asked how the schools were doing for children with disadvantaged backgrounds a Baltimore respondent claimed:

> They are doing an horrendous job. I mean, the kids that need it the most are the ones getting the least. . . . I mean it makes me sick when I go to some schools. I mean, that's why we need the Head Starts, that's why we need the full-day kindergarten, that why we need preschool programs, to give these kids a fighting chance. And they come in the school system behind . . . the teachers give up on them and just fall further and further and further behind, and all of a sudden in junior high school they are gone.

A similar view was expressed in Detroit: "The fact is that our school system is failing, failing our children and that's failing our future, and I think that is the most dramatic evidence that anyone would ever need to say that we've got to do much, much better."

It is possible, of course, that respondents in black-led and other cities would agree that education "is a problem" yet disagree significantly on what they *mean* when they say as much. For example, some national education reformers emphasize the importance of exposing more children to the types

---

[29] See chapter 1 for details.

[30] Of a total of 383 responses, 25 percent identified a lack of resources as a major problem in their community. Close behind were issues of education (22 percent) and crime (15 percent). No other issue area made up more than 10 percent of the responses. Responses were coded from an open-ended question on major problems facing their community.

of courses that might prepare them for college; however, it is possible that stakeholders in black-led cities might see other goals—such as training high school youth to move directly into the workforce; providing an atmosphere of order, discipline, and encouragement not available in some inner-city homes and neighborhoods; protecting relatively high status and high paying jobs for local teachers and educators—as equally or even more important. The third panel of Table 3.1 suggests some differences in problem definition in black-led cities: asked to name up to three major challenges in the area of children and youth, respondents in Atlanta, Baltimore, Detroit, and D.C. were more likely to mention workforce preparation and less likely to mention minority relations and teacher quality than respondents in the comparison cities. Here again, however, the similarities across the two types of cities are more striking than the differences.

AN ARRAY OF REFORM EFFORTS

If school authorities have failed to revitalize local education, it has not been due to an unwillingness to embark on reform. Change has been common. Education leaders report a number of important types of changes occurring within their systems. Frequently such changes were the result of specific actions of local political and educational leaders. The most common example cited was change in important actors within the school system. The second most common category was the implementation of some new educational reform.[31]

Of particular interest is the range of reported educational reforms. Table 3.2 provides a descriptive summary of the sorts of reforms that have been implemented in each city during the past decade. In very general terms these efforts can be organized around four broad themes: leadership, program, coalition formation, and structural innovation. As with any summary topology many actual instances will not fit completely in a single category. However, the listing does provide a framework to discuss the innovations.

Leadership Change

Popular dissatisfaction with public education is often directed toward the leadership of the local school system. Job security is increasingly limited for

---

[31] Of 282 total responses, 31 percent cited changing leadership as the most significant change in the education system and 23 percent mentioned some major educational reform. Declining quality, changing demographics, and decline in the effectiveness of school were all cited by 8 percent to 9 percent of the responses of those interviewed in the city.

TABLE 3.2
Typology of Education Reforms, 1988 to 1997

	Atlanta	Baltimore	Detroit	Washington
Program				
Curriculum reform	X		X	X
Graduation requirements	X		X	X
Strategic planning			X	X
Personnel				
New superintendent	X	X	X	X
Significant change in school board				
Coalition Strategies				
Business linkages	X	X	X	X
Community	X		X	
Parents		X	X	
Foundations		X	X	
Structural Innovation				
Site-based management			X	X
Charter schools			X	
Choice schools	X	X	X	X
Contracting		X		

Note: X indicates a serious effort in the city to implement the reform.

school superintendents in all large urban districts. This has certainly been the case for Atlanta, Detroit, Baltimore, and Washington. During the course of this study all have dismissed superintendents to hire "reformers" who are seen as having the appropriate vision to lead the district. Interestingly, three of these reform superintendents were themselves subsequently dismissed for failing to provide the board of education with desired levels of leadership.

Elected school boards are sometimes targeted as well. Both Atlanta and Detroit have seen reform slates sweep into office. In 1988 four Detroit reform candidates established a working majority on the board after their election. In 1993 Atlanta's *Erase the Board* was founded with a stated goal of replacing all members of the faction-ridden school board. External actors also target the authority of local school boards. In the District of Columbia the elected school board has largely been supplanted by an appointed set of trustees. In April 1997, the Maryland legislature enacted a school restructuring law and thereby created a new Baltimore school board jointly appointed by the mayor and the governor. The new law also replaced the school superintendent by splitting the duties formerly performed by the superintendent among three new positions: a chief executive officer, a chief academic officer, and a chief financial officer. The law mandated the new school board to adopt a comprehensive school reform plan.

The importance of leadership change is reflected in interviews with city elites. When asked to identify major changes in the education system, respondents often identified changes in leadership. For example, in Atlanta and Detroit major, reform efforts centered on electing new members to the Board of Education. An Atlanta school board member claimed: "The major change has been the election of the Atlanta School Board. The election of a new school board and the subsequent hiring of the new superintendent. Now we have to do something for the children. We got elected, now we have to do something for the children." Describing the outcome of a 1988 school board election, a Detroit respondent claimed:

> We've had a revolution you might say, in Detroit Public Schools that began in 1988 with a group of four board members who were elected on a platform of reform and one by one additional reform board members joined that group. At one time there were 10 reformers out of 11. The reform group hired Dr. Deborah McGriff who is a visionary superintendent who is interested in change empowerment, diversity, choice being the cornerstones of her change strategy.

Often expectations are particularly high when replacing the district superintendent. The superintendent is seen as source of potential fundamental change. Speaking of the superintendent in Atlanta, one observer noted: "We do have a new superintendent. I have his bio, but that is really not my issue. What we see in him, is a charge and a vision to really move us forward and the reflection is on him in that he is the number three African American that we have had over the system and he is talking about all children, not just black children, making Atlanta an international thrust. Dr. Canada is a visionary that I believe God sent." Similar hopes were also expressed when the Detroit Board of Education appointed Deborah McGriff: "I think that about five years ago, the people of Detroit decided they were ready for change and elected a reform minded school board which brought in a nationally recognized school superintendent. . . . And I think the new superintendent has really tried to present Detroit with a mission to educate all its children." A Baltimore economic leader also placed a good deal of hope in the potential for new leadership: "I'm hoping that with a new superintendent we'll see something. . . . There has been some progress and you could really see the progress of Dr. Amprey, who is the current superintendent, when he came on the scene. . . . Amprey has come with good ideas, lots of energy, willing to work with a lot of different constituencies to get things done and he is getting things done."

The potential of leadership change is, however, not accepted by all. Several respondents saw the emphasis on replacing the superintendent as naive. Indeed, some viewed it as distracting from a more serious substantive policy debate about reforms needed in the schools: "I don't really hear much being tried in Atlanta except 'let's get a new superintendent,' and that I guess is a little troubling to me. I guess I would rather people were arguing about 'maybe we should privatize or maybe we shouldn't,' but at least people are trying things. At least talk about it, at least some thinking about it, but the only solutions people seem to be grasping at is 'let's put a new guy in charge.' " There was even some concern that frequent recruitment of new leadership in the school system might serve to further reduce the capacity of the system by introducing instability: "Instability at the administrative level is a major concern. For years superintendents used to be in for ten or fifteen years. Now every three or four years there is a new superintendent with a set of assistant superintendents and so that is instability at the administrative level."

Program Enhancement

At the heart of the contemporary debate about education quality is the perception that student performance is inadequate. At various times political authorities at various levels have attempted to improve performance simply by requiring it. The implicit assumption in such efforts is that students are in fact capable of doing much better if they are given an appropriate set of incentives. Many look with amazement at the low expectations for students and seek to mandate a higher level of performance. According to one Washington D.C. respondent, "We wanted higher standards for graduation, higher requirement. I mean that the idea that many of our seniors take one history course, and an English course. The idea that they actually learned enough to leave school and go get a job or whatever is ridiculous."

Each city has also sought to implement a variety of curriculum innovations to stimulate academic achievement. These include a range of innovative programs in math, reading, and language instruction. Some of these reforms were introduced in explicitly racial terms. That is, efforts have been made in each city to introduce a more Afrocentric orientation into the core curriculum. Sometimes such efforts are very focused as in Detroit. Here a set of African-American academies was established. Other districts have attempted a more broad-based, if somewhat less intense, application. All four districts, however, have tried to use black heritage and pride as a means of reaching their students.

Coalition Strategies

In each district educational leaders have concluded that the formal educational system does not command sufficient resources to fulfill its mission. This has led to efforts to increase the capacity of the school system by linking it to key constituencies in the communities. Although the need to draw in actors outside the school system was expressed in a number of ways, one respondent in Detroit captured the feelings of many of those interviewed:

> I guess you know Detroit is using the phrase of an old African proverb, "that it takes a whole village to educate a child." I think it is really trying to be played out in the schools. And I think that it is really true. I mentioned the businesses and there are a number of Detroit businesses that have stepped forward in the Detroit Compact and other partnerships. I think that in Detroit we have very active church groups. There are a whole group of eastside pastors that are very active politically as well as in the lives of the schools.

A similar view was expressed in the District of Columbia:

> If you pull together a broad coalition then you need to hit each segment of society that would have an impact. You need to get your individual citizens, and you have your group of civic associations. In the District you have the [Advisory Neighborhood Commissions] and you get them to support. . . .
>
> You have your religious community who is usually out there supporting certain issues in one way or another. You obviously have your business community who a lot of things will impact one way or the other. You have your education community. That functions on different levels. You currently have a group of individuals I think in the past probably six or seven years who have been extremely supportive of elementary and secondary education and having been growing in strength since their inception over the past seven years.

While the definition of specific education stakeholders varies, it always includes business interests, local and state foundations, and parents. In addition, some districts see community and neighborhood groups as important partners.

The most visible coalition-building efforts have been directed toward engaging the interest of business in the schools. However, the terms of the engagement vary. A business often "adopts" a particular school and contributes to its educational program directly. In Atlanta, for example, a central administrator describes existing business linkages:

> Well, there are two categories of businesses that we work with. Simply those who are supporters, who provide donations and help us do our work. The Home Depot is a good example. Cox Communication is another good example. Then there are others with whom we have relationships such that they have an interest in a particular school or a particular community organization and they have an interest in us working with that school or community based organization, so they provide funding in order for that to happen.

Often an effort is made to link businesses to programs that train students to work in related sectors: "It's preparing students for careers and then we work directly with business in preparing. For example, we have a tech prep program. One of our high schools is food services. We have a desperate need for food preparation services. So we work directly with business in putting those programs together." Key to such efforts is the identification of job opportunities for graduates of these business-oriented programs.

> We've been working with an industry group for hospitality and tourism and particularly the managers of downtown hotels have told us they were having a very difficult time locating in this region, not just the city, but in this region who are interested in working their way through a career path in hotel management. . . . So we have instituted an academy program in one of the high schools to get students interested in the hospitality and tourism industry, helping to sort of grow that industry in Baltimore.

In addition to these more targeted programs, there have been some efforts to create a system-level relationship between the business community and the schools. Typically this linkage takes the form of a compact in which a business interest pledges a variety of direct incentives to students. These incentives usually include college support and/or job opportunities for students who perform at targeted levels. Currently school-business compacts operate in Atlanta, Detroit, and Baltimore.[32] Each provides college scholarships and guaranteed job interviews for students who meet the minimum standards set by the compact. In Detroit,

> The Compact is supported by about 12 different partner groups. Business is at the top of the list because business is providing most of the funding for the compact. It's this year about three million dollars. By the time we complete the process in 2003, business through the Detroit Renaissance group will have put into the Compact just under nineteen million. The state of Michigan is also a primary partner. They have been providing funds at about $500,000 a year. The other partner groups would include the major universities in the state who are providing college assistance.

In 1991 the Atlanta Chamber of Commerce founded the Atlanta Promise. The Promise is an umbrella organization of city businesses, nonprofits, city government, school system, housing authority, colleges and universities, and PTAs that provides a number of services to Atlanta students. These include tutoring and mentoring programs, awards and scholarships, and coordination of a variety of special programs. The compact was well received in the Atlanta

---

[32] There is an interesting difference among the compacts. In both Detroit and Atlanta the compacts were essentially a business initiative. In Baltimore the compact was created only after significant community pressure demanded an increase in business engagement in the problems of the local school system. In Washington, D.C., the Committee on Public Education (COPE) provided a citywide forum for business interests; however, it does not provide compact services to the district.

schools system. A high administrator noted: "If it's a power base to serve the well being of the students in the Atlanta Public School System, then it can't be anything but good. We in the education field would probably be the first to tell you we have serious problems in trying to meet the needs of the entire population we have to deal with. We want to serve all our children, and it can't be done alone."[33] The compacts are seen as important motivators for students as well as evidence of positive corporate engagement in the local educational system.

The limited capacity of such organizations to promote educational change is the focus of our analysis in chapter 6. For example, in Detroit the Compact is seen as being dominated by white-led industries. Efforts to recruit smaller African-American business into the Compact have met with very limited success. This failure not only threatens the financial future of the Detroit Compact, but it also generates some concern and suspicion among city residents as to the motivations of the Compact. These limits were brought into clear focus when the Chamber of Commerce tried to generate support for the re-election of the HOPE team by suggesting that if the reformers were turned out of office, the Chamber would have to reassess its involvement in the Compact. The community reaction to this tactic was very negative. Some black critics characterized the Chamber's action as an example of "plantation politics."

In all the school systems there is a strong formal commitment to increase the participation of other key stakeholders. However, efforts to actually engage such groups are episodic. This is particularly true with respect to parents. As noted by one administrator: "We are always working to mobilize parent groups more than they are. We believe that one of the keys to a successful education system, is strong parental involvement. So no matter how effective we may be, ultimately if we do not get parents involved we are not going to resolve too much." There is widespread rhetoric for this involvement, but relatively few concrete reforms promote it.[34]

Structural Reorganization

Based in part on widespread perception that earlier reforms were not effective, communities have sought organizational strategies that will bring meaningful changes to the school system. For some, education structure is the

---

[33] Betsy White, "Atlanta Corporations Make City Schools Their Business," 21 November 1991, D3. *Atlanta Journal-Constitution.*

[34] One exception is in Detroit: the board of education created what they sometimes call an "empowered" school, which has a strong community-based advisory committee. These reforms are discussed below.

central problem to be overcome.[35] Such claims rest on the general notion that the organization of schools interferes with their educational mission. School districts are seen as highly centralized bureaucracies, largely unresponsive to the needs and interests of parents.

In all four districts there has been strong symbolic support for the notion of site-based management. There seems to be broad support for the general notion that those closest to the delivery of educational services are better able to make specific budget allocations. However, in practice the degree of actual site-based management has remained modest in all cities. Detroit did implement a school empowerment program that granted considerable authority to the school principal; however, the program generated much union opposition and remained very small. Baltimore and Atlanta did demand some site-level planning, but it did not greatly expand school-level budget authority. In Washington, support for site-based management remained largely symbolic.

Some argue for a more radical restructuring that forces schools to be operated more as a market enterprise. Some local policymakers believe that market forces can effectively reform local education. The key assumption is, of course, that, by introducing more competition into the education system, educators will be forced to be more responsive to parent and student needs. A common strategy to introduce local competition is some form of school choice. Only Baltimore has not created a set of magnet programs open to all students in the district.[36] These magnets typically focus on a particular theme and offer specialized programs in that area. These schools are thought to give students valuable educational options as well as creating pressure for positive change in those schools losing students. Detroit has a liberal policy permitting student transfers to neighborhood schools, limited only by space availability. The logic in supporting transfers is, of course, the same. Schools are expected to compete for students by improving the quality of education.

A much more controversial scheme to restructure local education calls for the use of private firms to manage educational programs. The city of Baltimore explored the potential of such privatization by contracting with a private firm to run a set of elementary schools in the district. The decision was bitterly attacked by the city's teachers union and a number of important community organizations. Ultimately the contract was voided by the city on issues of excess costs and a lack of evidence of significant increase in student

[35] A useful overview of reform proposals is presented in Michael Mintrom and Sandra Vergari, "Recent Efforts to Improve Public Education in the United States: Intergovernmental Politics and Accountability Issues" (manuscript, 1997).

[36] Baltimore does have a set of citywide schools such as the City College, but these have been in place for many years. D.C., for the most part, does not use the term "magnet" to apply to its schools and programs that draw students from throughout the city.

performance.[37] About the time that Baltimore was embarking on its privatization experiment, the school superintendent in Washington was promoting a similar effort in the District of Columbia; however, the D.C. proposal was quickly withdrawn in the face of widespread public opposition.[38]

Charter schools provide a final source of local competition. Charter schools are privately established and administered schools supported with public funds. Authorization to create charter schools comes from either state or, in the case of the District, the federal government. At present charter schools are permitted in Michigan and the District of Columbia.[39] Although charters have been aggressively supported by state-level actors in Michigan, only a very modest number of charter schools directly serve the children from Detroit.[40] During the 1997–98 school year there were only three charter schools operating in D.C., but implementation of the congressionally mandated charter program accelerated rapidly, with eighteen schools in place by fall 1998.

THE FRUSTRATION OF REFORM

There is no question that all four cities have devoted much effort in pursuing educational reform. There are, of course, differences in the reforms sought. When asked to describe recent educational reform in their city, elites in Detroit and Washington are more likely to mention program changes (29 percent and 24 percent) than those in Atlanta and Baltimore (17 percent and 19 percent). Atlanta respondents stress leadership (21 percent) more than those in Baltimore (12 percent), Detroit (16 percent), and Washington (12 percent). Atlanta respondents seem less interested in structural reforms (19 percent) than Baltimore (37 percent), Detroit (28 percent) or Washington

[37] The issue of cost was particularly contentious. Originally the private form was to have been given "the same" resources available to the school district. However, through a series of miscalculations it was generally agreed that the private firm was receiving more resources than regular public elementary schools.

[38] It should be noted that efforts to contract with private firms to provide specific tasks, as opposed to the operation of entire schools, are more common. This is especially the case for support services. For example, in 1997 the Atlanta School District contracted with Marriot School Services to reorganize its maintenance workers.

[39] At present the state of Georgia only allows existing public schools to be charter schools. Of the twelve charter schools currently operating in Georgia, none are located in Atlanta. Efforts in the 1997 legislative session to liberalize the chartering laws were not successful. D.C.'s current charter law was imposed by Congress, but the local school board had initiated a modest public school-within-school charter program on its own initiative.

[40] In general, school districts have opposed school charters largely because such schools usually directly reduce the revenue of the regular district from which the charter student has left. In Michigan, for example, the full state subsidy follows the student to the school he or she actually attends.

(23 percent). Most striking, however, are not the differences but the relatively stable patterns of elite issue definition.[41]

There is little question that local school districts have been actively promoting a wide variety of school reform projects. More interesting, however, is whether these systems were actually engaged in efforts at systemic reform. As Anhalt, Di Gaetano, Fraga, and Henig have noted, terms like "systemic reform" and educational "restructuring" have "functioned, in the current national education policy debate, more as political symbols than as referents to a concrete programmatic agenda."[42] Although a precise definition of project-level reform and systemic change can be arbitrary, we believe the general distinction is clear. Systemic reform seeks to initiate broad restructuring of the education system. As such it is targeted to most or all of the school district. In addition to its broad scope, systemic reform typically demands a reconstruction of the decision-making elite that directs educational policy. Because this may require reorienting informal patterns of decision making, redesigning formal institutions, and reallocating power, systemic education reform requires more than careful attention to program design and implementation; it also requires a political process of coalition building.

A review of recent education politics in Atlanta, Baltimore, Detroit, and Washington suggests that in each city there have been periodic efforts to build a broad-based political coalition to support restructuring of the local education system. All shared a general commitment to restructure the political coalition around education. In part this restructuring was programmatic; districts experimented with a wide variety of programs and structures. However, the political element of reform was also quite clear as leaders sought to expand the set of actors central to the education policy. Although this political element was common across the cities, the contrast in who championed reform and how such efforts were framed was significant. In Atlanta educational politics remained in the hands of a broad public-private coalition that has long dominated Atlanta politics in general. Education reform in Atlanta was largely framed as an elite response to widespread pressures to desegregate the city's schools. In Baltimore reform was driven by the ambitions of a strong mayor. In Detroit it came from the election of a slate of

---

[41] It should be noted that these aggregated categories mask some important variation in city reform efforts. This is particularly true for potential structural reforms. Detroit respondents focus their attention almost exclusively on choice and school charters. In Baltimore there is an equally strong focus on privatization and contracting. In Atlanta and Washington respondents are much less focused and discuss a wide range of potential structural reforms. This suggests that, although, each city actively searched for a reform strategy, the outcome of that search was by no means the same.

[42] Bari Anhalt, et al., "Restructuring School Governance: Reform Ideas and Their Implementation" (presented at the annual meetings of the American Political Science Association, New York, August 31–September 4, 1994).

reform school board candidates. In Washington efforts were driven by a private coalition of interests, largely led by business elites. The frailty of such efforts is underscored by the collapse of internal reform efforts in each city at some point during the course of our study.

Systemic Reform in Atlanta: Elite Response to Desegregation

In 1973, Alonzo Crim became the first black superintendent of the Atlanta school district.[43] His selection was a key element of the Atlanta Compromise, which explicitly acknowledged the leadership role of Atlanta's African-American community in the local school system. Crim believed he had a mandate to bring fundamental educational reform to the city. A set of magnet programs was established to help stem the flow of whites from the system. However, key to Crim's strategy was expansion of the local constituency for education. He made a public commitment "to engage the community and APS system-wide and local schools in continuing partnership for identification of needs, goal setting, program implementation, evaluation, and program redesign." Such engagement was necessary to "provide learners with opportunities to attain higher levels of achievement and growth."[44] To gain community engagement in reform efforts, Crim embarked upon a strategy that put him in contact with civic associations, PTA presidents, social clubs, and almost any group that offered an invitation.[45] He also conducted a series of town hall meetings to obtain the public's views and to mend wounded relations between the school system and parents and students.

MOBILIZING THE COMMUNITY

Observers estimate that Crim met with more than ten thousand citizens who more often than not voiced their pent up anger and frustrations that they had not been permitted to voice during the previous administration. From these meetings, four priorities emerged: improve significantly basic skills in reading, writing, speaking, and math; assist students in handling their futures by providing job and opportunity counseling; allocate the system's resources equitably; and improve communications among Atlanta Public Schools

[43] The authors wish to acknowledge the contributions of Carol Pierannunzi (Kennesaw State University) to this discussion.

[44] *Your Schools* (October 1974), cited by David Blount, "An Analysis of Selected Indicators of Performance Effectiveness in the Atlanta Public Schools, 1968 to 1983" (Ph.D. diss., Georgia State University, 1985), 170.

[45] Before Crim could address these goals and other pedagogical issues, he had to comply with the federal court order to desegregate the school system and to balance the system's top administrators racially. Consequently, Crim's public meeting strategy was not underway until 1974–75.

(APS), the public, parents, and students and among school staff. By the 1975–76 academic year each of these goals were designated as formal APS goals.

There is little question that Crim's community efforts expanded civic support for local education. Several new education-oriented community organizations were created. The Northside Atlanta Parents for Public Schools (NAPPS) was founded in 1975, in part, to stem the tide of white parents away from the school system and to promote the public schools in North Atlanta. APPLE Corps (Atlanta Parents and Public Linked for Education) was founded by the Atlanta Chamber of Commerce as an educational advocacy group—a nonprofit, independent support group composed of parents, concerned citizens, business leaders, and representatives from educational organizations. During the school year APPLE Corps offers workshops and forums to increase parent and community awareness on educational issues, publishes a newsletter and a handbook to serve as school system guide, operates a telephone and resource center that links parents with each other and with school officials, honors outstanding teachers with awards, and operates a grants program, funded by donations, to support innovative classroom projects.

Crim's community-building efforts also prompted the Atlanta Chamber of Commerce to found the Atlanta Partnership of Business and Education,[46] a nonprofit, tax-exempt corporation whose mission is to "enhance the quality of education for students in the APS system by establishing and maintaining high caliber and creative partnerships between individual schools and the Atlanta area's businesses and institutions." The Atlanta partnership provides mentoring and role modeling, tutoring, student and staff recognition and appreciation, classroom assistance, funds for enrichment activities, career exploration, scholarships, and support for PTA activities. By the end of the 1983 school year, 167 schools had been adopted, and local businesses had contributed more than $2 million in services to the APS.[47]

Crim also actively recruited churches and existing civic organizations to work with the schools. Such engagement generally involved job placement, tutoring and mentoring, and enrichment services during school, after school, and on weekends; many offered scholarships. For example, the 100 Black Men in Atlanta—a group of prominent lawyers, doctors, educators, and politicians—adopted a class of twenty-eight students in one of Atlanta's poorest schools for the purpose of moving the students through high school graduation and into post-secondary enrollment and completion. Students

---

[46] The program was originally known as Adopt-A-School, but in 1980 it was brought under the umbrella of this larger organization, the Atlanta Partnership for Business and Education.

[47] Blount, "An Analysis of Selected Indicators of Performance," 192. See also Alonzo Crim, "A Community of Believers Creates a Community of Achievers," *Educational Record* 68, no. 4/69, no. 1 (Fall 1987/Winter 1988): 44–49.

attending a reputable college, university, or vocation program would receive full tuition each year until they graduated.[48]

The Crim administration required principals to ensure that there was a functioning PTA organization in each school. The PTA was seen as a mechanism by which parents, teachers, and community members could give input into each local school's decision-making processes.[49] This policy, by reversing the membership loss in 1976, produced a growth in PTA membership to 11,000 by 1978. By 1985, PTA membership of well over 26,000 included both white and black members.[50]

Each school in the system was also mandated to develop an ongoing program of volunteerism. Crim believed that "every human being has a circle of influence within his home, among friends, and in his community that could contribute constructively to the improvement of society. Many citizens believe that educational volunteering can substantially contribute to the uplifting of society, as well as improve the welfare of children."[51]

Each of these various groups and organizations made up what Crim called a "Community of Believers." Crim laid out what that meant to him in 1981: "Belief by the community at large must include these factors: 1) Each student is a valuable person fully capable of learning, 2) our school system can bring about learning, 3) the economic future of the nation is dependent on the academic achievement of all students, and therefore, 4) every person in the total community is a stakeholder and has a vested interest in the Atlanta Public School System."[52]

RAISING ACHIEVEMENT

As Crim expanded the community support for school reform, discussions about the substance of reform were being held at the school level. By the 1975–76 school year, each school was required to develop a plan for improving reading and math skills. For the first time the new testing program provided achievement data for all students that could be shared with students, parents, and teachers alike.[53] Prior to 1975, test scores had never been made public. Unfortunately the low standardized achievement scores for the 1975–76 academic year seemed to confirm popular opinion that the "public schools were bad."[54]

[48] This is just one example of civic participation in education. See Crim, "A Community of Believers," for more examples of this type of community involvement.
[49] When Crim arrived in Atlanta, there were separate PTAs for blacks and whites, although the state and national organizations had merged.
[50] Blount, "An Analysis of Selected Indicators of Performance," 179–83.
[51] *Atlanta Public Schools Volunteer Handbook* (Atlanta Public Schools, 1978).
[52] Alonzo Crim, "A Community of Believers," *Daedalus*, Fall 1981.
[53] Atlanta Board of Education, Minutes, September 1980.
[54] David Blount, "An Analysis of Selected Indicators," 75.

During the 1976–77 school year, another phase of Crim's systemwide improvement plan was implemented: a district-level committee was organized to advise local schools on their development plans. During the year, the review committee met with local school staffs every three months to review progress and suggested modifications to the plans, if needed. A pupil progression policy for elementary school students, which ended social promotion, was also implemented.[55] Students were not to be promoted until they had mastered a certain percentage of skills required to go on to the next level. These efforts seemed to produce modest increases, but scores were still below the national norm. Systemwide gains were clearer by 1978–79, and Crim ambitiously announced that the downward trend had been reversed. He claimed that a systemwide goal of reaching the national norm in basic literacy skills would be reached by 1985.[56] This announcement became a rallying cry for the business community, parents, teachers, and the Atlanta Public Schools.[57]

By 1983, the APS system announced that students had reached the national norm in reading and mathematics. Test results indicated that for the third consecutive year, California Achievement Test (CAT) results had improved, exceeding district goals. The projected goal in reading was for 43 percent of the students enrolled in kindergarten through tenth grade to score at or above the national norm. The results indicated that 50 percent of the students had met that goal. In math, test results indicated that 55 percent of students in kindergarten through tenth grade scored at or above the national norm.[58]

By 1985, citywide 56 percent of all students taking the standardized test scored at or above the national average for reading. And 63 percent scored at the national average for math. According to the *Atlanta Journal and Constitution*, all but five of the city's eighty-five elementary schools were at or above the citywide average. But six of the ten middle schools and twenty of twenty-two high schools were below the average.[59] Atlanta's success in raising test scores brought the school system a measure of national recognition. The *New York Times* called the system "Urban Education That Works." Joe Martin, a school board member with close ties to the business community, noted that the "system's accomplishment on the CAT was crucial for Atlanta schools, helping to refute the notion that a system with a large number of

[55] Ibid.

[56] Ibid., 91–100.

[57] See Tom Walker, "Investment in Schools Pays Dividends," *Atlanta Journal and Constitution*, 15 October 1984, c1.

[58] Ibid.

[59] Connie Green, "Atlanta Schools Don't Stack Up on Standardized Test Scores," *Atlanta Journal and Constitution*, 2 June 1986, A1.

poor and black children is inferior."[60] Critics, however, charged that the CAT overstated achievement. It was also later revealed that teachers were engaging in a number of strategies to improve scores. According to the *Atlanta Journal and Constitution*, "teachers admit[ed] privately that because of pressure to raise test scores, some in their ranks have taught the test, and have allowed students during testing to work together in groups so that the better students could help the low achievers."[61]

REFORM UNRAVELS

In 1986 a debate over the test erupted.[62] Through the Quality Basic Education Act, the Georgia legislature required the APS to shift to the Iowa Test of Basic Skills. Not only had the test been changed, but the state also mandated a key change in test administration. During the years the APS had used the CAT, tests were administered to students according to their ability level rather than their grade level. For example, a fifth grader with second-grade ability would take the second-grade CAT. This practice resulted in inflated and misleading scores. Under the state's reform legislation, all students would be tested uniformly at their grade level.[63] Not surprisingly, the combination of a new test and the more appropriate testing procedures contributed to a poor showing. In 1986, only 37 percent of APS students scored at or above national norms. According to reports, Crim was disappointed, but he also sought to reassure the public that things were not as bad as the test scores might make them seem. "There is no way to rationalize the scores," he said at the time. "Scores will improve but . . . the emphasis on testing [is] not the real measure of what happens to kids."[64]

In May 1986, to the dismay and surprise of the board, teachers, parents, the business community, and the wider Atlanta community, Alonzo Crim announced his resignation effective 1 August 1987, two years before his contract expired. Citing personal reasons, Crim said that when he was hired he promised the board he would remain in Atlanta for ten years and now he was going on fourteen. "I've had the most satisfying career with the Atlanta Public Schools but at this point I think I should be considering a change."[65]

---

[60] Ibid.

[61] Ibid.

[62] In 1981 the APS switched from the Iowa's Skills Test to the California Achievement Test. Crim contends that the change was made because the school system wanted a testing tool that followed students through the twelveth grade rather than the sixth as the Iowa's test. Critics charged the change was made because the CAT was easier than the Iowas test.

[63] Ibid. See also Connie Green, "Atlanta Schools: Some Improve, but Others on a Downward Slide," *Atlanta Journal and Constitution*, 1 June 1986, A1.

[64] Donna Williams Lewis, "Atlanta at a Crossroads," *Atlanta Journal and Constitution*, 5 January 1987, E1.

[65] Alonzo Crim cited by Peter Scott, "City School Chief Crim Resigns," *Atlanta Journal and Constitution*, 16 May 1986, A1.

Some speculated that "personal abuse" by some board members had taken a toll on Crim. Board member Joe Martin said that Crim had "struggled mightily and done a magnificent job in raising standards and improving the attitude and inspiring people to do better. . . . In recent years, the task has not become any easier."[66] A majority of the Board urged Crim to reconsider.[67]

Crim's departure revealed the fragility of the coalition he had built. Several respondents noted that specific reforms and innovations in APS came to a complete halt when Crim resigned. A former schoolteacher remarked that when Crim left she felt abandoned: "Things were changing. Parents were involved. Teachers had opportunities to use innovative techniques in their classrooms. New programs that exposed students to speakers from around the world simply stopped. It all stopped."

School board member Robert Raymer noted that Crim was the "only school superintendent in this system's history that [had] the respect of both the mayor and the governor. Plus he [had] the business community involved in education. He's built a support system in Atlanta like nobody else has."[68] In short, Crim created in Atlanta an environment that facilitated action.[69]

With Crim's departure, the Atlanta Board of Education fell into disarray. Suddenly the board would argue for hours over minor issues that had little to do with education, involve itself inappropriately in personnel matters, and become downright uncivil. The board became "the most criticized and ridiculed public body in the history of the city."[70] Without a strong superintendent at the helm, the board began to exercise its political authority in much the same manner as a political machine. Board members were often involved in micromanagement of the system, despite the presence of a superintendent. In controversies just prior to the 1993 elections, the board involved itself in the hiring and removal of principals and individual teachers, the salaries of specific individuals, and the discipline of individual students. New jobs in administration, services, and inventory were created to provide work for constituents.[71]

[66] Joe Martin cited by Connie Green, "Crim Denies Friction Led to His Quitting," *Atlanta Journal and Constitution*, 17 May 1986, A1. Some board members suggested that criticism may have become tougher and harsher since the retirement and subsequent death of longtime board president Benjamin Mays. Some contend that Mays had acted as a buffer between Crim and the board.

[67] Karen Harris, "Move Is on to Get Crim to Remain," *Atlanta Journal and Constitution*, 18 May 1986, C1.

[68] Robert Waymer cited by Jane Hansen, "From the Start, Crim Stood for Giving Poor Children a Chance," *Atlanta Journal and Constitution*, 17 May 1986, A12.

[69] See James Coleman, *Foundations of Social Theory* (Cambridge: Harvard University Press, 1990).

[70] Bob Holmes, "The Status of Black Politics in Atlanta," *The Status of Black Atlanta* (Atlanta: Southern Center for Studies in Public Policy, 1993), 15.

[71] Cynthia Tucker, "The City's School Board Needs a Lot of Educating," *Atlanta Journal and Constitution*, 20 January 1993, A13.

Two voting blocs formed on the board: one supported Joe Martin, a white businessman from an affluent neighborhood and president of the board during this period; the other supported D. F. Glover, a black social science professor representing a disadvantaged minority community. Almost every vote taken split along these divisions. Conflict on the board escalated to ridiculous proportions. At one board meeting it was reported that Glover asked Superintendent Butts to "meet him in the parking lot." One respondent noted that the council meetings were widely watched on the state's public television network because they were "better than 'Dallas.' "

REFORM ROUND #2: AN ELECTORAL STRATEGY

Following the resignation of Superintendent Crim, the business community, parents, and community leaders disengaged from active participation in the Atlanta school system.[72] Before the 1993 election, opposition to the board escalated to the point that various community actors began to form a coalition to remove some or all board members in 1993. For example, the Atlanta Federation of Teachers, the Atlanta Labor Council, Apple Corps, 100 Black Men, and the Atlanta Association of Educators ran the following advertisement in the local newspaper:

> Wanted: New Atlanta School Board! Nine positions now available. Qualifications include: integrity, dependable, courteous, ability to calmly discuss issues and make rational decisions, must be able to engage in collaborative decision making with fellow board members, must have a passion for excellence in education, educating Atlanta's boys and girls must be top priority, must be willing to receive excellent training, must have excellent interpersonal skills. For further details and AFT Screening Application write: Atlanta Federation of Teachers, 374 Maynard Terrace, Suite 202, Atlanta, GA 30316.[73]

Each of these groups sought to stimulate interest among the voters and recruit and fund reform-minded candidates. The executive director of Atlanta

---

[72] The metro Atlanta Chamber of Commerce has also involved itself in the operations of the school system by funding a study of the financial condition of the schools. The report, released in February 1993, was surprisingly supportive of the system, although it noted many ineffective policies. One criticism of APS was the higher rate of pay received by Atlanta School employees when compared to other local districts. Criticism was also directed toward the state policy that uses the same formula to evaluate both suburban and urban schools while ignoring neighborhood differences and students' needs. The report further criticized the business community itself for failing to address problems associated with the schools and relying instead on graduates of suburban districts to meet their needs for trained employees. See Betsy White, "Chamber Finds City Schools Better Than Many Had Feared," *Atlanta Journal and Constitution*, 14 February 1993, A16.

[73] Betsy White, "Groups Seek New Blood for Atlanta School Board," *Atlanta Journal and Constitution*, 2 April 1993, D5. Also groups involved in the efforts to unseat all the board members were Erase the Board and Concerned Black Clergy.

Committee for Public Education, a business group, said that people were concerned about the future of Atlanta based on what was not happening in the schools.

> You don't normally see this level of interest in a school board election, but it appears that voters have as much, if not more, interest in the school board as they do in the mayor's race. I can't think of a more important election to the future of Atlanta because the incoming board will make policy for the next four years that impacts 60,000 students. They will also manage a construction program involving millions. . . . Everybody has a vested interest in this political process because it affects all of us whether or not we have children in school.[74]

The Chamber of Commerce also became active in the campaign, creating EDUPAC, a biracial political action committee, to recruit, endorse, and fund candidates.[75] Erase the Board, a grassroots, community-based organization was created with the goal of removing all sitting board members. Other existing organizations were also active in efforts to recruit new board members. These included Concerned Black Clergy, 100 Black Men, and the Atlanta Council of PTAs (a racially mixed but majority black organization), the Council of Intown Neighborhoods and Schools (also racially mixed), APPLE Corps, and the education division of the (Jimmy) Carter Center's Atlanta Project. The efforts of these groups were noteworthy: among other things, black and white citizens joined together in this effort, as did labor unions and business leaders, affluent neighborhoods and disadvantaged ones, parents and educators.

The endorsements by these groups differed. EDUPAC's final slate of endorsements included incumbents. Most noteworthy was Martin's endorsement by many organizations allied with the business community. One member of the business elite stated that they were not ready to oust Martin and "throw the baby out with the bath water." However, Erase the Board advocated the wholesale termination of all incumbent board positions. Neither group endorsed Glover or his frequent ally, Ina Evans. While the business community seemed embarrassed by the actions of these board members, black community members also joined in the criticism, specifically men-

---

[74] Betsy White, "They're Hot and Getting Hotter," *Atlanta Journal and Constitution*, 22 July 1993, D1.

[75] By some reports, EDUPAC was slow to get started, perhaps as a result of its recent organization, see Julie Hairstop, "Restoring Faith in City Schools," *Business Atlanta* 22 (September 1993): 14–15. With as little as ten weeks until the election, EDUPAC was still an organization only on paper. However, it eventually was able to endorse a slate of candidates and raise $53,000 in cash and $100,000 in in-kind contributions. Among the top contributors was Guy Millner, who later ran as the Republican gubernatorial candidate. M. Saporta, "Town Talk," *Atlanta Journal and Constitution*, 24 October 1993, D1.

tioning that Glover was "a catalyst for the cat fight" and the "main foot drag-
ger" in matters of educational reform.[76]

Some measure of support from the city's black leadership was essential to
the success of groups promoting change on the school board. Because the
board itself was a symbol of black political power, criticism of black board
members could be difficult. In particular, criticism of single members of the
board who were seen as problematic, especially Evans and Glover, could
have created a backlash in black communities. So an anti-incumbent theme
was adopted in order to avoid overtones of casting out only black board
members.[77] EDUPAC was more successful than Erase the Board in its endorsement of candidates. All the EDUPAC-endorsed candidates won their
elections outright or in the runoff election. In all, three incumbents were
reelected (Joe Martin, Midge Sweet, and Carolyn Yancey). Two were defeated in runoff elections, and four chose not to run. Herman Reese of 100
Black Men called the election outcome "a new day for Atlanta."[78]

In 1994, the new reform board hired Benjamin Canada as superintendent.
A Louisiana native and the former superintendent of Jackson (MS) Public
Schools system, Canada rekindled the "can-do" spirit that had not been present since the Crim administration. Like Crim, Canada began his tenure with
a series of community meetings to assess the views and opinions of all facets
of the APS community, including business, parents, principals, teachers, and
staff. In December, he announced the reorganization of the system—all departments would focus on students and instruction. He envisions more
"shared decision-making" on the school level and hopes the new plan will
translate into fewer administrators between the schools and the superintendent. Board members believe these changes will "empower employees to
be more creative in instructional strategies." Canada's goals are ambitious:
improving all students' performance; increasing safety; raising standards, reviewing and assessing people and programs continuously; developing and
recruiting innovative leaders, aligning the system to promote partnerships
and communication; enhancing shared decision making and adopting enabling policies and practices.[79] In February 1997, Canada unveiled the school
system's strategic plan that claimed that the system "was well into the process of retooling for reform."[80] A cornerstone of the strategic plan gives indi-

    [76] Carol Pierannunzi, Desiree Pedescleaux, and John Hutcheson, "From Conflict to Coali-
tion: The Evolution of Educational Reform in Atlanta," (manuscript 1993).

    [77] Ibid.

    [78] Betsy White, "School Board Newcomers Trounce Evans, Glover," *Atlanta Journal and
Constitution*, 24 November 1993, D1.

    [79] Gail Hagans, "Atlanta School Chief's Reorganization Expected to Affect All Parts of the
System," *Atlanta Journal and Constitution*, 22 December 1994, E11.

    [80] Gail Towns, "Three More Years: Atlanta Superintendent Sets His Course," *Atlanta Journal
and Constitution*, 21 February 1997, E4.

vidual school administrators the authority to individualize their programs to meet student and community needs. One indicator of this new authority is that principals must give written approval for staff assignments to their schools. Likewise, some spending discretion has been given to local schools.[81] As the basis of a set of performance audits, Canada reorganized two low-performing schools with new staffs and curriculum. Several others were "refocused" by updating curriculum, increasing staff training, and targeting efforts to increase community participation.

Systemic Reform in Baltimore: The Education Mayor

The 1987 election of Mayor Kurt L. Schmoke seemed to consolidate school reform on the local political agenda. Schmoke made education his top campaign issue and vowed to make it his administration's priority. In his first inaugural address, Schmoke vowed to make Baltimore "the city that reads." He initially expressed his vision for the schools in terms of site-based management (moving more decision-making authority from the central administration to the school site) and the increased involvement of outside interests in educational policy making. The initiative had broad support from the black church community, leading corporate and civic elites, and the Baltimore Teachers' Union (BTU).

Schmoke aggressively used his authority to influence education policy making. He rejected his school board's initial choice for superintendent and asked its members to name Richard Hunter, an education professor who had served as superintendent in Richmond, Virginia, and Dayton, Ohio, to replace the retiring Alice Pinderhughes. Hunter's tenure in Baltimore was tumultuous. Consistent with a long tradition among professional educators, he was uncomfortable with outside involvement in school affairs. Not only did Hunter fail to reach out to local stakeholders, but he also publicly disagreed with Schmoke on several policy issues. For example, the mayor and the superintendent clashed over a proposed collaboration between a Baltimore public school and a local private school.[82] Barclay School, which encompasses kindergarten through eighth grade, is located in the center city, where the student population is 94 percent black and 82 percent of the students receive free or reduced-price lunch. During the mid- to late 1980s, Barclay's principal and parents had become very concerned that the students at their school were not achieving at the city or national averages on a variety

---

[81] *School Talk* 19 no. 4 (summer 1997): 3.

[82] See Marion Orr, "Urban Politics and School Reform: The Case of Baltimore," *Urban Affairs Review* 31 (January 1996): 314–45, and Marion Orr, *Dilemmas of Black Social Capital: School Reform in Baltimore, 1986–1998* (Lawrence: University Press of Kansas, forthcoming).

of measures. Gertrude Williams, the African-American principal at Barclay, had become interested in the correspondence curriculum of the elite private Calvert School. Perhaps the most unique features of the curriculum are the intensive writing program (students write every day on a variety of topics and are taught how to write in cursive in the first grade) and the requirement that all work be revised until the students' product contain no errors. Supported by a grant from The Abell Foundation, the two schools developed a proposal to implement the entire Calvert program at Barclay. The program was to be implemented by the Barclay faculty. In 1989, Schmoke simply ordered a reluctant Hunter to approve the Barclay-Calvert collaboration.[83] The conflict, widely reported in the local media, is said to have greatly embarrassed Hunter.

Schmoke also had to overcome opposition from the Baltimore Teachers Union to the Barclay-Calvert collaboration. Irene Dandridge, BTU president, was concerned that the rigorous curriculum and the requirement that students rewrite essays until they are free of errors would increase the teachers' work load. According to one observer, the BTU opposed "the move to the new curriculum because it would increase their management responsibilities at the schools."[84] DiConti also notes that the dispute about the Barclay proposal also took on "racial overtones." According to DiConti, Joann Robinson, a white activist who had no children enrolled in Barclay, took on the role of chief spokesperson for the project so that Barclay's principal would not have to defy Superintendent Hunter in public. DiConti observed that some members of the black community "grew suspicious" of Robinson and believed that she was pushing the proposal to provide an elite school for white students.[85]

In December 1990, citing Hunter's lukewarm support of decentralization, Schmoke asked the school board not to renew his contract. In August 1991, the school board followed Schmoke's advice and named Walter G. Amprey as superintendent. Amprey was a Baltimore native, a graduate of the city's schools and Morgan State University. He started his career as an educator in the BCPS. In 1973, he moved to neighboring Baltimore County and eventually became a well-regarded associate superintendent. While working in

---

[83] The collaboration seems to have been quite successful. A four-year evaluation of the collaboration shows standardized test scores for Barclay students at or above national averages. In addition, the percentage of Barclay students achieving "satisfactory" scores in writing and language usage on the very demanding Maryland School Performance Assessment Program are more than double the city's average, and they are at the state average. See Sam Stringfield, "Fourth Year Evaluation of the Calvert School Program at Barclay School," a report prepared by the Center for the Social Organization of Schools, Johns Hopkins University, n.d.

[84] See Veronica D. DiConti, *Interest Groups and Education Reform* (Lanham, MD: University Press of America, 1996), 146.

[85] Ibid.

the Baltimore County schools, Amprey maintained contact with school administrators, teachers, and black leaders in Baltimore city. In a sense, Amprey arrived in his new job as both an insider and an outsider. Eventually, Amprey would become an ardent supporter of the controversial experiment that turned over the management of nine city schools to a private firm.

By the time Superintendent Amprey took over, Mayor Schmoke had become frustrated by the slow pace of change in the schools. Since his election in 1987, the BCPS had changed very little. Opposition from teachers and principals slowed and weakened the city's school-based management proposal. The teachers and administrators were successful in "capturing" and "eviscerating" several school governance reforms.[86] Veronica DiConti, in her study of the role and influence of interest groups in school politics in Minnesota and Baltimore, argues that the teachers' union incorporated school-based management into union contract negotiations and eventually stacked the process in favor of the teachers.[87]

The teachers' union also played a role in delaying the Barclay-Calvert collaboration. The BTU took the position that adopting the new curriculum would increase teachers' responsibilities at Barclay. The union opposed the collaboration, although Barclay's parents and teachers (union members) supported the proposal. Only through the intervention of Mayor Schmoke was the proposal adopted.

EAI: PRIVATE MANAGEMENT OF PUBLIC SCHOOLS

In 1992, Baltimore gained national attention when school officials, with Mayor Schmoke's support, hired a private firm, Educational Alternatives, Inc. (EAI), to operate nine (eight elementary schools and one middle school) of its public schools. Mayor Schmoke believed that EAI could show that public personnel, using private management techniques, could improve performance and the quality of education in the BCPS. Schmoke also saw EAI as way around both the teachers' union and school bureaucracy that were finding ways to "slow down" and "choke" efforts to decentralize the schools. Finally, Schmoke viewed private management of the nine schools as consistent with his goal of giving schools more autonomy so that decision making is on site. As he explained: "Baltimore's privatization initiatives are in keeping with this overall strategy of liberating schools from what is often an unwieldy and unresponsive central bureaucracy. By signing a five-year contract with Education Alternatives Inc., we literally cut off nine

---

[86] Ibid., 155.

[87] Teachers had definite strong opinions about the direction of school-based management. In particular they wanted resources distributed from the central administration to the schools and the teachers themselves. Their proposal, originally introduced as a way to increase parental and neighborhood involvement, evolved into a device for increasing the authority of teachers in relation to the central administration of the schools.

schools from the central bureaucratic hub, and put them under private management. While this was a controversial move, we felt that we had to jump-start the emancipation process, particularly given the increasing resistance to change."[88]

Prior to the Baltimore contract, EAI ran two private schools in Minnesota and Arizona and one public school in Miami.[89] EAI's trademark instructional model, known as the Tesseract method, relies on a second adult in each classroom to intensify teaching and lower student-teacher ratios, the use of computers and other technology, individual education plans for each student, and heavy parental involvement. Each student is tested and given an individual learning plan. This "personal education plan" is developed with input from the child's parent or legal guardian. EAI also provides facility maintenance services and managerial and financial expertise.

EAI officials promised to improve student performance in the Baltimore schools and to make a profit, without increasing either the per pupil cost or the number of teachers and staff. Under the terms of the Baltimore contract the school system retained authority over the assignment of all professional staff; EAI could "recommend" assignments and transfers and set final staffing levels. Paraprofessionals—namely, teacher aides—could be hired by EAI. The five-year contract could be terminated at any time with ninety-days' notice.

When the contract was announced, a number of Baltimore's civic and political leaders praised the decision. The editors of the *Sun* wrote that Mayor Schmoke, the school board, and the city's new school superintendent, "should be applauded for being willing to try this new approach."[90] Business leaders, who had long advocated implementing private management techniques in the operation of the schools, liked the idea of having a business firm operating public schools. Although soon to turn hostile, the teachers union had been impressed by EAI's record in Miami. The BTU president appeared in public session before the school board to endorse the contract.[91]

The Tesseract schools underwent extensive renovations. EAI painted the buildings, installed new carpeting, replaced broken window panes, fixed leaky faucets, repaired broken toilets, and cleaned and landscaped rubble-strewn school yards. Teachers and principals in the schools were pleased with the additional resources EAI provided: bright new tables and chairs in each classroom, a telephone on each teacher's desk, and a working copier in

---

[88] Remarks by Mayor Kurt L. Schmoke, American Federation of Teachers' Quest Conference (Washington, D.C., 9 July 1993), 4.

[89] For a thorough discussion of EAI, its corporate structure, investors, and background of its founder John Golle, see Craig E. Richards, Rima Shore, and Max B. Sawicky, *Risky Business: Private Management of Public Schools* (Washington, D.C.: Economic Policy Institute, 1996).

[90] Editorial, "Schools in Another Dimension," *The Sun*, 11 June 1992, A12.

[91] Galerah Asayesh, "Baltimore Board Weighs Private School Operation," *The Sun*, 17 May 1991, 2D.

each school. Students and parents were excited about the new computers—four in each classroom and a new computer lab in each school. Initial reports showed that students' attendance increased.[92]

This broad support for the privatization of public schools proved unsustainable when one of the school system's most powerful constituents, the teachers' union, withdrew its support. After EAI transferred ninety teacher's aides from the Tesseract schools and replaced them with less experienced, hence less costly, recent college graduates, the BTU launched an aggressive campaign to kill the experiment. The BTU questioned the wisdom of replacing experienced teacher's aides—people who lived near the schools and were among the few who held jobs in those neighborhoods—in favor of college "interns" who were willing to work for less money and no health benefits. EAI officials argued that the interns, all of whom were college graduates, were better qualified than the BTU teacher's aides. The episode concerning the teachers' aides—combined with EAI's earlier decision to reassign union custodians from the nine schools and replace them with nonunion janitors—convinced BTU's leaders that EAI's strategy was to save money and make a profit by replacing relatively expensive union personnel with less costly nonunion personnel. It also heightened the BTU's concern about the long-term job security of its membership.

In response, the BTU boycotted EAI's teacher-training sessions.[93] The BTU filed a lawsuit claiming that the contractual agreement with EAI violated the city charter in that it was approved without competitive bidding and without consideration of the city's minority set-aside provisions. The American Federation of Teachers (AFT), BTU's parent organization, asked the federal government to investigate the impact of privatization on public schools. BTU called for Superintendent Amprey's resignation and organized a protest march on school headquarters.

Baltimoreans United in Leadership Development (BUILD), which in 1983 helped mobilize community support for school reform and worked closely with Mayor Schmoke on several policy issues, also took a strong stance against the EAI experiment. BUILD's leaders claimed to have been left out of the decision-making process. "The mayor has not really consulted with us," one BUILD member told reporters.[94] The day before the vote to approve the EAI contract, Schmoke attended a meeting that drew over 450 BUILD volunteers; BUILD leaders argued against turning to the private sector to rescue the public sector. To "turn to the market sector to bail out

---

[92] Mark Bumster, "Nine Schools Start to Mend," *The Sun*, November 15 1992, B1.

[93] Mayor Schmoke eventually stepped in to negotiate an agreement that left some aides in the nine schools (some EAI classrooms now had three aides) and found jobs elsewhere in the school system for the rest.

[94] Mark Bumster, "Schmoke Facing Challenge Tonight on School Reform," *The Sun*, 20 July 1992, B1.

the public sector is dangerous," asserted an influential BUILD organizer.[95] BUILD asserted that EAI's major concern was not schooling but generating a profit. A BUILD leader told the mayor, "We will fight you on this because the whole thing is contrary to public education."[96] The Interdenominational Ministerial Alliance (IMA), an organization representing about 166 black ministers, complained that city officials failed to consult with them before announcing plans to hire EAI. The IMA joined with BUILD and the unions to stop EAI.

Finally political opponents of Mayor Schmoke joined the chorus of opposition. Mary Pat Clarke, then the president of the city council and later an unsuccessful challenger to Schmoke in the 1995 mayoral election, vocally opposed EAI. As a member of the Board of Estimates, Clarke voted against the EAI contract. Other city council members also criticized the experiment. The city council eventually voted to urge Mayor Schmoke to delay any expansion of EAI before an independent evaluation of the experiment was completed.[97]

THE DEMISE OF EAI

The first set of standardized test scores, released in 1994, showed that the Tesseract experiment failed to significantly improve student performance in the two years since EAI began managing the schools.[98] Student performance on standardized test results provided further ammunition for opponents of Tesseract. Superintendent Amprey argued that test scores alone should not determine the experiment's success or failure. However, heavy resistance from teachers, some parents, and the city council forced Amprey to announce that no further expansion of EAI would occur without a comprehensive evaluation. Moreover, preliminary financial analysis showed that despite EAI's initial claims, the Tesseract schools were receiving more money per pupil than the other schools in the system.[99]

These initial test scores intensified critics' opposition and led the BTU to call for an immediate end to the contract. City Council President Mary Pat Clarke, campaigning to unseat Mayor Schmoke, increased her opposition to EAI. With an election looming, Mayor Schmoke was forced to announce that EAI's fate depended primarily on student test scores and the results of an independent evaluation.

---

[95] Ibid.

[96] Ibid.

[97] Gary Gately, "Council Members Call for a Delay on EAI Expansion," *The Sun*, 26 May 1994, A1.

[98] Gary Gately and JoAnna Daemmrich, "EAI Fails to Improve Elementary School Scores," *The Sun*, 17 June 1994, A1.

[99] For a detailed analysis of spending in the Tesseract schools, see Roberts, Shore, and Sawicky, *Risky Business*, 79–124.

In August 1995, the first outside evaluation of the EAI experiment was completed. The report, conducted by the University of Maryland, Baltimore County, found that the Tesseract schools showed little difference from comparable city-run schools on test results, attendance, parent involvement, or even cleanliness.[100] Three years into the experiment, the evaluation found that student scores on the Comprehensive Test of Basic Skills were about the same as in 1992, the year of EAI's arrival, for the Tesseract schools, the control schools, and the city as a whole. Significantly, the evaluation found that BCPS was spending about 11 percent more (approximately $628) per student in the Tesseract schools than in comparison schools.

EAI's management of the Tesseract schools ended on 4 March 1996, a year and three months short of the original five-year contract. In announcing the end of the experiment, Mayor Schmoke and Superintendent Amprey pointed to the researchers' financial information. The report asserted that "the promise that EAI could improve instruction without spending more than Baltimore City was spending on schools has been discredited."[101] In actuality, the contract termination came after Mayor Schmoke and EAI failed to agree on a renegotiated contract. Schmoke offered to continue the contract at a rate 16 percent less than EAI was projected to receive under the average per-pupil cost formula, but EAI would not accept these new terms.[102] Mayor Schmoke maintained that the city, facing a budget deficit, could not afford to keep EAI. Superintendent Amprey told reporters, "We have only so many dollars."[103]

Systemic Reform in Detroit: School Board-Led Reform

In 1988 the Detroit Public Schools (DPS) seemed poised on the brink of comprehensive change. Four new school board members, popularly referred to as the HOPE team, defeated veteran members on election pledges to restructure the city's school system.[104] These members quickly established a working majority and began to translate their electoral victory into policy changes. Their vision primarily focused on three venues of policy innovation:

[100] Lois C. Williams and Lawrence E. Leak, *The UMBC Evaluation of the Tesseract Program in Baltimore City* (Baltimore: Center for Educational Research, University of Maryland, Baltimore County, 1995).

[101] Ibid., 115.

[102] Lois C. Williams and Lawrence E. Leak, "School Privatization's First Big Test: EAI in Baltimore," *Educational Leadership* 24 no. 2 (October 1996): 57.

[103] Jean Thompson, "City School Board Ends Effort to Privatize," *The Sun*, 1 December 1995, A1.

[104] HOPE was a campaign slogan (Frank Hayden, David Olmstea, and Larry Patrick for Education). The slate later added Joseph Blending.

a school compact with area business, broad-based school-level decentralization, and the expansion of schools of choice. As a first step in realizing these
goals, the new board removed the long-standing superintendent and hired
a nationally prominent reformer.

THE DETROIT COMPACT

Formed in 1988, the Detroit Compact has become a cornerstone of school
reform in the city. The Compact grew out of the recommendations of the
Detroit Strategic Planning Initiative, financed by a powerful private foundation in the city, Detroit Renaissance. It has had strong support at both city
and state levels. The Michigan Department of Commerce provided $500,000
of seed money to the Compact. The new school board quickly endorsed the
Compact concept and incorporated it into their reform agenda.

The Compact guarantees students either four-year tuition scholarships at
Michigan's public universities or interviews for career-track jobs if they
maintain minimum grade requirements, test scores, and attendance standards. The Compact also provides students with summer job opportunities,
tutoring, and many other resources. Compact operations are directed by a
council of fourteen stakeholder groups including the State of Michigan, City
of Detroit, Wayne County, organized labor, Board of Education, DPS superintendent, Detroit Federation of Teachers, the Organization of School Administrators and Supervisors, parents and students, and representatives from
the community, business, and higher education. Each participating school
has a Local Compact Council (LCC) that meets monthly; it is a "mini" version
of the systemwide Compact. The LCC representative from each patron
group along with the school principal oversees the Compact budget and
coordination at its school. There is no set Compact program. Each school is
provided with the flexibility and capacity to adjust the partnership to best
suit local school needs. To become a Compact school the partnership requires a commitment from the principal, two-thirds of the faculty (including
union representatives), and 50 percent of the students.

A number of observers claim that the Local Compact Councils have been
successful in engaging community actors long absent from local education.
The monthly LCC meetings and the bimonthly stakeholder meetings provide vehicles where community input is accepted and conflict by stakeholders can be resolved. This process is well described by a representative from
the Chamber of Commerce:

> The schools really were a closed community. What is happening now and again,
> I think because of the Compact, the schools are becoming more open communi-
> ties. For example, in each Compact school there is a council that replicates the
> major stakeholders group so that the schools now have business people and

community people and union people and higher education people who visit the school regularly, who work with the schools. I think the schools are realizing that their success in the future really lies with being an open community, taking advantage not only of the resources that they want but also of the expertise and the volunteers that really are required to get involved in education. So, yes I do think there's a significant shift going on there.

From its inception in 1989–90 through 1993–94, the Compact provided 4,216 jobs to on-target Compact students and 214 college tuition awards. A survey conducted by the Greater Detroit Alliance of Business revealed that 93 percent of employees who hired an on-target Compact student would so again. Preliminary results indicate that the Compact is making a positive difference in many city schools. The longer a school participates in the Compact, the better the performance is at that school. The four schools with the highest rates of on-target twelfth graders are those which have been in the Compact for three or more years. According to a Chamber official, the Compact has already realized an important educational reform by creating easily measured outcome standards.[105]

SCHOOL EMPOWERMENT

The HOPE-dominated school board was committed to a fundamental decentralization of the district. Indeed, site decentralization was seen by the board as the primary reform vehicle for the district. Schools granted site management authority were designated as empowerment schools if the principal, 75 percent of teachers, and 50 percent of support staff voted for empowerment. Each empowered school was given wide discretion over how funds were to be spent. The empowerment schools were to be governed by a School Empowerment Council/Team whose members were to define and implement an educational agenda for that school.[106] The school board had hoped to make every school

[105] Observers suggest additional benefits from the Compact. A number of business partners have made substantial direct investments in specific schools. For example, Mumford High in Detroit opened a $725,000 high-technology laboratory with twenty Apple and twenty IBM computers. Michigan Bell and Ameritech donated $400,000 for the project, and the Detroit Compact funded another $105,000 (*Detroit Free Press*, 22 May 1991, 3B). Without the help of the business community, Detroit Public Schools could have never even considered such facilities. McKenzie High School's Compact partner, IBM, followed suit and donated more than $500,000 in equipment, software, and technical services for the McKenzie/IBM Science Technology Wing. The new wing includes seven classrooms and three presentation rooms. IBM also trained school employees to use this technology.

[106] Any school is eligible to become an empowered school if the following representative numbers vote yes: administration and teachers: 75 percent (by secret ballot); parents: 55 percent; support staff: 55 percent, and students: 55 percent. David L. Sneed, *Design for Excellence* (Detroit, Detroit Public Schools, 1993).

in the district an empowered school. In all, twenty-six schools became formally empowered; in addition, a number of other schools adopted some form of shared decision-making governance structure.

Empowerment seemed to get off to a promising beginning. Although the pace of implementation was slow, a number of observers saw an emerging consensus supporting empowerment. Problems began when HOPE members grew impatient with the pace of reform. A former superintendent states:

> I would say that my position on empowerment was, you can't push that. That's something that's got to germinate on its own. We had about 21 schools as part of that initiative when I left. They tried to push it contractually. My response to you is that I didn't think there was anything wrong with the way we started empowerment. It's just that it wasn't something you could push on people . . . in many public meetings. I told them, I said, "look, you don't understand." I said, "if you put the unions up against the wall, you're gonna lose." I said, "we created a very delicate, successful balance here and it's something that has to be cultivated and it can't be something you can force." They didn't listen.

The school board moved quickly to implement the empowered school concept, trying to force some changes contractually upon the union. A Wayne State University respondent contended, "changes were occurring too quickly without the membership. . . . If you want to use the word . . . you know . . . the union." A former board member illustrated the union's ability to play both sides of the issue:

> I also find it's kind of interesting, just a couple weeks ago there was an item in *The Detroit News*. There was a Harvard study going back and evaluating the aftermath of desegregation litigation in Detroit. It might have been interesting for you to note, that the Harvard folks were charging that the Detroit Schools were performing abysmally and John Elliot (president of Detroit Federation of Teachers) is quoted in there, in the back and he said, "well, they're not all performing abysmally," says John Elliot. The schools of choice, empowered schools, are really showing progress, words to that effect. For the person who killed the blueprint, I find that quite ironic to have him make the statement.

By the end of 1991–92 school year, nearly all DPS's unions went on record against empowerment, stressing concerns over job security, privatization of some school services, and transfer of staff. Representatives of a number of community organizations also opposed empowerment; they claimed they were not given much information on empowered schools and feared those schools would be elitist. A four-week strike at the beginning of the 1992–93 school year further widened the gulf between the unions and administrative leadership. Expansion of self-governing schools was put on hold in the 1993–94 school year as the $1.3 million slated for the creation of new empowered schools was used to balance the 1993–94 budget. Although representatives of the school district continue to express formal support for the concept of site-based management, the term "empowerment" has virtually disappeared from official DPS rhetoric. Only one additional school voted for empowerment during the first eighteen months of David Snead's tenure. The Office of Empowerment, Diversity, and Choice was renamed the Office of Research, Development, and Coordination.

Leaders at some empowered schools remain enthusiastic supporters. A principal of one of the twenty-six empowered schools claims she has been overwhelmed with the kind of interest and participation in the school. "I've tried innovation in other schools. Sometimes it was very difficult to get ten people to come to a school meeting. I think some of that has to be our responsibility to break down some of those old walls and make it a place where people aren't intimidated to come and feel very welcome when they get here and know that their presence is not just a token." A key frustration for district administrators is the failure of many empowered schools to accept the goal of shared decision making. Some empowered schools have emphasized union rights rather than the reworking of school governance and academic programs. Some empowered schools are described as wanting only budget control but not change. A DPS administrator stated:

> So we have these schools, a few of them, not many, that are not intent on really implementing any change. That's my frustration. We don't have the staff to really follow up all the time. Six months later we find out the principal has not convened an empowerment council meeting. If the parents don't complain it may not come to our attention. In conversation with a noncomplying principal, I really get frustrated. The next week I find out the principal has spent money without involving the stakeholders, "but you just told me you didn't spend any money." "Well, I needed the books in order to operate my curriculum." "Yes, but if you become empowered, you cannot make decisions about money without involving the council." "Yes, but it is my curriculum and I needed to . . ." . . . for a few principals, personally they just want the control over the money.

Even worse, a few months after this discussion, a principal of an empowered school, was charged with embezzling over $140,000 in funds.[107] Reinforcing the perils of implementation, a school administrator stated:

> This office has only been in existence for a year and it started a year ago in August and when I am naive, I can be real naive. I just assumed that folks were doing things that they said they were doing. Some weren't doing anything. Now the two new schools that are becoming empowered the 25th and 26th, have

---

[107] *Detroit Free Press*, 24 August 1994, 3B.

already written on to the empowerment contract. I will make sure they won't get a dime until I am sure that there is compliance. I've been burned, now I want to come out and talk to the group. So you learn.

DIVERSITY AND CHOICE CHOICE

The HOPE board also sought to create specialized schools of choice. Increasing school options for parents was the primary reform advocated by Superintendent McGriff.[108] Such schools offered parents a range of alternatives for their children. The value of this choice rested on the assumption that parents would choose programs that best served their children's needs. Successful schools would thrive; poor ones would fail.[109]

A number of observers claim that expanding parental choice has been a benefit to children in the DPS. An area superintendent for DPS sees the variety of schools and programs as providing a better match to the complex needs of Detroit's children. A similar theme was struck by a Detroit minister who stated that "diversity is good while trying to meet the kids' needs; rather than trying to have one box of cereal for everybody, let's get the 12-pack."

Schools of choice are not neighborhood schools, although most choice schools give first choice to neighborhood residents. A few schools such as Cass Tech and Renaissance High were created as citywide institutions. Others have adopted specific themes and used excess capacity to recruit students from across the city. Critical to this process are efforts to ensure that parents have sufficient information to make an appropriate choice:

> We need to get our parents more involved, we need to have parent resource centers. We need to make sure that the processes for new initiatives is fair and equitable. Because all we need is one incident and it can blow great ideas and months of planning right out of the water. This year we had our third choice fair. Our first one we had about 800 parents; our second one we had 2,000; this year we had 6,000 parents. I know next year we won't be able to handle, it will be so big. People can't make good choices if they don't have any information. So at our choice fair, every one of our choice options is represented. And they have a booth. Parents walk around and ask questions of staff and that is just great.

[108] The relative emphasis to be given to school empowerment and schools of choice became an important issue dividing the reform board and their superintendent. Soon after McGriff was hired a number of board members were openly complaining that she was substituting her own priorities for the board's.

[109] The board experimented with variety of choice models including Comer School Development Schools, African-Centered Academies, and Professional Development Schools. In addition, the number of theme schools grew, focusing on mathematics, science and technology, foreign language, multiculturalism, examination schools, business education, allied health, and fine and performing arts.

It is hardly surprising that the dramatic reforms proposed by the HOPE board would generate substantial controversy. Even Deborah McGriff, the board's superintendent, recognized this: "In the past, nothing happened and people were very, very safe. They believed innovations come and go. They might outlive me, but while I'm superintendent, I'm going to promote programs I know work and that I believe in."[110]

Her prophecy would be realized as public resistance all but destroyed the reform coalition that had brought her to Detroit. The school board elected in 1992 eventually provoked her resignation. After beginning a national search for her replacement, the new board of education abruptly canceled it, instead, the board hired a school system insider to a long-term contract. Both the board and its current superintendent, David Snead, appear more focused on facility conditions and student safety than on innovative approaches to bringing comprehensive change to the system. A former board member commented:

> You win the battle but lose the war and lose your organization and lose everything you're fighting for. The HOPE team had not learned that lesson and we all pleaded with them to slow down. It's not what they wanted to do. It was how they did things not the mission, where the reform group split up on the board. Some of us who consider ourselves deep, passionate reformers could not go along with how things were being done. Because they were in power on the board as president and vice president and chair of the finance committee and chair of the most important committees, they were able to run the board in a way that even left out their own allies.

The HOPE coalition provides dramatic evidence that electoral office does not necessary permit one to dictate or impose change upon a community. A DPS administrator stated, "It is necessary to have buy-in from the community every step of the way. It takes longer to do that. It probably takes five times as long. You have to be skilled in knowing when to move forward. That is a mixed bag. In the past we were heavily criticized as moving too slowly. Clearly Dr. McGriff was criticized in some circles for moving too rapidly. So it is a skill, but it is necessary to build support along the way and take some risks."

THE END OF REFORM

Detroit's reform-minded Board of Education demonstrated an ability to formulate innovative policies but a limited capacity to actually implement such efforts. The HOPE team swept into power and solidified a reform majority on the school board. Innovation was short-lived, however, as reformers met

---

[110] Ron Russell, "McGriff Gives Herself High Marks for Reform," *Detroit News*, 22 June 1992, A1, A4.

an entrenched labor community's stiff opposition, peaking with a month-long, bitterly contentious teachers' strike in the months prior to the November 1992 school board election. The board of education has proven to be a stage for larger political conflict, with polarized electoral contests and shifting governing coalitions. With the erosion of the HOPE coalition in 1992–93, a mood of reform backlash predominated: "clean, safe, and healthy" neighborhood schools prevailed over pilot approaches for specialized schools. The appointment of David Snead as superintendent signaled a return to business as usual.

The Detroit Federation of Teachers (DFT) and related school unions were widely acknowledged as presenting the greatest institutional barrier to school reform. Several interviewees remarked that DPS is "owned by the unions." A Detroit church leader stated:

> I think that probably the strongest influence on the Detroit Public School system is the teachers' union, and what that says is that it's the self-interest of the teachers that gets first attention. Compensation and work rules and hours of work and all those factors and supervision and evaluation, all of that is set by the very people who are mostly affected by it, not by people who are on the outside asking what they're getting for that. . . . I'd say, even up until this last election (1992), they've demonstrated clearly that they're in charge. The system is in the hands of the professionals, the unions.

During the 1992 teachers' strike and subsequent HOPE reelection campaign, the DFT successfully rallied the Detroit labor community (the UAW and the AFL-CIO), along with sympathetic, antireform grassroots organizations, to kill the empowerment movement and cripple the HOPE reformers. A former HOPE-team school board member offered a telling account of the unions' entrenchment in Detroit: the DFT reversed itself by rejecting a *Memorandum of Understanding: Empowerment and School of Choice* written by the American Federation of Teachers after originally endorsing the memo.[111] Similarly, without even presenting the proposal to its members, the Organization of Supervisors and Administrative Staff (OSAS) rejected a plan to expand the work year, salary, and authority of principals as being "against the best interest of its members." Many observers claim the unions were destined to strike in reaction to HOPE reforms.

Detroit churches are perhaps the most important community-level organizations in the city. Churches and their leaders are often principal actors in community decision making and coalition formation. Churches frequently

---

[111] On 5 June 1990 Interim Superintendent John Porter and the Detroit Board of Education received the endorsement of the administrators and teachers unions through a *Memorandum of Understanding: Empowerment and School of Choice*. By February 1992 the unions had issued an embargo on empowerment, which virtually blocked further implementation of the concept.

function as arenas for political debate and election campaigns. Political actors in all sectors of the city—city government, the board of education, and the general superintendent—take care to seek advice and support from senior church leaders. Church leaders, very supportive of the HOPE team in the 1988 elections, often provided a forum for the candidates to present their views; however, most grew disillusioned with the team's perceived exclusionary tactics. The political importance of local churches was revealed in the remark by a HOPE coalition member that they knew that their reelection bids would not be successful when the ministers refused to allow their churches to be used as forums in the 1992 elections.

Systemic Reform in Washington, D.C: Private Initiative

COMMITTEE ON PUBLIC EDUCATION

Between 1989 and 1991, Washington, D.C., also seemed on the verge of building the kind of broad-based coalition and wide-reaching agenda for school reform that proponents of systemic change envision. Business leaders, who historically had lobbed criticisms from the sidelines, sponsored a new organization to set education goals, provide support, and monitor progress. This group—the Committee on Public Education (COPE)—quietly built bridges to the most significant parents' advocacy organization (Parents United) while publicly gaining media attention that helped to propel school reform onto the public agenda. In 1991, this nascent coalition helped orchestrate the hiring of Superintendent Franklin Smith, who had established a record as a proven reformer in another district and moved to articulate an agenda for radical change linked to a strategy of gradual but steady, certain progress. The failure of this promising beginning to generate unambiguous results culminated in a dramatic rejection of the potential for indigenous reform efforts. In 1996, with the implicit support of business leaders and the resigned acceptance of many parent activists, the congressionally appointed financial control board fired Smith, disempowered the elected school board, and appointed its own agents to take over responsibility for the District's public schools.

The formation of the D.C. Committee on Public Education in 1989 marked a new stage in the nature of the relationship between local businesses and the public schools. Prior to 1989, with a few exceptions,[112] most

---

[112] Even before the District was granted home-rule powers, it had experienced a brief experimentation with a serious attempt at a large-scale public-private partnership. In Spring 1971, after just four months on the job, Superintendent Hugh Scott approached the Metropolitan Washington Board of Trade and asked its help in recruiting business executives to advise the system on a wide range of management issues. H. Gayle Shaffer, a community relations officer for IBM who was a participant, summarizes this effort in her August 1973 report, "A Case

links between the business community and the District's schools had been on an individual rather than systemic level. COPE provided a new and more unified focus. Organized by the Federal City Council—a select group of civic and corporate leaders—COPE had more than sixty members drawn from business, government, universities, and community groups. Its first major report, *Our Children, Our Future* (June 1989), combined some of the first reliable data analysis of the schools' performance with an ambitious agenda for reform. Committee members visited schools, held town meetings, surveyed more than twelve hundred teachers, interviewed principals and administrators, collected comparative data from districts in surrounding jurisdictions, visited at least eight other districts along the east coast, and consulted with national experts. Peat Marwick Main & Co., as part of the effort, reviewed internal management operations. Outside consultants reviewed testing procedures, curriculum, and quality of instruction.

The tone of the initial report was measured, and COPE took care to emphasize some positive things it had found in its intensive study. Nonetheless, its message was unambiguously calling for reform. Its ambitious agenda combined conventional proposals and structural change. Conventional reforms included adopting new assessment tests for mathematics; mandating art, music, physical education, and foreign language instruction in all elementary schools; requiring at least two years of foreign language, two years of laboratory science, and world history for high school graduation; expanding the use of computers; lengthening the school day and the school year; and instituting career ladders and incentive pay for teachers. More fundamental were its proposals for altering the basic governance structure. Citing as models Dade County, East Harlem's District 4, and suburban Prince George's County, COPE issued a strong call for shifting the locus of authority from the central office to the school level. "This effort," it indicated, "will be the centerpiece of the reform effort, and will involve providing greater authority to individual schools for such items as budgeting, curricula, facilities, and personnel."[113] Second, COPE identified another key to reform: in D.C. a structural ambiguity blurred lines of authority and accountability, produced in part by the school system's awkward mix of independent policy authority with fiscal dependence on the mayor and council; that Congress retained ultimate author-

Study: D.C. Public Schools/Board of Trade Coalition" (archival files, Greater Washington Board of Trade, George Washington University's Gelman Library, Box 294). See also Jeffrey R. Henig, "Civic Capacity and Urban Education in Washington, D.C.: Second year report" (Washington, D.C.: Center for Washington Area Studies, 1994). The collaboration resulted in a number of internal improvements in the system's budgeting, personnel, and financial reporting systems, but the interaction was not without conflict; the formal relationship ended in December 1972.

[113] D.C. Committee on Public Education, *Our Children, Our Future: Revitalizing the District of Columbia Public Schools* (Washington, D.C.: D.C. Committee on Public Education, 1989), 105.

ity blurred matters more.[114] COPE recommended that both policy and financial responsibility should rest with a single entity—namely, the Board of Education. Finally, COPE identified some specific goals and committed itself to monitoring progress toward those goals.

BUSINESS LINKS TO PARENT ADVOCATES

While its ties to the Federal City Council gave it something of an elitist caste, COPE worked hard to present a multiracial face and to reach out to some organizations with experience and established credibility in the school reform arena. Parents United, founded in the midst of a 1980 public school budget crisis, in its early years defined its mission primarily in terms of ensuring that DCPS received adequate funding.[115] Subsequently, Parents United broadened its focus to include such issues as improving deteriorating school facilities, providing health and medical services in the schools, making teachers' salaries competitive with suburban jurisdictions, and extending the school day. While continuing generally to support the superintendent and board, Parents United adopted more of an arms-length relationship with them toward the end of the 1980s; the group's leadership recognized that growing perceptions that the district was being mismanaged could undermine Parents United's credibility if the group was seen as too much of a booster. Over time, Parents United became a launching pad for several reform activists who subsequently were elected to the school board. Well before COPE launched its efforts, Parents United had earned the reputation as having the only relatively reliable data and the only personnel capable of translating the vague and confusing budget information released by the system. This data collection and analysis was almost exclusively the responsibility of one person, Mary Levy.

Although Parents United initially was skeptical of COPE as a Johnny-come-lately in the school reform battle, COPE showed that it was willing to work with PU, and Levy played a major role in helping COPE staff make sense of the data it acquired. This combination was potent. As admitted by one school board member, "frankly, in terms of real educational policy and direction—and this is part of what I was saying before about the school system either being pushed as opposed to really taking initiative—I think you've got more expertise and knowledge across the board among some of the COPE and Parents United and all that than within the school system."

[114] Ibid., 108.

[115] Reflecting its orientation, the group initially was called Parents United for Full Public School Funding. This discussion of the history of Parents United draws from Anna Speicher, "Community Involvement in Public Education: Parents United for the D.C. Public Schools," Center for Washington Area Studies, George Washington University, Occasional Paper 11 (August 1992).

A REFORM SUPERINTENDENT ARRIVES

In July 1991, COPE and Parents United welcomed the arrival of Franklin Smith as the new superintendent.[116] Smith, who entered on the heels of his predecessor's controversial ouster, was the first outsider appointed to the position in about two decades. For the previous five years he had served as superintendent in Dayton, Ohio, where he had been credited with developing a successful magnet school program, increasing parent participation, introducing site-based management, raising academic standards, and working with the Dayton Chamber of Commerce to link every school with a local business partner.

In addition to fairly conventional curriculum and management reforms,[117] Smith identified himself with an ambitious agenda for systemic reform, one that dovetailed with the goals of COPE and Parents United and reflected the reigning notions of the national reform movement about the need for radical organizational change. Smith proposed a set of three broad education reforms. First, he called for a significant decentralization of the decision-making process, by cutting back central bureaucracy and instituting a mechanism for shaping policy at the individual school level. On 17 January 1992, he announced the creation of a new unit—the Center for Educational Change (CEC). Besides serving as the superintendent's contact point for all systemwide restructuring efforts and new educational initiatives, he designed CEC to oversee implementation of the superintendent's plans for moving the local schools "to center stage" and redefining the role of central administration so that its "primary purpose becomes that of meeting the needs of local schools."[118]

Second, he advocated public school choice. In July 1992, Smith announced a "revolutionary proposal" to institute a policy so that "all children in our public school system can attend whatever public school in the city they and their parents or guardians choose."[119] As superintendent in Dayton, Smith had turned to choice, in 1987, as a means of responding to a court order to desegregate; reports indicated he had overseen the development of magnet programs in 80 percent of that city's schools. His July 1992 proposal went even further. "In essence, every public school in Washington would

---

[116] According to some respondents, COPE and the Federal City Council had played a substantial behind-the-scenes role in orchestrating the search and in promoting Smith a leading contender.

[117] For example, Smith quickly challenged the teachers union and successfully expanded the school day. In the face of intense localized opposition, he spearheaded an effort to close schools for fiscal savings. See Henig, "Civic Capacity and Urban Education in Washington, D.C."

[118] Districtwide Restructuring Team, "Planning Guide for Local School Restructuring Teams" (Washington, D.C.: D.C. Public Schools, June 1992), 1.

[119] Franklin L. Smith, "Give D.C. Kids a Choice," *Washington Post*, 12 June 1992, C1.

be expected to develop, function, and 'sell itself' as a magnet school to the entire city."[120]

Third, and subsequently most controversially, Smith's platform involved contracting with a private firm to manage some D.C. schools. A strong partisan of public schools, Smith seems to have somewhat reluctantly been drawn to contracting-out as a kind of "shock therapy." His conversion to the strategy of contracting-out seems at least in part a response to growing impatience with the pace of change, especially among the business constituencies of the Committee on Public Education who would be particularly sympathetic to the logic of this approach. He first learned about Baltimore's plan in the fall of 1992, at a conference in Milwaukee, but he later told a reporter that the idea was so foreign to him that it took a year before he could really embrace it.[121] Seemingly frustrated by the slow pace of his reforms to date, Smith viewed contracting-out as a way to bring about more radical change. "When we look at our overall performance, it is clear we cannot continue to tinker around the edges of educational reform," he noted.[122] "I need help. . . . I need changes right away."[123]

Smith reportedly neither informed the mayor or council nor waited for board approval before announcing, in the fall of 1993, his proposal to contract-out as many as fifteen schools by the following academic year. But once he announced the initiative, he set out aggressively to build a constituency for the change. In the week following the announcement, a group of about twenty parents, politicians, and school officials were given tours of two Baltimore schools. Then school board president R. David Hall pronounced, "I'm impressed. . . . I'm willing to try it." And council member and former and future mayor Marion Barry, said, "I feel energy in these schools. You know something is going right here."[124]

A DISAPPOINTING FINISH

For all its promising starts, by late 1996 the D.C. school reform movement was discredited and in disarray. Smith's careful approach to decentralization and choice was too timid and incremental to build much enthusiasm. His plan for contracting-out met a hostile response from a vocal minority that cast its opposition in racial terms and forced Smith to back down.[125] Cracks

---

[120] Ibid.

[121] Sari Horwitz, "Why Smith Decided to Call in the Cavalry: Baltimore Schools Convinced D.C. Superintendent There is a Way Around the Bureaucracy," *Washington Post*, 4 December 1993, A1.

[122] Sari Horwitz, "Private Firm Eyed to Run D.C. Schools," *Washington Post*, 8 December 1993, A1.

[123] Horwitz, "Why Smith Decided."

[124] Paul W. Valentine and Sari Horwitz, "D.C. Group Tours Baltimore Schools," *Washington Post*, 9 December 1993, C1.

[125] See chapter 6 for a discussion of the racial backlash to the contracting-out plan.

in the proreform coalition emerged. A cover story in the *City Paper*, a widely read alternative newspaper, began its 1994 review of Smith's tenure in quite favorable terms but then sounded sharp chords of dissatisfaction:

> But when you look at a balance sheet, reinventing education has achieved about the same result as the federal campaign to reinvent government. So far, Smith has generated lots of jargon, written reams of position papers, and held dozens of meetings. He has done very, very little to improve student performance. Test scores fell again last year. Dropout rates remain astronomical. The school closings that were supposed to save the system $10 million conserved only a few hundred thousand dollars. . . . And the much-trumpeted school-based management has barely dented the system. . . . The restructuring teams that are supposed to revolutionize local school management barely exist.[126]

A school board member, who was not always in Smith's camp, said: "He's talking about the slow migration from the way that his organization structure was before to the way that he would like to see it go. He doesn't have a lot of time."

While Smith was the main potential vehicle for change, reform-oriented allies muted their criticisms. But with the emergence of the financial control board as a new power point, impatience that had been expressed *sotto voce* was more publicly aired. In August 1996, the National Science Foundation rescinded a $13.5 million grant for math and science instruction, citing a concern that management problems were so severe that it could not be assured that the money would be well spent. When Smith attempted to pass some of the blame onto the control board, the board and other key actors turned on him aggressively. "It is absolutely outrageous that every time something happens a finger is pointed everywhere else," the executive director of the control board responded. "We've met with Dr. Smith quite often, and he's never said, 'I've got a problem with this grant.'" "I don't understand why, frankly," added a CEO of an investment firm who was serving as co-chair of COPE. "The superintendent must be held accountable," a member of the City Council chipped in.[127] When the control board stepped in to displace Smith and the school board, many local reformers expressed dismay at the incursion on Home Rule, and some leaders within COPE and Parents United protested that Smith was being unfairly cast as the scapegoat. Their righteous indignation, however, was held in check by the widespread consensus that the indigenous reform efforts had come up short. A Ford Motor Company vice president and COPE co-chair called for cooperation with the control board plan. "The last thing this community needs is a divisive and counterproductive debate about school governance. . . . We are prepared to

---

[126] David Plotz, "School-house Rock," *Washington City Paper*, 1 November 1994, 22.

[127] Michael Powell, "Lots of Finger Pointing Over Loss of School Grant," *Washington Post*, 20 September 1996, A1.

work with the control board and General Becton."[128] At least for the near term, the responsibility for school reform was being relinquished to outside actors; indigenous efforts had failed. But outside intervention would not prove the panacea that some envisioned.[129]

WHY IS REFORM SO DIFFICULT?

Given the poor performance of urban schools, the widespread demand for improvement, and the many efforts begun by school districts, how is it that educational reform is so elusive? In particular we are curious about the failure of each school district to move from project-based reform to true systemic reform. There is certainly no simple answer as to why reforms fail to transform local educational systems. Contributing factors include insufficient resources, inadequate program design, and finally a lack of community capacity to build a genuine reform coalition. The issue of resources would seem to be most straightforward. Although it is certainly true that large urban school districts such as Atlanta, Baltimore, Detroit, and Washington do have large budgets, it is also clear that these districts are significantly underfunded, especially when one considers the special problems they face. In spite of serious state efforts over the past decade to make district spending more equitable, disparities remain. Such differentials obviously reinforce and exacerbate existing academic differences in student populations. Resource issues can be defined more generally than simple expenditure data. For example, each school system studied here displays a genuine lack of administrative capacity.

A second source of the failure of educational reform in our four cities is rooted in the inability of specific reforms to bring about the dramatic effects predicted by their more ardent supporters. Sometimes this perceived failure is a function of unrealistic expectations. For example, it is certain that no "silver bullet" will reclaim urban education. Improving urban education requires attention to a wide range of issues. Thus, any reform effort will be

---

[128] David A. Vise and Cindy Loose, "D.C. School Officials Lash Out at Control Board," *Washington Post*, 7 November 1996, C01.

[129] By spring 1998 General Becton had resigned in frustration. In spite of being granted much more formal authority than Superintendent Smith had enjoyed, Becton foundered in some highly publicized ways. As outlined later, a major embarrassment was tied to his failure to open schools on time for the 1997–98 school year. In announcing his retirement, he attributed some of his problems to his failure to engage a broader segment of the community in his efforts. His successor, Arlene Ackerman, came into office with a much stronger background in education and a seemingly stronger understanding of the need to work with external constituencies. But only eleven weeks into her tenure, the *Washington Post* was reporting that she, too, was finding obstacles more daunting than she had expected. See, for example, Doug Struck and Valerie Strauss, "D.C. Special Ed System Still in Disarray, Report Says," *Washington Post*, 20 July 1998, B1.

labeled a failure if the evaluation standard demands a complete transformation of the school system. That problem is exacerbated when the idea of systemic school reform is linked directly to expectation of sharp, quick, and measurable results in student performance on standardized examinations. The overwhelming weight of the evidence on school performance suggests that the link between what schools teach and how well students score on standardized tests is rarely clear and dramatic; when key political interests indicate that their support for reform initiatives ultimately is contingent upon evidence of quick improvement on that particular "bottom line," they may be setting the stage for frustration. Note, too, that unrealistic expectations of specific reforms are often the fault of supporters' exaggerated claims. Examples of such an "oversell" are common in each of our cities.

We believe that the failure of education reform in Atlanta, Baltimore, Detroit, and Washington reflects a lack of civic capacity. By civic capacity we mean the ability to assemble a broad-based set of community actors who might have the collective capacity to design and implement educational reform. Too often local actors who agree on abstract goals become much less united when these abstractions are turned into concrete educational policy. Stressing civic capacity highlights the distinction between formal administrative power and the ability to implement policy. Civic capacity moves beyond formal authority to determine education expenditures and directs attention to the political capacity to reallocate existing resources and to generate new ones. Effective schools clearly require not only adequate budgets but also programmatic cooperation and collaboration of other institutions and groups in the community. Although the existing black leadership has formal authority to make school policy, it has not yet been able to gather a working community coalition around education.

But linking the failure of education reform with a lack of civic capacity is not an explanation, it is only a label that helps direct us to the appropriate questions we need to ask to gain an understanding of the determinants of genuine education reform. For example, what patterns of alliances and interactions have provided the context in which school policies are formed? What factors have inhibited (or facilitated) the development of cooperative and complementary activities in the area of human investment and education? What is the role of the private sector in education reform? How have external actors effected this process? What steps may be taken to stimulate the cooperative interactions and build the alliances conducive to broad and substantial education and human investment efforts? And how does race permeate the processes by which these issues of coalition building and dissolution are played out where local public authority is in the hands of black leaders, but private investment and higher levels of government remain predominantly in the hands of whites? It is to these questions we now turn.

CHAPTER FOUR

Race and the Political Economy of Big-City Schools: Teachers and Preachers

> There is a power struggle—the principal and the teachers' unions or the teachers and the parents—but most likely the problem is either a principal or union representative who is disgruntled because of past histories and so you can't get anything moving.
> *(D.C. school administrator)*

> The teachers are not advocates of students. The teachers say they're advocates of students, but the teachers have to cover their priorities as professionals. That's a large part of it.
> *(Baltimore community activist)*

THOSE who study urban politics have long recognized the importance of tangible, material incentives as tools for building political alliances and supplementing formal authority with informal mechanisms of influence and control.[1] Big-city school systems are a major source of economic benefits to individuals, companies, and neighborhoods. As Wilbur Rich aptly put it: "The school pie feeds many families, and slicing it is a major event in the local economy."[2] But the connection between this insight and the challenge of urban school reform has been ignored or treated in one-dimensional terms.

One cannot understand the politics of school reform without first understanding the important role that school systems play in the local political economy. But understanding this role means moving beyond the simple observation that teachers and other school system employees have a clearly defined interest in resisting reform initiatives that threaten their jobs, impose new work demands, or limit their discretion. The inclination and capacity of school employees—or, more precisely, the unions that typically represent them in large urban school districts—to delay, diminish, or derail systemic school reform, has been noted loudly and often.

---

[1] Clarence Stone, *Regime Politics* (Lawrence: University Press of Kansas, 1989).

[2] Wilbur C. Rich, *Black Mayors and School Politics: The Failure of Reform in Detroit, Gary, and Newark* (New York: Garland Publishing, Inc, 1996), 5.

Commentators from across ideological perspectives have blamed professional educators and especially the unions that bargain for them for blocking reform. A cover story in the *U.S. News & World Report* asserted: "At a time when corporate leaders and others are calling on schools to hold students to significantly higher standards, the intransigence of the unions has slowed the pace of school reforms."[3] The more liberal *Washington Monthly* magazine argued: "Throughout the country unions used their formidable political clout to perpetuate the status quo."[4] And Cynthia Tucker, a liberal African American and editorial page editor of the *Atlanta Constitution*, criticized teacher organizations in Atlanta for putting the interests of students second. "Teachers' organizations," she writes, "would have you believe they are dedicated to only one thing: ensuring the best possible educational environment for the students they teach. Yet, if you watch local teachers' groups closely enough, you will see a pattern of behavior that suggests a very different mission— ensuring the highest wages and laxest standards for schoolteachers."[5]

In the academic literature, public choice theorists and others have emphasized the role that unions and the public school bureaucracy can play in blocking school reform. Chubb and Moe blame the failure of many American public schools on teachers' unions, organizations representing principals, school boards, superintendents, administrators, and professionals, private vendors and many other "beneficiaries of the "institutional status quo." They argue that "the root of the problem" is the institutional force of vested interests in public school systems.[6] Similarly, Myron Lieberman asserts that teachers' unions "threatened by reform become very active to prevent the reform from taking place." The unions, he argues, are "political organizations" that are "devoted to economic ends."[7]

Even sympathetic scholars have criticized teacher unions for being intransigent obstacles to meaningful school reform. In his recent book on school reform in Detroit, Gary, and Newark, Wilbur Rich found that efforts to achieve equity and excellence in the classroom failed in the face of powerful opposition from professional educators, school board members, and community activists. Rich called this group the "public school cartel." These entrenched and powerful interest groups, Rich argues, maintain control of school politics not for the sake of children but to promote the economic

---

[3] Thomas Toch, "Why Teachers Don't Teach," *U.S. News & World Report*, 26 February 1996.

[4] Joshua Wolf Shenk, "The Public Schools' Last Hurrah?" *Washington Monthly* 28 (March 1996): 8–17.

[5] Cynthia Tucker, "Kids' Interests Come Second" (editorial), *Atlanta Journal and Constitution*, 20 October 1993, A13.

[6] John Chubb and Terry Moe, *Politics, Markets and America's Schools* (Washington, D.C.: Brookings Institution, 1990), 12.

[7] Myron Lieberman, *Beyond Public Education* (New York: Praeger Press, 1986), 36.

interest of its members.[8] Rich's analysis also reminds us that racial transition of school personnel and union leaders in big-city school districts alone will not improve educational opportunities for black students. "There is no evidence that the poor are better off under black-led school boards," says Rich.[9] Black school board members in his three cities viewed their role as steering school contracts to black businesses and vendors and expanding black economic opportunity by increasing the number of blacks on the school system's payroll. "The black takeover of school boards signaled no fundamental change in policy," Rich asserts.[10] Even black teachers and school administrators, according to Rich, abdicated the progressive role they could be playing as champions for inner-city children. By adopting narrow, ultimately self-defeating stances, the unions representing professional educators made themselves unavailable as a reliable ally in reform coalitions.

There is little doubt that professional educators, especially their local union chapters, have been formidable obstacles to many school reform initiatives in Atlanta, Baltimore, Detroit, and Washington, D.C. At best, professional educators are politically marginalized; at worst, they are direct obstacles.

If our goal is to understand fully the elusiveness of school reform, however, bemoaning the unhelpful role of the local teachers' unions can only take us so far. In both private and public sectors, unions have experienced a long-term erosion of their power and support. In large and historically Democratic central cities, like Chicago, Philadelphia, Los Angeles, and New York local employees have found themselves faced with tough-minded, fiscally conservative mayors who stand up to the unions and expand their political support by doing so. Given this context of declining union power, the widespread sense that urban schools are critically important and in critical danger, and the apparent interest in systemic school reform on the part of a broad array of parents, businesses, foundations, and politicians, the interesting question is why reluctant and resistant teachers' unions have not been more seriously challenged.

Moreover, if our goal is not simply to catalogue the obstacles to reform but to identify opportunities for making things better, then it will almost certainly be necessary to work *with* teachers, not simply *around* them. The fact that divided and somewhat marginalized unions still do exercise clout is testimony to their central role as a key leverage point in translating ideas about education into practice. Running over teachers' unions with a steamroller might succeed in getting reform initiatives on the books, but implementing and institutionalizing those initiatives will be extremely problematic

[8] Rich, *Black Mayors and School Politics*, 5.
[9] Ibid., 208–14.
[10] Ibid., 208.

unless teachers become a part of the reform regime. Our goal is to gain some insight into how that can happen.

RACE, JOBS, AND POLITICS

In this chapter, we expand upon the conventional explorations of schools as large employers in three ways. Rather than looking at schools and their jobs in negative terms—as sources of patronage, inefficiency, intransigence, and waste—we take seriously the positive roles that schools play in the local political economy, as sources of citywide economic development, community identity and stability, and upward mobility for individuals and groups. Blocked by opportunities in the private sector, African Americans in our four cities have historically depended on public-sector employment, including public schools, for economic opportunity and mobility. Today, in Atlanta, Baltimore, Detroit, and Washington, African Americans occupy a huge percentage of the school districts' workforce, including the top administrative positions.

The role of public schools as large employers affects the politics of school reform in all large districts, but we illustrate how the legacy of racial polarization and racial sensitivities gives it a particular spin in Atlanta, Baltimore, Detroit, and D.C. where African Americans occupy key positions in the school systems. Rather than looking at the political economy of urban schools through a deracialized lens, we consider how institutional and perceptual legacies linked to race overlay and alter the political dynamics as they play out in black-led cities.

Many conventional analyses look at school reform as a two-actor game— pitting intense, united, and highly mobilized teachers against a loose and amorphous collection of concerned parents and do-gooders. In this study, we conceptualize school reform as a multi-actor game in which battles to mobilize or neutralize important third parties—to expand or contract the scope of conflict—play a critical role. In Atlanta, Baltimore, Detroit, and Washington, for example, teachers' union influence must be seen as part of a picture that includes African-American churches, ministers, and other community activists.

The Economics of Big-City Schools

Big-city school reform must be viewed within the context of urban political economy. For example, all four of our school districts are currently major employers in their respective cities. Table 4.1 lists the largest private employers in Atlanta, Baltimore, Detroit, the District of Columbia and the num-

TABLE 4.1

Major Employers in Four Black-Led Cities

	Largest Private Employer	Number of Employees	Number of School District Employees
Atlanta	Delta Airlines	22,900	6,466
Baltimore	Baltimore Gas and Electric	8,000	11,414
Detroit	Chrysler Corporation	13,659	18,822
Washington	Georgetown University	5,756	14,235

Source: Atlanta, Atlanta Chamber of Commerce, 1995; Baltimore, Greater Baltimore Committee, "Survey of Members" (Baltimore, Maryland, 1995), and Department of Planning, Detroit, Craine's Detroit Business (Detroit, 1995).

ber of workers each employ. Also listed is the number of workers on the payroll of each school system. What may be surprising to some readers is that in three of our cities—Baltimore, Detroit and Washington, D.C.—*the public school systems are the* largest employers.[11]

Among the four school systems, the Detroit Public School system (DPS) has the largest number of employees. With 18,822 workers, the DPS employs more workers than the Chrysler Corporation (13,000 workers), the city's largest private employer. Similarly, the Baltimore City Public Schools (BCPS) employ more workers (11,400) than the city's largest private-sector employers—Baltimore Gas and Electric Company and Johns Hopkins University Hospital, with 8,000 and 6,500, workers, respectively. With more than 14,000 employees, no private employer in the District of Columbia comes close to the number of workers employed in the D.C. public schools. Georgetown University, the city's largest private employer, has a payroll of nearly 5,800. Only the federal government and the District of Columbia general city government rival the D.C. public schools in terms of number of employees.

Atlanta is the only city among our four where the school system does not have more workers than the city's largest private employer. Atlanta is situated in an economic boom region that has attracted a number of growing service industries. Atlanta Public Schools (APS) employ about 6,500 workers. Delta Airline's huge payroll exceeds 22,000 employees. Although the number of workers in the APS is significantly smaller than the number of school employees in the other three cities, APS is Atlanta's sixth largest employer, with more workers than Coca-Cola Company, Georgia Power Company, and Grady Hospital. The thousands of positions in the Atlanta Public Schools are vital to the city's local economy and especially to the city's black middle class.

[11] Public schools were also the top employer in two of the six comparison cities for which we have data. In five of the six comparison cities, the public schools were among the top five largest employers.

In Detroit and Baltimore, the emergence of the school systems as major employers is tied to the decline of manufacturing and heavy industry. Today the residents of the Motor City and Baltimore are more likely to work for the public school system than for the Big Three automakers or any local manufacturing firm. As we discuss in greater detail below, the rise of the D.C. school system as a major employer is tied largely to efforts by Mayor Marion S. Barry and other black politicians to help build a broader black middle class. The D.C. school system's payroll swelled even as the number of students enrolled fell precipitously.

What does the emergence of our school districts as major employers have to do with school reform? Substantive school reform involves changes in school governance, institutional structures, and personnel. As one Baltimore school administrator explained, "reform means you have to change." The emergence of schools as major employers means that systemic school reform and reform ideas that are perceived to threaten job security, change the favored way of doing things, or upset organizational routine are likely to be viewed with skepticism and often resisted. As we shall show, in Atlanta, Baltimore, Detroit, and D.C., the organizations representing professional educators were joined by a broad network of organizations, ministers, and politicians throughout the city to delay, derail, or diminish initiatives perceived to destabilize the historic *economic* role the school systems have played—and continue to play—in the black community.

RACE, SCHOOL EMPLOYMENT, AND PATRONAGE POLITICS IN FOUR CITIES

African Americans comprise a majority of the top ten school administrative positions in the four cities:[12] in 1993, in Atlanta, Detroit, and the D.C. public schools blacks held nine posts, and in Baltimore, seven. All four school systems employ hundreds of other central office administrative, professional, and clerical workers. The Baltimore central office numbers between 600 and 700 employees.[13] When D.C. Superintendent Franklin Smith left office in 1996, the central office staff numbered about 400; down from the nearly 900 when he arrived in July 1991.[14] In Atlanta about 730 professional administrators, directors, and coordinators are housed in the school system's central

[12] We classified the top ten administrative positions to include superintendent and such positions as associate superintendent, assistant superintendent, deputy superintendent, finance director, personnel director, and curriculum director. The composition of these ten positions varied across the four school districts.

[13] "A Report of a Management Study of the Baltimore City Public Schools," Associated Black Charities, 26 June 1992, II-1.

[14] Vernon Loeb and William Casey, "Work Force a Family Affair for Many," *Washington Post*, 17 February 1997, Appendix B.

TABLE 4.2
Total Number of Teachers and Proportion of Minority Teachers

	1989	1990	1991	1992	1993
Atlanta	3,815	3,851	3,779	3,740	3,701
	(82%)	(82%)	(82%)	(82%)	(82.4%)
Baltimore	6,452	6,400	6,450	6,590	6,590
	(67%)	(67%)	(66%)	(64%)	(62%)
Detroit	8,333	8,239	8,273	6,541	7,035
	(65%)				
Washington	6,055	5,950	6,087	5,809	5,595
	(93%)	(85%)	(84%)	(85%)	(83%)

Note: Reports total number of teachers in each district. Parenthetical percentage indicates the proportion of African-American teachers.

office.[15] In all four cities, African Americans comprised more than 70 percent of central office administrators.

In terms of overall numbers, the top administrative personnel represents a small component of the school districts' employment base. However, these well-paid professionals are important politically and economically, especially in the African-American community. For example, in Atlanta six assistant superintendents each earned more than $83,000; ten supervisors of operation earned $70,680 each; and nineteen directors each took home $68,261.[16] These administrators, each earning well above the 1990 median income ($18,353) of black households, are a part of the nearly 8,100 (or 9.6 percent) black households with annual incomes of between $50,000 and $100,000 or more.

Meier, Stewart, and England have demonstrated the relationship between black access to administrative positions and the hiring of black teachers.[17] Table 4.2 shows the total number of teachers and the percentage who are African Americans in the four cities from 1989 to 1993. Clearly, blacks dominate the classrooms in all four school systems. Over the five-year period black teachers represented on average 86 percent of the instructional work force in the District. During the same period, the black percentage of the teaching force in Atlanta remained steady at about 82 percent. African Americans comprise about 65 percent of the teaching positions in both Baltimore and Detroit.

[15] Good Government Atlanta, *Program of Financial Reform of the Atlanta Public Schools* (Atlanta: Good Government Atlanta, 1995), A1.

[16] Ibid., Appendix B.

[17] Kenneth J. Meier, Joseph Stewart, Jr., and Robert E. England, *Race, Class, and Education* (Madison: University of Wisconsin Press, 1989).

Teaching and administrative positions represent only part of the school systems' employment picture. In addition to the hundreds of other employees that have contact with students everyday—counselors, aides, psychologists, principals, librarians, and the like—the school systems have painters, janitors, security officers, school secretaries, office assistants, chauffeurs, food workers, cafeteria managers, bus drivers, and even piano tuners. Blacks also dominate these positions.

Bonds of Personalism: Black Professional Educators

In many cases, the teachers and administrators in our four cities, have spent their entire careers in their respective school systems. Management is highly durable, especially below the position of superintendent. Central office administrators are typically men and women who worked their way up the system—perhaps as teachers, assistant principal, principal, then central staff administrators. In Baltimore, seven of the top ten school administrators have spent almost their entire career (an average of twenty-three years each) as educators in the Baltimore schools.

Previous research has shown that average years of experience among teachers are largely a function of the growth and shrinkage in student enrollment.[18] Fast-growing districts are likely to have younger teachers; however, school districts experiencing enrollment losses, the case in our four cities, are more likely to have teachers with more years of experience who have worked in the school system for many years. In Maryland, the statewide average of teachers with more than twenty-one years experience is 28 percent; in Baltimore that percentage is nearly 35, and only 22.5 percent have less than ten years experience. In the District of Columbia, the median age of teachers is forty-seven; that is, they typically have been in the classroom for more than twenty-five years. As one top Baltimore central office administrator explained: "If you come through the system you have some conception that there are opportunities within the system, and you tend to stay, and then once you stay you get tenure, and then you start thinking about retirement benefits."[19]

The teachers and administrators in our four school systems are a tightly knit group who have developed a personal affinity, a bond. The bonds of personalism, however, did not begin, nor do they end, at the school headquarters or at the school building. The majority of the teachers and adminis-

---

[18] Robert E. Slavin, "Funding Inequities Among Maryland School Districts: What Do They Mean in Practice?" (paper, Johns Hopkins University, October 1991).

[19] Will Englund, "Tightly Knit Group of Survivors Controls Power," *The Sun*, 3 May 1988, 1A.

trators in Atlanta, Baltimore, Detroit, and D.C. share similar middle-class backgrounds. Many of them attended the same colleges and universities. For example, in Atlanta many administrators and teachers graduated from the historically black colleges at the Atlanta University Center—Spelman, Morehouse, Morris Brown, and Clark colleges. Many of Baltimore's black educators attended Coppin State College or Morgan State University, two historically black institutions located in Baltimore.[20] In Washington, Detroit, and many other big-city school districts in the Northeast and Midwest that underwent racial change in the 1960s and 1970s, local officials recruited teachers from predominately black colleges and universities in the South.[21]

African-American teachers and administrators are frequently members of the same social, fraternal, and religious organizations. For example, many black professional educators, especially those who are alumni of predominately black colleges, are members of the same black fraternities (Omega Psi Phi, Kappa Alpha Psi, Alpha Phi Alpha, and Phi Beta Sigma) and sororities (Alpha Kappa Alpha, Delta Sigma Theta, Zeta Phi Beta, and Sigma Gamma Rho). Reportedly, when Alice Pinderhughes was Baltimore's school superintendent (1982–1987), her sorority, Alpha Kappa Alpha, was well represented among the professional staff. As one black Baltimore administrator remarked: "You've got to recognize a little bit of tradition in terms of blacks. Many of us went to black colleges and universities, and the social outlet there was the fraternities and sororities. That was the orientation for us."[22] Furthermore, the bonds of personalism are strengthened by the fact that many African-American teachers and administrators attend the same middle-class black churches. In each of our cities many prominent African Americans active in school affairs are leaders of these large, influential religious institutions.

School Affairs and Patronage Politics

In the school affairs of each city, strong evidence suggests patronage politics. In Baltimore during the 1970s and 1980s, an enduring alignment and relationship developed between black professional educators, City Hall, and the

[20] The tendency to hire educators trained at local colleges was also discovered in St. Louis, one of the ten cities in the larger Civic Capacity and Urban Education Project. Many teachers and administrators in St. Louis public schools attended the local teachers' college, Harris-Stowe. A 1976 study found that 97.5 percent of the principals in St. Louis were in fact graduates of Harris-Stowe. See Lana Stein, "Site Report: St. Louis, Missouri," 1 December 1994, 11.

[21] Rich, *Black Mayors and School Politics*, 10; Jeffrey Mirel, *The Rise and Fall of an Urban School System* (Ann Arbor: University of Michigan Press, 1993), 260.

[22] Quoted in Will Englund, "Tightly Knit Group of Survivors Controls Power," *The Sun*, 3 May 1988, 1A.

school system. Mayor Schaefer (1971–1986) helped solidify this relationship. As the white mayor of a largely black city, Schaefer sought to strengthen and maintain black votes by appointing his African-American supporters as school administrators, principals, and other professional positions as rewards for their political support. African Americans were also hired in lower-level positions as janitors, secretaries, and teacher-aides. Wong described it, "Increasingly, the school district resembled a patronage base. Personnel that orchestrated mayoral activities were put on the school system's payroll. Central office administrators critical of the administration were either demoted or transferred. Not infrequently school resources were allocated in a politicized manner to serve as warnings to dissenters at the school building level."[23] Evidence indicates that this patronage culture persists under Mayor Kurt L. Schmoke, who was elected in 1987 on a platform to reform the schools. A 1992 study of the management of the BCPS found that "personal relationships rather than competence, experience, or performance . . . [are the] primary factors that determine who is promoted. . . . Exemplary performance is rarely perceived to be the reason that an individual is promoted."[24]

In the District of Columbia, the hiring and promotion of school system personnel have been described as a "family affair."[25] "It was no secret," says a former staff member of the D.C. City Council's Education Committee, "that school officials did get jobs for their relatives. . . . This goes back to one of the major flaws of the system—it became an employment agency."[26] An extensive study of the family and personal relationships of D.C. school employees conducted by *The Washington Post* found "a host of connections" among principals, assistant principals, central office administrators, clerks, secretaries, and other school employees.[27] For example, the *Post* reported that school board member Angie Corley, who made $15,000 a year was joined on the DCPS payroll by her daughter, Gwenellen, a $49,096-a-year vice principal, and her son, William, a $35,054-a-year science teacher.[28]

In an effort to protect the jobs of friends and relatives, D.C. school officials kept "two sets of books" that allowed them to spend millions of unauthorized dollars to employ more people than the D.C. Council and Congress officially approved.[29] Between 1990 and 1995 the school system spent an extra $54 million on personnel that should have been spent on textbooks, field trips,

    [23] Kenneth Wong, *City Choices* (Albany: State University of New York Press, 1990), 115.
    [24] Associated Black Charities, "A Report of a Management Study of the Baltimore City Public Schools" (June 1992), III-32.
    [25] Loeb and Casey, "Work Force a Family Affair."
    [26] Ibid.
    [27] Ibid.
    [28] Ibid.
    [29] Sari Horwitz and Valerie Strauss, "A Well-Financed Failure: Systems Protects Jobs While Shortchanging Classrooms," *Washington Post*, 16 February 1997, A1.

athletics, facilities, and other student items. "The money goes to create a middle-class community. It goes to salaries," says Abdusalam Omer, the school system's chief financial officer hired by the congressionally approved D.C. Financial Control Board to clean up the school system's finances. In a scathing report, the Financial Control Board found that the "DCPS' personnel operations are in disarray."[30] Many local observers suggested that the lack of adequate administrative controls was intentional, designed to obfuscate.[31]

Not only top school administrators play the patronage game. In Atlanta, Detroit, and D.C., the elected school boards are heavily involved in the hiring of school personnel. In an interview with Wilbur Rich, a former Detroit school board member admitted that "our role was more than just to educate but to give blacks positions and jobs, so that they can hire other blacks in the future."[32] Washington, D.C., school board member R. Calvin Lockridge, who represented the city's poorest area from 1978 to 1990, reportedly saw it as part of his job to expand the number of professionals living in Ward 8. He is quoted in an interview as saying: "Sometimes I feel like I run a job placement service."[33] In Baltimore, where the mayor has a stronger formal role in education governance than in most U.S. cities, the patronage game historically has been centered in the mayor's office rather than the school board. For the most part this is still the case, although Mayor Schmoke is generally a less avid player than was his predecessor.

A recent report on Atlanta schools' finances found that the APS has many more employees when compared with other school systems in the region and nation of comparable size.[34] It criticized the school board for adopting employment policies that squeezed the system of its finances. For example, the board has consistently tied nonteacher employees' compensation to teachers' pay; if teachers' pay goes up, so does that of every other person working in the public school system. Cafeteria workers were paid higher rates than in surrounding jurisdictions and for purposes of fringe benefits classified as full-time employees although they work only part-time. Finally when the system's bus drivers, who technically worked for a private firm, went on strike and demanded medical benefits, a coalition of school board members voted to provide the benefits over the objection of a minority of board members who argued that it was the responsibility of the private firm.

[30] District of Columbia Financial Responsibility and Management Assistance Authority, *Children in Crisis: A Report on the Failure of D.C.'s Public Schools* (November 1996), 16.

[31] The D.C. school system's personnel records were so inadequate that top school officials admitted that they did not know how many workers were on the schools' payrolls. Michael Powell, "No Accounting for Some Workers in D.C. Schools," *Washington Post*, 15 September 1996, A1.

[32] Rich, *Black Mayors and School Politics*, 145.

[33] Loeb and Casey, "Work Force a Family Affair."

[34] Good Government Atlanta, *Program of Financial Reform*, June 1996.

Following the board's vote, members who voted in favor of the school system paying the benefits reportedly were heard to remind the bus drivers to vote for them in the up-coming elections. A black journalist described the Atlanta school system as "an employment agency of last resort."[35]

School Contracts and Patronage Politics

The economic benefits that a big-city school system provides to a community go beyond school personnel. Big-city school districts enter into contracts for everything: cafeteria services, school construction and repairs, janitorial and maintenance services, legal services, accountants and auditing, data processing, school security, and so on.[36] With the ascendancy of black elected officials and the appointment of black administrators, more black businesses have obtained contracts. The opportunity to enter into a huge contract with the school district offered various African-American businesses and professionals opportunities that were severely limited prior to the 1970s.

After Mayor Marion Barry took office in 1978, D.C. schools switched suppliers for breakfast cereal and fuel oil to black businesses. School officials also withdrew the school system's trash contract from a white firm and gave it to a black-run company.[37] In Atlanta and Detroit, efforts were made by black school officials to increase the number of black vendors receiving contracts for goods and services. Wilbur Rich observed that in Detroit some black school members were "very proud" of their "role in steering contracts to black vendors."[38] In many instances, these school contracts are huge. For example, in 1996 D.C. school officials signed a food service contract with a private firm for $21 million; a janitorial service was awarded a $5-million contract.[39] In 1991, Baltimore schools signed a contract with Education Alternatives, Inc. (EAI), a white-owned firm, for $25 million to manage nine of its public schools.

In most instances these contracts have been good for the school districts; they provide needed services in a cost-effective manner. However, in a number of cases the steering of contracts to favored vendors has been problematic

[35] Cynthia Tucker, "Ousting School Board May Not Be So Simple," *Atlanta Journal and Constitution*, 20 January 1993, A13.

[36] Other functions and services would include, but are not limited to, the following: advertisement of public notices; architectural services; data processing; evaluation services; executive searches; fleet or vehicle maintenance; insurance services; medical/nursing services; moving services; paving services; parking lots and garages; public relations services; vehicle towing or storage; and solid waste collection or disposal.

[37] Harry S. Jaffe and Tom Sherwood, *Dream City* (New York: Simon and Schuster, 1994), 152.

[38] Rich, *Black Mayors and School Politics*, 145.

[39] *Children in Crisis*, 30.

and costly. For example, before Mayor Barry changed vendors the schools had been buying cornflakes for $8.00 a carton; the new contract increased the cost to $13.50 a carton. Likewise, the cost of heating oil went up 25 percent. Jaffe and Sherwood recounted an exchange between Barry and then-Superintendent Vincent Reed:

> "I understand that you want to give contracts to black companies," Reed said, "but when you tell me to take food out of a black kid's stomach so some black dude can get rich, I have to ask what's your rationale?"
>
> "Black entrepreneurs are at the top of my agenda," Barry responded. "We have to do it this way. It's the only way to get them into the mainstream."[40]

The racial transition in four school districts did not bring about fundamental change. As one former D.C. school board member put it: African-American school officials simply decided "to do what white folks had been doing for some time."[41] In terms of the typology introduced in chapter 1, we can say that the more immediate and material incentives associated with education as an employment regime engendered a pattern of "politics as usual," in which schools functioned more as a source of patronage and personal security than as a institutional vehicle for investing in human capital or leveraging economic growth.

UNIONS AND REFORM

Teachers' unions have been a significant force in school politics since the late 1960s and early 1970s.[42] The teachers' organizations in Atlanta, Baltimore, Detroit, and D.C. maintain higher profiles than the unions representing school administrators, possibly reflecting the difference in membership. For example, the teachers' union in Washington, D.C., has 5,500 members while the Council of School Officers, which represents the District's principals, has only 370 members. The Detroit Federation of Teachers has more than 7,000 members, while the Organization of School Administrators and Supervisors (OSAS) represents about 1,200 administrators in the Detroit Public Schools. However, the economic and political influence of school principals and the respect that many in black community hold for them magnify their

---

[40] Jaffe and Sherwood, *Dream City*, 153.

[41] Loeb and Casey, "Work Force a Family Affair."

[42] Paul Peterson, *School Politics, Chicago Style* (Chicago: University of Chicago Press, 1976); Alan Rosenthal, *Pedagogues and Power: Teacher Groups and School Politics* (Syracuse, NY: Syracuse University Press, 1969); William J. Grimshaw, *Union Rule in the Schools* (Lexington, MA: Lexington Books, 1979); Susan Moore Johnson, *Teacher Unions in Schools* (Philadelphia: Temple University Press, 1984); Maurice R. Berule, *Teacher Politics: The Influence of Unions* (Westport, CT: Greenwood Press, 1988).

influence beyond what would be predicted by their numbers alone. The principals' organizations tend to become most vocal over issues that directly affect their members. Certain teacher contract provisions, for example, can limit the principal's control over the school site.[43]

In chapter 2, we presented data indicating that organizations representing professional educators were more likely to be seen as major players in general political decisions making than in the other seven cities. This is the case, also, when respondents are asked specifically about education decision making. Indeed, respondents in the Atlanta, Baltimore, Detroit, and Washington, D.C., were three times more likely to identify teachers' unions as major education stakeholders than respondents in the other seven cities. Unions, however, were *less* likely to be named than other actors—business leaders, mayors, and the nonprofit community—who are presumed supportive of systemic big-city school reform. Although respondents in the four black-led cities acknowledge the influence of labor unions in school affairs, they do not view the unions holding a monopoly.

Figure 4.1 summarizes the respondents' perceptions of the role of school unions as general stakeholders in local politics and as key players in education-specific policy decision making. In Atlanta, where most respondents characterized education decision making as a closed arena, not a single respondent spontaneously mentioned teachers' unions as key players.[44] Respondents in Detroit—by history and culture a quintessentially pro-union town—were the most likely to perceive the unions as playing a central role in city politics generally and in educational decision making specifically. Only 3 percent of the respondents in Baltimore and Washington mentioned unions when asked to name important actors in school affairs.

Some will consider the overall low assessment of unions' power to be surprising, even shocking. That well-informed respondents are slow to think of teachers' unions when asked about influential actors in educational decision making runs directly counter to so much of the commentary that identifies the unions as a powerful, almost omnipotent, obstacles to meaningful school reform. We do not think that the conventional wisdom is wildly inaccurate; as we detail in the sections to follow, teachers and the organizations representing them *are* important actors in the arena of school politics. But our findings suggest that this conventional wisdom needs rethinking in some key respects. That our respondents were slow to think of teachers unions,

[43] For an insightful analysis of the dimensions of teacher and principal relations, see Betty Malen, "The Micropolitics of Education: Mapping the Multiple Dimensions of power relations in school politics," in *The Study of Educational Politics*, ed. Jay D. Scribner and Donald H. Layton (New York: Falmer Press, 1995), 147–67.

[44] The "players" question was asked only of those who indicated that education was an open arena with multiple players. Coders recorded the first five responses, but it was rare for more than three interests to be mentioned.

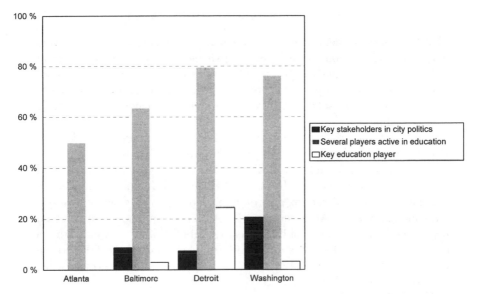

Figure 4.1 Role of school unions in city/education politics. Percentage of respondents identifying school unions as key stakeholders in city politics, agreeing that education politics has several key players, and if they agree that education has several players, seeing school unions as key players.

we believe, reflects the increasingly peripheral role they play in debates about school reform. This peripheral role is prompted not only by factors outside the unions' control, but it also results from some tactical decisions (we think misguided ones, by and large) made by local union leadership. Outside union control has been a broad historical erosion of the myth of neutral professionalism; the public is no longer willing, as it was earlier in the century, to grant educators the discretion to run schools as they see fit, based on the premise that teacher knows best. But within union control has been the decision to remain at arms' length from local school-reform coalitions; teachers have tempered their vague agreements to the goals of reform with sharply etched skepticism about specific reform proposals that might reduce their numbers, salaries, independence, or status.

Teachers unions, as a result, have become somewhat peripheral and politically isolated from discussions about change and reform. Yet, as we also show, the unions remain able to exercise some veto power at critical points. Rather than reflecting their internal power, however, we suggest that this residual veto power rests in good measure on their ability to mobilize support from other actors. And this ability, in turn, is augmented in our cities by ties of loyalty and perception that are related to race.

THE DETROIT FEDERATION OF TEACHERS (DFT)

That Detroit respondents considered the school unions as significant players in educational decision making is not surprising. Detroit is the birthplace of industrial unionism, and the power of the unions is still felt throughout city. The schools are no exception. Compared to our other cities, in Detroit there is a broad sense that school employee unions form a major force in setting educational policy.

In Detroit, the principal union player in education politics is the Detroit Federation of Teachers (DFT).[45] Its president, John Elliott, is the undisputed education labor leader in Detroit. Elliott is the first African American to hold the DFT's top post, a position he has held since 1981. In public John Elliott, typically skeptical of reform and pilot initiatives, instead advocates systemwide approaches. An executive with AT&T Telephone Company who has worked on several school initiatives described Elliott as "a nice human being but he's into the status quo." Elliott has not moved the DFT to the forefront of school reform. DFT's central role in derailing reform was discussed in some detail in chapter 3.

The DFT claimed that the school empowerment program undermined the union contract and personnel rules. The great fear among teachers was that site-based management would give the principal and the school site committee the power to replace or remove underperforming teachers without due process stipulated in the teachers' contract. In addition, many teachers viewed the school board's empowerment agenda as requiring them to perform more tasks without additional resources. OSAS, the principals' union, joined DFT in opposing the empowerment program. "Because they were not trained as facility managers, most principals would prefer such functions to remain in the hands of the central administration."[46] The principals themselves were skeptical of site-based management.

Thus, the conflict over many of the HOPE team's reforms was not based in either pedagogical issues or philosophical concerns about how best to run a school or teach children; the conflict focused on jobs and job security. This distinction was clear to one HOPE member: "Typically the conflict is between those folks who have a vested interest in continuing their relationship with the school board that provides them a job or source of income. That's one group which is typically in conflict with the group of folks that are interested in quality education for children. Often it is union leaders who are trying to get as much money as possible for their members in opposition to community activists and leaders who are trying to see that as much money as possible results in quality education for children." DFT was successful in

---

[45] Mirel, *Rise and Fall of an Urban School System*, 152–202.
[46] Rich, *Black Mayors and School Politics*, 41.

painting the school board as "union busters." Detroit's labor community, including the United Auto Workers and other nonschool unions, joined to help defeat the HOPE slate in the 1992 elections.[47] Out of this opposition movement emerged a group of candidates that sought to depose the HOPE team incumbents. The challengers, although not running on a single slate, were determined to put into office candidates who would respect the hegemony of professional educators in educational decision making. A community leader who worked closely with the school system during this period explained why she believed the HOPE coalition was ousted in the 1992 election.

> This reform board for all its zeal and passion did not bring along the unions, the bargaining units, or the community with them and were perceived as union busting when they tried to push too fast on certain reforms like merit pay, privatization and empowerment. Included in empowerment was a provision that individual school buildings could waive portions of the union contract if 75 percent of the teachers agreed. At one point they were talking about 51 percent of the teachers. Well, this just enraged the union. You have to remember—this is Detroit, the birthplace, you know, the stronghold of unions if not the birthplace—the union successfully painted these four school board members as union busters, and this is the kiss of death in Detroit and the community. It was a perfect political play, and they pulled it off masterfully. And I believe the voters would have elected David Duke [a Louisiana politician widely regarded at the time as representing a racist strain in Southern politics], you know, to replace them.

In the November 1992 election three of four HOPE reformers were defeated. Advocates for a return to the basics and equalized school improvement across the school district, with emphasis on "neighborhood schools," replaced the reformers.

THE BALTIMORE TEACHERS' UNION

Labor unions have never been as strong in Baltimore as they are in Detroit. Still, unionism has thrived, especially among municipal workers. And although only 3 percent of our Baltimore respondents named school unions as key players in educational decision making, this probably reflects local observers' sense that the unions have lost control over the broad agenda of school reform rather than their daily influence on school affairs.[48]

---

[47] The UAW even opposed one of their own. In 1988, Joseph Blanding, a high-ranking black in the UAW, was added to the HOPE slate after he won the runoff election. In 1992, labor opposed the HOPE team, including Blanding. Blanding lost his bid for reelection in 1992.

[48] Interestingly, nearly four times as many (12 percent) Baltimore respondents named "educators" as being central players in school affairs than the unions.

The Baltimore Teachers' Union (BTU), the major labor group active in school affairs, is also the largest municipal union in Baltimore. The BTU represents about 6,800 teachers and 1,800 paraprofessionals or teacher aides. During our research, Irene Dandridge was serving her sixteenth year as president of the BTU. In May 1996, Dandridge was ousted by another black woman, Marcia Brown, amid allegations of misuse of union funds.[49] The real power in the BTU, however, is copresident Lorretta Johnson.[50] For nearly a quarter-century Johnson has led the paraprofessional unit of the union. Johnson is also a vice president of BTU's national organization, the American Federation of Teachers (AFT). Several Baltimore respondents told us that Johnson's political influence was driven by her position in the AFT and the close relationship that she developed with the late AFT president Albert Shanker. One knowledgeable school administrator noted that "Lorretta has a direct line to Al Shanker. And he takes her calls."

Dandridge and Johnson are African Americans. As discussed in chapter 3, the Baltimore union strongly opposed, or sought to undermine, several reforms pushed in Baltimore, including the Barclay-Calvert collaboration and the EAI private management. The unions representing school employees in Baltimore have spent the bulk of their energy on traditional union concerns: working conditions, salaries, and fringe benefits. An African-American entrepreneur, a former BCPS teacher and BTU member, expressed disappointment in what he considered the union's overemphasis on "traditional" union concerns.

> When I joined BTU I was very contented with the organization. But once we began to do things that were more along the lines of union striking, picketing, and that type of thing, my philosophy of education didn't allow me to participate. So I was very glad that I was able to move on. I would like for them to be spending their time concentrating on trying to encourage and help these parents work with these students and be more up on a professional level where you're training and helping your teachers and your principals and that type of thing.

When asked to describe how he would go about gaining the support of teachers for a reform idea, a Johns Hopkins University researcher who has worked closely with the BCPS made a telling statement that reflects on the BTU's priorities.

> Depends on what kind of things you're talking about. Because in some cases you'd want to get to teachers in particular schools and you would want to have them involved early on. In other cases, it might be the union that you'd need to

[49] Jean Thompson and Joe Matthews, "Stormy Transition at the BTU," *The Sun*, 24 May 1996, A1.

[50] Mike Bowler, "BTU's Two-woman Team Sees Success and Failure," *The Sun*, 15 August 1994, B1.

get involved with in dealing with the larger policy. For example, let's say, as it's been in the news recently, your intention was to weed out ineffective teachers. Now that would be a top, hot button for the union and if you were going to try to do that, you've got to get the union involved on day one. Whereas, let's say, you were trying to implement a new reading program in particular schools. Then the union doesn't care so much about that. You want to involve the particular teachers in those particular schools that you're interested in supporting it.

THE WASHINGTON TEACHERS' UNION

The Washington Teachers' Union (WTU) maintains a high profile in D.C. school politics. The WTU is headed by Barbara Bullock, a black teacher. In 1994, Bullock defeated the incumbent president Jimmie C. Jackson after losing to her in a 1993 election that was subsequently ruled invalid.[51] The WTU has not been part of a major reform effort. Instead, the unions representing teachers and to a lesser extent the Council of School Officers (CSO), the union representing school principals, have resisted systemic school reform. As shown in chapter 3, the WTU and CSO opposed D.C. Superintendent Franklin Smith's initiative to lengthen the school day by thirty minutes. As in Baltimore and Detroit, efforts to implement site-based management in the District encountered stiff union resistance, especially from principals who did not wish to relinquish or share their authority over the school site.[52] The unions representing D.C.'s professional educators were vehement in their opposition to Superintendent's Smith proposal to hire a private management firm to operate fifteen D.C. schools.[53]

Our D.C. respondents consistently portrayed the school unions as being especially concerned about issues such as wages and working conditions. This assessment was confirmed by the response of a top officer in the CSO when asked to comment on recent changes and educational innovations in the Districts' schools. He told us: "I don't know if I can speak intelligently about that [new initiatives in education] because in the past seven or eight years I've been more involved in union operation than I have in so much the new concepts of education."

[51] First elected in 1991, Jackson's presidency was controversial to say the least. The *Washington Post* accused her of raising race as an issue as a political tactic. She reportedly predicted that D.C. School Superintendent Franklin Smith would be last black superintendent in the District and that "Euro-Americans" controlled the D.C. school board and the D.C. city council education committee. Sari Horwitz, "D.C. Teachers Elect New Union President," *Washington Post*, 17 January 1994, C1.

[52] Districtwide Restructuring Team, *Planning Guide for Local School Restructuring Teams* (Washington, D.C.: D.C. Public Schools, 1992), 9.

[53] Sari Horowitz, "Private Firm Eyed to Run D.C. Schools," *Washington Post*, 8 December 1993, A1.

A former D.C. school board member argued that in earlier decades the WFT was involved in "a broad array of professional and administrative issues. Staff development was one of the major issues. They're no longer talking about those things. They're now clearly talking about pay raise and maintaining their working hours." A staff member who monitored education issues for the D.C. city council believed that the school unions could play a positive and effective role in school affairs but lamented that he believed the unions would remain an impediment: "They [school unions] should play a major role in education right now, but frankly the role they are playing in many respects is a negative one because they are unfortunately an obstacle to a number of reforms that have a great deal of support throughout the city. Frankly, given the present leadership of the teachers' union, I don't think anything is going to change in the near future."

THE ATLANTA FEDERATION OF TEACHERS

In Atlanta, organizations representing professional educators have not played a major role in efforts to reform the public schools. As in the other three cities, the Atlanta Public Schools (APS) system is an employment regime for the African-American community. Protecting jobs, fighting school lay-offs, and securing fringe benefits have been the dominant concerns of the Atlanta Federation of Teachers (AFT) and its allies.

The Atlanta Compromise required APS to balance top administrative positions by race (see chapter 2). Some twenty-four new administrative positions were created, which increased administrative costs from $3.959 million in 1973 to more than $4.820 million in 1974. A 1995 study showed that the school system never eliminated the extra jobs created to implement the Compromise.[54]

The practice of protecting and expanding the APS employment base was firmly established during the fifteen-year tenure of Alonzo Crim. Under Atlanta's first black superintendent, the school system went through a number of reorganizations, but cutbacks in administrative positions were accomplished through attrition, including resignations, retirement, and death, rather than firings or layoffs. When an administrator died or retired, the position went unfilled and duties shifted to other positions. Some high-level vacant positions were eventually abolished.[55]

The employment base of the school district has remained relatively steady even as student enrollment has declined and financial difficulties have set in. In 1971, when the system enrollment was more than 100,000, APS main-

[54] Good Government Atlanta, *Program of Financial Reform*, 14.
[55] David Blount, "An Analysis of Selected Indicators of Performance Effectiveness in the Atlanta Public Schools, 1968 to 1983" (Ph.D. diss., Georgia State University, 1985), 137–69.

tained 2,133 support employees, mostly custodians, cooks, and so on. By 1992, although enrollment had declined 40 percent, the school system still maintained more than 1,500 support employees, a reduction of only 25 percent; administrative and teaching staff had declined by only 14 percent. As a result, a recent report notes, the number of students per employee declined from 13 to 1 in 1972 to 10 to 1 in 1992.[56]

In 1993, the AFT supported Superintendent Benjamin Canada's proposal to close underutilized schools as a cost-saving effort, but with one significant caveat—no teacher should lose her job. An AFT officer told us that she believed closing some schools was necessary; however, she quickly added: "I don't want him to fire anybody in the process. And that is another issue. Reduction in force would be a way of going, but we have been asking [the school administrators] to find places for these employees, the teachers." Georgia's Fair Dismissal Act permits school systems to terminate teachers and administrators to reduce staff size because of shrinking enrollments. Despite declining enrollment and a sizable personnel budget, APS has never invoked the law. The school system remains committed to a no-termination policy.

In addition, Atlanta has the highest paid teachers in the state. Two separate reports issued by private groups in Atlanta note that the salaries of Atlanta's teachers exceed by 40 percent those required by state law. Likewise wages and salaries in Atlanta are 29 percent higher than the average of other big-city school districts, including Denver, San Francisco, San Antonio, New Orleans, Austin, and Nashville.[57] Atlanta's average public school teacher receives approximately $38,500 plus benefits of $9,500 a year. Veteran teachers earn around $52,000 plus benefits. The starting salary for a teacher fresh out of college is a little more than $28,000, "which is higher than the state mandated salary for a teacher with eighteen years of classroom experience, and $3,000 higher than the annual combined incomes of 49 percent of households in Atlanta."[58] A starting teacher with a master's degree earns $32,000.[59]

In a comparison of starting salaries, an Atlanta police officer makes about $5,000 less than a starting teacher. The top pay for Atlanta police officers is approximately $33,636 a year—$6,000 less than the average pay of Atlanta teachers and $19,000 less than teachers at the top of the pay scale.[60] Certainly

[56] Good Government Atlanta, *Program of Financial Reform*.

[57] See ibid., and Atlanta Committee for Public Education, "Atlanta's Overpaid Teachers" (Atlanta: ACPE, 1993). Also see Randy Jay, "Atlanta Teacher's Pay Tops State," *Atlanta Journal and Constitution*, 4 June 1987, E1.

[58] Good Government Atlanta, *Program of Financial Reform*, 11.

[59] According to the Good Government Report, the best example that APS salaries are higher than need be is that few Atlanta teachers leave before retirement even though disgruntled. With a workforce of more than 4,600, the school system hires less than 200 in any given year, an indication that turnover is low. "At the current rate of turnover, it would take more than 23 years to replace the teaching staff of the APS."

[60] Ibid.

Atlanta teachers deserve to be paid well for their performance; however, APS's compensation package is based on neither performance evaluations nor merit. Instead, pay is based on the number of degrees held by the teacher and length of service. Atlanta's teachers and their unions have opposed performance measures. Being required to prove their worth, according to one teacher, would be like forcing teachers to "do a monkey dance."[61]

In spite of teachers' exceptional salaries, each year during APS budget preparation, Atlanta teachers' unions listen for two words: more money. In fact, they prescribe pay raises for improving everything from low teacher morale to high teacher absenteeism. In 1992 when the school board decided that no pay increases would be forthcoming, some two hundred teachers and AFT members rallied at the school board, chanting "we deserve a raise." In 1995, teachers crippled the school system when more than fourteen hundred called in sick to protest the school board's failure to give them a raise. Parent volunteers, substitute teachers, central office administrators, and school board members filled in for absent teachers at a cost that exceeded $95,000. According to an Atlanta Association of Educators representative, "there is a direct correlation between teacher satisfaction and student achievement. A happy teacher is a productive teacher." The Professional Association of Georgia Educators condemned the sick-out: "anything that takes away from the process of teaching and learning, anything which distracts us from that mission, is not productive."[62] But AFT leaders contend that "the rising cost of living and lack of salary supports have many of [Atlanta teachers] looking for part-time jobs to help support their families and pay their bills."[63] In fact, AFT estimates that 33 percent of Atlanta teachers hold part-time jobs. "They have to make ends meet and support their families. But it takes a lot out of them . . . that spark of enthusiasm that many teachers have," said then AFT president Mary Lou Romaine.[64]

Moonlighting teachers may explain why absenteeism is so high in Atlanta. An *Atlanta Journal and Constitution* article estimates that teachers are absent 6 percent of the school year, that is, more than ten days each year. Noting that the average U.S. worker misses only seven days a year, the article ob-

[61] "Too Many Atlanta Teachers Get Away With Playing Hooky," *Atlanta Journal and Constitution*, 30 May 1996, A16.

[62] Gail Hagans, "Pay Protest," *Atlanta Journal and Constitution*, 23 May 1995, B1.

[63] Bernadette Burden, "200 Teachers Protest Atlanta School Budget: Union Member Rally for Pay Raise," *Atlanta Journal and Constitution*, 5 May 1992, C4.

[64] Susan Laccetti, "Moonlighting Teachers: Help or Hindrance," *Atlanta Journal and Constitution*, 14 March 1988, A1. Moonlighting seems to be driven primarily by self-preservational, though some moonlighting teachers contend that their outside work informs their teaching. Some students note teachers napping and lacking enthusiasm. Teachers themselves note that they are tired the next day after working two jobs and comment on their lack of extracurricular time with students. One teacher said, "I don't stay after school" and often miss PTA or faculty meetings if they are held at night or afternoons.

serves that absenteeism cost APS more than $3 million in 1995 on substitute teachers who do little more than babysit classes.[65]

UNIONS IN CONTEXT

Given the widespread belief that the school systems in our four cities are failing, and given the apparent interest in systemic school reform on the part of a broad array of school activists and civic leaders, the interesting question is why teachers' unions, whose stance seems narrow and reactionary, have not been more seriously challenged.

Many commentators address this question by thinking of the school reform challenge as a two-actor game: a unified and highly mobilized organization of professional educators challenges a small, unorganized collection of concerned parents and well-intentioned but ineffectual reformers. Business leaders, an important constituency when education reform is under consideration, are especially likely to subscribe to the view that educators are an obstacle to progress. In one national survey, 86 percent of business executives agreed (49 percent strongly) with the statement that "usually, educational reforms are resisted by unions and administrators who like to keep things the way they are."[66] As we have noted, our research suggests that this view overstates the influence of unions to some extent; we find that teachers' organizations, when considered on their own, tend to be on the periphery of political and activism regarding school reform. Racially influenced differences in perceptions, however, make it easier for organizations representing teachers and school administrators to rally community support even when their stance seems narrow and reactionary. In the four cities we have studied, union power is never an isolated strength. Union influence must be seen as part of a picture that also includes African-American clergy, black community activists, black politicians, and a set of personal bonds rooted in shared racial experiences.

BLACK MINISTERS AND SCHOOL AFFAIRS: 1960–1980

Historically, African-American ministers in each of our cities have been major political actors involved in many issues, including public education.[67]

---

[65] "Too Many Atlanta Teachers Get Away With Playing Hooky."

[66] Steve Farkas, *Educational Reform: The Players and the Politics* (New York: The Public Agenda Foundation for the Charles F. Kettering Foundation, 1992).

[67] For a good account of the role the black church and black church leaders in the politics of the black community, see C. Eric Lincoln and Lawrence Mamiya, *The Black Church in the African American Experience* (Durham, NC: Duke University Press, 1990); Charles V. Hamilton, *The Black Preacher in America* (New York: William Morrow and Company, 1972); Aldon Morris, *The Origins of the Civil Rights Movement* (New York: Free Press, 1984); Doug McAdam,

In the middle 1960s, black ministers in the District of Columbia, organized as the League for Universal Justice and Goodwill, played a prominent role in mobilizing community opposition to the school system's student tracking system.[68] The group's primary goal was "enhancement of the quality of education in Washington's schools."[69] After home rule, black ministers continued to play an important role in electoral politics, and a few maintained a focus on education, most notably the Reverend David Eaton, who played a leadership role on the elected school board.[70] But, as we show, D.C. religious leaders have been most involved when issues are framed in terms of a moral crusade. With both integration and home rule, education politics lost some of that edge of moral fervor, and the involvement of the religious leaders became more episodic and reactive.

In Detroit, the most prominent black minister involved in school issues during the 1960s and 1970s was the Reverend Albert Cleage, Jr., a Congregational minister, whom historian Sidney Fine has described as "the most articulate spokesman among the black militants and the central figure in the development of a 'strident' black nationalism in Detroit during the 1960s."[71] As chairman of the Inner City Parents Council, Cleage fought for the removal from black schools all "incompetent and racially prejudiced" white educators who, according to Cleage, were "often guilty of 'a condescending attitude' toward black students and their parents."[72] More moderate black ministers were also actively involved in Detroit's school affairs in the 1960s. In March 1965, the moderate Ad Hoc Committee Concerned with Equal Educational Opportunity was formed to examine racial discrimination in the Detroit schools.[73] Headed by the Reverend William Ardrey, pastor of the St. Paul AME Zion Church, and supported by other prominent black ministers in-

Political Process and the Development of Black Insurgency, 1930–1970 (Chicago: University of Chicago Press, 1982); and Frederick C. Harris, "Religious Institutions and African American Political Mobilization," in ed, Paul E. Peterson, *Classifying by Race* (Princeton: Princeton University Press, 1995), 278–310.

[68] Floyd W. Hayes, III, "Race, Urban Politics, and Educational Policy Making in Washington, D.C.: A Community's Struggle for Quality Education," in *Exploring Urban American: An Introductory Reader*, ed. Roger W. Caves (Thousand Oaks, CA: Sage Publications, 1995), 479–93.

[69] Ibid., 484–85.

[70] Eaton, pastor of All Souls Church, had a long background in local battles for civil rights and home rule. A frequent Barry ally, he helped officiate (with the Reverend Walter Fauntroy, another religious leader who made the transition into local politics as the District's long-time delegate to the House of Representatives) the service at Barry's first marriage in 1973. Jaffe and Sherwood, *Dream City*, 101.

[71] Sidney Fine, *Violence in the Model City: The Cavanagh Administration, Race Relations, and the Detroit Riot of 1967* (Ann Arbor: University of Michigan Press, 1989), 25.

[72] Ibid., 45.

[73] Ibid., 299.

cluding Rev. Nicholas Hood, Sr., and Rev. James Wadsworth, the Ad Hoc
Committee produced a report that called on school officials to take specific
actions to desegregate public education in Detroit.[74] In the 1980s and 1990s,
a number of prominent black ministers continued to work on school issues.
But they have emphasized electoral politics, especially the endorsement of
school board candidates. Gone are the battles with the school board and the
teachers' union over the elimination of incompetent teachers or educators
who have low expectations of their inner-city students.

Throughout much of the post–World War II period, the Baltimore
NAACP took the lead on most black education issues in that city. From the
mid-1930s until the mid-1970s, the Baltimore NAACP was headed by Lillie
May Jackson, a fiercely independent woman who, along with her preacher
husband, built a "real estate empire" in Baltimore's black community.[75] In
the early 1930s, Jackson's activism inspired her daughter, Juanita Jackson,
to form the Citywide Young People's Forum, an organization designed to
encourage black youths to participate in the civil rights struggle. Among the
black youth that rose to leadership positions within the Forum was Clarence
Mitchell, Jr., a reporter for the *Afro-American*. When Mitchell and Juanita
Jackson later married they created something of a civil rights dynasty. From
the 1940s and into the 1980s the most powerful black name in Baltimore
was Mitchell.

During the civil rights movement of the 1960s, leading ministers like Vernon Dobson often consulted with Martin Luther King, Jr., and his staff and
helped spark a wide-ranging series of successful protests for desegregation
of public facilities in Baltimore.[76] But the NAACP was usually out front on
issues that concerned blacks. Whenever the NAACP undertook a fight, the
Afro-American, then one of the nation's most prominent black newspapers,
gave it great publicity. Black ministers underscored the issue by preaching
sermons and distributing literature to be used in church services.[77] Activists
often planned tactics at the Bethel AME, Union Baptist, and Sharp Street
Methodist, and other black churches. Black ministers increased their influence on education issues through the long tenure of Mayor William Donald
Schaefer (1971–1986). In 1970, for example, black clergy encouraged the
school board to appoint Roland Patterson, as the first black, school superintendent. In 1974, City Hall and the white-majority school board attacked

[74] Ibid., 44.

[75] George Callcott, *Maryland and America, 1940–1980* (Baltimore: The John Hopkins University Press, 1985), 147. The two eventually married.

[76] Harold A. McDougall, *Black Baltimore: A New Theory of Community* (Philadelphia: Temple University Press, 1993).

[77] Callcott, *Maryland and America*, 146.

the superintendent, black ministers ardently defended Patterson and mobilized the black community to support the embattled school chief.[78]

During the 1983 mayoral campaign, the influential Interdenominational Ministerial Alliance (IMA), an organization representing about 166 black churches, in a divided vote endorsed Schaefer's black challenger, William Murphy. The Reverends Vernon Dobson, Marion Bascom, and Wendell Phillips, key leaders in the IMA, supported Murphy's claim that Schaefer had built a glittering downtown at the expense of basic services, including public education.[79]

Around 1984, organized under the organization Baltimoreans United in Leadership Development (BUILD), black clergy became outspoken advocates for school reform.[80] BUILD developed a reform plan for the schools that included site-based management and the creation of neighborhood school autonomy.[81] However, the policy activism and reform orientation of BUILD and Baltimore's black clergy were short lived. By 1986, the black preachers joined black teachers to oppose a number of reform initiatives.

Black ministers have always played a role in educating black Atlantans. Both Spelman and Morehouse colleges were founded in the basements of churches. In addition, black churches, along with fraternal societies and various self-help groups, provided kindergarten, vocational classes, and established free libraries. When the Atlanta Public Schools System opened in 1872, some black schools were incorporated into the public school system on a "separate but equal" basis.[82] Eventually, black ministers successfully petitioned the Board of Education to replace the northern white missionaries with black teachers in all of Atlanta's black schools.[83] Black ministers also were part of the negotiations of the Atlanta Compromise in 1973.

In the 1980s and 1990s, African-American clergy and churches continue to play a role in educating black Atlantans. Indeed the APS coordinates the educational efforts of more than seventy-five churches, mosques, and other religious institutions that participate in the School/Church Collaborative.

[78] Hugh Scott, *The Black School Superintendent: Messiah or Scapegoat* (Washington, D.C.: Howard University Press, 1980), 102–18; see also Barbara L. Jackson, *Balancing Act: The Political Role of the Urban School Superintendent* (Washington, D.C.: Joint Center for Political and Economic Studies, 1995).

[79] Kevin O'Keeffe, *Baltimore Politics 1971–1986: The Schaefer Years and the Struggle for Succession* (Washington, D.C.: Georgetown University Press, 1986), 98–99.

[80] Vernon Dobson and Wendell Phillips were founding members of BUILD.

[81] Marion Orr, "Urban Politics and School Reform: The Case of Baltimore," *Urban Affairs Review* 31 (January 1996): 314–45.

[82] David Plank and Marcia Turner, "Changing Patterns in Black School Politics: Atlanta, 1872–1973," *American Journal of Education* 95, no. 4 (August 1987): 589. See also R. Bayor, *Race and the Shaping of Twentieth-Century Atlanta* (Chapel Hill: University of North Carolina Press, 1996).

[83] Ibid., 592.

This partnership was established to provide quality education and community experiences for all students in the schools. Activities of the Collaborative include workshops on parenting skills, student/parent relations, latch-key kids, as well as direct involvement with students through tutoring and mentoring during and after school. In addition, some churches have adopted schools through the Adopt-A-School program. For many black churches, this is a long-term commitment because most adopted their first schools in the 1970s.

In addition to these individual church efforts, black ministers formed Concerned Black Clergy to uplift the poor, speak for the speechless, improve the economic conditions of African Americans, and challenge the educational system.[84] A coalition of 125 churches and mosques, representing more than 100,000 people, Concerned Black Clergy urged the Atlanta school board to improve the educational opportunities for Atlanta's youth. When things failed to improve they joined with Erase the Board to unseat the obstructionist board. Ministers used their pulpits to get people to the polls. However, for some ministers, the general aim was to get folks out to increase voter turnout—not to target the black incumbents. Some obstructionist board members had strong support among poor and lower-income blacks because the obstructionists were perceived as "one of them" articulating their interests. One of those board members told us that he was targeted during the election because he continually pointed out the disparities between the "haves" and the "have-nots" in the APS. He said "it was [his] intention to make education practical for the inner-city people, to get those people who had been left out, to make certain that *our* [emphasis added] major goal was included. They didn't like that."

Since 1994, Concerned Black Clergy has waited for changes in the APS. Some individual ministers see change on the horizon. For example, Rev. Horace Andrews of Mt. Ephraim Baptist Church noted that things have changed, particularly at Pitts Elementary School, the new science and technology theme school: "We couldn't see his [Canada's] vision. What we heard was just so far-fetched. When I go to Pitts now, I see a different atmosphere. Somehow the desire has been rekindled in them [students] to want to learn. I can't put my finger on any specific thing, but there is a marked change."[85] Other members of Atlanta's black clergy are more critical of the school board and the school administration. They argue that there is much planning but little implementation. Curiously, the leadership of Concerned Black Clergy has not challenged incumbent board members in their reelection bids. In

[84] William H. Boone with Bob Holmes, "Atlanta's Black Civic Organizations," in *The Status of Black Atlanta 1996–1997* (Atlanta: The Southern Center for Studies in Public Policy, 1997), 52.

[85] Dan Sadowsky, "Fresh Air: Will Reforms Breathe New Life Into Atlanta's Worst Public Schools?" *Creative Loafing*, 31 May 1997, 1, 26.

the November 1996 board elections, black ministers found themselves in a precarious position. D. F. Glover, an obstructionist board member who was unseated in the 1993 election, sought to regain his old seat. With strong support in the black community, particularly among working-class parents, Glover was able to win the endorsement of a number of key black ministers.[86]

A recent development suggests that the involvement of black ministers in school affairs is likely to increase. In 1994, a new interfaith, biracial organization emerged. Atlantans Building Leadership for Empowerment (ABLE), the new organization formed to deal with the city's social ills, it is composed of seventy religious congregations. Since its formation, more than nine hundred individuals have gathered for training sessions and small group meetings to build relationships aimed at developing grassroots political power.[87] In 1996, ABLE established two specific goals for its education action team: audit a sample of schools, and establish school-to-work opportunities. ABLE members made some twenty visits to public schools to ascertain what improvements were needed. In addition, ABLE has developed an after-school program strategy.[88] ABLE leaders have promised to continue addressing educational issues.

A Holy Communion: Black Teachers and Black Preachers

Black church leaders continue to play an important role in school issues. Interview data from the larger Civic Capacity and Urban Education Project show that in black-led cities, church leaders were more likely to be seen as major players in both general politics and educational decision making than in the other cities (refer to Table 2.3). Respondents were four times more likely to identify church leaders as major education stakeholders in our four cities than respondents in the seven comparison cities.

Although the particular role played by black clergy varies with issue and city, the black religious community usually opposes school reform if the proposed change is seen as a threat to local control and jobs. When asked why the broader black community is not more active in demanding school reform, a Baltimore education consultant suggests: "They ain't mobilized because the preachers ain't gonna let them. See, the preachers got to have their cut. And if the preachers are not adorned then they don't help get their people revved up about any one issue. That's the problem; you got too many of them [who are] corrupt."

[86] However, he was unable to unseat the incumbent. Glover received 41 percent of the vote vs. 59 percent received by incumbent Jean Dodd.

[87] "New Interfaith Group Begun," *Atlanta Journal and Constitution*, 16 March 1994, B2.

[88] William Boone with Bob Holmes, "Atlanta's Black Civic Organizations," 56–62.

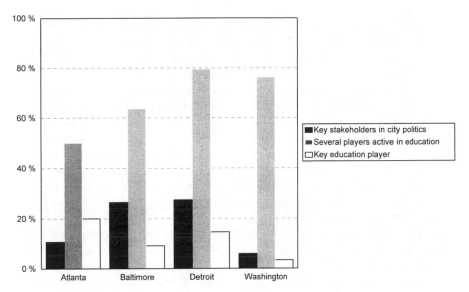

Figure 4.2 Role of church groups in city/education politics. Percentage of respondents identifying church groups as key stakeholders in city politics, agreeing that education politics has several key players, and if they agree that education politics has several players, seeing church groups as key players.

We are much less inclined than this commentator to see corruption and venality as the cementing force. Rather, we suggest that the failure of the religious community to play a stronger role in demanding better school performance is rooted in a black preacher-black teacher bond that has deep roots in local history and racial experience.

Figure 4.2 presents respondents' perceptions of the role of church groups and religious leaders as general stakeholders in local politics and as key players in education-specific policy decision making. Here we find an interesting pattern where perceived influence in politics generally and education politics specifically are not closely linked. Respondents in Atlanta were less likely than those in Detroit or Baltimore to mention religious leaders when asked about general stakeholders in local politics, but, of those who indicated that education was an open arena involving multiple interests, they were the most likely (20 percent) to name church organizations and religious leaders as being major players in school affairs. In Atlanta, churches and ministers were ranked just below business leaders as the most active nongovernmental group in educational matters. In Detroit and Baltimore, where churches were much more likely to be named as general stakeholders, their involvement in education-specific decision making is relatively less pronounced. In

Detroit, 14 percent of our respondents identified church leaders as major education players. Among our Baltimore respondents, 9 percent named churches and their ministers as being actively involved in school affairs. And only 3 percent of the respondents in the District of Columbia viewed the clergy as playing a major role in educational decision making.

Our data on the proportion of respondents identifying clergy as important actors in general city politics probably understate their clergy's indirect impact. Katherine Tate's analysis of black electoral behavior indicates that religious institutions form an important organizational resource for disseminating information about elections, encouraging church members to vote, providing individuals a base from which to work with political campaigns, and allowing individuals to financially contribute to political candidates.[89]

Politicians in all four cities recognize the capacity of the churches to mobilize voters. In his study of Atlanta, Clarence Stone found that the black ministers were "important gatekeepers for the black electorate in citywide elections" and "an integral part of the city's electoral politics."[90] A Detroit business leader described the black ministers in the Motor City as "extraordinarily powerful. . . . I would say the single most powerful organization in Detroit is the Baptist church," he added. In Baltimore, "unified support" from black church leaders is considered a must for any successful citywide election.[91] "They may not be able to elect you but they can keep you from being elected," explained a Baltimore business leader. And in D.C. black ministers have played a central role in Mayor Marion Barry's electoral coalition.

The key black preachers in Atlanta, Baltimore, Detroit, and Washington are not only political figures and leaders in the African-American community, but they are also spiritual leaders and personal friends of black teachers, principals, and school administrators. There is a kind of "holy communion" between prominent black clergy and the members of their churches whose livelihood is schooling and for whom the school system is a source of wages, professional development, and economic advancement.

In Baltimore, Union Baptist Church, Saint James Episcopal Church, and Bethel African Methodist Episcopal Church (11,500 members) are three of Baltimore's most prominent African-American churches whose congregants include principals, teachers, administrators, and other school system personnel. In Detroit, the Hartford Memorial Baptist Church is a seven thousand–member congregation whose minister, the Reverend Dr. Charles Adams,

[89] Katherine Tate, *From Protest to Politics: The New Black Voters in American Elections* (Cambridge: Harvard University Press, 1993). See also Frederick C. Harris, "Something Within: Religion as a Mobilizer of African-American Political Activism," *Journal of Politics* 56 (February 1994): 42–68; and Ronald Brown and Monica Wolford, "Religious Resources and African-American Political Action," *National Political Science Review* 4 (1994): 30–48.

[90] Stone, *Regime Politics*, 167–68.

[91] O'Keeffe, *Baltimore Politics, 1971–1986*, 95.

was described by one respondent as "a black minister of a huge middle-class church in Detroit, which is supported by many city and school employees." In churches like these in each of our cities, black professional educators tend to be prominent members.

Thus, in our cities, the politics of school reform is not simply a matter of reactionary unions resisting the reform efforts of business and other civic leaders. The challenge of school reform is much more complex. There are, for example, more important players. An important third party—the black church—typically supports the position of the professional educators. The basis of this support is also more complicated than simple self-interest.

Black Preachers and School Reform in Detroit

Detroit's black ministers play a central role in electoral politics. For example, in the 1970s, Reverend Cleage (now known as Jaramogi Abebe Agyeman) created the Black Slate—a list of candidates for elected offices endorsed by the church leaders—as a political arm of his church, now called the Shrine of the Black Madonna.[92] The other important black religious organization in Detroit is the Council of Baptist Pastors, a 250-member body acknowledged by many observers to be "the most powerful religious leaders" in Detroit.[93] Candidates for mayor, city council, school board, and other offices submit eagerly to the Council of Baptist Pastors and the Shrine of the Black Madonna's Black Slate as they seek endorsements.

African-American church leaders in Detroit have supported education-related programs such as "Each One, Reach One," an effort by churches to link with schools in their community by opening their buildings to young students before and after school. Black church leaders were also strong proponents of the African-American Male Academies. Nevertheless, Detroit's black preachers have not used their political clout to push for systemic change within the DPS.

Indeed, a number of our Detroit respondents questioned the black clergy's commitment to reforming the public schools. The sentiment seems reflected in that of a former member of the HOPE team who told us that the black clergy are "not necessarily positive." Another school activist described the Reverend Jim Holley, a former president of the Council of Baptist Pastors and major player in schools and related issues, as "controversial because everybody says he's politically tied in and then some of his motives are not pure." In 1988, shortly after the reform-minded HOPE team won

[92] Wilbur C. Rich, *Coleman Young and Detroit Politics* (Detroit: Wayne State University Press, 1989), 82.

[93] Carol Hopkins, "Pulpit Power," *Detroit Monthly* (December 1990): 57–61.

election to the school board, the lame duck board members attempted to appoint Holley, who opposed the HOPE team, to fill out the remaining term of a school board seat that had become vacant shortly before the elections. According to Rich, "Holley was promoted as the grassroots candidate [for the vacant post] but seen by the HOPE supporters as a defender of the status quo."[94] Holley's effort to gain a seat on the board failed.

Many key members of the Council of Baptist Pastors—Charles Adams, Jim Holley, Frederick Sampson, and Charles Butler (the late Mayor Coleman Young's personal minister)—all lead churches whose members include schoolteachers, principals, school administrators, and others who work for the school system. These ministers opposed many reforms instituted by the HOPE team. In 1992 school board elections, many black church leaders in Detroit joined the DFT and opposed the reelection of the HOPE team. "I knew we were going to lose the election; we were not allowed to come into the churches to campaign," recalled a former HOPE team member.

Black Preachers and School Reform in Washington, D.C.

In D.C., the involvement of the religious community in school politics has been episodic and reactive. Although respondents acknowledged the important political role of black ministers, they only occasionally mentioned them in terms of education issues. The religious community is seen as being most involved with school issues relating directly to issues of values and behavior. A key foundation executive indicated that, although she worked with them on occasional projects, she did not have a close relationship with leading religious leaders and did not think of them as key actors when it came to generating political support for human investment issues: "Well, I think certainly in D.C. politics, the role of prominent ministers and their ability to deliver votes is absolutely critical to win an election or it used to be. I think in my world here I sort of vaguely know of the power of the church. . . . I sort of know who you would put in a room, but I don't have chatty relationships with any of them and I would almost bet that these, of the other players that we mentioned, don't either." According to one black minister who *does* want to see the religious community more involved in school issues: "From the political side, the religious community has always been viewed as a place to get votes, not a place to implement change. Okay. When politicians would run for office, they sought out the church. But in the implementing of policy, day-to-day policy, [they] never included the church, or synagogues, or mosques, in any planning or any forethought of that."

[94] Rich, *Black Mayors and School Politics*, 46.

In an organized manner black ministers have spoken out on issues of school prayer, distribution of condoms in public schools, and on the general need to curb violence among the city's youth. Many churches have had a long history of involvement in direct service provision to low-income children and their families, often under contract with the D.C. government; in alliance with other local nonprofits, black ministers have also spoken out about the need to maintain public funding for such efforts. But, with relatively few exceptions, the organized religious community has not been a proactive force in measures to reform the District's schools. More often, they have led opposition to reforms that are seen as threats to local control and local jobs. As one black minister sees it, once power was transferred into local hands, the religious community found it difficult to maintain the activist role it adopted in the battle for civil rights and home rule.

> But I think for the black church, major emphasis in the past was put on civil rights, and it was a major, major drive. And due to the composition of the, the color of the District of Columbia, once home rule stepped in, I mean, we had major, we had mostly African Americans in position. That wasn't such a huge issue, so the church actually kind of sat back after that.
>
> And then there's also a notion that grew up with, which was, which has hurt us as African Americans, there was a notion of, there was an unspoken rule that you couldn't criticize your own. Because the way it looked to the white community was that we were fighting amongst ourselves. Whereas the white community always did fight amongst itself and still held its unity. That the white community has always allowed within it a Strom Thurmond, a Kennedy, a Dole, an Agnew. It's always allowed that, a Nixon, a Reagan. There's a tension, but it always held together. Within the African-American community, everyone had to look alike; and if someone did not look alike it was this tension that we can't really say anything about it because it looks like we're fighting amongst ourselves.
>
> So a politician could go wrong or go bad, and the community never spoke out about it because it said, "hey, it's going to look like we're fighting against one another." They [the politicians] gave us, you know, an invitation to their house for a picnic now and then, they gave us a photo opportunity, and that was sufficient. And that was sufficient. We went back and preached the gospel. Communities never got better, the education system went down, and we never held them accountable. . . . But I think that's changing. And, you know, they were, the churches were very strong in the civil rights movement here, but I think what's happening now is the churches are beginning to say, "we're going to hold you accountable, be 'you' black or white, male or female."

While many D.C. residents either welcomed or acquiesced in the Control Board's involvement in local and school affairs, a few black ministers have been the focal points for sharp efforts to resist. Most visible was the Reverend

Willie Wilson, leader of the six thousand–member Union Temple church. A major Barry supporter, Wilson organized a prayer vigil outside the Control Board offices in June 1996, where he criticized congressional Republicans for "whipping and beating" the District; based on their actions, he suggested "maybe their names ought to be Ku Klux Klan." Another key protest figure was George Stallings, archbishop of the African American Catholic Church, a group he started after breaking away from the Catholic church in 1989. In announcing his ultimately unsuccessful bid for the Ward 6 city council seat in December 1996, Stallings linked schools and the race issue indirectly through a powerful symbol of black culture and pride: "Our schools are under siege. Our financial structure is under siege. Home rule is under siege. . . . We need a voice that is forceful on the city council . . . a voice of truth. A voice that will, as Spike Lee said, 'Do the Right Thing.' "[95] While D.C.'s religious leaders feel that they can speak out forcefully on moral issues, many find that their congregations have much less tolerance for their involvement in more controversial issues. When the Reverend Albert Gallmon decided to run for the school board, for example, many members objected. Prompted by the Mount Carmel Baptist Church trustees—some of whom felt he had neglected his duties at the church and failed to consult with the congregation before taking public stands—Gallmon stepped down.[96]

A spokesperson for a coalition of churches noted that the narrow and diverse agendas of many of the city's religious leaders make it difficult for them to coalesce around complicated issues.

> Clear-cut issues . . . are easier then, clear-cut issues, issues of the moment. It's hard to keep them [the city's religious leaders] focused and sustained on more complicated issues. Unless it's very clear, easy issues, it's hard for them to stay focused and organize. Death penalty. Those are clear and moral issues for the churches. Gambling. Clear and moral issues. Clear and moral issues are easier for them to deal with than long-term, economic, fundamental, bureaucratic change. Obviously, it's easier to galvanize a winning coalition with something that's coming to a vote with definable ends and definable results than long-term neighborhood change, bureaucratic change, governmental change. That's a lot harder. . . . We stay with social, neighborhood, service issues. We avoid some of the larger philosophical debates. All the debates that go on that I couldn't get a consensus on, they don't affect the local. So I keep the churches focused on local issues, and it helps, a lot, to gain consensus.

The failure of the black churches to unite around school reform proposals also reflects division within the religious community. It is hardly surprising

[95] Debbi Wilgoren, "Stallings Seeks Ward 6 Seat," *Washington Post*, 9 December 1996, B3.
[96] Laurie Goodstein, "Pastor Quits to Follow Political Call," *Washington Post*, 1 September 1993, D6.

that some very strong personalities emerge among the District's most visible ministers. Often these leaders find it difficult to work together. Indeed, some critics charge that personal ambition rather than the public good may motivate a few of these church leaders.

Black Preachers and School Reform in Baltimore

African-American church leaders in Baltimore continue to be influential in school issues. The fact that only 9 percent of Baltimore respondents named ministers as being key stakeholders in school issues almost certainly understates the role church leaders play in school issues. Many respondents indicate that the black clergy offered critical support in mobilizing for a policy goal. When asked how he would go about building support for an educational reform program, a Baltimore Urban League official immediately stated: "I would present it, first of all, to the preachers in this town. The black clergy is a very, very, critical force of mobilizing. The preachers are critical." In the 1990s, the black clergy's role in Baltimore's school affairs remains important.

Despite their widely recognized influence, however, church leaders in Baltimore are viewed as being unreliable partners in a school-reform coalition. More often, key church groups and influential black ministers have allied with the school unions and opposed most major school-reform initiatives, especially those that threaten local control and jobs. For example, when the decision was made to award EAI a five-year contract to manage nine Baltimore schools, about six hundred supporters attended a meeting BUILD held to express to city officials its opposition to the experiment.[97] The Interdenominational Ministerial Alliance (IMA) also opposed EAI. It is instructive that BUILD and IMA opposed EAI from the outset, long before any independent evaluation of its impact on the students and their performance. Indeed, the thrust of the African-American church leaders' opposition was similar to that of the BTU: Tesseract represented a potential loss of jobs. An active and influential black minister affiliated with BUILD told us that EAI could destabilize the city's employment base: "It destroys some of the employment base in the city. Tesseract then has the authority to hire and fire, to reallocate, to reassign employees at will, that's very threatening to a person. That's their livelihood in the school system." When we asked about his position if a credible and independent evaluation confirmed that the quality of education and student achievement in the EAI-operated schools improved appreciably, he responded: "We'd still be leery of privatization of a traditional government function."

[97] Mark Bomster, "Schmoke Facing Challenge Tonight on School Reform," *The Sun*, 20 July 1992, 1B.

In 1997 the Maryland legislature adopted a five-year school-aid package that would send a billion dollars in aid to the Baltimore schools. The legislation also greatly increased the state's role in the management of the schools. Mayor Schmoke, reluctantly endorsing the legislation, believed that the increased funds would ultimately benefit the city's youth. The legislation was also supported by a majority of Baltimore legislators. The BTU and the Public Administrators and Supervisors Association (PSASA) denounced the partnership as usurpation of local control. BTU opposed provisions in the legislation that allowed the restructured school board to reopen contract talks. BTU and PSASA leaders objected to the requirement that certain central office supervisors reapply to the new school board for their old positions.

Baltimore's black ministers, however, were the loudest critics of the legislation. The Reverend Arnold Howard, president of the IMA, noted that the ministers opposed the legislation because they believed the amount of additional funds was "not enough" to warrant state oversight of Baltimore's largest municipal department.[98] The Reverend Frank Reid, pastor of Bethel A.M.E. (and Mayor Schmoke's stepbrother), also spoke out against the legislation. Paraphrasing a verse from the scripture, Reid asked: "What does it profit a city to gain $254 million and lose its soul?"[99]

For many African-American ministers, sharing administrative authority of the school system with state officials was their central reason for opposing the legislation. In an open letter to state legislators, the ministers and other community leaders denounced the school-aid package as "anti-democratic" and "racial paternalism."[100] "We will not accept Baltimore becoming a colony of the state, with its citizens having no say in the education of their children. African-Americans, in particular, have fought a long, hard battle for equality. Over the years, too many paid the ultimate price for community empowerment. We will not stand and allow the gains those people sacrificed and died for to be given away. We have earned the dream of quality education for our children, and local autonomy in decision making."[101]

Howard "Pete" Rawlings, an African-American Baltimore legislator who sponsored the school-aid package, lambasted the ministers for putting adult concerns before the concerns of children: "These folks are being led and fed information by people who do not have the interest of Baltimore children at heart. The interest of the children should be the bottom line."[102] In June 1997 the new Board of School Commissioners was jointly announced by

---

[98] Jean Thompson, "Ministers Join PTA Group in Opposition to Giving Up Control of Baltimore Schools," *The Sun*, 26 March 1997, 5C.

[99] "Two Ministers join effort to defeat city schools deal," *The Sun*, 1 April 1997, B3.

[100] The open letter was printed in *The Sun*, 5 April 1997, 1A.

[101] Ibid.

[102] Tony White, "Community Leaders Oppose School Settlement," *Baltimore Afro-American*, 5 April 1995, 1.

Mayor Schmoke and Governor Parris Glendening. It is too soon to develop conclusions about student performance. However, the new board developed a long-range reform plan that includes reducing class sizes in grades one through three and establishing "after school" academies to improve student achievement. To recruit new teachers the BCPS launched a major effort that includes raising the salaries of starting teachers. To help reduce class sizes and staff the after-school programs hundreds of retired teachers were hired on a part-time basis to tutor students in reading and math. In May 1998, following a nine-month search, the school board named Robert Booker, the top financial officer for San Diego County, California, as BCPS first permanent chief executive officer. An African American, Booker previously worked for the Los Angeles Unified School District as its chief business and financial officer. Booker's experience in financial management reflects the school board's and state official's desire to dramatically improve the management of the BCPS. When Booker assumed office on 1 July 1998, he promised to institute a series of management and financial changes designed to make the system run more efficiently.

Black Preachers and School Reform in Atlanta

Church leaders in Atlanta have been the least engaged in the overall political process of educational reform. More often local churches have forged partnerships with a specific school. For some churches, this has been a long-term commitment. These programs generally entail direct educational services such as tutoring, mentoring, and after-school programs. Systemwide church efforts are virtually nonexistent.

Concerned Black Clergy's primary focus has been homelessness, not educational reform. Prominent religious leaders have made some efforts to become more active in education politics. The Reverend Joseph Lowery of the Southern Christian Leadership Conference (SCLC) called for a "movement akin to the civil rights struggle of the 1960s to focus attention on the plight of 'miseducated' black youths." Citing tracking and low test scores, he said, "we recognize now what has happened. Until we free our children to have access to quality and meaningful educational opportunities, we will not be able to overcome social ills that plague our communities."[103] To date, no such movement exists. In fact, the SCLC itself continues to emphasize a direct service approach to education by offering a number of mentoring and after-school programs.

[103] Hollis R. Towns, "A New Movement: Lowery Calls for Education Reform," *Atlanta Journal and Constitution*, 13 May 1996, B4.

REFORM WITH TEACHERS AND JOBS IN MIND

Teachers are perhaps the most organized stakeholders in most urban school systems. Without exception their unions have wide power and influence. For the most part, however, unions representing professional educators (but especially teachers' unions) in Atlanta, Baltimore, Detroit, and Washington, D.C., have not deviated from the traditional role of labor unions. They have not been progressive advocates for the thousands of inner-city children; rather they focus on the direct material interests of union members. This focus often pits teachers' unions against progressive educational reform. Such opposition is often fatal to reform. Education historian David Tyack observes that "teachers were the group with greatest power to veto or sabotage proposals for reform. No realistic estimate of strategies for change in American education could afford to ignore teachers or fail to enlist their support."[104]

For those interested in building a broad-based reform coalition that includes teachers it may be necessary to distinguish between reforms that raise apprehension on the part of teachers and administrators—management efficiency, cost-saving mechanisms, and rigorous testing of students, for example—and other kinds of reform. Simply stated, professional educators are not likely to support reforms perceived either to threaten jobs or to radically change the favored way of doing things.

The Atlanta, Baltimore, Detroit, and Washington experiences show that school reform is a complex multi-actor game in which the effort to mobilize or neutralize important third parties plays an important role. Black preachers, for example, have a personal relationship with many schoolteachers, principals, and school administrators. These *bonds of personalism* encourage black preachers to align with black teachers even when their stance seems at variance with generally accepted notions of good school policies. This communion between black preachers and black teachers allows school unions to draw upon an especially broad and powerful constituency, also including African-American politicians and other black community leaders. The resulting coalition of teachers' unions and organizations representing school administrators and black churches and preachers is very powerful indeed.

Race and racial consciousness sometimes make it easier for teachers and school administrators to rally community support even when their stance seems narrow and reactionary. Often many African-Americans are reluctant to publicly criticize other black leaders. As we discussed, in the 1960s, before the schools underwent a racial transition, African-American clergy were among the most vocal advocates for improved educational opportunity for black youth and for holding teachers and administrators accountable. As po-

---

[104] David B. Tyack, *The One Best System: A History of American Urban Education* (Cambridge: Harvard University Press, 1974), 289.

litical scientist Wilbur Rich recently observed, today the situation has changed. Three decades ago, when civil rights leaders included public schools on their protest agenda, African-American protesters were fighting the white establishment. As Rich notes: "When blacks took over City Hall, it was difficult to rally people against the black establishment."[105]

This capacity of teachers' unions to block reform has been widely noted in the existing literature on school reform. However, such traditional literature not only fails to take seriously the important role that big-city school districts play in the local economy but also tends to take a deracialized and ahistorical view of the economic significance of some big-city school districts. The bureaucratic resistance school-reform literature is not wrong, but it is incomplete. The story is much more complex.

Prospects for coalition building for school reform in Atlanta, Baltimore, Detroit, and Washington, D.C., are affected by the broader economic and employment environment. Where quality private-sector jobs are increasingly scarce and racial discrimination is still a reality, the employment opportunities available to blacks in the public schools are vital to the stability of African-American community.[106] If jobs are leaving and employment opportunities bleak, then the perception that reform initiatives could threaten wages and fringe benefits in the public sector are heightened and likely to engender greater resistance from teachers, principals, and other school-system employees. Moreover, the ability of teachers to rally black preachers, politicians, community activists, and other nonteacher groups to their side may be greater. School reformers cannot ignore the fact that in many black-led cities the public school systems form an important source of jobs, economic opportunity, and social status for African Americans.

Robert Merton, reflecting on the persistent attack that "reformers" launched on the much-maligned big-city political machines of the late nineteenth and early twentieth centuries, states the case as well as anyone:

> We are here concerned with documenting the statement that moral judgments based *entirely* on an appraisal of manifest function of a social structure are "unrealistic" in the strict sense, i.e., they do not take into account other actual consequences of that structure, consequences which may provide basic social support for the structure. . . . "[S]ocial reforms" or "social engineering" which ignore latent functions do so on pain of suffering acute disappointment and boomerang effects.[107]

The leaders of school employee unions, black religious leaders, black politicians, and other community leaders in our four cities believe that the public

---

[105] Rich, *Black Mayors and School Politics*, 150.

[106] William Julius Wilson, *When Work Disappears: The World of the New Urban Poor* (New York: Knopf, 1996).

[107] Robert K. Merton, *Social Theory and Social Structure* (Glencoe, IL: Free Press, 1957), 72.

school system as a black employment regime plays a "latent function." An important issue in Atlanta, Baltimore, Detroit, and the District of Columbia is whether school reformers can improve systemwide performance without destabilizing the historical and racial legacy of its employment base.

Finally, black professional educators continue to retain a special status and influence within the African-American community. Because the vast majority of African-American students in the four school systems come from socially and economically deprived backgrounds (see chapter 1), their teachers and principals constitute one of the few examples of success that they (and often their parents) know. From this perspective, it is little wonder that the prospects of African-American parents rising up in opposition to black teachers are slim.

CHAPTER FIVE

Parental and Community Participation
in Education Reform

The evidence is clear that parental encouragement,
activities, and interest at home and participation in
schools and classrooms affect children's achievements,
attitudes, and aspirations, even after student ability
and family socioeconomic status are taken into
account. Students gain in personal and academic
development if their families emphasize schooling,
let the children know they do, and do so continually
over the school years.
(Joyce L. Epstein)

Parental guidance continues to be a critical and
decisive factor in the education of children, and I
suppose it goes without saying there's a perception
on the part of many people that given the extent of
family disorganization in the black community that
the community is without that center of education.
(Detroit school administrator)

ONE OF the most consistent and seemingly uncontroversial findings in the
education literature concerns the importance of parent involvement for children's learning and schools' success.[1] Parents, teachers, principals, and public officials readily subscribe to the premise that partnerships between parents and schools make a potent combination. This view has encouraged
various reform efforts at the local level, including policies to improve communication from the schools to homes, to encourage teachers to make home
visits, and to institute school-based decision-making teams comprising principals, teachers, parents, and community representatives. The federal government, too, has signed on to the parent involvement movement; the eighth
National Education Goal, indicates that "by the year 2000, every school will

---

[1] E.g., James Coleman et al., *Equality of Educational Opportunity* (Washington, D.C.: U.S.
Government Printing Office, 1966); Joyce L. Epstein, "Parent Involvement: What the Research

promote partnerships that will increase parental involvement and participation in promoting the social, emotional, and academic growth of children."

At least on the face of it, such calls for parent involvement should fall on willing ears in black-led cities, where many of today's public leaders cut their political teeth on calls for community involvement and broadened participation. Spurred by the civil rights movement, social activists during the 1960s challenged our democratic society to be more inclusive. Black power activists furthered the participation theme and called for "black people to consolidate behind their own, so that they [could] bargain from a position of strength. The goal of black self-determination and self-identity . . . [was] full participation in the decision making processes affecting the lives of black people."[2] One of the first manifestations of this determination occurred in urban public schools.

The call for the African-American community to participate in the schools was given impetus by the recognition that the schools had failed their children. Demands during the 1960s by parents and civil rights groups had forced school systems to reveal test scores for the first time, and they revealed what parents had feared—massive failure. For example in Washington, D.C., four out of every five students were behind in reading.[3] Fueled by this knowledge and research showing that low expectations held by white middle-class teachers and administrators caused poor performance,[4] Preston Wilcox called for a "community presence [in public schools so that] an instrumentality be developed which assures minority group parents direct access to the channels of informed opinion and power."[5] Carmichael and Hamilton strongly stated the case in *Black Power*:

> Control of the ghetto schools must be taken out of the hands of "professionals," most of whom have long since demonstrated their insensitivity to the needs and problems of black children. These "experts" bring with them middle class biases, unsuitable techniques and materials; these are, at best dysfunctional and at worst destructive. . . . Virtually no attention is paid to the wishes and demands of the parents, especially the black parents. This is totally unacceptable.[6]

Says to Administrators," *Education and Urban Society* 19:2 (1987): 119–36; S. S. Purkey and M. Smith, "Effective Schools: A Review," *Elementary School Journal* 83 (1983): 427–52.

[2] Stokely Carmichael and Charles Hamilton, *Black Power* (New York: Vintage Books, 1967), 47.

[3] Maurice Berube and Marilyn Gittell, eds., *Confrontation at Ocean Hill-Brownsville* (New York: Praeger, 1969), 3.

[4] R. Rosenthal and L. Jacobson, *Pygmalion in the Classroom: Teachers' Expectations and Pupils' Intellectual Development* (New York: Holt, Rinehart and Winston, 1968); William Ryan, *Blaming the Victim* (New York: Vintage, 1976), chapter 5.

[5] Preston Wilcox, "The Controversy over I. S. 201," *The Urban Review* 25 (1966): 13.

[6] Carmichael and Hamilton, *Black Power*, 166–67.

Detroit and Washington, D.C., were among the nation's leaders in early reform efforts to translate the concept of community control into working examples in the public schools.[7]

Such background lends credibility to the view, discussed in chapter 1, that local-level racial transition may set the stage for a broad new coalition incorporating parents and community advocates along with elected leaders—a coalition in which shared racial identity and experience would be the glue, and human capital development, rather than simple economic development, would be the unifying theme. Yet by most indications, hopes for a more participatory, human capital–oriented regime have not developed in these cities. The impetus for systemic reform, where it has emerged, has more often been located in either the business community or external actors, such as the federal or the state government. Even popular leaders with grassroots constituencies have had a difficult time mobilizing parents for more than short bursts or at a single school. When parents *have* mobilized, they have often defended the status quo and rejected systemwide substantial reform.

The absence of a strong, readily mobilizable parent and community constituency has important consequences for local capacity to initiate and sustain systemic school reform. In the previous chapter, we discussed some ways in which the role of schools as an employer can induce a patronage-style politics that imposes an obstacle to some varieties of school reform. The direct and material incentives associated with jobs make it likely that teachers and principals will be mobilized and vigilant about the direction of school policies. As individuals, these educators often moderate their self-interest in protecting their jobs, salaries, and independence with professional values and a personal commitment to helping their students. The unions that become the organizational manifestation of their more material concerns and the institutional manifestation of their political clout, however, often crystallize this focus on jobs and money in a more unadulterated form. Politicians and community leaders, who are inclined to challenge the unions directly, need to know that there is an alternative constituency to which they can turn for support. Although many other commentaries attribute the elusiveness of reform to the overwhelming clout of the unions, we suggest that the absence of such a counterconstituency is of equal if not greater import.

This chapter examines the role of family and community in the schools and partially explains the difficulty in translating rhetorical commitment to the benefits of participation into practice. This review identifies certain fail-

---

[7] W. R. Grant, "Community Control vs. Integration: The Case of Detroit," *Public Interest* 24 (1971): 62–79; G. R. LaNoue and B.L.R. Smith, *The Politics of School Decentralization* (Lexington, MA: Lexington Books, 1973).

ures of vision, tactics, and leadership within our four cities, failures that have left reform movements weaker and more episodic than they ought and need to be. Just as emphatically, however, our analysis also highlights limitations in the way reformers think and talk about parent and community involvement. By failing to distinquish among *types* of involvement and by implicitly adopting the premise that key stakeholders share goals and perceptions— with differences limited to misunderstandings or quibbles over the most effective means—many proponents of parent involvement grossly oversimplify the challenge of building more inclusive coalitions. In black-led cities— where racial identity and experiences complicate political interrelationships, where the schools are invested with special status as symbols of black aspirations as well as concrete manifestations of the relationship between power and jobs, and where well-trodden paths of suburbanization and flight make exit a powerful alternative to the exercise of political voice—naive affirmations of the importance of parent involvement are more likely to lead to dashed expectations than sustainable reforms.

WHAT KIND OF PARTICIPATION AND ON WHOSE TERMS?

Most contemporary literature celebrating the importance of parent participation focuses on modes of participation that are *individualistic*, in the sense that parent energies are targeted directly at their own children, or *collaborative*, in the sense that parents' goals and activities are presumed to be in harmony with those of others (parents, teachers, principal, etc.) within the local education community.[8] Participation of these sorts—reading at home to one's own child, monitoring homework, attending parent-teacher conferences—not surprisingly, is seen as something of a "mom and apple pie" enterprise to which few could reasonably object. In practice, however, parent and community participation often involves broader targets, including school and system organizations and programs and often represents values and claims that produce conflict among interested parties.

Individual versus Collective Participation

Figure 5.1 distinguishes varieties of participation along two dimensions. The horizontal dimension relates to the *degree of social aggregation* at which the participation takes place. At one extreme, parents' participation may be

[8] W. Perry and M. Tannenbaum, "Parents, Power, and Public Schools," in *Education and the Family*, ed. L. Kaplan (Boston: Allyn and Bacon, 1992), 100–115; Joyce Epstein, "School and Family Connections" in *Families in Community Settings*, ed. D. G. Unger and M. Sussman

Degree of Social Aggregation			
		Family	School	System

		Family	School	System
Relation Between Parent and Educator Interests	Cooperative	Child centered Monitoring homework; selecting a school; meeting individually with teacher	Parent-school partnerships PTA; fund-raising; help in classroom	Compacts and systemic collaborations Lobbying/support for pro-education school board, etc.
	Conflictual	Home/school conflict Individual parents versus classroom teacher on priority of homework; their child's need for attention; more(less) demanding work	Community/school conflict Parents vs. principal and teachers on spending priorities within schools; implementation of discipline policies; grading complaints	Systemic conflict and hyperpluralism Intra-community conflict and community vs. educators...on curriculum, tenure, funding levels and equalization; length of school day

Figure 5.1 Varieties of parent involvement.

highly individual, oriented around the needs and interests of their own children. Such individualized participation might involve activities such as providing proper nutrition and a safe and nurturing home environment, building self-esteem and high aspirations in their children, reading to the child at home, showing interest in school and monitoring homework, attending parent-teacher conferences, and the like. At the other extreme, parents may work collectively to encourage reforms in the broader educational system; this can include efforts to hold public officials responsible for poor performance, to promote new visions of curriculum and school organization, to press for a greater public investment in education and human development, and so on. Intermediate along this dimension of social aggregation would be reform efforts focused on single schools rather than the entire system.

The strongest empirical support linking parent involvement to educational success involves more individualized family support. James Coleman remarked, "if there is one thing that recent research has shown it is that a child's education depends on what goes on in the child's life, not merely

(New York: Haworth Press, 1990); and "How Do We Improve Programs for Parental Involvement?" *Educational Horizons* 66 (Winter 1988): 58–59.

on what goes on in that child's school."[9] His 1966 analysis of educational opportunity is still the most prominent example of quantitative research suggesting a strong causal link between students' achievement on standardized tests and characteristics and behaviors of their parents. More recently, in attempting to explain why private school students appear to outperform public school students, researchers have added support to this observation with evidence that parents in private schools are more likely to volunteer time and join in school-based activities.[10] Voucher and school choice proposals are intended to give even greater leverage to this individualistic form of participation; by making it more feasible for parents to withdraw their children from poorly performing schools, some reformers expect that cumulative shifts in demand will provide market pressures upon schools to improve the product they provide.[11]

According to this family-centered model, parents have basic obligations to make children ready for school, including building the child's self-confidence, self-concept, and self-reliance. Likewise, they provide home-based learning activities such as reading to their children. Schools, in turn, are expected to devote considerable energy and resources toward nurturing this basic parental motivation and giving parents the information and access they need.[12] Central to this view is the observation that, as Walberg notes, "twelve years of schooling add up to about 13 percent of a child's waking life in her first eighteen years. During the same time period, parents nominally control 87 percent of the student's waking time."[13] Consequently, participation in the educational life of the child occurs primarily at the home and away from the school.[14]

While interesting and important, the finding that children whose parents love, nurture, stimulate, support, challenge, and encourage them do better in school and life is not particularly surprising. More important, because we lack real understanding about how to make parents act in this manner, the policy implications are far from clear. Research shows a strong relationship

---

[9] Coleman et al., *Equality of Educational Opportunity*. The Coleman quote is cited in Robert Crowson, *School-Community Relations, Under Reform* (Berkeley: McCutchan Publishing, 1992), 195.

[10] E.g., Anthony Bryk, Valerie Lee, Peter Holland, *Catholic Schools and the Common Good* (Cambridge: Harvard University Press, 1993).

[11] John E. Chubb and Terry M. Moe, *Politics, Markets and America's Schools* (Washington, D.C.: Brookings Institution, 1990). But see also Jeffrey R. Henig, *Rethinking School Choice: The Limits of the Market Metaphor* (Princeton: Princeton University Press, 1994).

[12] The parent-teacher conference is relevant to this model. Schools are obliged to inform parents about school programs and their child's progress. They send memos, calendars of the school year, and notices of special events.

[13] Cited in Crowson, *School-Community Relations*, 195.

[14] See the writings of Joyce Epstein, including "Parent Involvement," 119–36.

between such supportive behavior and socioeconomic class, particularly parents' level of education. But to conclude that the best way to improve school performance among poor urban students is to raise the education level of their parents would be begging the question. There is some evidence that schools *can* take steps to increase the participation of poor parents, but that evidence is still rather spotty, and claims of dramatic and long-term success are more often based on anecdote than systematic analysis.[15]

Our interest in this book is focused more on the kinds of collective and system-oriented activities evidenced on the right side of Figure 5.1. In the politics of urban education reform, families and communities are perhaps the most crucial of coalition members whose participation, or lack thereof, often determines the success or failure of systemic school reform. Sirotnik and others have argued that to ignore the "ties that bind" between schools, parents, and community in reform efforts is to "condemn such attempts to almost certain failure."[16] Consequently, both family and community participation in efforts that are channeled through and targeted at broader institutions—not just directly supportive of the needs of their own children—is central to our analysis. We argue that civic capacity provides the foundation for building alliances and networks that "recognize the inherent interdependence" of education stakeholders. Our assumption is straightforward: as parents, communities, schools, businesses, government agencies, and so on learn to cooperate and trust one another, by acting together they can accomplish goals that could not be accomplished either separately or competitively.[17]

The direct link between more collective forms of participation and student performance is not as clear or empirically validated as that associated with parents' participation in their own children's education. The School Community Relations Group at the University of Wisconsin—Madison conducted a series of case studies and found virtually no link between the level of family and community participation on advisory councils and student achievements. Likewise, Fantini suggests that research on governance confirms that

[15] Nancy Vaden-Kiernan, *Statistics in Brief: Parents' Reports of School Practices to Involve Families* (Washington, D.C.: National Center for Education Statistics, 1997), (NCES 97–327). Available at http://www.ed.gov.NCES/pubs/97327.html.

[16] Kenneth Sirotnik, "Improving Urban Schools in the Age of 'Restructuring,'" *Education and Urban Society* 23, no. 3 (May 1991): 264. See also M. Gittell, "Institutionalizing Community Participation in Education," in *Community Participation in Education*, ed. Carl A. Grant (Boston: Allyn and Bacon, 1979), 47–64.

[17] J. G. March and J. P. Olsen, *Rediscovering Institutions* (New York: Free Press, 1989); S. Kelman, "Adversary and Cooperationist Institutions for Conflict Resolution in Public Policymaking," *Journal of Policy Analysis and Management* 11 (1992): 178–206; E. Ostrom, *Governing the Commons* (New York: Cambridge University Press, 1990); and W. W. Powell and P. J. Dimaggio, *The New Institutionalism in Organizational Analysis* (Chicago: University of Chicago Press, 1991).

for "parents as decision-makers, no direct evidence was found to confirm or reject the basic hypothesis about impacts on children, although there is evidence of benefits in participating adults."[18] Fine also suggests that there is no link between improvement and parent power. She contends "while empowered parents may 'stick with a school' longer, they do not, in and of themselves, produce in the aggregate improved student outcomes in the area of retention, absenteeism, [test] scores, or grades."[19] A 1995 study by Lewis and Nakagawa similarly supports these findings.[20]

The difficulty in empirically documenting the nature of the relationship between collective participation and individual student performance suggests a complex and indirect relationship. One reason that the link between collective, system-oriented participation and school performance may be empirically elusive is that the pay-off for parental involvement constitutes a public good; that is, the children who stand to benefit include those whose parents have *not* been involved. This same fact may also account for why sustaining such parental involvement is so problematic.[21] From the standpoint of rational self-interested parents, it may be more rational to devote energy and resources to the types of participation targeted narrowly at their own children. Yet, from the overall community standpoint, participation that reshapes the broader system may be more desirable. By generating positive spillover effects that accrue to the children of families that are less active and involved, systemic participation has the potential to target benefits toward the families and neighborhoods most in need and least able to provide for themselves. Just as important, but less widely understood, because the pay-offs from individualistic participation accrue to families that are also more likely to be geographically mobile, cities may find that they cannot capture the benefits of their investments into promoting individualistic participation. If the families and children with the greatest inclination and ability to participate eventually take their energy, along with what they have learned, and move to the suburbs, the central-city schools systems will be like a balloon with a slow leak; in spite of much huffing and puffing at the mouthpiece, the balloon may never inflate. Systemic reform, in contrast, has the potential to improve the institutional and civic infrastructure and in that way bolster a city's competitive edge.

[18] The School Community Relations groups and Fantini studies are found in M. Fullan, *The New Meaning of Educational Change* (New York: Teachers College Press, 1991), 237–40.
[19] Michelle Fine, "[Ap]parent Involvement: Reflections on Parents, Power, and Urban Public Schools," *Teachers College Record* 94, no. 4 (summer 1993): 689.
[20] Dan Lewis and Kathryn Nakagawa, *Race and Educational Reform in the American Metropolis* (New York: State University Press of New York, 1995).
[21] Mancur Olson, *The Logic of Collective Action* (New York: Schocken, 1965).

Cooperative versus Conflictual Participation

Considerations of the consequences of parental involvement often take for granted that parents and teachers are all working toward the same goals. When this is not the case, the relationship between participation and children's performance in the schools becomes more problematic as well. As Popkewitz notes, the

> focus on outcomes tends to eliminate consideration of the substantive political dimension of participation. Discussion tends to proceed upon a belief that there is a general consensus about what school should do. Reforms are limited to such devices as forming advisory councils. . . . Rather than considering how organizational beliefs and procedures prevent meaningful parent [and community] participation, student outcome arguments make the current assumptions and priorities of the institution unproblematic.[22]

The second dimension underlying the typology in Figure 5.1 broadens our typology of parental and community participation to incorporate instances in which values and priorities are in conflict. Under such circumstances, the prospects of parental mobilization may appear threatening to educators, and the consequences of mobilization may be destabilizing and unsettling.

Whereas the 1960s call for parent participation and community control was premised on the existence of conflict of interest and values between minority families and white educators and officials, the contemporary conceptualization of parent involvement within the education literature adopts a language of "partnership" and "collaboration" that wishes away still prevalent real differences. Parents and teachers might agree in the abstract about the value of making the home and school environments reinforce one another, for example, but disagree vehemently about what the content and emphasis of the learning process ought to comprise. What teachers consider necessary homework for the purpose of reinforcing classroom lessons may appear to parents as stultifying repetition or a time-consuming impediment to other activities that they believe their children ought to engage in. What teachers consider to be an exercise in thinking analytically about law and customs and beliefs may be seen by some parents as a direct assault upon their own authority and values.

Failure to anticipate such value clashes is one reason why many seemingly propitious opportunities for reform get stalled or spark damaging backlashes. Education commentators and administrators, in relatively closed communities of similarly trained and similarly situated professionals, may come to broad agreement about the desirability of a longer school year or a national

---

[22] Thomas Popkewitz, "Schools and the Uses of Symbolic Community Participation," in *Community Participation in Education*, ed. Carl A. Grant (Boston: Allyn & Bacon, 1979), 207.

testing framework, for example. Failing to understand the potential points of conflict and believing their reasons to be good and solid and convincing, they may plant new initiatives without bothering to prepare the soil the way any good farmer—or smart politician—would know to do. When lines of conflict over reform initiatives overlap lines of race and class cleavage—or *appear* to overlap them or can be *made* to overlap them—the potential for politically crippling polarization is increased.

In small, relatively homogenous school districts, families may share basic situations, experiences, and values. Their local political institutions may have effectively translated those values into a school system staffed with public officials who know what the public wants and who expect to be held account-able to that vision. In such a context, individual and cooperative participation may be the norm and the most effective form of involvement. Cooperative involvement at both school and system levels may occasionally be necessary to insure that matters stay on course. In larger, economically and socially more diverse districts, visions about what schools ought to be doing may be directly at odds. Even where broad goals are fundamentally compatible, differences in style, barriers to communication, historically brewed suspi-cions, and the politics of symbolism may make it exceedingly difficult for parents and educators to recognize and articulate their shared interests. In such contexts, conflictual modes of participation are more likely and may even be necessary prerequisites to participation of the more cooperative type.

PATTERNS OF PARTICIPATION IN BLACK-LED CITIES

When it comes to setting the agenda and shaping broad policies, parent and community groups are not the first political actors that come to the mind of respondents in Atlanta, Baltimore, Detroit, and D.C. Respondents were asked whether educational decision making in their city was a "specialized arena" or an "open arena" in which general decision makers were active; those who indicated decision making was open were asked to name key "players." As we explained in chapter 2, black-led cities as a group were significantly more likely to be labeled open arenas than were the comparison cities. But the fact that decision making is open does not necessarily translate into access and involvement for parent and community groups. When asked to name key education players, only about 6 percent of respondents in the four black-led cities mentioned either community groups (3.5 percent) or parents' organizations (2.5 percent) first, compared to 13.6 percent who mentioned the mayor, 11.6 percent who made a general mention of "city government," and 8.5 percent who mentioned business. A substantially higher proportion of respondents mentioned parents or community groups

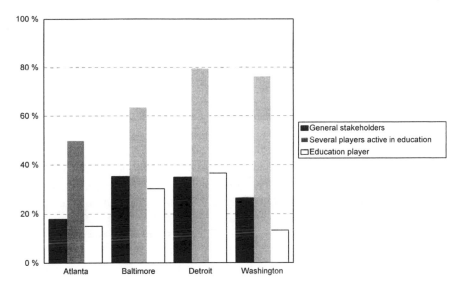

Figure 5.2 Role of community groups in city/education politics. Percentage of respondents identifying community groups as key stakeholders in city politics, agreeing that education politics has several key players, and, if they agree that education politics has several key players, seeing community groups as key players.

as among the top five education players (43 percent), although by this measure too, parents and grassroots actors are consistently less visible than general city officials, school officials, or the business community, each of which is mentioned by at least half of all respondents. These responses differ across the four cities, however (see Figure 5.2). Parent and community groups arc more likely to be mentioned in Detroit and Baltimore than in either Atlanta or D.C.

In this section we review some major developments in parent and community participation in educational decision making in the four cities. Some observers have suggested that parent involvement is most lacking where it is most needed—in central cities. They attribute this to parental indifference, educators' inhospitality, lower-income citizens' lack of power and resources in many political spheres. Yet we find evidence of serious efforts to mobilize parent and community support in all four cities. Nonetheless, participation tends to be episodic rather than sustained, reactive rather than proactive, and individual rather than systemic. These similarities mask some differences, however, in political tactics and style. Following our account of these similarities and differences, we consider some possible explanations for the generally disappointing showing. Some explanations that we find compelling would apply to many school systems, regardless of size and racial composition; others, as we suggest, may be more specific to, or more potent in, the kind of racial and political environment that characterizes the four cities under scrutiny here.

Atlanta: A Promising Initiative Fizzles Out

Compared to the other three case cities, parent organizations and community groups in Atlanta appear to play a more peripheral role. As we see in Figure 5.2, Atlanta respondents are most likely to characterize educational decision making as a specialized arena; when they do indicate that decision making is open, they are less likely than respondents in the other three cities to name parent or community groups as key education players.[23]

This low level of visible parent involvement of the collective sort cannot be attributed to lack of effort on the part of school officials to encourage family and community participation in the schools; indeed, under former Superintendent Crim Atlanta launched a substantial effort to overcome the traditionally low levels of involvement, particularly in the black community. With the black community enthused about its new access and authority and the predominantly white business community supportive,[24] Crim's efforts appeared to be bearing fruit. The unraveling of that initiative suggests that maintaining such systemic reform may be difficult when collaborative forms are superimposed on a situation in which latent cleavages are unacknowledged.

Believing that input from parents and the community was important in order to create a sense of ownership, Crim engaged the community and Atlanta Public Schools (APS) in a partnership: identifying needs, setting goals, and implementing programs, evaluating, and redesigning. To facilitate this partnership, Crim created a cabinet-level position to act as a liaison between the school system and the community. Family and community participation also was included as an objective of APS for the 1975–76 school year. Additionally, Crim encouraged volunteerism in the school by recruiting and training family and community volunteers to assist teachers in the classrooms and "provide many children with the individual attention they so des-

---

[23] Asked to name education players, almost every Atlanta respondent (95 percent) mentioned either the mayor, council, or city government in general; half mentioned business or the Chamber of Commerce, and just under half mentioned the superintendent or school board.

[24] According to Crim, the business community "summoned" him and delivered the message that they wanted to help him get "the resources needed in order to get the job done."

perately need[ed]." Principals were required to report quarterly on their volunteer programs and activities.[25]

At the same time, Crim launched a PTA membership campaign for the school system. During the twenty years of desegregation, PTA membership declined considerably and in some schools had ceased to exist. Believing that there was a relationship between the degree of parent and community participation in the classroom and day-to-day activities of the school and student achievement, Crim almost single-handedly reversed the decline. The PTA grew from an all-time low in 1976 to 11,000 by 1978 and to well over 26,000 by 1986. Crim preferred working with the PTA simply because it was the largest grassroots organization oriented toward the schools: "I felt that I needed all the resources that they could give me to help develop our parents' support of the schools. Every month I would report to the PTA presidents on the progress of the school system and I could try out new initiatives with those dedicated and interested parents who were willing to go back and share that information with the parents at each of the schools." APS was recognized nationally as having the fastest growing PTAs of any large city school system. Because of their sheer numbers, Atlanta's PTAs were able to elect the first black president of the state PTA. Impressively, this growth occurred at the same time enrollment was declining.[26]

To encourage even greater and more meaningful participation in the school, during the 1979–80 school year, the Atlanta Board of Education established minimum requirements for systemwide parent and community participation. At the school level, the principal was charged with the responsibility of ensuring a viable parent and community organization. And to facilitate systemwide participation, APS adopted a policy stating that family and community members should be involved any decisions affecting their children. The policy statement reads:

> Parent and community representatives shall, in situations where decisions are being made that will affect their children's education, be selected to participate in this process. Such activities as serving on screening committees for recommending administrative personnel, development of school programs and objectives, planning the school's budget, etc. are some possible areas that this group could address.[27]

---

[25] The discussion about the Crim years is based on the work of David Blount, "An Analysis of Selected Indicators of Performance Effectiveness in the Atlanta Public Schools, 1968 to 1983" (Ph.D. diss., Georgia State University, 1985), 169–90.

[26] During this period of PTA growth, the number of operating schools declined. The number of elementary schools declined by twenty-one and high schools by three. PTA participation is often higher in elementary and middle schools than in high school. See Ibid., 183.

[27] "Minimum Requirements for Systemwide Parent and Community Involvement," Atlanta Public Schools, 1978.

Dr. Crim and the Board of Education were neither just accommodating demands from already mobilized parents nor adopting the symbols and ceremonies of participation to coopt or distract groups seeking deeper or more genuine reforms. The high priority they placed on family and community participation, their proactive rather than reactive stance, their formal adoption of an inclusive policy, and the creation of a cabinet-level position all suggest that they wanted meaningful, sustained participation in the schools.

Crim's efforts initially expanded civic support for local education. A number of new education-oriented community organizations were created, including APPLE Corp., Council of Intown Neighborhoods and Schools, and Northside Atlanta Parents for Public Schools, to name a few. Each organization continues to provide a host of services and activities to increase parent and community participation in APS. The Atlanta business community also joined in Crim's community efforts by establishing in 1981 the Atlanta Partnership for Business and Education. This partnership works to harness the resources of businesses, higher education, governmental, religious, and human service agencies for the benefit of youth. Its goal is to "improve the quality of life for the people of [Atlanta] by improving their educational attainment level." Joining with the APBE are numerous other community and civic organizations, including the Atlanta Council of PTAs, the Religious Community Partnerships, the Kappa Boule, and 100 Black Men, to name a few. The centerpiece of APBE and other civic and community efforts is the Adopt-A-School Program. Activities take a variety of forms but are generally child-centered and school supportive, including mentoring and assisting in the classroom.

In 1982, Mayor Andrew Young created a Task Force on Public Education to promote increased cooperation between city government, the schools, and the community in an effort to expand educational and career opportunities for APS students. Chaired by Jean Young, an educator and wife of Mayor Young, one hundred citizens made up the task force. The task force's most notable accomplishment is the Dream Jamboree, which continues today. The jamboree is a two-day educational and career fair where thousands of Atlanta ninth, tenth, and eleventh graders and their parents meet with representatives from colleges, vocational schools, the military, and employment centers. Inspirational speakers and young celebrities also are on hand to provide entertainment and encouragement. Held annually in May, some fifteen thousand students and their parents attended in 1996.

With Dr. Crim's resignation in 1988, much of the family and community momentum declined. Many programs founded during the Crim years continued but often went unnoticed among the bickering of the school board. Some business leaders, parents, and community groups limited their participation with APS. In fact, family participation dropped to an all-time low. For instance, the *Ultimate Atlanta School Guide* reports that 58 percent of the city's elementary schools rank in the lowest quartile among metropolitan area schools in parent and family participation; only one percent of the city's elementary schools ranked in the highest quartile.[28] And although every school in Atlanta has a parent center, they are underutilized annually, except for an occasional workshop or seminar.

Where systemwide community involvement has emerged, it has tended to be centered in the business community and nonprofit civic improvement organizations. Usually these reform partnerships adopt a cooperative style and limit themselves to uncontroversial activities. In 1991, for example, the Atlanta Chamber of Commerce founded the Atlanta Promise, which in structure and aspiration, is similar to the Baltimore Commonwealth and the Detroit Compact (see chapter 3). Former President Carter linked the Promise with his Atlanta Project. School officials welcomed this alliance.[29] Likewise in 1993, the Chamber formed another organization, the Atlanta Committee for Public Education (ACPE). Chaired by Clark-Atlanta University President Thomas Cole, the organization's purpose is to build a bridge between the community and public schools. Cole said, "Atlanta deserves a more involved community working to improve the quality of the Atlanta public schools and the education of our children."[30] ACPE also identifies resources to help APS and lobbies the state on Atlanta's behalf, raises public interest in Atlanta schools, and conducts research to facilitate a more efficient operation of APS.[31] The committee has a liaison to the superintendent's office and has been supportive of the reform board.[32] We discuss the limits and potentials of such public-private partnerships in chapter 6.

Sporadically, some reform partnerships have adopted a more aggressive posture toward the school system. Usually, this has involved electoral strategies designed to alter the composition of the school board. Spurred primarily

[28] *The Ultimate Atlanta School Guide* (Atlanta: Atlanta Journal and Constitution, 1996).

[29] Betsy White, "Atlanta Corporations Make City Schools Their Business," and "Atlanta Promise Leaders Vow to Lose Egos," *Atlanta Journal and Constitution*, 21 November 1991, D3, and 22 November 1991, G2.

[30] Mana Saporta, "Business Group Seeks Closer Ties with City Schools," *Atlanta Journal and Constitution*, 25 March 1993, E1.

[31] Betsy White, "Chamber Finds City Schools Better Than Many Had Feared," *Atlanta Journal and Constitution*, 5 September 1993, G1, and "A Passing Grade for Atlanta Schools," *Atlanta Journal and Constitution*, 14 September 1993, A14.

[32] It is important to note that in 1996, ACPE issued a midterm assessment of the board and the superintendent that was critical, though not scathing. ACPE criticized the board for not having a strategic plan or yearly operational priorities to guide staff and board decisions. Likewise, the report said that the board needed better quality information in order to monitor, manage, and evaluate the system and student performance and needed to upgrade the quality of teachers. As a result of this criticism, the superintendent stepped up strategic planning for the APS and ordered performance evaluations. See Greg Land, "It Takes a Village. . . . But Atlanta Needs More," *Creative Loafing*, 14 May 1996, 1. Also see a Letter to the Editor, *Creative Loafing*, 18 May 1996.

by the antics of the previous school board, a number of groups, including EDUPAC, the Atlanta Federation of Teachers, the Chamber of Commerce, APPLE Corp., and Good Government Atlanta, combined in an effort to unseat members of the previous board who were considered obstructionists. Since that time, they have issued reports critical of APS and drawn attention to problems. Presently, they are directing efforts at making the school system operate more efficiently. Through their various efforts, each has pushed for some type of school reform, including site-based management, shared decision making, curriculum reform, performance audits, and evaluations of faculty and administrators. Likewise, they have suggested several cost-cutting measures, such as outsourcing, staff reductions, restructuring of the tenure system, and reducing the salaries of beginning teachers.

These systemic reform initiatives, however, do not appear to have penetrated very deeply into the grassroots community or to have generated much enthusiasm among lower- and middle-income black parents. To the contrary, when the reformers focus on cost-cutting efficiencies, a schism becomes apparent that frequently pits the elite reformers against some grassroots activists who portray the reforms as attacks on minorities and the poor. For example, school closings, one of the most controversial recommendations offered by Good Government Atlanta, became part of the superintendent's reorganization plan, which recommended closing fifteen elementary schools and three high schools. According to Canada, the system schools were built to educate 110,000, and the system now educates only 60,000. "That adds up to a $20 million a year in extra cost that could otherwise be spent directly on educating children." The business community praised the Board of Education and urged the support of the business community as "APS makes tough calls on school closings." Kent "Oz" Nelson, then chairman and CEO of UPS, said, "we business people ought to be supporting people who are willing to take those bold steps" and named Superintendent Canada. However, parents, teachers, and students were not so gracious. Hundreds turned out to vent their frustration at a public hearing on the school closings. Some parents contended that the school closings were a "breach of faith" because they had voted for a school bond referendum to renovate the schools, many of which would now be closed.[33]

Parents almost always can be counted on to resist school closings, regardless of race, but in Atlanta this schism between efficiency-oriented reformers and grassroots stakeholders had a racial dimension that was difficult to ignore. Many key figures promoting broad efficiency-oriented reform initiatives were whites, who either lived in the suburbs or sent their children to private schools. Most, if not all, of those who opposed the schools closings

[33] See a number of *Atlanta Journal and Constitution* articles on the subject including 20 and 27 April and 10 May 1995.

were African Americans with children and family members in APS. After much public debate the number of actual closings was reduced from eighteen to thirteen.[34]

Nevertheless under the new superintendent, momentum among family and community members is on an upswing, particularly around strategic planning. More than five hundred parents, business leaders, civic leaders, teachers, and administrators turned out to "reinvent the learning process" in APS. One parent remarked that she "gets the sense that people see a ray of hope. We're about making some real changes, and the fact that the school system is trying to involve the entire community means there's some real interest."[35] She goes on to say, "we, as parents, want some immediate and drastic changes in the way our kids are being educated. Some have asked me if this is just another new initiative and what's different about it. *The difference is that this time everybody has an opportunity to be included in the process* [emphasis added]."[36] Superintendent Canada noted that "this is not just about Atlanta public schools. This is about Atlanta. If we're not successful and the community isn't involved, then Atlanta loses."[37]

Baltimore: BUILD Raises the School Reform Issue, Then Loses Leverage

Baltimore comes closest among our cities to have realized—albeit ephemerally—a model for a progressive, school-reform regime linking black city and school leaders to a broad, grassroots coalition. During the early 1980s, BUILD (Baltimoreans United in Leadership Development) demonstrated that a strong, aggressive advocacy movement, rooted in the black churches rather than the business community or among elite civic groups, could propel school reform onto the citywide agenda and—just as significantly—shape a definition of reform that was anchored in a vision of the special needs of low-income and minority youth. While the joining of hands between BUILD and Kurt Schmoke hinted at the potential for a human capital regime, the subsequent unraveling of that relationship helps to illustrate reform's elusiveness. The contingent alliance and superficial veneer of consensus between candidate Schmoke and BUILD proved difficult to sustain once Schmoke was elected. As their relationship unraveled, both were weakened. Without a clear ally in the mayor's office, BUILD, a multi-issue organization,

[34] Teachers were relatively quiet on the school closing issue because most would simply be transferred to fill vacancies elsewhere in the system.

[35] Gail Towns, "Atlanta Parents Join School Officials to Try to Reinvent Learning Process," *Atlanta Journal and Constitution*, 14 February 1996, D3.

[36] Gail Towns, "Groups Organize to Fight for City's Students' Future," *Atlanta Journal and Constitution*, 8 February 1996, XJD9.

[37] Ibid.

turned its attention to matters other than school reform; its role in educational decision making became one of a veto group, which joined the teachers' union to oppose the mayor's privatization experiment. Without a grassroots ally to provide ballast, Mayor Schmoke found himself more dependent upon the business sector and more vulnerable to intervention by external actors in the state legislature.

Formed in 1977 as an Alinsky-type organization, BUILD's membership consists of fifty churches, the majority of which are African-American congregations, and three unions—the Baltimore Teachers' Union (BTU), the union representing school administrators and principals, and the hospital workers union.[38] BUILD began to focus its attention on schools in 1983, after an investigation revealed a shortage of paper, textbooks, film projectors, typewriters, and an array of other school essentials. Determined that something had to be done, BUILD's leadership identified disparities in spending between city and suburban schools. They took their findings to the legislature but were met with resistance.[39]

Undeterred by this defeat, BUILD developed an ambitious education reform plan that called for site-based management and neighborhood school autonomy. Joined by the Coalition for School Reform,[40] the Greater Baltimore Committee, the League of Women Voter, and the District Advisory Council, BUILD issued a report that called for a school-based management pilot plan to begin with one high school, one middle school, and one elementary school. The mayor favored the plan, but the superintendent rejected it in its entirety. However, after a year of meetings and becoming a part of the Baltimore Teachers Unions contract negotiations, school-based management was adopted by BCPS in September 1991.[41]

BUILD provided the impetus that eventually led to the establishment of the Baltimore Commonwealth, a public-private partnership in which BCPS pledged to produce job-ready high school graduates while the business community pledged to provide job opportunities and college scholarships.[42] In most cities where such an education "compact" has been pursued, the initiative has come largely from the business community. The Baltimore case

---

[38] This discussion relies heavily on Marion Orr, "Urban Politics and School Reform: The Case of Baltimore," *Urban Affairs Review* 31, no. 3 (1996): 314–45. For an extended account, see Marion Orr, *Dilemmas of Black Social Capital* (Lawrence: University Press of Kansas, forthcoming).

[39] Ibid.

[40] This coalition was formed in 1988 as BUILD, the Baltimore Teacher Unions, and the Public School Administrators and Supervisors Association joined together to push school restructuring. See Veronica D. DiConti, *Interest Groups and Education Reform* (Lanham, MD: University Press of America, 1996).

[41] Ibid., 144–54.

[42] Marion Orr, "Urban Regimes and Human Capital Policies: A Study of Baltimore," *Journal of Urban Affairs* 14, no. 2 (1992): 177.

is distinct in that BUILD pressured the Greater Baltimore Committee, an organization representing the city's largest businesses, to take such a step. Orr suggests that BUILD managed to alter the way the business community defined the problem of urban education, by "connecting systemic school reform to economic development, thus reorienting the business community's understanding of the benefits a good school system can bring the entire community."[43] The Greater Baltimore Committee "wanted the public school system to graduate students that could participate in and help create a productive labor force." And BUILD "wanted a guarantee that Baltimore's minorities would not miss the promising employment opportunities created by economic development."[44]

Furthermore BUILD and the Greater Baltimore Committee created Project CollegeBound, which serves students who do not normally think about going to college. CollegeBound assists students with applying for college and provided financial aid.[45] According to DiConti, each of these programs— the Partnership, Commonwealth, and Project CollegeBound—"increased the role of the individual school in the policymaking process. By setting up programs at the school site, each school would receive resources tailored to its specific needs. In the process, individual schools, as well as the groups they served, would participate in policymaking."[46]

BUILD's aggressive stances often put it at odds with Mayor Donald Schafer, but initially BUILD and Schmoke occupied common ground. Schmoke oriented his 1987 election campaign largely around the theme of education reform; he wanted to make Baltimore "the city that reads." This dovetailed nicely with BUILD's agenda; during that same time period, the group was collecting more than seventy thousand signatures in support of its school-reform proposals. "Candidate Schmoke enthusiastically embraced BUILD and its school agenda," and during his first term, the mayor continued to meet with the group on a regular basis.[47]

But Schmoke's insistence on making the contract with EAI to manage Baltimore schools the centerpiece of his school-reform initiative helped erode the working relationship. When BUILD challenged him, Schmoke recalls, "I simply said that it is BUILD's job to be an advocate; it is my job to govern."[48] Since then, BUILD's stance in education reform has been more

[43] Orr, "Urban Politics and School Reform," 322.

[44] DiConti, *Interest Groups and Education Reform*, 120.

[45] Ibid., 135–36. DiConti notes that both CollegeBound and the Commonwealth achieved only limited success. By 1992, Project CollegeBound had raised only half of its original $25-million goal. Even worse, very few students qualified for the Commonwealth program, which later modified some of its qualifications to allow more students to qualify.

[46] Ibid., 173.

[47] Orr, "Urban Politics and School Reform," 322.

[48] Quote appears in ibid., 323.

reactive and sporadic. The group played a role in the effort (chronicled in chapters 3 and 4) that ultimately succeeded in killing the contracting-out program. A multi-issue organization by design, however, BUILD has refocused its attention in other areas. As explained by one school activist, "I don't think they are particularly involved in the schools right now. . . . They were really involved with us for a while. Now they've moved on to other issues."[49]

Absent this organizing fulcrum, community and parent participation has waned. Only 65 of the 177 schools in Baltimore have "active" PTAs or PTOs.[50] Acknowledging the importance of family participation, a community activist noted that "the key indicator of a successful school is the amount of parent involvement." Yet, another respondent notes, "my concern is that many of the parents do not realize the power that they have." Similarly a white general influential adds: "The kinds of schools we work with are places where on Back to School Night . . . you may get a half dozen or a dozen parents who will show up or there may be very low participation in PTA or PTO programs. So the normal, if you don't do anything about it, is that there's relatively low parental participation."

Programs that have been designed to facilitate parental and family participation are often haphazard and nonsystemic. No systemwide programs designed to involve parents in the education activities of their children exist in Baltimore. A white general influential laments the lack of systemwide support for family and community participation in the schools:

> I don't see an awful lot of grassroots leadership taking place in the city school system in general. I think essentially the agenda for city school education . . . is set by the mayor . . . and the business community in the form of the GBC. . . . There are particular schools where parents are organized, where the staff is a strong one because of a strong principal and they've organized and motivated to create things for their individual school and there are other schools where there is a complete vacuum. . . . Middle class parents with a commitment to public education in the city tend to be well connected politically. They can call their council people and their legislators and many of them can call the mayor and make a fuss if they don't like something. They're in a position to shake things up . . . someone will get it done as opposed to some place else where they don't have a PTA, where you can't even get a dozen parents into a church basement.

Some efforts, however, are being made to establish programs to encourage parental involvement, but their pay-off remains uncertain. Since 1987 the Baltimore Public Schools have been collaborating with Johns Hopkins University and the Fund for Educational Excellence, a community foundation,

[49] Ibid.
[50] M. Orr, "Urban Politics and School Reform: The Case of Baltimore" (ms., second year report, December 1994).

to establish a project called the Baltimore School and Family Connections Project. It is designed to help teachers increase and improve parent and family involvement in the schools. By the 1995–96 school term, the project had enlisted almost fifty schools and hired two salaried interns. Baltimore's Enterprise Schools, formed as the basis of the site-based management program, include school improvement teams, composed of the principal, families, teachers, and other staff members. These teams are required to develop detailed school plans that specify how to achieve student learning, what performance measures to use, and how to configure the support staff. Nevertheless, we found that no mechanism was created to monitor the extent to which the school decision-making process was actually collaborative. In fact, in a number of interviews, respondents mentioned that parents were not invited to attend meetings of the local school council and that the decision-making process was dominated by the principal and school staff. These facts are surprising because prior to adopting the enterprise schools, "parents voiced concern about their input"; they feared their help would only be "requested after the fact."[51]

One of the more visible and well-funded efforts to involve parents among our case cities was associated with the EAI experiment in Baltimore. Parent involvement is a major feature of the Tesseract curriculum and methodology that EAI promoted. EAI schools were required to develop personalized education plans for each student, and extensive efforts were to be made to draw the parents into the process of developing those plans. Yet one evaluation found that parent participation declined each of the three times plans were developed. In the third phase of their development only 11 percent of the plans were completed and signed by a parent or guardian.[52] Indeed Ascher and her colleagues note that Tesseract schools obtained an average rating of 2.54 on a 13-point scale of parent involvement activities, with a range of 1.92 to 3.17. The average rating for Baltimore schools not participating in the Tesseract experiment was 2.63.[53] Although parents had an opportunity to participate, the challenge was mobilizing them to take advantage of these opportunities.

Detroit: The Fragmenting Politics of Empowerment and Choice

Like respondents in Atlanta and Baltimore, Detroit observers acknowledge both the importance of parental and family participation in the schools and

---

[51] Department of Research and Evaluation "Report on Enterprise Schools Network: Focus Group Survey Responses" (Baltimore: Baltimore City Public Schools, 1993), 31.

[52] S. Ruffini, L. Howe, and D. Borders, "The Early Implementation of Tesseract : 1992–1993 Evaluation Report" (Baltimore: Baltimore City Public Schools, 1994), 14–16.

[53] Carol Ascher, Norm Fruchter, and Robert Bern, *Hard Lessons* (New York: A Twentieth-Century Fund Report, 1997), 124.

their lack of participation. Only seventeen percent of Detroit respondents mentioned parents as being among the top three players in education policy making. According to one general influential:

> Parental involvement is probably the largest single weakness of the system because they don't put the pressure on by showing up and demanding answers and expressing themselves in terms of their expectations. So the system is left in the hands of the professionals who give us what they think you need, not what you as the customer wants.

Almost one in five of those we interviewed indicate that the lack of parental and community participation is a major challenge facing Detroit Public Schools (DPS).

Detroit respondents' expressions of frustration over the lack of community and parental involvement echo those in our other cities. Yet among the nation's school districts, Detroit is distinguished by having been the focus of one of the earliest efforts to institutionalize community control. During the late 1960s, frustrated by the unresponsiveness of the entrenched school bureaucracy, some leaders within Detroit's African-American community came to see "community control as a 'black power' goal." As Rich reports, Citizens for Community Control, a citywide black group, "endorsed community control as the salvation of Detroit public schools."[54] Not long afterward, State Senator Coleman Young, later to be elected the city's first black mayor, helped press the Michigan legislature to pass a major decentralization act for the Detroit public schools. More recently, Detroit again joined the vanguard of the movement to encourage parents and communities to become actively involved in shaping their schools. The Hope Coalition and superintendent Deborah McGriff saw decentralization as a potential catalyst for the systemic reform they advocated.

"Empowerment schools" and schools of choice were key elements of the Detroit strategy for drawing parents and communities more directly into the process of education and school reform. Initially popular across a broad swath of the community, the attempt to use school-based efforts as stepping stones toward systemwide changes ultimately backfired. One obstacle was the predictable assertion of conventional patronage politics: some educators at the central office and school-level saw parental involvement as threatening their status and prerogatives, and some communities saw empowerment and choice as draining resources out of *their* local school. Moreover, exposure of racial and class cleavages led to polarization of opinion and the unraveling of the reform coalition as detailed in chapter 3. Ironically, the empowerment and choice efforts—intended to stimulate lacking parent participation—foundered in part because a small but vociferous group participated "too

---

[54] Wilbur Rich, *Black Mayors and School Politics* (New York: Garland, 1996), 29.

much" by playing upon racial symbolism to challenge the reform-oriented administration's plans.

In the late 1980s the Detroit Board of Education sought to deflect widespread public criticism by charging two study commissions with the responsibility to consider appropriate educational policy for the city. Through a conscious effort, both committees incorporated representatives of parents and community groups. In 1986 the Parental Task Force's report called for a significant expansion of choice available to parents. Formed in 1987, the Citizens Education Committee (CEC) brought together prominent, yet disparate parts of the Detroit community. One member of the CEC claims there had never been a more impressive collection of leaders assembled in Detroit.[55] The committee provided recommendations on educational quality, fiscal stability, and managerial accountability. Their report began: "The tenure of the Citizen's Education Committee coincided with a period of unprecedented focus on the leadership and governance of the Detroit Public Schools. Public debate, newspaper and television scrutiny, contested ballot issues, and political intrigue have sustained an environment where schools and schooling are prominent issues for anyone concerned with the future of our city." The Citizens Education Committee proposed a general strategy of decentralizing DPS operations with emphasis on the creation of empowered and choice schools.[56] It explicitly endorsed empowerment as part of a reform strategy. The CEC recommends that empowered schools should:

have considerable discretion over curriculum, instruction, and other activities;

be encouraged to use their creativity and talent to design their program in a way they believe will be effective;

have significant control over the allocation of the school's budget, personnel, and other resources; and

be expected to involve parents and the community and to be held accountable for the results of the school's program, the most important result of which is student learning.

Although the commissions were established by the Board of Education before the HOPE team came to power, their reports were widely cited by

[55] There was also a link between the CEC and the Detroit Strategic Planning Group. Both co-chairs of the CEC, Donald R. Mandich, chairman and chief executive officer of Comerica Inc., and Howard F. Sims, chairman and chief executive officer of Sims-Varner and Associates, Inc., played key roles in the Detroit Strategic Planning Process a year earlier, with Sims chairing the Education Task Force of the Detroit Strategic Planning Process from which the Detroit Compact originated. The increasing activism of the business community coincided with the goals of various civic, religious, and community leaders who wanted to see change.

[56] In fact, the district has an extensive history of efforts to promote decentralization. In addition to legislated decentralization plan implemented in 1971, School Superintendent Jefferson (1980–88) attempted to introduce a number of decentralization plans.

the reformers to justify their program. For example, HOPE board member Lawrence Patrick cited the Task Force's report as providing clear and convincing evidence that an overwhelming demand for additional schools of choice existed in Detroit.[57] HOPE reforms did try to expand the community and parent participation. Each major reform called for institutional representation. For example, parent and community groups were guaranteed representation on both the Compact's Stakeholder Council and school level Local Compact Councils (LCC).

Detroit's empowerment schools were designed to provide opportunities for family and community participation. The empowerment agreement granted individual schools authority to define their mission, goals, and objectives. Empowerment schools—created to enhance authority and responsibility within the parameters of existing board policies and union contracts and to increase ownership, commitment, and accountability among parents, community members, principals, teachers, and students—are governed by a School Empowerment Council/Team. These councils/teams have the authority and responsibility to determine curriculum decisions, school finances, general policies, student and parental support, and community involvement. Although some pressure was placed on individual schools to come forward, empowerment was voluntary. Only a small proportion of schools responded. By the mid-1990s, approximately 26 of Detroit's 225 schools were empowerment schools. With respect to empowerment, a board member noted:

> More than anything else, I'm concerned with us having policies here in Detroit that would assure that decision making can be at the local school level whenever and wherever possible. . . . The principal, teachers, parents, support staff, and even students where possible at local schools, are able to decide for themselves how to get the job done. As opposed to having decisions made by a far away bureaucracy that doesn't have the knowledge or perhaps even the interest to make the same quality decisions and is really not in a position to be accountable or responsible for the outcome.

In practice, however, not all empowered schools operated on the basis of shared decision making. In particular, some principals regarded efforts to involve teachers and parents in school-based decision making as a threat to their traditional role. A Detroit Public School administrator states:

> We have these schools, a few of them, not many, are not intent on really implementing change. We find out that the principal has not convened an empowerment council meeting. If parents don't complain, it may not come to our atten-

---

[57] To be sure, the independent impact of these reports might easily be overestimated. To some extent, the school reformers were led to cite the conclusions of the report because they were consistent with their own preconceptions.

tion. . . . The next week I find out the principal has spent money without involving the stakeholders, "but you just told me you didn't spend any money. Well, I needed the books in order to operate my curriculum. Yes but if you become empowered, you cannot make decisions about money without involving the council."[58]

Schools of choice became the second piece in Detroit's strategy to increase family and community participation. In the national debate about school choice, the "choice" label is generally associated with efforts to bring more market forces to bear on public schools, but in Detroit the term was more closely associated with efforts to diversify the curriculum to meet the particular needs of specific groups. Choice schools were created around very specific curricular offerings or academic themes, such as business and commerce, citizenship, fine and performing arts, gifted and talented and math, science and technology.

Building a community coalition in favor of districtwide schools of choice proved to be a problem because support for the abstract concept of choice was diffuse and unfocused. Residents tend to coalesce around specific choice schools, but no districtwide mechanism linked school-based coalitions into support for districtwide reform. Likewise, some segments of the community saw specific curricular innovations as appealing, while others viewed them as potentially divisive or discriminatory. Choice became the main vehicle through which proponents of Afrocentrism and single-gender schools pursued their visions. Thus, the choice coalition was itself seriously divided. Some reformers who were generally in favor of choice opposed plans for Afrocentric schools and boys-only schools. Supporters of African-centered schools of choice were not necessarily supporters of professional development schools. In addition, primary supporters of the empowerment strategy often quarreled with primary supporters of schools of choice.

Many in the community enthusiastically embraced DPS efforts to move toward a more multicultural curriculum. Community advocates stressed the importance of cultural centering in education in a city that is 76 percent African American and a school population that is 92 percent African American. The overwhelming response of parents to the expansion of African-centered education is evident in the March 1992 opening of the Mae C. Jemison Academy; with only 120 seats available in this school, which offers pre-kin-

[58] Richard Hula, Richard Jelier, and Mark Schauer, "Making Educational Reform: Hard Times in Detroit 1988–1995," *Urban Education* 32, no. 2 (May 1997): 213. Rich's study is informative here. He contends that the empowerment school plan assumed that "principals wanted more control over the management of school facilities. Because they were not trained as facilities managers, most principals would prefer such functions to remain in the hands of the central administrator. . . . Others may not want to share the newly acquired power with teachers and the community." See Rich, *Black Mayors*, 41.

dergarten and kindergarten classes, nearly 800 applications were submitted. There was even greater demand when Malcolm X Academy opened as the first African-centered school a year earlier. According to a principal of one of the nine African-centered schools, all the schools have long waiting lists.

African-centered academies did have significant community support; however, they also drew venomous opposition. The first African-centered academy, Malcolm X, was placed in a school surrounded by a mostly white enclave in the city, near the Dearborn border. Local neighborhood groups, mounting legal challenges to the proposed all-male academy, charged that the curriculum was sexist and contained religious ceremonies violating separation of church and state.[59] The main opposition, however, to the single-sex requirement of the academies came from longtime guardians of civil rights interests including the NAACP, the National Organization of Women, the American Civil Liberties Union, and the Legal Defense Fund. A city council member who opposed the Malcolm X academy commented: "The premise was wrong to begin with because some of the little boys were saying they needed a male academy because the girls were distracting to them. If you can't learn with girls in the elementary school, then God help us." Board members were divided with four opposing the plan. Individual leaders such as Horace Sheffield, executive director of the Detroit Association of Black Organizations and a key community leader in forming the Detroit Compact, strongly opposed the single-sex exclusion. He argued there is "no rationale for bringing any form of segregation back into the schools. . . . The law of the land is that school segregation is unconstitutional and inherently unequal." The plan was struck down in October 1991, by U.S. District Judge George Woods, who ruled it was unconstitutional because it discriminated against females. This decision opened the academies to girls, but few, in the immediate aftermath, enrolled.

In addition to the initial single-sex plan for the academies, some community leaders objected to the emphasis on culture over basic education. Although the African-centered academies overall have maintained majority support in the city, the schools remain divisive. Controversial black scholar Leonard Jeffries, who heads the black studies department at the City College of New York, has been invited four times to Detroit by the DPS to lead a series of seminars on African-centered education.[60] Opponents suggest this

---

[59] Bloomfield Hills lawyer Constance Cumbey sued the DPS claiming the Malcolm X Academy violates the First Amendment by allegedly teaching anti-Christian religion. Students at Malcolm X Academy practice meditation as part of harambee, Swahili for "a coming together ceremony." She claims the meditation at Malcolm X is a sacrament of a new religion and the African-centered curriculum "racist propaganda." Opponents in the mostly white Warrendale neighborhood surrounding the school see that argument as the best hope for closing the school. Amy Wilson, "The Message of Malcolm X," *Detroit Free Press*, 8 November 1992, 1D.

[60] Jeffries has come under fire since the mid-1980s for comments perceived as anti-Semitic and challenged for his belief that skin pigmentation contributes to intellectual superiority. Rich-

indicates how Afrocentrism can too easily become a tool of monoculturalism rather than multiculturalism.

In addition to the debates surrounding African-centered education, the choice schools sometimes fought amongst themselves. A number of existing choice schools—including Boyton Magnet Middle, Erma Henderson Institute, Catherine Blackwell and Malcolm X academies—have been battling for new buildings. McGriff's expansion of five new schools of choice in 1993–94 added to the mix of schools competing for new buildings. James Humphries, parent group president at the Erma Henderson Institute of International Studies, Commerce and Technology states: "I will be watching very closely to see what facilities that they're offering to the new schools. I am concerned that they will be opening more schools when the current schools that exist do not have adequate, efficient and proper facilities for their educational programs."[61]

As support remained fragmented, the reforms drew vitriolic opposition by the DPS unions, which contended that the traditional neighborhood schools were being neglected. In response to growing opposition, McGriff created the Office of Empowerment, Diversity, and Choice in 1992; headed by Assistant Superintendent Sharon Johnson Lewis the office diffused criticism, built support, and generated positive public relations for the reform agenda. A Special Committee on Empowerment, Diversity and Choice was also created on the DPS Board of Education. However, the momentum in support of the reforms had been lost. A DPS administrator stated: "We allowed the media to pit schools against each other. That's what happened to some of the McGriff initiatives. Then we fell into the trap. So now we talk about our schools as a neighborhood schools vs. choice schools. I mean we give these classifications. We allowed the media to frame the issue in a way that was very unfavorable."

Perceptions that choice would starve traditional neighborhood schools of resources began to resonate among a number of community leaders. The reformers reintroduced the controversy regarding neighborhood schools versus specialized schools that first erupted under Arthur Jefferson when he established the magnet academies and the examination schools.[62] A community advocate expressed her disdain for the magnet schools.

---

ard Lobenthal, Michigan region director for the Anti-Defamation League, called the visit part of a growing anti-Jewish sentiment in the Detroit district. Debra Adams, "District Picks Controversial Scholar to Lead Seminars," *Detroit Free Press*, 12 May 1994, 8B.

[61] Debra Adams, "Detroit May Add Schools of Choice," *Detroit Free Press*, 29 June 1993, 1B.

[62] For example, Cass Tech and Renaissance High School (examination schools) were created under Jefferson. In addition, Jefferson decided that King High School would change its image and focus, which at that time, was one of the worst high schools in the city. Many opinions contrary to his own view in regard to the creation of the magnet academy resurfaced during implementation of Empowerment, Diversity, and Choice.

> The way they became examination schools was they just threw everybody out
> that didn't meet their criteria. I don't know how much more elitist you can get
> than that. There are still attempts by the elitists within the district to isolate the
> 'really good kids' from the other kids. I am not for examination schools of any
> type. I think there needs to be pure random selection for choice schools. The
> parents like the heterogeneous groupings when they are outside of the school,
> but once they are on the inside, they are happy to test to keep others less quali-
> fied out.

Other community members expressed concerns often raised by choice opponents: reforms were elitist; poor families who have less information and more
prohibitive obstacles such as transportation and distance find their involvement in choice schools problematic. Critics also objected to extra resources
targeting the specialized or innovative schools at the expense of the neighborhood schools. The original decision to target empowerment and choice
to schools already judged effective magnified these concerns. Even though
McGriff moved quickly to remove restrictive qualifications, perceptions that
the reforms were elitist endured.

A small group of activists, self-proclaimed grassroots of the community,
mounted a particularly vitriolic attack on the choice initiatives. They came
to every board meeting, expressed adversarial, often hostile, attitudes toward
DPS leadership, and especially criticized the "Empowerment, Diversity,
and Choice." Leaders of other organizations were reluctant to attend board
meetings given their unpleasant nature. A community advocate noted that
the constant bickering back and forth for three hours at every board meeting
each month solves nothing. Participant observation of a number of board
meetings confirms this view.

All, past and present board members, former superintendents, and many
community activists alluded to this group. The activists' significance derives
from their monopolization of both discussion and press coverage throughout
and following every meeting; their comments about the educational leadership
are always negative. A former HOPE school board member described them:

> There's a group of women that come down to the Board meetings on a regular
> basis and their main goal in life is to be printed in the newspaper or be viewed
> on television. They will do almost anything to capture that. They have no agenda.
> They have no direction. They are loud. The papers give them what they want.
> They get quoted more than Board members. They aren't community leaders.
> Most of them haven't had children in the school system for twenty years but
> they claim themselves to be parents. . . . You can't reason with them, you can't
> talk logically to them, and they lie.

While it is difficult to ascertain how much influence they really have, a leader
claims that she has an underground network and takes primary credit for

"getting out the vote" against the reformers. She shouted at a DPS board meeting in April 1995, "You want war, we'll give you war! We've already shown you will lose. We've done this before. Do you want to do this again?" As a leader of this group, she described her tactics, "We are noted for embarrassing people on the board and the staff members only to make the community aware of what's really going on so now they begin to be a little more open about things." Respondents have linked some agitators directly to union leadership and DPS board member and former board president April Howard Coleman. Another board member critical of their presence commented, "There is this self-appointed watchdogs who've made a career out of following the board. Probably they spend ten to twenty hours a week each, a group of five to ten people, who attend every committee meeting and every gathering of anything that has to do with the board. They snoop around in the schools and come up with gossip and just make our lives miserable."

It is clear that these constant personal attacks, if nothing else, diverted the attention of the board. An influential Detroit minister saw the agitators as doing a grave disservice to education, by preventing anything from getting done. He contends these relatively few agitators seem to take the rhythm of the whole. A former superintendent complained about the board groupies: "It's just annoying and serves no purpose other than obstruct. It doesn't build a sense of community. We had high school students who would attend our board meetings as part of their government class and these kids would stand up and reprimand adults for their behavior. As an adult you're supposed to set a model for kids in terms of appropriate public decor. High school students would stand up and tell these detractors, I would be expelled from school for the behavior you're displaying."

Washington, D.C.: Limits of a Legalist Approach

Compared to some other cities, there is no long or deep tradition of grass-roots community mobilization over citywide education issues in the District. Where parental involvement has occurred, most often it has been focused at the school level. For a number of years, the D.C. Congress of Parents and Teachers was reputed to have wielded significant clout. But by the mid-1970s the combination of outmigration from the city of black middle-class parents and weak leadership left the group without focus; as one community advocate observed, "its political effectiveness waned away to almost nothing." Into this vacuum Parents United (PU) emerged in 1980 as a significant force. Without question PU became the most widely recognized voice for community input; it eclipsed the Congress of PTAs, established a credible, generally moderate community voice, and sought to work within the system as a partner (albeit occasionally critical) of the public school system. While

PU's pragmatic stance and use of the courts as a lever for reform have made it an effective voice—even in times when public officials have been unresponsive and public interest has waned—these same attributes may have contributed to periods of isolation and left the group, and to some extent the city, without the kind of grassroots base that may be necessary for sustainable reform. More disaffected and more confrontational groups of parents occasionally emerge, but so far they have proven to be short-lived and lacking in political muscle.

Founded in the midst of a public school budget crisis, Parents United originally defined its mission in terms of ensuring that DCPS received adequate funding.[63] During the summer of 1980, seven hundred public school teachers had been laid off, and Mayor Marion Barry was proposing to cut the Board of Education's budget request by about 10 percent. PU was initiated by The Washington Lawyers' Committee for Civil Rights Under Law, a private organization founded "to provide high quality pro bono legal services to victims of discrimination and poverty" in Washington by focusing on the areas of employment, discrimination in public accommodations, housing, refugee and immigrant rights, and public education, and child care.[64] Washington Lawyer's Committee Director Roderic Boggs, recognizing that "there was not an effective citywide [education] advocacy group in existence" to challenge the mayor's actions,[65] worked to assemble a coalition of parents.

Parents United used the air of crisis to mobilize attention and concern. According to Speicher,

"the organizers were remarkably successful in attracting parents both to the rallies and to the hearings to testify. Approximately 1,000 parents attended a rally held at the District Building on 30 October 1980. Parents from fifty schools testified to the needs of their children's schools at hearings held by the D.C. Council. Through these efforts Parents United was able to draw media—and therefore, public—attention to the school budget process in an unprecedented way. The end result was two separate increases in the fiscal 1982 school budget amounting to $28 million."[66]

Subsequently, Parents United broadened its focus to include such issues as deteriorating school facilities, lacking health and medical services in the

---

[63] Reflecting its orientation, the group initially was called Parents United for Full Public School Funding. This discussion of the history of Parents United draws heavily from Anna Speicher, "Community Involvement in Public Education: Parents United for the D.C. Public Schools," Center for Washington Area Studies, George Washington University, Occasional Paper 11 (August 1992).

[64] Washington Lawyers' Committee for Civil Rights Under Law, program brochure, Washington, D.C., n.d.

[65] Roderic Boggs, Washington, D.C., 19 September 1992, quoted in Speicher, "Community Involvement."

[66] Speicher, "Community Involvement," 12–13.

schools, making teachers' salaries competitive with suburban jurisdictions, and extending the school day. While continuing to adopt a generally support-ive stance toward the superintendent and board, Parents United adopted more of an arms-length relationship toward the end of the 1980s. The group's leadership recognized that growing perceptions that the district was being mismanaged could undermine Parents United's credibility if the group was seen as too much of a booster. Although Parents United continued to believe that the schools required an infusion of additional resources to meet the serious needs of some of its children, it adopted the position that calls for substantial new resources would have to be delayed until the system could demonstrate that it was capable of making tough decisions and providing a quality product. In this vein, Parents United supported Franklin Smith's undertaking to close schools and reduce the central bureaucracy. When the Control Board initiated the ouster of Smith and the institution of a new chief executive officer and board of trustees, leaders within Parents United quietly grumbled; they felt that Smith, in spite of faults, was being caste as the scapegoat. And they were unhappy to find that they—in spite of their long engagement in the reform process and deep familiarity with the system's flaws—were treated with suspicion by the new overseers of the system, who appeared to regard them as part of the problem rather than a key ally.

In terms of political tactics, the group has only occasionally reverted to the broad public mobilization attempts that characterized its origin. Instead, it has tended to rely on two tactics that reflect the particular skills and orien-tation of the Lawyers' Committee that spawned it and continues to sponsor its activities. First, the group self-consciously looks for issues that require selective use of lawsuits or the threat of lawsuits. As one group official puts it: "What I'm saying is we can find an issue and work it most easily when there is a law." For example, when the organization realized that some local school-based parents' groups that were supposed to be spending on educa-tional enrichment were actually using their resources to hire licensed practi-cal nurses, they encouraged the city council to pass legislation requiring that each school have nurses available; PU then used that legislation to file a suit when the school district did not comply. Second, PU collects, analyzes, and disseminates data concerning the schools and their performance. Well before COPE launched its efforts, Parents United had earned the reputation as having the only relatively reliable data and the only personnel capable of translating the vague and confusing budget information released by the system.[67]

Its self-conscious efforts to play from its strengths in legal and research expertise and its orientation toward coalitional rather than confrontational

[67] This data collection and analysis has almost exclusively been the responsibility of one person—Mary Levy—a lawyer employed by the Washington Lawyers Committee, who occa-sionally has had part of her salary paid through Parents United, but who has primarily under-

politics led Parents United to limit its policy agenda. Although its leaders were concerned about teacher quality, for example, they decided that this is something that very little can be done about in the near term. There is no law requiring that teachers be good at what they do, they observe. According to one of its founding members, the group focuses on "issues that unite and don't divide"; its executive director characterizes its focus as issues of "God, Motherhood, and Country."[68]

Parents United's tactical decisions to focus on legally enforceable goals and to eschew outright confrontation for a coalition-building strategy and a stance as critical-but-cooperative ally of the school system help account for the group's successes and longevity. According to one assessment, PU's efforts have "either directly or indirectly resulted in a host of reforms including smaller classes, a full day pre-kindergarten program, testing of incoming teachers, the extension of the teacher work day by a half hour, an increase in the availability of texts and supplies, implementation of teacher evaluation procedures, building and repairs, and improved nursing services."[69] Equally important, PU was influential in the passage of the D.C. Public Schools Act, which mandates regular public hearings on the schools.

But this pragmatic, legalistic approach at times has limited the organization's capacity to broaden its base. The clearest illustration of the double-edged sword of a judicially oriented strategy can be seen in the group's up-and-down experience in addressing building code violations in D.C. public schools. In one sense, Parents United's battle to make D.C.'s schools safe can be seen as a testimony to the effectiveness of community advocacy and a stunning vindication of the organization's emphasis on using research and the courts as levers for reform. Frustrated by the city's failure to deal with inadequate facilities, Parents United first carried out its own research to determine the nature and scope of the problem. Its 1985 survey found many shortcomings, ranging from leaky roofs to doors that could not open to lack of playground equipment; but "through legal research, we learned that students have no right to a 'good school.' The only 'right' they have is to a school that complies with the city's fire code (with semi-annual inspections by the fire department) and that meets the standards of the Office of Consumer and Regulatory Affairs for kitchens and boilers."[70] When PU looked into matters, it found that some schools had not been inspected for at least fifteen years and that about eleven thousand fire code violations had accumulated.[71]

---

taken the task as a concerned parent. Levy played a major role in helping COPE staff make sense of the data it acquired.

[68] Speicher, "Community Involvement," 19.

[69] Ibid., 22.

[70] Delabian Rice-Thurston, Letter to the *Washington Post*, 3 September 1996, A14.

[71] Serge Kovaleski, "Progress Slow at D.C. School," *Washington Post*, 8 September 1994, A1.

Armed with such information, PU first tried to work with city and school officials to get them to acknowledge and tackle the problem head on. When the system response proved inadequate, PU went to court.

In 1994, D.C. Superior Court Judge Kaye Christian ruled in the group's favor and began a process of close oversight of the system's practices. In both 1994 and 1996, as noted in chapter 3, many D.C. schools opened late when Judge Christian issued orders blocking school openings until fire code violations were repaired. These strong steps got people's attention. Not only did PU manage to leverage repairs that might not otherwise have taken place, but its suit succeeded in expanding the public discussion to broader issues related to inadequate funding. Rather than dismiss PU's concerns, then-superintendent Franklin Smith tried to use the case to convince the community that the problem was greater than most imagined. "If we believe the fire code problem will go away once the book is closed on the Parents United lawsuit, we are naive," he wrote in *The Washington Post*. "Until we address the root cause of this problem—aging buildings and deferred maintenance—we will not rid ourselves of fire code violations." And doing so, he estimated, would cost millions more than the school system's budget could sustain. "In other words, we have a $500 million problem with only $30 million to fix it."[72]

Having succeeded in raising the issue and enlisting the muscle of the courts on its behalf, Parents United suddenly discovered that it had lost control of matters. Although PU considered Smith to be an ally, other important stakeholders—including the media, much of the public, and, eventually, the congressionally instituted control board—came to regard the delayed school openings as evidence of Smith's managerial incompetence.[73] Ironically, the PU lawsuit became a key catalyst to the control board's intervention, a move that PU considered illegitimate and one that greatly limited the organization's access to the decision-making process. In addition, Judge Christian's strict standards had consequences that PU neither anticipated nor desired. Keeping schools closed until they were certified as free of even—seemingly—minor violations in some instances appeared extreme; angry parents sometimes blamed Parents United.

[72] Franklin L. Smith, "After the Fire Drill Is Over," *Washington Post*, 14 September 1994, A21.

[73] Smith can rightly be faulted for failing to act with sufficient urgency and failing to build a broad enough coalition to allow him to act more authoritatively when trying to bring to heel recalcitrant members of his own bureaucracy. But subsequent events reveal that the scapegoating of Smith was part and parcel of an overly simplistic view of the obstacles to school reform. The Control Board's hand-picked successor, warmly welcomed by most of those who cheered Smith's ouster, foundered on many of the same shoals—in spite of being granted considerably more formal authority than Smith had enjoyed.

Matters came to a head in the fall of 1997. Chief Executive Officer General Julius Becton had made elimination of violations and opening schools on time a high and very public priority for his externally imposed regime. When he failed, he tried to shift responsibility. Becton blamed Judge Christian, who had insisted that no school could be opened while repair work on roofs was still underway (Becton argued that such work could be done without risk to the students). Rather than open some schools while others remained closed, Becton decided to delay the opening of all schools for three weeks, a decision that generated considerable anger on the part of parents. Becton and the board of trustees then responded by blaming Parents United. They publicly asked the group to drop its suit and suggested that the courts were no longer needed to insure responsiveness; Becton argued that a once-appropriate tactic had now become an obstacle to genuine reform.

> D.C. school and financial control board officials [on 10 October 1997] yesterday joined a united front of teachers, principals and PTA representatives and emotionally denounced a lawsuit that they said has given too much power to D.C. Superior Court Judge Kaye K. Christian and hampered their ability to operate and repair the city's public schools.
>
> "The blood is on the hands of these people who continue to deny our children an education," Joyce A. Ladner, the control board member who oversees school reform, said . . . . "Shame on you," Ladner and emergency school trustees . . . chanted at Parents United's executive director . . . who stood quietly in the audience and did not respond. "Shame on you, Delabian Rice-Thurston."

PU, which also disagreed with Christian's interpretation, felt caught between a rock and a hard place. While the organization desperately wanted to have schools open on time, it was reluctant to relinquish the one tool that it had found to be effective. Finally, however, it accepted a compromise and dropped the suit.

The dilemma faced by Parents United mirrored, in some ways, a more general problem that Lipsky has suggested confronts all community groups trying to balance the need to attract and energize grassroots membership against the need to earn and maintain credibility with more established third-party organizations that may be important allies. To attract and mobilize membership, particularly among lower-income individuals who often have developed a certain cynicism or fatalism about the political process, organizations may need to adopt strong rhetoric, make big promises, paint the world in stark black and white with good guys and bad guys, eschew compromise, and favor confrontation over negotiation. But to maintain credibility with the media, and to convince more established groups of the legitimacy of their claim, the same groups may be pulled in different directions: to base their claims on empirical data, to limit exaggeration, to avoid extreme claims, to enlist the help of technical experts.[74] Lipsky is not optimistic that groups can maintain such a balance in the long run.

Although some might criticize Parents United for moving too far in the direction of moderation and legal expertise—and therefore abandoning the opportunity to nurture a broader grassroots constituency—its decisions in some sense reflect an accommodation to constraining political realities. Absent a more broadly mobilized community and aware that efforts to mobilize more broadly might expose latent race and class cleavages, Parents United's opted for a more tenable approach. PU's leaders express frustration about the difficulty of getting D.C. parents to turn out in numbers; the decision to avoid calls for demonstrations and the like was due in large measure to concern that the organization's credibility might be damaged if it "called a demonstration and nobody came." This problem is exacerbated by the racial context. Parents United's executive director and primary spokesperson is black, but many of the organization's founders and long-term mainstays are white; the group's strongest base is in the city's whiter and wealthier sections. In spite of the fact that the group has worked hard and had some success, at involving black middle-class professionals in its leadership core, the association of Parents United with the privileged "West of the Park" constituencies sometimes has been exploited by more radical voices as a way to undermine its legitimacy in the eyes of lower-income black parents.

THE DOG THAT HASN'T BARKED: ACCOUNTING FOR THE ABSENCE OF A STRONGER COMMUNITY-BASED MOVEMENT

The impulse to reform may come from public officials and civic leaders (top-down) or from grassroots community pressure (bottom-up), but it is likely that sustained and effective reformed efforts require a little of both. Genuine reform almost always imposes some costs on at least some key segments of the community. These can be financial costs, felt ultimately by taxpayers asked to support higher spending. But they also can include a range of other costs associated with disruption and change: costs felt by teachers asked to work longer hours or alter teaching routines; costs felt by administrators asked either to sacrifice authority or to accept greater authority; costs felt by children and parents asked to meet new and possibly more demanding expectations; costs felt by neighborhoods asked to accept the closing or fundamental reorientation of a key community institution. Public officials and civic leaders who seek to promote a top-down reform agenda can expect mobilized resistance from those interests that feel such costs directly and immediately. Unless they simultaneously develop a supportive constituency

---

[74] Michael Lipsky, *Protest in City Politics* (New York: Rand McNally, 1971).

in the broader community that stands to benefit from long-term reform, they will face that resistance alone. Exposed and isolated, they are likely to fail.[75] In a famous story, Sherlock Holmes suggests to Watson that the key to the mystery had to do with barking dogs. But the dogs did *not* bark, the puzzled Watson replies. Precisely, Holmes observes. In our view, the absence of a broad, reliable, readily mobilizable, community and parent-based movement as a reform partner in part explains the elusiveness of school reform.

What, then, accounts for this nonevent? One of the most commonly held views is that key stakeholders fail to recognize the value of community and parent involvement. Another is that parents and community groups lack sufficient will and commitment to respond to the opportunities for involvement that school districts provide to them. The first view promotes an overly optimistic notion that stimulating parental involvement may be a relatively simple matter of "giving it a try." The second promotes a generally fatalistic notion that building a broad reform coalition is unlikely unless and until residents of inner cities undergo a dramatic change in their political culture.

The evidence from Atlanta, Baltimore, Detroit, and D.C.—along with supporting data from some recent national surveys—challenges both explanations, however. Regardless of race or position, respondents in each city generally believe that family, school, and community participation is important and potentially beneficial to both children and their schools. In each city, too, the sporadic reform initiatives discussed above and in chapter 3 have included a call for greater involvement, usually linked to a plan to give parents a greater decision-making role at the individual school level. Each city has at least some formal programs and some personnel whose primary responsibility is deemed to be expanding parent involvement.

Cynics charge that such initiatives can be merely symbolic, lacking in substance or real commitment, and we found support for such a jaded view. "Offices" of parent involvement sometimes turn out to consist of one or two individuals; phone calls to those offices go unanswered or unreturned; functions relate more to public relations than citizen mobilization. Yet national evidence suggests that urban schools and schools with high proportions of minority children may be doing a better job than other schools at carrying out various practices that experts recommend for increasing parent involvement. As part of the 1996 National Household Education Survey more than sixteen thousand parents of first through twelfth graders were asked how well their child's school performed seven different practices.[76] Hispanic par-

---

[75] This, perhaps, is the lesson to be drawn from the short tenures of many superintendents, including nationally recognized reformers like Joseph Fernandez in New York City, John A. Murphy in Prince George's County, and Deborah McGriff in Detroit.

[76] The seven practices involved letting parents know between report cards how well their children are doing, making parents aware of chances to volunteer at the school, providing information about how to help with homework, providing information about why their child was

ents, on average, reported 3.6 of the practices were done "very well." Black, non-Hispanic parents indicated that 3.3 practices were done very well. White parents, the least satisfied, reported only 2.8 practices were done very well. Parents living in urban areas were slightly more likely to indicate that family involvement practices were done well than were those in more rural or suburban communities.[77]

Nor do we find convincing an off-hand assertion that many inner-city parents and residents simply lack the interest to sustain high-level participation in school affairs. National data indicate that black parents are almost as likely as white parents to belong to a parent-teacher organization (PTO) and considerably more likely to report attending meetings of such groups; 30.4 percent of black, non-Hispanic parents of eighth-graders belong to a PTO, and 47.8 percent attend, while the comparable figures for white, non-Hispanics are 34.3 percent and 33.3 percent. Black parents were only marginally less likely than white parents to report that they had contacted school officials about their child's academic performance (52.1 percent to 53.7 percent).[78]

In our four cities we find many examples of parental and community activity. Some of the broader and most significant of these we discussed above. With the possible exception of BUILD, however, these broad, systemwide collective efforts have featured elite partners—business, civic organizations, public officials, middle-income parents—who carried the greater burden of initiating, planning, and implementing a reform strategy. In each city, however, we also found evidence of speedy and intense mobilization concentrated in lower-income, minority communities. The most common catalysts to such eruptions were proposals to close schools or fire teachers. When D.C. Superintendent Franklin Smith proposed closing ten underenrolled schools in 1993, for example, an article in *The Washington Post* observed that: "Previous efforts to close schools have met with bitter resistance. . . . This round has been no exception."[79] Four years later, when D.C.'s new emergency board of trustees proposed closing sixteen public schools "hundreds of angry, scared parents and dozens of children" packed a hearing to

---

placed in particular classes, providing workshops and materials about helping children learn at home, helping parents understand what children at their child's age are like, and providing information on community services to help the child or family. Vaden-Kiernan, "Statistics in Brief: Parents' Reports of School Practices to Involve Families."

[77] It is possible, of course, that this reflects lower expectations on the part of urban and minority parents rather than objectively better performance by the schools with which they deal. We know of no reliable and systematic data on actual practice that would enable us to test this possibility.

[78] U.S. Department of Education, National Center for Education Statistics, National Education Longitudinal Study of 1988, "Base Year Parent Survey." Hispanic parents had considerably lower levels of involvement.

[79] Sari Horwitz, "10 D.C. Schools Proposed for Closing," *Washington Post*, 27 April 1993, D1.

protest the plan. "The hearing was raucous, with frequent angry outbursts from the audience. . . . Groups broke into chants of 'Save Keene' or 'Petworth' [two of the affected schools]."[80]

While belying the notion that poor parents do not care or are incapable of political mobilization, episodes like these underscore the fundamental dilemma that this chapter has posed. Rather than a proactive voice for an alternative vision of schooling, community and parental mobilization has tended to represent a reactive, and indeed often reactionary, stance. Rather than a reliable and consistent ally for other reform elements, community and parental mobilization has tended be sporadic and unpredictable. While some reasons for this are idiosyncratic to each city, driven by the personalities of key individuals and parochial political history, we believe some broad factors may be of general import.

We highlight four of these factors: (1) class cleavages in the black community as they become reflected in the stance of educators toward low-income parents, (2) relocation to the suburbs as an "exit" option that diminishes the viability of political voice, (3) school-based efforts as a form of "within system exit," and (4) the confounding role of race.

Black Educators versus Black Parents

One perspective about the consequences of racial transition rests on the presumption that barriers between families and schools are grounded in the racial differences between white educators and black parents; this leads to an optimistic vision of black educators and black parents linking hands in a common crusade to improve inner-city schools. Jean Anyon's research in Newark found that black educators could be extremely abusive and condescending to their black students; shared race did not erase sociocultural gaps.[81] In each city we studied, too, respondents reported that—rhetorical commitments to parental involvement aside—black principals and black teachers often engage in behaviors that discourage parental participation.

A story relayed by a Baltimore community advocate is worth quoting at length. It is unusual in the extent of detail but not in the experience it recounts.

> Last year there was a big emphasis on empowering parents. . . . I got into a lot of hot water with the principal at my children's school. I was doing it right. She didn't like the way that I was doing it because she thought that the school and

[80] Debbi Wilgoren, "D.C. Parents Assail School Closing Plan," *Washington Post*, 4 April 1997, C3.

[81] Jean Anyon, "Race, Social Class, and Educational Reform in an Inner-city School," *Teachers College Record* 97, no. 1 (fall 1995): 70–94.

she could tell the PTA how they could function in the school in which I told her that they did not set the calendar for the PTA. The calendar for PTA was set by the PTA; and she still thought that was her responsibility and once she found that I was correct, I was in her target of revenge. . . . Once our parents started speaking out on everything, it was like shunning from the principal. They want us to be empowered. Amprey [the superintendent] preaches "Empower parents—let parents be involved." But we still have principals here in the city that will not let the parents in the school. Two years ago, I was president of the PTA. I had so many parents in that school I didn't know what to do with them and all. . . . We did very well [but] near the end of the school year, one of the parents had a confrontation with one of the teachers. . . . We couldn't get the situation resolved. . . . The parent transferred her child out of the school because her feelings were hurt. As a result, five other parents (they did not transfer their children) they just stopped coming. . . . Then over the summer, different things happen and when we came back to school the next year, they was real crazy stuff going on at my school and a lot of parents just came to me and they just said, "Well, I'm not coming up to the school. If you need me to volunteer to help with something, just call me but I will not be in the school." Why? Because of the principal.

Another Baltimore respondent from the education community put it this way: "Well, I think what happened over the years [was that] school systems . . . certain schools, principals, whatever tended to discourage parental involvement at certain levels. They felt that parents were a nuisance. They were asking questions that they didn't want to answer."

A community activist in Detroit notes "some schools are not receptive to parent groups": "These are actual parent groups and they [teachers and administrators] don't want to deal with them. Silly them, you know, they want this and that. Parent groups want things for their children. That's an annoyance to some." Another respondent believes the Detroit Public Schools practice isolationist policies that he describes as a "power thing": "I don't know how much you know about education, but teachers are essentially isolationist and a bit power hungry. . . . [T]hey are not real open to new ideas, nor are they open to having people in the classroom and they are not really eager to share their turf." Yet another respondent notes that "working with the city and the Detroit Public Schools has been very difficult. I wonder how long they expect people to bat their heads against the wall before they leave." And a community activist in D.C. observes: "Many times educators and administrators can be hesitant about parents being involved because they either feel that the parents are trying to take over the school or they don't know enough to be really helpful too them."

That educators should attempt to assert and maintain their professional sovereignty should not be surprising; sociologists have noted the same tendency among doctors, lawyers, accountants, academics, and other professionals, as well. In one study, most teachers simply wanted parents to defer to their professional judgment. As one teacher said: "The parents that I enjoy working with the most were the ones who would listen to how the child is and what they needed to work on and didn't criticize you."[82] Similarly, in their communications with parents, teachers often send mixed messages. On the one hand, teachers ask parents to be involved in education, but, on the other hand, teachers often keep key aspects of schooling within their exclusive control. For instance, Henderson notes that, "it is still not unusual to hear experienced educators say that since children are in school, their education is best left to the professionals—that untrained parents may unwittingly interfere with today's sophisticated teaching techniques, or even that turf battles between parents and teachers might disrupt the learning environment. They also argue that the extra time it takes to work with parents would place an intolerable burden on already overworked teachers and principals."[83] When parents do become involved in the school, teachers and administrators often view this participation as a sign of disrespect or a threat to the status quo. The fact that such games continue to be played when both parents and educators are black suggests that race is not the key variable here.

In place of the common sense of purpose that some hoped would bond black educators and parents, we encountered evidence of a class cleavage within the black community; the division manifested itself in black educators' disparaging and condescending attitudes toward the parents of their lower-income students, an attitude that may have intimidated some parents from taking a more active role. Although teaching may no longer be as dominant a path to upward mobility as it once was for American blacks now that other avenues in the public and private sectors have become more open, teachers, even with their shortened work year, still draw salaries well above the median income earned by black households in our four cities.[84]

Educators sometimes expressed a feeling that lower-class parents present the problem rather than the solution. A black Baltimore educator observed:

Plus, the other fact is we're starting to see a large number of parents who were not successful students. So they were so glad to get out of school or leave school, that as far as they were concerned, it was nothing they wanted to go back there

[82] Annette Lareau, "Parental Involvement in the Schools: A Dissenting View," in ed. C. Fagnano and B. Werbere (Boulder, CO: Westview Press, 1994), 62–63. *School, Family, and Community Interactions*, 62–63.

[83] Anne Henderson, *The Evidence Continues to Grow* (Columbia, MD: National Committee for Citizens in Education, 1987), 2. See also Pedescleaux, et al., "Urban Education as An Arena of Reform" (paper presented at the annual meeting of the American Political Science Association, 1–4 September 1994, New York).

[84] Based on 1989 school year salaries (1990 for Atlanta) and 1989 census data, the ratio of teacher salaries to median black household income is: Atlanta (173 percent), Baltimore (135 percent), Detroit (179 percent), D.C. (130 percent).

for even if it was their child. Then the other side of it too, I think, is when we look at education, those of us who have been successful in negotiating the educational process, we tend to place more emphasis on what that education can do for us. Those who have not been successful, if anything they blame the education system for their failure. Why would they go and try to change it or to be involved with it.

A black public official who helped to organize an Atlanta convention to encourage parental involvement said that "the only difference in the schools now and fifteen years ago can be tied to the fact that we don't have the same level of involvement on the part of the parents. We can surely hold parents responsible for the education of their children."[85]

One D.C. respondent, a black woman who works for the school system but identifies closely with the low-income parents in the city's Head Start program, complained about the haughty attitudes of middle-class black teachers who take excessive pride in their higher status. She included "disrespect of poor parents" as one of the three aspects of her job that was most frustrating. "See we tell our parents the school belongs to them and then they go to kindergarten and find out that the school doesn't belong to them." Making a disparaging reference to their expensive clothes and grooming habits (specifically, the fact that many have long, brightly colored fingernails), she labeled such teachers the "long fingernails ladies" and implied that these teachers aggressively acted to erode the self-confidence of their low-income students and their parents.

Suburbanization As an Exit Option

In a classic analysis, Albert O. Hirschman outlined the ways in which the option to exit from an undesirable situation can serve as an alternative to political mobilization. When exit becomes easier, mobilization becomes relatively less attractive to rational individuals. Because voice requires responsive institutions and a continuous application of energy and innovation, Hirschman suggests that there may be "an important bias in favor of exit when both options are present."[86] Over time, the availability of an easy exit option can erode the basic foundations for collective political action.

The figures on population and school enrollment trends presented in chapter 2 show clearly that many residents in these metropolitan areas have chosen suburbia over the central cities. While dissatisfaction with the city schools certainly is not the only factor going into such decisions, it also is

[85] Marc Franklin, "Schools Hold Parent Power Convention," *Atlanta Journal and Constitution*, 23 February 1997, D2.

[86] Albert O. Hirschman, *Exit, Voice and Loyalty* (Cambridge: Harvard University Press, 1970), 43.

clear that families with school-age children are especially likely to make that choice. In Atlanta, Baltimore, and D.C., the rate of population loss among children (under the age of nineteen) between 1960 and 1990 was almost exactly twice that of the population at large.[87] The relative loss of parents to the suburbs can undermine political pressure for reform of schools in several ways. First, given the absolute numbers of those opting for suburbia, parents of school-age children become a smaller share of the central-city electorate; then, public officials may find it relatively easier to push school issues off the agenda in favor of competing priorities, including that of keeping taxes low. Other possible impacts derive from the specific characteristics of those who leave. If those who leave tend to care the most about their children's education and have the socioeconomic status that makes exit more feasible, suburbanization may selectively deplete the supply of those who are most likely to constitute an effective leadership core around which a political movement for reform might be built.

During the 1950s and 1960s, while the black population was rapidly growing in these cities, various informal factors, including blatant as well as subtle racial discrimination, combined to make the suburbs an either infeasible or unattractive option to many black middle-class families.[88] The fact that exit was at least partially blocked may have helped to bolster efforts to mobilize black-middle class residents in the effort to convert demographic change into political power. During the 1970s, the growing economic well-being of the black middle-class and the puncturing of some racial barriers in the suburbs widened opportunities for exit. While black suburbanization began in earnest, particularly in D.C., the appeal of living and working in a black-run city may have offset the appeal of exit for some black households that financially could have born the cost of moving. Hirschman refers to such a counterforce to exit as "loyalty," which "can neutralize within certain limits the tendency of the most quality-conscious customers or members to be the first to exit."[89] Thus, although exit systematically erodes the capacity for political voice among white residents of these cities, the desire to live in a city in which blacks have full access and control of the levers of self-government may keep the potential for political voice alive within the black community. However, as the black suburban population grows and begins to assert its political presence in the suburbs, the unique appeal of black-led cities may be watered down. This may be an especially important factor in the D.C. area; blacks recently captured the leading elected offices in suburban Prince

---

[87] The total loss in persons eighteen and under and total population for each of the cities was Atlanta (37.7/19.2 percent), Baltimore (43.9/21.6 percent), Detroit (42.5/38.4 percent), and D.C. (47.9/20.6 percent).

[88] Douglas S. Massey and Nancy A. Denton, *American Apartheid: Segregation and the Making of the Underclass* (Cambridge: Harvard University Press, 1996).

[89] Hirschman, *Exit, Voice*, 79.

George's County, and simultaneously the institution of the District's financial control board and the emergency education board of trustees diminished the authority of the local offices that black elected leaders hold. Suburbanization, a prominent force in accounting for the flimsiness of collective reform efforts within the white community, may be emerging as an important factor in the black community as well.

Exit can be an alternative to voice even among those who remain in the central city. Many have pointed to the option of private schools as an additional way in which concerned parents might solve their problems individually rather than collectively. Overall, exit to private schools does not seem to be an especially prominent factor in our four cities. According to 1990 census figures, an average of 84.5 percent of all school children living in the four black-led cities were attending public schools; this compared to 78.8 percent in the seven comparison cities. In D.C., where yearly figures are available, private school enrollment declined more than twice as steeply as public school enrollment between 1983 and 1992.[90] Although the proportion attending private schools may not be large, there is reason to suspect that those who do opt for this private-sector exit option are among those with the resources that might otherwise have made them valuable allies of a movement to reform the public schools. In the four black-led cities, for example, only about half of white school children attend public schools; this compares to 57 percent in our seven comparison cities and about 82 percent in the one hundred largest school districts in the United States.

Within System Exit–School-Focused Participation As an Alternative to Systemic Reform

Some parents in Atlanta, Baltimore, Detroit, and D.C. may be intimidated or manipulated by educators, and other parents may move to suburbs or private schools instead of staying to fight for the general improvement of urban public schools. But many others *do* assert themselves, either collectively or individually. The considerable energies that they muster, however, are too often channeled in directions that make them less available as potential partners in a citywide coalition for systemic education reform. Much of today's literature on parental involvement and school reform celebrates the notion of school-based decision making as a tool for stimulating reform; decentralized authority, it is argued, gives parents an opportunity and incentive to participate with

---

[90] Between 1983 and 1992, private school enrollment declined by 24.4 percent, while public school enrollment declined by 6.1 percent. D.C. Office of Policy and Evaluation, *Indices: A Statistical Guide to the District of Columbia* (Washington, D.C.: District of Columbia Government, various years).

TABLE 5.1
Racial and Economic "Enclaves" (percent)

	Atlanta	Baltimore	Detroit	Washington
Schools with less than 5% of students eligible for free lunch	0.9	0.9	NA	21.3
Schools with less than 15% of students eligible for free lunch program	4.4	5.2	NA	31.1
Schools with more than 40% of students eligible for free lunch program	78.1	73.6	4.6	6.6
Schools less than 35% black	NA	13.0	4.6	6.6
Schools more than 90% black	NA	58.2	67.6	78.1

Source: National Center for Educational Statistics, U.S. Department of Education, School District Data Book, CD-Rom Version (November 1994).

their energy, resources, and new ideas. Without gainsaying some potential advantages of decentralization, we feel it is necessary to offer a somewhat contrary view. We believe that the focus on improving individual schools in our four cities may actually erode the potential for broader reform efforts particularly among both white and black middle classes.

As the proportion of white and middle-income students has dwindled, it has also become concentrated in a relatively small number of "enclave" schools. In chapter 2, we illustrated this phenomenon as it unfolded in Washington, D.C. Table 5.1 presents relevant data from all four cities, drawn from the 1990 common core of data on all U.S. school districts. When defined in terms of socioeconomic class, it appears that the enclave phenomenon is much more pronounced in D.C. than in the other two cities for which this data is available. In racial terms, the enclave phenomenon is most apparent in Baltimore, where twenty-three schools (13 percent) are about two-thirds nonblack in a system in which more than 80 percent of all students are black.

Parents in these enclave schools are extremely active and involved, but most of their energies are targeted at improving the relative position of their school versus others, rather than aiming for changes that might benefit the system at large. The most dramatic manifestation of this can be seen in the will and capacity of the parents in some of these schools to raise extra money to enrich the educational experience for their children when resources from the central administration do not suffice. Reliance on school-level initative goes hand-in-hand with great disparity in levels of parental financial support. As one Atlanta community advocate recalled:

> They had on the PTA [membership form] a chance for you to just pay your dues, or you might want to just contribute to help on a certain fund. Some of those

pay the dues and then write another check for $200 just to help with school funds, to supplement the school budget. . . . And a lady next to me said, "well, this is not a high price to pay for a good education for your child, and when they need things." And she said, "My little girl is in the third . . . grade and they said that they needed rain coats on hand in case it rained . . . . so my husband and I, we just donated $2,000 to buy raincoats for the children in case they needed to go to the bus."

In Atlanta PTA budgets range from a high of $68,000 at a predominately white elementary school in north Atlanta to a low of $200 at a predominately African-American elementary school in northwest Atlanta.[91]

Fund-raising activity at the school level appears to be highest in Washington, D.C., particularly among the middle- and upper-income neighborhoods of Ward 3. When the water fountains rusted and were not repaired by the school system, parents in one of these schools raised the money to replace them. When the school system failed to cover hot pipes, parents bought insulation and wrapped them. And when parents heard that teacher's aides would be cut from six to three, parents assessed themselves $500 per child to keep the teacher's aides at six. Although parent groups in the District's poorer neighborhoods are providing some services, their fundraising ability does not approach that of their counterparts.[92] Toomey suggests that these kinds of family involvement activities tend to increase educational inequality.[93] In fact, Ward 3 parents were concerned about the "perception of fairness," with some parents agonizing over the expenditures A Ward 3 parent and PTA co-president said: "We wondered whether it would help the city change faster if we were suffering more. We felt like we weren't part of the school system by doing so much. But in the end, the decision came down to one thing: we didn't want our kids to suffer."[94] Ward 3 parents eased some of their anxiety over the equity issue with the rationalization that Title I money provides for aides in schools with large numbers of poor children. Many also believe that central authorities are less likely to give them the resources they need *because* central authorities think of their schools as relatively white, affluent, and self-sufficient. The paradox for these parents, Loose suggests, is that if they did not spend their own money to supplement

[91] Diane Stepp, "Strong PTAs Raising More than Money, Teachers Say," *Atlanta Journal and Constitution*, 23 May 1996, C2.

[92] Cindy Loose, "Parents Dive In to Save Sinking Schools," *Washington Post*, 9 June 1996, A1.

[93] D. Toomey, "Home-School Relations and Inequality in Education," cited in *Families and Schools in a Pluralistic Society*, ed. Nancy Feyl Charkin (Albany: State University of New York Press, 1993), 4.

[94] Cindy Loose, "Parents Dive In to Save Sinking Schools."

the school budget, their school would be even poorer than schools in the District's impoverished neighborhoods.[95]

In D.C., the presence of these enclave schools also serves as a within-system exit option for middle-class black parents who do not live in those attendance zones. During the 1970s, when white flight began to depopulate some predominantly white west-of-the park schools, concerned parents feared that low enrollments would be used as an excuse by central authorities to close their neighborhood schools. They addressed this challenge, in part, by seeking ways to attract middle-class black children from other neighborhoods.[96] Out of disinterest or for tactical reasons, the central administration chose to look the other way. Over time, DCPS informally adopted a liberal policy of allowing out-of-boundary transfers to parents aggressive enough to seek the opportunity. With almost no central guidance, local principals have had substantial discretion in determining which students are encouraged to follow through when they have inquired about transfer possibilities and which are accepted once they have applied.[97] Some black parents, who might otherwise be vocal advocates for reform in their own neighborhood schools, instead opt to transfer into schools that have fewer poor children, more active parent organizations, and much higher test scores. We had this exchange with a black D.C. school board member:

> Q: Is there a class dimension here though too?
> A: Yeah, oh yeah.
> Q: Even within the black community?
> A: Oh yeah, that's what I told you. Yeah. Oh yes.
> Q: How do you see that in terms of the sort of the politics of what gets done?
> A. That is, well the majority of your middle-class blacks will send their children to the Ward 3 schools.

In March of 1993 more than 30 percent of the students at the sixteen D.C. elementary schools with fewer than 25 percent of their students eligible for school lunch were registered out-of-boundary, compared to only 12 percent at the more than one hundred elementary schools that had higher proportions of poor children.[98]

---

[95] Ibid.

[96] See, for example, Judith Denton Jones, *The Six Schools Complex: A Successful Innovation in Washington, D.C.'s Public Schools* (Washington, D.C.: Six Schools Council, 1987).

[97] A black D.C. school board member notes that political connections play a role in these transfer decisions: "Now, while I was here I found out that board letters had great weight. And who you knew in administration had great weight. . . . First come, that's how they were supposed to do it, first come first serve, but that didn't necessarily mean that Johnny was getting in there. Because he may not have had a letter of recommendation to accommodate him and somebody who could have applied in June the following year, but had a letter of great weight, because it was a political connection, actually could get in. I don't like that."

[98] Original calculations based on school level data compiled by WESTAT, Inc.

Although some parents at these schools also choose to participate in efforts to improve the broader system, the overall impact of these school-based efforts usually diverts some potentially important resources away from the citywide arena. Parents and teachers have a limited store of time and energies. When school-based efforts achieve results, the pay-off to the children at that school is immediate and clear. Systemwide reform efforts, in contrast, demand more of the participants, are less likely to succeed in the short-run, and, when they do succeed, may have dispersed benefits not readily perceivable at the school level. Small successes at the individual level can undermine citywide reforms in another way as well. Parents, teachers, and principals who believe that they have managed to gain extra resources or special dispensations for their school may hesitate to ally with other schools, for fear they will lose those special benefits if attention is drawn to them.

This tendency to channel energies into school-based activities is not re-stricted to enclave schools with more privileged parent and student bodies. In all four cities, PTAs are a channel of first resort for concerned parents, and in all four cities the PTAs operate relatively independently, rarely, if ever, linking aggressively into a systemwide voice. After Crim's resignation, the Atlanta system's commitment to family and community participation al-most ceased to exist. As we have seen, compared to our other cities, Atlanta has a stronger tradition of professional domination and elite decision making. Without strong insistence on grassroots involvement from the top, these tra-ditions apparently reasserted themselves. At least for a while, the burden for developing PTA participation fell to the principals. However several of our respondents noted problems associated with this approach. As one commu-nity advocate observed, PTA activity is often dominated by the principal and teachers: "Unfortunately people have hidden agendas . . . at the local school level. . . . There is a feeling on the part of some people that the PTA is too often dominated by the school administrator. . . . Principals can sometimes get persons they can control in PTA leadership positions. . . . The same could be true on the part of teachers in terms of student involvement. Teachers select students who will simply mimic what they want them to mimic." To maintain their own independence and control, principals sometimes work hard to ensure that parent involvement not extend to systemic initiatives that might link them to parents at other schools. Such linkages can lead to more informed parents, who return to the principals and ask awkward ques-tions about why their schools does not have programs or resources that they have discovered exist elsewhere in the system. Likewise, some principals are anxious to avoid antagonizing central authorities and seek to restrain parents from making aggressive demands.

The obstacles to building system-oriented movements out of school-based initiatives can also be self-imposed. In D.C., the Washington Parent Group Fund (WPGF) is a citywide organization that works with PTAs in areas of self-improvement. Rather than becoming a vehicle for developing a broader movement, WPGF systematically avoided taking up general policy issues. According to one leader, the broad diverse membership includes schools and parents with very different needs and perspectives; it would be impossible to try to speak with a unified voice on behalf of the members. "I want to get them revved up about two things only: How to give support at home, and how to help their school." Although some parents at the affected schools wanted WPGF to take a position against the 1993 school closings, it did not do so because "it could become too political within the organization." By way of contrast, in suburban Montgomery County, Maryland, school PTAs are part of an active systemwide council of PTAs that aggressively lobbies the school board and County Council with the goal of increasing school spending and maintaining important services.[99]

Ironically, the tendency of national school reformers to emphasize school-based decision making, adopt-a-school programs, and partnerships between individual schools and businesses and nonprofit groups may consequently channel parent and community involvement further away from systemwide reform efforts. In Atlanta, for example, hundreds of churches, businesses, and civic groups participate in the adopt-a-school program. The type of participation is agreed upon between the churches or groups and the principals and generally involves job placement, tutoring and mentoring, and enrichment services during school, after school, and on weekends. Some churches and civic groups also offer scholarships. For example, the 100 Black Men in Atlanta are currently sponsoring their third class of students.[100] Activities like these may substantially contribute to the life and learning of individual students, but participating organizations often become frustrated by their inability to make a dent in the broader, more pervasive problems.

The overall impact of these school-based efforts may be to divert potentially important resources away from system-based reform. Indeed, school-level efforts may prevent teachers, administrators, and parents from forming coalitions with their counterparts across the school system for fear of losing benefits, the school-based approach encourages a zero-sum mentality and a wariness of cooperation with other schools that might exploit shared information to gain a competitive advantage in the battle over resources. Also, school-based efforts produce immediate results; by contrast, systemwide reform is slow and demands more diverse participation.

[99] Connie Hill and Cheryl Jones, "Race, Class, and Education Policy in a 'Good Government' County" (paper prepared for the annual meeting of the Urban Affairs Association, 3–6 May 1995, Portland).
[100] This is just one example of civic participation in education. See Alonzo Crim, "A Community of Believers Creates a Community of Achievers," *Educational Record* 68, no. 4/69, no. 1 (Fall 1987/Winter 1988): 44–49, for more examples of this type of community involvement.

Community Leadership and the Confounding Role of Race

By and large, the factors that we have considered as possible explanations for the fitful and unreliable nature of parent and community mobilization in our four cities are not tightly linked to the concept of black-led cities or the issue of race. The ambivalent and even hostile stance of black teachers toward participation by black parents is little more than a recapitulation of a general relationship between education professional and parents regardless of race; it is of interest to us primarily because some argued that this pattern would be broken once black parents were confronted with black educators bound to them by experiences and outlooks shared by virtue of their common race. Exit by parents and residents who might otherwise opt for the weapon of political voice is a condition facing most U.S. central cities, including those in which the key offices of local authority continue to be held by whites. The potential for neighborhood-level activity to deflate the potential for broader mobilization and more ambitious targets has historical roots that predate racial transition; this was, for example, a major point of tactical debate within the radical left during the 1960s, pitting those who favored starting with issues of immediate concern to neighborhood residents against traditional Marxists, who saw battles over garbage collection and service delivery as distractions from the important task of building a class-based movement.[101]

Yet, the context of demographic change and transition in racial control interacts with these other factors in interesting and consequential ways. As discussed in chapter 4, many black residents in these four cities worry that school reform initiatives offered in the name of increased efficiency and stricter educational standards are *de facto* and *sub rosa* strategies to scale back the gains that they have made through public programs, public employment, and the use of public power. Even black respondents who hold positions of authority and power occasionally express this view. A general influential in Baltimore, reflecting on the administration of the city's first black superintendent, put it in these stark terms: "They ran Patterson out—killed the poor man. They killed him. But he was a black man who knew what it took to make black kids learn, and he came in here to be about the business of making that happen. And the white folk ran him out." Asked about the groups that have been most effective in shaping Atlanta school policy, a black leader who had served on the school board, answered:

I think the most effective, and that is unfortunately, would be a group called Apple Corp. Have you heard of it? . . . Apple Corp has been the most effective

---

[101] See Todd Gitlin and Nanci Hollander, *Uptown* (New York: Harper & Row, 1971) for an account of this debate as it unfolded within the Students for a Democratic Society. Also see, Robert Fisher, *Let the People Decide* (Boston: Twayne Publishers, 1984).

in getting out their hidden but supposedly public agenda. They have a hidden agenda and people don't [know] that Apple Corp really came about after integration and after the PTAs turned black. Those are the white folks who were PTA members and they formed that organization to do some of the same things that they were doing at the white PTA organizations.

Such concerns make it easier for teachers to mobilize support in opposition to certain reform proposals; they also make it possible for others within the black community to build constituencies by playing on fears that out-numbered white elites will use their greater financial leverage and external ties to protect their priviliged status. For example, in 1993, a new organization—the Association of Black Parents (ABP)—emerged in D.C., directly tied to resentment over the school closings orchestrated by then-Superintendent Franklin Smith. ABP initiators charged that the closings had been orchestrated to protect schools in the west-of-the-park neighborhoods. ABP's first newsletter suggested "that there were only three (3) white children affected in this event because the schools that would have put those parents into the fight were taken off the consideration list long before the final process was enacted."[102] According to a founding officer of APB, "The school board is controlled by the money ward. I'm not saying this because Erika Landberg, Karen Shook, and Jay Silberman [members of the school board] are white. . . . I wish it was that simple because then it would be something that we could work with. I think that it's green and they represent the green and they just happen to be white. If you had three black people sitting there and they were in that money ward, then they would have the same credibility." One result is a highly charged political atmosphere in which potential parent and community leaders must worry whether their involvement will be characterized in racial and class terms. "But absolutely, between black and white, there are racial undertones to almost every single thing that goes on in Atlanta. I think that is a little particular southern, but that exists."

Several white parent and community leaders in these cities expressed a special frustration about implicit constraints that made them less willing or able to exercise leadership more publicly and on a systemwide scale. The simple fact of their involvement, they believed, had the potential to frame the issue of school reform as an issue of white versus black. One white community-based reformer in the District of Columbia made it clear that racial inhibitions made it extremely difficult for groups to openly criticize black officials and seriously constrained the political tactics they could employ. "It's been costly to the city. Very costly. Because if you can't say the emperor is naked . . . and if you always feel you have to work from the inside . . . you're limited."[103]

---

[102] Association of Black Parents, "A Ray of Hope," I: 1 (n.d.).

[103] This phone conversation with a D.C. advocate took place after the formal data-gathering.

One way parent and community school-reform groups seek to de-fuse the racial issues is by aggressively seeking black parents to take on public leadership roles. But the racial backdrop limits the effectiveness of these tactics in at least two ways. First, some activists in the black community do not hesitate to attack blacks that take on such positions by labeling them as either witting or unwitting dupes of white elites. Sometimes this charge is framed in racial terms, as when one black accuses another of being an "Uncle Tom" or a "house Negro."[104] When the black principal of D.C.'s Marcus Garvey Public Charter School got into an altercation with a white reporter, she allegedly referred to one black police officer who came to the scene as "a slave to the white man" and told another detective that his "blackness was in doubt."[105] Both white and black community activists sometimes draw distinctions about the *degree* to which some black leaders can be considered "truly" black; the distinction is based on political position, not the color of their skin. Second, fear of being subject to such personal attacks combined with concern that even legitimate criticisms of black public officials might be exploited by some to make the case that blacks are incapable of effective self-rule creates tremendous pressures on potential black reformers. The white coleader of one school reform organization related the story of how her black coleader eventually succumbed to this pressure and resigned her leadership post. "It is very difficult for the group that normally would have a voice about issues like standards and quality of education—middle-class African Americans—to take on that role," she observed, referring to the emotional stress her former partner had felt when placed in the position of publicly criticizing black leaders.[106]

Black opponents of biracial reform alliances often characterize the battle lines in terms of class rather than race. This enables them both to conform with broad public norms against starkly racial appeals and to attack black supporters of reform in a way that conjures the "Uncle Tom" label without using it directly. One black activist in D.C., for example, linked moderate black officials to the white [Ward 3] interests in this manner:

[104] For example, in an intraneighborhood conflict over planned development in D.C.'s Shaw neighborhood, one black member of the local Advisory Neighborhood Commission charged another with being a "house negro," adding "I will continue to use that term as long as it applies to people who act the way they act. . . . I already know that I'm a field Negro, because I want to be free." Linda Wheeler and David Montogomery, "Many Voices, No Harmony in D.C.'s Shaw," *Washington Post*, 25 July 1997, B3.

[105] Bill Miller, "Anigbo Voiced Racial Insults, Prosecution Documents Allege," *Washington Post*, 8 February 1997, C3; Joel Thurtell, "Detroit Principal Charged with Paying Bills, He took $140,600, Prosecutors say," *Detroit Free Press* 21 September 1994, 3B. The principals' racial framing of the issue earned her condemnation from some elements in the black community but simultaneously gave her hero status to some.

[106] See note 103.

> People like John Ray [black city councilman] get voted in because they have
> that real estate interest. People like [Harold] Brazil [black city council member]
> probably gets voted in because they have the interest of the . . . development
> here in Ward 6 and so forth and so on and it can go on down the line. So it is
> not a matter of race, it's where the special interest is and we all know that in
> that Ward 3 area, that's the richest section of the city so, you know, and those
> people, it's like tentacles that go through the rest of the city.

The complexities of these racial overtones can be seen in the generally well
regarded Barclay-Calvert reform initiative in Baltimore. When a group of
parents, community leaders, teachers, and the principal at the public Barclay
School decided to adopt the curriculum of the Calvert School, a private
middle school with mostly white and affluent students, the superintendent
turned down their request. But this rejection did not deter these participants. Rather, they became more determined and pressed for the approval
of their proposal at every opportunity. As a result, Mayor Schmoke ordered
the superintendent to work out a compromise with the Barclay parents and
staff.[107] After seven years, students at Barclay were performing at or above
the national average on standardized tests. But the Barclay experience high-
lighted a schism in the Baltimore education community. As parents pushed
for the Barclay school proposal, the dispute began to take on racial overtones.
When a white community activist agreed to become the spokesperson for the
Calvert project, some members of Baltimore's African-American community
began to see the effort as having an elitist caste. Speaking of this white community activist, the union president indicated: "I think her vision and my
vision were totally different. My vision includes the worst child in the school
system." According to DiConti's account, these voices in the black community—voices primarily from outside the Barclay school itself—feared "that
the [white activist] was trying to start a private school for whites," in spite of
the fact that the school was 87 percent black at the time.[108] Blacks contended
that the white activist spoke with one voice and held one vision while they
held another.

   The complexities are also revealed in Detroit, where the "elitist" label
served a dual function for those seeking to undermine the HOPE reform
agenda. Rich explains that the black proponents of the status quo used the
"whispered theme . . . that whites are attempting to embarrass 'us'," in an
effort to mobilize blacks to rally to their support in the 1988 election. But a
public reliance on that racial pitch would not have much leverage in light of
the fact that the most visible proponent of reform, Superintendent McGriff,
was black. Formulating the charge in terms of elitism allowed opponents
of the McGriff/HOPE agenda to more subtly link black reformers to the

[107] DiConti, *Interest Groups and Education Reform*, 145–47.
[108] Ibid., 146.

predominantly white business community and had the added advantage of conjuring the image of class-based conflicts of interest in a city with a long, strong tradition of unionism.

FIZZLED EXPECTATIONS

One image of a progressive coalition for systemic school reform calls for a strong, reliable, fully mobilized citywide parent and community component to support elected officials who are willing to fight for human development policies, to counterbalance the politics of patronage that can result when the school system becomes a source of jobs rather than a tool for social improvement, and to act as a steady voice for the interests of all children including those from less advantaged circumstances. There were some reasons to hope that the transition to black control of local power might facilitate the emergence of such a force. Whereas white central-city politicians and educators may have been wary of public involvement during the period of racial and demographic change, the new black leadership could see parents and community groups as their natural allies. The formative experience of the civil rights movement might have left black parent and community groups with a clearer appreciation of the value of political mobilization and a greater understanding of its tactical side.

Measured against such a hopeful image, Atlanta, Baltimore, Detroit, and D.C. each fall short. Although parent and community groups are a constant force in some schools and neighborhoods and strong initiatives with a systemwide perspective occasionally emerge in every case, the overall pattern of mobilizations is sporadic, narrow, unpredictable, and ephemeral. The strongest outbursts are at least as likely to rally around the status quo as they are to prod for meaningful change.

There are good reasons to ask whether the image, in itself, of a continually mobilized parent and community reform movement is realistic. After all, even in the more conducive socioeconomically advantaged suburbs, parent and community involvement at the system-level is often a fairly desultory and nonsubstantive exercise that only occasionally penetrates beyond a thin core of activists.[109]

At the same time, these cities especially *need* a collective reform movement; their problems are more daunting, and the presumption of clear and

---

[109] Montgomery County is an affluent Maryland suburb just outside of Washington, D.C., and its parents are noted for their high levels of civic awareness and concern about schools. Yet, in the 1996 primary elections, more than one out of five of those who went to the polls chose not to cast a ballot for the at-large school board seat, even though the election was a competitive one. Barbara Goffman, "Primary Voter Turnout Lowest in 20 Years," *Montgomery Journal*, 7 September 1996.

common goals is more doubtful. Public leaders and others who want to see genuine change need a constituency if they are to tackle the difficult and politically risky job of providing leadership in the systemic reform effort. Right now, those who scan the horizon in search of potential allies cannot draw much optimism from the account in chapter 5. It is not surprising that potential reform leaders—looking for partners with straightforward goals and some resources—often turn to the business community. As we discuss in chapter 6, however, that course of action has its own problems.

CHAPTER SIX

Black Leaders, White Businesses:
Racial Tensions and the Construction of
Public-Private Partnerships in Education

We urge business to become a driving force in the
community on behalf of public education and a prime
advocate of educational initiatives for
disadvantaged youngsters.
(Committee for Economic Development, 1987)

Business leaders, often accused of short-term
thinking, are taking the lead in a long-term revolution
to save public education.
(Ann B. Morrison, *Fortune, 1990*)

Despite the enormous stake businesses share in
maintaining an educated work force, only a few
business people pay more than lip service to the
ongoing challenges of running a public school system.
(Joe Martin, Atlanta, school board president, 1993)

There isn't a very good, in my opinion, a very good
dialogue between business and the city right now so
that inhibits good decision making. One of the tough
things in the city is that business is looked at as a
white, essentially male suburban group and the city,
our city is somewhat different than other major urban
areas in that it's so predominantly black and it's
getting so predominantly poor that dialogue between
the two groups is often difficult and limited.
*(Black member of the Greater Detroit
Chamber of Commerce, 1993)*

ADVOCATES of systemic school reform frequently include public-private partnerships on the list of initiatives that they believe are critical if urban school
systems are to be turned around. Business is seen as a potentially valuable
partner in the reform movement for at least three reasons. First, business is

seen as a source of *information and expertise*. Corporate leaders are well-placed to provide guidance on the types of knowledge and job skills that graduates need to be employable and prosperous in the coming decades; in addition, corporate employees may have particular skills in accounting, information systems, and other management tools that could help public school systems operate with greater efficiency. Second, business is an alternative source of *financial and in-kind support* during a period when local public school revenues are often eroded by cuts in intergovernmental transfers, stagnant local economies, and public resistance to tax increases. Business partners—at either school or system level—are potential sources for cash grants to teachers, scholarship offers as incentives to students to get good grades and remain in school, classroom volunteers, computers and software, and the like.

The third mode of business partnership has received less attention, although it may be the most significant. Business can be an important ally in *constituting a governing coalition* with the capacity to set community goals, allocate resources, and sustain initiatives over time. As Stone has argued, "public officials can govern *with* the grain of business cooperation but cannot govern very effectively against that grain."[1] As we noted in chapter 1, illustrations of public officials successfully working productively with corporate leaders to define and pursue a common agenda are most apparent in the area of local economic development. Business leaders have often joined hands with elected officials to build political support and raise financial backing for high visibility projects—convention centers, sports stadiums, and the like—that some consider critical catalysts to the revitalization of aging downtown areas.[2]

Often, as in the first two epigraphs at the chapter opening, the business community itself has been most vocal in declaring that the private sector can and should play a leadership role. Groups like the Business Roundtable, the National Alliance of Business, the Committee for Economic Development, and the U.S. Chamber of Commerce have recommended that business and schools ally in pursuit of a common agenda of education reform.[3]

---

[1] Clarence Stone, *Regime Politics* (Lawrence: University Press of Kansas, 1989), 196

[2] For generally enthusiastic accounts, see, for example, Scott Fosler and Renee Berger, eds., *Public-Private Partnerships in American Cities* (Lexington, MA: Lexington Books, 1982), and Harvey Brooks, Lance Lieberman, and Connie S. Schelling, eds., *Public-Private Partnerships: New Opportunities for Meeting Social Needs* (Cambridge, MA: Ballinger Publishing Co., 1984). For a more critical reading, see, for example, Susan S. Fainstein, *The City Builders: Property, Politics, and Planning in London and New York* (Cambridge, MA: Blackwell, 1994).

[3] See, for example, Rochelle L. Stanfield, "School Business," *National Journal*, 27 July 1991, 14. A Spring 1990 special issue of *Fortune* was devoted entirely to the issue of business involvement in school reform.

Several cities in the eleven-city study of Civic Capacity and Urban Education have been celebrated as national leaders in this movement toward public-private partnerships in education reform. The Boston Compact, in which
business leaders signed a formal agreement to increase their hiring of local
public school graduates in return for promises by school officials to reduce
drop-out rates and increase academic standards, has been hailed as "a national success story that annually attracts scores of visitors seeking to find
out how to begin similar ventures in their own cities."[4] Business leaders
in the Pittsburgh area, through the Allegheny Conference on Community
Development, were among the first to self-consciously shift their policy focus
from a solely bricks-and-mortar approach to urban redevelopment to a plan
that includes public education and other social issues. As part of a broader
coalition, this business effort has demonstrated some notable successes.[5]

Yet, as the last two epigraphs underscore, translating high hopes and good
intentions into working collaborations has proven far more elusive than most
school reformers expected. In each of our case cities, some business and
political leaders sought to emulate the Pittsburgh and Boston examples; their
efforts, however sincere and well intentioned, have been tentative, halting,
and generally short-lived. This chapter shows why business involvement is
difficult to sustain.

Part of the problem, we argue, has almost nothing to do with race at all.
In their eagerness to counter a prevailing sense of fatalism and despair, proponents of urban school reform have been too quick to assume a unitary
interest linking the fates of businesses and other urban actors and too quick
to presume that successful collaborations in the arena of economic development can readily be translated into the murkier world of social and educational reform. The business community's stake in quality public education is
more indirect and long-term than its stake in downtown development, and
the cultural gap between business leaders and public educators is wider than
that separating them from their counterparts in local economic development
agencies.

Race, however, makes a tough job even tougher. Blacks now hold most
key public policy positions within the general local government and school

[4] Eleanor Farrar and Anthony Cipollone, "After the Signing: The Boston Compact 1982 to
1985," in *American Business and the Public School: Case Studies of Corporate Involvement in
Public Education*, ed. Marsha Levine and Roberta Trachtman (New York: Teachers College
Press, 1988), 89–120.

[5] Valerie S. Lies and David Bergholz, "The Public Education Fund," in *American Business
and the Public School*, 77–80. For a detailed analysis of Boston and Pittsburgh, that contrasts
their relative successes with the far more limited role of business in St. Louis, see John Portz,
Robin Jones, and Lana Stein, *Urban Education and Civic Capacity in Pittsburgh, Boston and
St. Louis* (forthcoming).

systems in Atlanta, Baltimore, Detroit, and D.C., but the major positions within the corporate community continue to be occupied by whites. One scenario that we introduced in chapter 1 predicts that this racial cleavage will necessarily dominate local politics and make cross-sector collaboration all but impossible. According to this perspective, race is the interest that trumps all others. This view projects a volatile and unpredictable arrangement in which business-based reformers are vulnerable to isolation and attack. Wary of being tagged as white "colonialists" or profit-maximizing exploiters, business may be reticent to become involved in any leadership role. If business does take an aggressive role, opponents may use the issues of race, jobs, and ideology to rally a corps of opposition that is too broad and too intense for elected leaders to stand up to.

Our findings suggest a more complex reality, one that supports a more skeptical view than most proponents of public-private partnerships offer, but that holds out a bit more hope than a stark racial cleavage model. Shared interests in the economic well-being of the city provide real and important contact points. Among the black elites in the political arena and the white elites in the economic arena, we find evidence that some historical and social barriers to cross-race cooperation are losing their edge. Perceptions of the nature of the educational challenge do not differ dramatically, and black leaders and activists are surprisingly supportive of the notion that business should play a leadership role. Yet, in several ways that we detail, race continues to affect perceptions, calculations, loyalties, and concerns in ways that tug at the thread of collaboration and erode civic capacity to undertake meaningful and sustained reform.

BUSINESS-SCHOOL PARTNERSHIPS: THE RALLYING CRY

The notion that business might take an active role in support of public education is nothing new.[6] But business involvement has been episodic. The 1960s and 1970s witnessed something of a lull in visible business involvement, at least in the larger and older central cities. A combination of sharply changing demographics, broad economic restructuring, and volatile issues involving desegregation and race made many business leaders uncertain of their stake in the cities and wary of stepping into a political hornets' nest.

Calls for reasserting corporate leadership intensified in the 1980s.[7] To some extent this reflected a crystallization of a national sense of crisis in

[6] See, for example, Samuel Bowles and Herbert Gintis, *Schooling in Capitalist America*, (New York: Basic Books, 1976); Ira Katznelson and Margaret Weir, *Schooling for All* (New York: Basic Books, 1985); Joel Spring, *Education and the Rise of the Corporate State* (Boston: Beacon Press, 1972).

[7] Michael Timpane, "Business Has Rediscovered the Public Schools," *Phi Delta Kappan* 65 (February 1984): 389–92.

American education following the publication of the report of the National Commission on Excellence in Education and its infamous warning that the "educational foundations of our society are presently being eroded by a rising tide of mediocrity that threatens our very future as a Nation and a people."[8] To some extent, the message reflected the Reagan administration's emphasis on the limits of government and the importance of private initiatives, voluntarism, and self-help.[9] According to a White House survey, the number of partnerships between individual schools and private organizations of one type or another increased from 40,000 to 140,000 between 1983 and 1988; about 60 percent of the partnerships involved business corporations.[10]

Dire characterizations of existing crisis paradoxically have been linked to high levels of optimism about the potential for quick and dramatic gains if business becomes engaged. Problem-definitions and priorities are presumed clear and shared by all well-meaning actors. Solutions are presented as if they are readily at-hand; problems melt when confronted by corporate resources and technical expertise. The task is simple: business people must roll up their sleeves, and educators must let them do their thing. Even the titles signal the optimism of some of these accounts:

"Solving Educational Problems Through Partnerships"[11]
"Schools and Business: Partners for Reform"[12]
"What the Boardroom Has to Offer the Schoolroom,"[13]
"Business and Schools: A Dynamic Duo"[14]
"Grab Your Partner"[15]
"How Business Helps the Schools"[16]
"Business Bites the Education Apple!"[17]
"How Business Can Help the Schools"[18]

[8] The National Commission on Excellence in Education, *A Nation At Risk: The Imperative for Educational Reform* (Washington, D.C.: April 1983), 5.

[9] Renee Berger, "Private-Sector Initiatives in the Reagan Era: New Actors Rework and Old Theme," in *The Reagan Presidency and the Governing of America*, ed. Lester M. Salamon and Michael S. Lund (Washington, D.C.: Urban Institute, 1984), 185.

[10] Rose G. Foltz, "Big Business Is Backing You," *Learning* (February 1990): 65.

[11] Alice McDonald, "Solving Educational Problems Through Partnerships" *Phi Delta Kappan* 67 (June 1986): 752–53.

[12] Donald M. Clark, "Schools and Business: Partners for Reform" *Education Digest* 53 (December 1987): 23–25.

[13] Ellen Flax, "What the Boardroom Has to Offer the Schoolroom," *Working Woman* 14 (December 1989): 26–28.

[14] John C. Rennie, "Business and Schools: A Dynamic Duo," *Personnel* 66 (November 1989): 40–44.

[15] John LeBaron, "Grab Your Partner," *Electronic Learning* 10 (September 1990): 18.

[16] Joel Keehn, "How Business Helps the Schools," *Fortune*, 21 October 1991, 161–80.

[17] Nicole Achs, "Business Bites the Education Apple!" *American City & County* 106 (May 1991): 42–46.

[18] Nancy Ramsey, "How Business Can Help the Schools," *Fortune*, 16 November 1992, 147.

"Business and Schools Helping Each Other"[19]
"Business-Education Partnerships Take Off"[20]
"Schooling, Business, and the New American Dream"[21]
"School-Business Partnerships: A Win-Win Proposition."[22]

There are, however, at least three ways in which the literature on business-school partnerships may be overly naive in its optimistic projections. First, by emphasizing consensual goals, such accounts risk underestimating potential points of contention where the interests, norms, and perspectives of public and private actors do not so neatly align. Second, by highlighting anecdotes of successful collaboration, such accounts risk overselling the benefits of partnerships and thereby setting the stage for frustration and disillusionment. Third, by de-emphasizing the extent to which corporate interests up the ante when they move from providing support to reshaping governance, such accounts may fail to recognize the potential for political backlash from those who see such an incursion as a threat to democratic institutions and processes as well as from those seeking to protect their own privileged access.

Emphasizing Shared Goals

Many of those calling for public-private partnerships in education presume that businesses, elected local officials, educators, and citizens are coming to recognize that they have a shared stake in making central-city schools more effective and efficient. They suggest two reasons for business rallying to the support of central-city schools. First, even though corporate leaders may meet their own children's schooling needs by moving to the suburbs or withdrawing into private schools, they continue to depend on the central-city school systems to provide them with entry-level workers who have the requisite skills, knowledge, and discipline. Second, business leaders are presumed to be concerned about the potential for poor schools to undermine the general reputation of the metropolitan area; a poor reputation might make it harder to attract or relocate upper-level employees, reflect badly on corporate image, and to make it less likely that the local economy will thrive.[23]

---

[19] Julie Hutchinson, "Business and Schools Helping Each Other," *Colorado Business Magazine*, December 1992, 38–40.

[20] Joseph J. Krautheim and Anne T. Walsh, "Business-Education Partnerships Take Off," *Vocational Education Journal* 67 (January 1992): 24–27.

[21] Phillip C. Schlechty, "Schooling, Business, and the New American Dream," *Business Horizons* 36 (September 1993): 3–8.

[22] Paula Blake and Scott Pfeifer, "School-Business Partnerships: A Win-Win Proposition," *NAASP Bulletin* 77 (September 1993): 28–32.

[23] See, for example, David A. Zacchei and Jill A. Mirman, with others, *Business-Education Partnerships: Strategies for School Improvement* (Andover, MA: Regional Laboratory for Educa-

Similarly, partnership proponents imagine that school officials and local politicians, who in other days and situations might have resented and resisted business involvement, possess a newly emergent appreciation for the potential for business to help them meet public needs in these tight fiscal times. As one article puts it: "Schools need help. Business is in a position to provide that help."[24]

Emphasizing Success Stories

The literature is sparkled with success stories. *Fortune* magazine, for instance, describes a Fannie Mae program at D.C.'s Woodson High, in which employees serve as mentors to promising youngsters, and the corporation ensures that the students get summer jobs and support for college tuition. "Since its inception 18 months ago," the article reports, the program "has boosted the number of A and B students at [Woodson] from 33 to 130."[25] Coca Cola's similar program in San Antonio is said to have reduced the dropout rate among a high-risk group of low-income seventh and eighth graders from 95 percent to less than 5 percent.[26] "Everyone has come out ahead," the article proclaims.

The U.S. Department of Education, in the mid-1980s, sponsored publications intended to showcase examples of successful partnerships from different regions of the country. One publication, for example, includes descriptions of fourteen partnerships from New York State and New England, all of which "are noteworthy because they have achieved a high level of collaborative planning and resource sharing. They conduct a variety of activities aimed at strengthening the capacity of schools to provide students with meaningful educational experiences. They recognize the positive role that the private sector can play in preparing students for life out of school. And they strive to involve the community at-large in educating students for productive lives."[27] Many case descriptions make claims about successful impact on student outcomes as well.

Thomas Toch identifies business involvement as one of three keys to the emergence of an educational excellence movement in the 1980s.[28] Toch

---

tional Improvement of the Northeast & Islands [sponsored by the Office of Educational Research and Improvement, U.S. Department of Education] 1986), 6; Janean G. Gilbert, "Education is Everybody's Business," *Educational Leadership* 40 (November 1982): 8–11.

[24] Kathleen Sylvester, "The Strange Romance of Business and the Schools," *Governing* (April 1991), 66.

[25] Brian Dumaine, "Making Education Work," *Fortune* [special issue] 121 (Spring 1990): 13.

[26] Ibid., 14.

[27] Zacchei and Mirman, *Business-Education Partnerships*, 34.

[28] Thomas Toch, *In the Name of Excellence* (New York: Oxford University Press, 1991), 20–22. The other two were support from the nation's governors and presidential politics.

singles out for attention corporate programs to reward students with a promise of jobs in return for good school attendance and grades, in Boston, Oak-
land, New Haven, Baltimore, and Dallas. He notes education foundations
formed by BankAmerica in 1983 and Metropolitan Life Insurance Company
in 1985 and emphasizes the fact that "scores of businesses [have] established
'partnership' and adopt-a-school' relationships with individual schools, sup-
plying them with resources ranging from tutors to lab equipment."[29] He
places just as much emphasis on a political partnership that led business
interests to lend their weight to public educators' call for greater funding.
"When chambers of commerce and leading corporate executives came out
in favor of increased appropriations and tax hikes for education, the opposition of their budget-minded allies on city councils and in the state legislatures began to dissipate."[30]

From Supporting Schools to Restructuring Governance

Somewhat anomalously, the literature on public-private partnerships in education jumps from stories of dramatic successes to business complaints about
how slow and difficult it is to bring about "real" change. "I see a lot of [busi-
ness] programs going on in the schools, and I don't see anyone saying the
schools are doing great," says the president of a foundation established by a
large corporation to stimulate school reform.[31] "Unfortunately, most business
activities on behalf of education reform during the middle to late 1980s can
only be described as cosmetic, not radical surgery; and with each passing
year, the health of American education continues to deteriorate," bemoans
a Cato Institute report.[32] "We have spent tens of millions dollars," notes a
Chicago businessman about reform efforts in that city, "yet despite this almost heroic effort, both public and private, Chicago's 410,000 school children remain short-changed by the city's poor and deteriorating public education system. The schools are not improving."[33] When *Fortune* polled Fortune
500 and Service 500 companies in 1990, 98 percent claimed that they were
making some contribution to education, but only 6 percent felt corporate

---

[29] Ibid., 22.

[30] Ibid., 21.

[31] Thomas Donahue, president of the Pacific Telesis Group foundation. Quoted in Gary
Putka, "Learning Curve: Lacking Good Results, Corporations Rethink Aid to Public Schools,"
Wall Street Journal, 27 June 1989, A1.

[32] John Hood, "When Business 'Adopts' Schools: Spare the Rod, Spoil the Child." *Policy
Analysis* (a publication of the Cato Institute), 153 (5 June 1991): 52

[33] Vernon R. Loucks, Jr., "The Failing Business Drive in Education R&D," *Stanford Law &
Policy Review* (Winter 1992/93).

involvement was making a big difference, and 55 percent indicated they felt it had little or no impact at all.[34]

Reflecting on the failure of public-private partnerships of the adopt-a-school mode to generate broad change, business leaders and some educators have begun to argue that corporate involvement must be far more proactive and more forceful. Business, they say, needs to move—beyond a focus on individual schools to a focus on systemic change, from facilitating incremental reform to forcing for radical change, and beyond a stance of passive support of public educators to an aggressive leadership role. "Adopting schools and buying chic uniforms for school bands and school basketball teams made some local people happy," reflects one business spokesman for a more radical approach, "but business leaders began to realize that they did nothing for true educational reform."[35] "Unless there are fundamental reforms going on," says another, "we're convinced there will be little long-term good."[36]

This transition, from the role of generous uncle with deep pockets—a role in which business lets public leaders continue to set the goals and lets educators continue to choose the means—to a role that envisions private actors from the business community taking a seat alongside elected officials at the policy-making table, typically has been treated as natural, incremental, pragmatic, and unobjectionable. According to *Governing* magazine, business response "to the slow progress of educational change in the 1980s has not been to withdraw but to plunge in deeper. There is almost no one who says this is a bad idea."[37]

SOME CAUTIONARY NOTES

Urban scholars began paying attention to public-private partnerships in addressing the problems of large central cities well before the burst of attention on education partnerships. As we pointed out in chapter 1, reports of successful development-oriented partnerships have bolstered the optimistic projections for education partnerships. But a more careful look at the urban development literature suggests that the process of building and sustaining partnerships may be more problematic than typically acknowledged—even in an area, like economic development, where the common stake linking

[34] Susan E. Kuhn, "How Business Helps Schools," *Fortune* [special issue] 121 (Spring 1990), 1.

[35] Preston Townley, "Business and Education Reform: Lots of Action . . . Any Impact?" *Vital Speeches of the Day*, 1 April 1989, 355, quoted in Hood, "When Business 'Adopts' Schools," 5.

[36] Thomas Donahue, president of the Pacific Telesis Group foundation, quoted in Gary Putka, "Learning Curve," 1.

[37] Sylvester, "The Strange Romance of Business and the Schools," 66.

private actors and public leaders is especially apparent and the special expertise of business especially apropos.[38]

As noted by Marc Levine, the literature on public-private partnerships in
urban redevelopment falls into two groups. "The studies in one group,
chiefly written by economic development practitioners, begin with the
premise that public-private partnerships are an indispensable tool of urban
revitalization."[39] Their methodology tends to be anecdotal and descriptive,
and their research tends to assume—rather than empirically test—the presumption that partnerships generate public benefits. These studies have had
the greatest influence on the education partnership literature, which echoes
them in style and tone.

A second group of studies, frequently undertaken by urban political econ-
omists, is more instructive about the potential for conflicting interests among
the relevant actors and more sensitive to the dangers that might follow from
an uncritical pursuit of public-private partnerships. Even in cities noted for
cooperative development endeavors, the interests of corporate actors and at
least some sectors of the broader community do not neatly align. Business
leaders, it appears, are more likely to define the development problem in
terms of physical infrastructure, while community activists and some of their
elected officials define it more in terms of social services and financial support. Shearer refers to the typical business perspective as an " 'edifice complex,' which equates progress with the construction of high-rise office towers,
sports stadiums, convention centers, and cultural megapalaces, but ignores
the basic needs of most city residents."[40] Another point of contention involves
the spatial distribution of reinvestment activities, with neighborhood activists charging that redevelopment partnerships overemphasize the downtown
central business district at their expense. Moreover, because public-private
partnership arrangements are seen by some analysts as establishing
"shadow" governments in which business's bricks-and-mortar, downtown-
centered perspective is given privileged status, this more critical group of
studies emphasizes the potential threat that partnerships may represent to
norms and institutions of democratic governance.[41]

Considered in this light, some of the gushing celebrations of business-
school partnerships may warrant a more skeptical reappraisal. Is it true that

---

[38] Paul Peterson, *City Limits* (Chicago: University of Chicago Press, 1981).

[39] Marc V. Levine, "The Politics of Partnership: Urban Redevelopment Since 1945," in *Unequal Partnerships: The Political Economy of Urban Redevelopment in Postwar America*, ed.,
Gregory D. Squires (New Brunswick: Rutgers University Press, 1989), 13.

[40] Derek Shearer, "In Search of Equal Partnerships: Prospects for Progressive Urban Policy
in the 1990s," in *Unequal Partnerships*, 289–307.

[41] Ibid., 13; Clarence N. Stone and Heywood Sanders, ed. *The Politics of Urban Development*
(Lawrence: University Press of Kansas, 1987); Norman I. Fainstein and Susan S. Fainstein,
Restructuring the City: The Political Economy of Urban Redevelopment (New York: Longman,
1983); Susan S. Fainstein, *The City Builders* (Cambridge, MA: Blackwell, 1994).

business and local public leaders share a common stake in central-city schools and a common vision for bringing about education reform? The growing suburbanization of America's businesses, the increasing attractiveness of cheap foreign labor for the kinds of tasks that in earlier decades were the province of lower-skilled products on inner-city public schools, and the gradual obsolescence of the home-grown, locally owned and locally loyal business with a long-standing commitment to the civic weal, raise the possibility that the tether linking the fate of business and central-city schools may be strained and frayed.

There is reason, too, to be wary of claims that business-school partnerships are as robust and successful as is sometimes claimed. "The inference to be drawn from the literature on successful partnerships," as Joy has noted, "is that collaboration is desirable and possible in all sites." Yet, "few studies have undertaken any systematic evaluation to document the outcomes of the projects."[42] Joy's analysis of education partnerships in ten cities discovered that many involved only sporadic interaction between business and educators, were limited in scope, and failed to move beyond an incrementalist and largely symbolic agenda. Existing public-private partnerships in education typically do not involve business in an active role in setting policy directions, and only rarely do they evolve into systemwide arrangements or draw corporate leaders into broader debates about the priority and direction that should be set for local school policy.[43] For example, while 78 percent of the 305 large businesses responding to a *Fortune* survey indicate they contribute money to support public education, only 22 percent indicate they lobby legislatures for reform and only 18 percent support tax increases or bond issues.[44]

Almost without exception, the literature on public-private-partnerships in education fails to revisit programs to determine whether short-term enthusiasms stand the test of time. A Hawthorne Effect phenomenon is common with policy innovations, in education and other fields as well: bursts of success in the early years of an innovation can be followed by regression once the sense of mission and the stimulation of change begin to wane. Claims of success typically are based on the enthusiasm of participants, rather than measurable gains in student achievement. For example, indicators of success cited for the fourteen partnerships in New York and New England, mentioned earlier, included: "the first graduate of the program became employed in a local restaurant," "increased business support," "parents and students expressed regret at the end of their involvement," "partners report a high

[42] Myra Ficklen Joy, *Public-Private Partnerships in Education: A Study in Implementation* (Ph.D. diss., George Washington University, January 1990), 6.

[43] See, for example, Gary Putka, "Lacking Good Results, Corporations Rethink Aid to Public Schools," *Wall Street Journal*, 27 June 1989, 1. Donald M. Clark, "Has Business Flunked Out on Education Reform?" *Business and Society Review* 46 (Summer 1990): 15–19.

[44] Susan E. Kahn, "How Business Helps Schools," *Fortune* [special issue] 121 (Spring 1990): 91.

degree of satisfaction," "the program has been successful in that the level of participation has increased." D.C.'s Woodson High, which was cited as a glowing success in the 1990 *Fortune* article, subsequently experienced an erratic pattern in test scores. Eleventh graders' math scores on the Comprehensive Test of Basic Skills (the primary standardized test employed by the D.C. Public Schools) rose from the 40th percentile to the 42nd between 1986 and 1992, but reading scores fell from 38th to the 31st percentile over the same period.[45]

Finally, there are good reasons to be wary of the tendency in the education literature to draw sustenance from stories of successful collaborations in the redevelopment arena. As we noted in chapter 1, business-public cooperation may be more difficult in issues like urban education, where the corporate stake is more diffuse, where business expertise is less relevant, where measurable success may be more elusive and long-term, and where polarizing issues of race and ideology are more likely to intrude.

BUSINESS AND SCHOOL REFORM IN BLACK-LED CITIES

By comparing Atlanta, Baltimore, Detroit, and Washington, D.C., to the other seven cities in the Civic Capacity project, we can provide some preliminary answers to these questions: How prominent a role is business playing in local decision making in general and in educational decision making in particular? Does the high level of need in black-led cities prompt a proportional business response, or have shifting demographic trends and racial tensions caused business to take a more hands-off role? To the extent that business *is* involved, does it bring a unique set of perceptions and values that places it at odds with other key actors in black-led cities? For example, are respondents from the business and economic development communities more critical of the public schools' efforts? Are they more likely to emphasize problems tied to workforce preparation and less likely think of schools as a vehicle for addressing broader social problems or as a means of nurturing self-esteem in a disadvantaged population? Do white and black respondents differ markedly in their perception of the legitimacy of corporate involvement in educational decision making?

Corporate Response to Racial Transition

Business leaders in all four cities fairly quickly recognized the significance and irreversibility of the racial shift in political control and pragmatically

---

[45] DCPS data compiled by WESTAT Corporation under contract to the U.S. Department of Education.

sought to adjust. This adjustment included the adoption of a low-key, low-visibility role in seeking to influence public policy through quiet lobbying and selective financial support of emerging black candidates. Throughout the 1970s and early 1980s, the business community returned to a more traditional focus on issues tied to economic development and downtown revitalization. But, by the early 1990s, public education reform had become prominent on the business agenda.[46]

Atlanta was unusual in the openness with which business adopted a early hands-off policy toward education. Business had long exercised substantial informal power through its organizational arm, Central Atlanta Progress (CAP),[47] but as the racial composition of the city shifted, business leaders gradually shifted away from civic issues and focused on issues more narrowly concerned with economic development. This position was formalized in the Atlanta Compromise, in which local black leaders agreed to back away from their push for massive, mandatory school busing, in return for which, the settlement "required that the board of education appoint a black superintendent . . . and it reserved 50 percent of all administrative posts in the system for blacks."[48] As summarized by Pierannunzi and others, "Facing enforced busing or white flight, business leaders and black citizens agreed that suburban schools would be excluded from all future busing proposals, and that control of the schools system, its financial matters and curriculum would be taken over by the black community."[49]

Over the ensuing fifteen years, the school board operated without much attention from either the mayor and council or the business community. Following the Atlanta Compromise, according to a member of school board, "the general leaders in the community walked away from education for twenty years. . . . The general civic and business leaders just decided to walk away from it, so it was left to the employee organizations." A city official interviewed for this study noted that business leaders would speak of school policy as "none of our business." According to Joe Martin, a businessman

[46] The following discussion relies heavily on the following second year reports to the Civic Capacity and Urban Education Project, 1994: Carol Pierannunzi, Desiree Pedescleaux, and John D. Hutcheson, "From Conflict to Coalition: The Evolution of Education Reform in Atlanta"; Richard Hula, Richard Jelier, and Mark Schnauer, "The Politics of School Reform in Detroit"; Marion Orr, "Urban Politics and School Reform: The Case of Baltimore"; Jeffrey R. Henig "Civic Capacity and Urban Education in Washington, D.C." Other sources include Stone, *Regime Politics*; Richard Hula, Richard Jelier, and Mark Schnauer, "Making Educational Reform" (paper presented at the annual meeting of the Urban Affairs Association 3–6 May 1995, Portland, OR); Marion Orr, "Urban Regimes and Human Capital Policies: A Study of Baltimore," *Journal of Urban Affairs* 14 (1992): 173–87; Marion Orr, "Urban Politics and School Reform: The Case of Baltimore," *Urban Affairs Review* 31, no. 3 (January 1996): 314–45.

[47] See Stone, *Regime Politics*.

[48] David N. Plank and Marcia Turner, "Changing Patterns in Black School Politics: Atlanta, 1872–1973," *American Journal of Education* 95, no. 4 (August 1987): 600.

[49] Pierannunzi et al., "From Conflict to Coalition," 11.

and former president of CAP who served on the board during much of this period, business involvement remained disappointingly limited at least into the 1990s. "It has always puzzled me why business is not more interested. During the time I've been on the board of education [sixteen years], until about 6 months ago, there was never any business leader who appeared before the board on any issue." Some of this business disengagement may be attributable to structural changes in the local business community. As Newman observes, "Large corporations were leaving the downtown area in a process of disinvestment which gathered momentum after 1988. Corporate acquisitions and mergers resulted in a loss of commitment to the downtown area. . . . These relocations combined with a leadership vacuum as the long-time Executive Director of Central Atlanta Progress stepped down."[50]

In 1993, however, prompted in part by embarrassing reports of school system corruption and waste, business took a more prominent role in a reform coalition. The Chamber of Commerce created a political action committee—EDUPAC—and helped oust some long-term board incumbents who were seen as obstructionists. It also helped to establish the Atlanta Committee for Public Education, which has attempted to serve simultaneously as a source of additional support and a friendly critic.[51]

Baltimore's corporate involvement in civic affairs is centered in the Greater Baltimore Committee (GBC), which was formed in 1955. GBC played a major role in supporting the highly visible Inner Harbor redevelopment, but its involvement in the public schools "has been sporadic."[52] Although this arrangement was less formal and explicit than the Atlanta Compromise, a GBC official admits that by the mid-1970s, the business community "abandoned the school system and gave it to a segment of the black community."[53]

Slightly earlier than in the other three black-led cities, the Baltimore business community began to reinvolve itself in the schools on a systemwide basis in the early 1980s. In 1982, the GBC performed a management study; the next year, it came out in support of school-based budgeting and hired a staffperson as a liaison to the school community. Baltimore's early adopt-a-school program linked particular business firms with individual schools and provided a way for the business community "to get involved in the schools [without] commit[ing] too much energy." Lacking clear program, the program had limited impact and "amounted to little more than a few factory

[50] Harvey K. Newman, "Black Clergy and Urban Regimes: The Role of Atlanta's Concerned Black Clergy," *Journal of Urban Affairs* 16 (1994): 23–33.
[51] Gail Hagans, "New Atlanta School Board Gets High Marks," *Atlanta Journal and Constitution*, 30 January 1995, B4.
[52] Orr, "Urban Politics and School Reform," 327.
[53] Orr, "Urban Regimes and Human Capital Policies," 178.

tours for school children."[54] The adopt-a-school program was upgraded to the "Partnership Program" during the 1980s at the request of then Superintendent Pinderhughes. This reconstituted program eliminated the need to work with the BCPS bureaucracy and allowed businesses to interact with individual schools directly. According to DiConti, the businesses that participated made commitments to provide not only materials, supplies, and computers to the schools with which they worked but also mentor and scholarship programs. "Most important, however, the Partnership program began a movement towards providing school based services in the city's schools rather than programs sponsored and overseen by the school system's central bureaucracy."[55]

In 1987, as we related earlier, GBC joined with BUILD to launch the Baltimore Commonwealth. Modeled after the Boston Compact, Baltimore's Commonwealth included guaranteed job interviews or college scholarships for students with 95 percent attendance in their junior and senior years. And in the early 1990s it was a supporter of the school district's experiment with privatization and a partner in establishing a management academy designed to train principals in budgeting and management techniques.[56] While its involvement was early and substantial, GBC often has played a background role, leaving the public leadership role occasionally to BUILD, more often to the Abell Foundation and to Mayor Schmoke, who has made education reform a central theme of his administrations.

In Baltimore, the most active foundation is the Abell Foundation. The foundation is the legacy of the A. S. Abell Company, which for a century and a half owned the Baltimore *Sun* and *Evening Sun* papers. Abell, one of the few foundations that has delved into the venture capital arena, makes grants in education, health and human services, arts and culture, conservation, economic development. "No other organization," writes one local observer, "has nearly the same impact or influence as the Abell Foundation."[57]

Abell, one of Maryland's largest foundations, with assets of over $150 million,[58] focuses the bulk of its resources on Baltimore. As a result, it has become an enormous force in the community, particularly in education reform. For example, between 1989 and 1993, more than 40 percent of Abell grant dollars went to education-related projects. The vast majority of these expenditures—80 percent—went to education programs and projects in Baltimore.[59] As a school administrator put it, "The Abell Foundation has millions

---

[54] Ibid., 127.

[55] Ibid., 129–39.

[56] Orr, "Urban Politics and School Reform," 327–28.

[57] Alex Friend, "The Kingdom and the Power: Inside the Abell Foundation," *Warfield's Business Record*, 18 December 1992.

[58] Orr, "Urban Politics and School Reform," 314–45.

[59] Ibid., 330.

of dollars and money talks. When you have a financially strapped school district, and you put money some place then that money is power in terms of influencing the process of education."

Abell's interest in education and school issues in Baltimore reflects the preoccupation of its president Robert Embry. Embry is a Baltimore native and graduate of Harvard Law School. Embry has children who attend BCPS schools. He served a brief stint on the city council in the 1950s, was the city's first housing commissioner and worked at HUD during the Carter administration. A trusted and close aide to Mayor Schaefer, Embry was Baltimore's school board president in 1985–86. Embry resigned from the school board in 1986 to explore the possibility of running for mayor after Schaefer became governor. Local observers speculated that with two black candidates in the Democratic primary, Embry could win the party nomination by capturing the white vote while the other two candidates split the majority black vote. Early polls, however, showed Embry behind both candidates, even among white voters. Embry decided not to enter the race. "I felt it was not healthy for the city and not likely that I could win," he said.[60] When Schaefer became governor, he named Embry to the Maryland state board of education, where he served as president from 1990–1994.

According to a GBC official, "the Abell Foundation sees itself as a change agent and a catalyst. It's essentially rolling out ideas, and whatever sticks they will go with and what doesn't, they'll pass on and come up with a couple of new ones." The successful Barclay-Calvert program is an Abell-supported program; reportedly, Embry was influential in encouraging Mayor Schmoke to overrule his superintendent who opposed the program. The Center for Educating African-American Males at Morgan State University is a project that came to Baltimore after Embry read about a similar program in Washington, D.C. Embry alerted a state legislator who is active in education about the project, and Abell provided funding to host a fact-gathering reception for the program's founder. For three years an Abell grant totaling nearly $435,000 helped support the black-male academy.

As discussed in more detail elsewhere in this book, Embry played an influential role initiating the process that eventually led the city to contract out the operation of nine of its public schools to EAI. Embry read about EAI in a national newspaper, contacted the head of the firm, and urged Mayor Schmoke to consider hiring the firm. An Abell grant paid for a delegation of school officials and teacher union representatives to visit an EAI-operated school in Miami.

However, a number of black school administrators and community leaders complain that Embry has been determined to run the schools from his posi-

[60] Quoted in Robert Barnes, "Schmoke Tilts Scales in Baltimore," *Washinton Post*, 22 January 1987, D1.

tion as the Abell president. Alice Pinderhughes, who served as superintendent during Embry's brief stint as school board president, "was often forced to take back seat to Embry, who envisioned grand and controversial plans to combat the schools problems."[61] Pinderhughes commented on the role of the foundation in school affairs, "The big question is that people are trying to control the direction of the school system. [Bob] Embry would have loved to be superintendent or mayor of Baltimore. Now he realizes that neither are possible he is trying to do what he can."[62] A former teacher and administrator, fearful of Embry's influence in school affairs, asserted that "he is one of the ones who try to rule the city with his money. . . . He means well, I guess, as all white folks do, but he is racist. How is he racist? The kinds of decisions he makes. The kinds of decisions he makes and who he wants to be where. Have you ever seen Bob Embry take anybody black and try to help them move to a high position? No, he goes and gets these white boys and white girls out of them Ivy League schools and bring them in here and put them in charge of black folk."

Some school observers perceived that Superintendent Richard Hunter's initial decision not to approve the Barclay-Calvert proposal was an attempt to set limits on Embry's influence in school affairs. "Dr. Hunter reportedly needed to show that he would not take orders from Embry."[63] When Governor Schaefer's successor announced in 1994 that he would not reappoint Embry to another term on the state school board, the *Sun* observed that the new governor's decision was "a nod to Embry critics." The *Sun* editors went on to note that "Mr. Embry is never short of plans, advice or suggestions. This can rub people the wrong way, raising suspicions that he is determined to run the schools."[64]

Despite his critics, however, many Abell-backed programs have been successful. The collaboration of the private Calvert School with the city's Barclay School has received "widespread praise and virtually no criticism."[65] An evaluation of the experiment found that student test scores have increased. In the fall of 1994, the Calvert collaboration was expanded to another city elementary school.

As in Atlanta and Baltimore, both the conceptual model and the institutional vehicle for business involvement in Detroit schools grew out of the experience of businesses in public-private partnerships for urban redevelopment. Detroit Renaissance, a powerful private foundation overseen by the chief executive officers of many of the city's largest corporations, historically

[61] Veronica D. DiConti, *Interest Groups and School Reform* (Lanham, MD: University Press of America, 1996), 139.
[62] Interview with Marion Orr, 4 December 1990.
[63] DiConti, *Interest Groups and Education*, 146.
[64] Editorial, "Bob Embry's Ideas," *Baltimore Sun*, 29 January 1996, 6A.
[65] Gary Gately, "The 'Calvert Way' Gets High Marks," *Baltimore Sun*, 22 January 1995, A1.

had been more interested in downtown development; another group that involved some business leaders, New Detroit, Inc., paid more attention to social issues.

But after fifteen years in which business involvement was limited to individual school-based, adopt-a-school efforts, 1988 witnessed the emergence of a two-pronged education reform strategy by the Detroit business community. The first, represented by The Detroit Compact, emerged out of a strategic planning initiative launched by Detroit Renaissance.[66] Modeled on Boston's version, the Detroit Compact guarantees scholarships or interviews for career-track jobs and helps to provide summer jobs and tutoring services to students with good attendance and academic records. Although business certainly plays a central role, other stakeholders are directly involved, including organized labor, the Detroit Federation of Teachers, Board of Education, the DPS superintendent, the State of Michigan, parents, community representatives, and higher education. Framed simply as a collaborative arrangement, business is one of many groups providing a helping hand, but, according to one member of the Chamber of Commerce, there is more at stake: "Now, a hidden agenda is to reform the Detroit Public Schools because they're obviously having to make substantial changes in the way they do things in order to be able to get kids to meet these standards and, of course, the parents are putting the pressure on the individual schools to do that because they want their kids to receive the awards. So it's kind of a multifaceted approach."

Second, businesses garnered support for a reform-oriented slate of candidates (the HOPE team) for the 1992 School Board election. After the HOPE slate had won with business support in 1988, it quickly hired a new superintendent and launched a series of initiatives, including a controversial effort to grant substantial autonomy as a selection of "empowerment schools." But the HOPE initiatives foundered, three of the original slate were defeated in 1992, and the new superintendent resigned in 1993. Public resentment of continued business support for the increasingly unpopular HOPE agenda, combined with its support for Republican Engler's school financing reforms and its subsequent opposition to a $1.5 billion capital bond referendum, left business somewhat isolated from other groups in the education reform coalition.

The District of Columbia has never had so rich, diverse, and loyal a business community as some cities have enjoyed. Its economic development has been closely tied to the growth of the federal government. Absent a traditional industrial sector, it lacks the kind of large, local corporate patrons who

---

[66] Marion Orr, "Urban Regimes and School Compacts: The Development of the Detroit Compact," *Urban Review* 25 (June 1993): 105–24; Marion Orr and Gerry Stoker, "Urban Leadership and Regimes in Detroit," *Urban Affairs Quarterly* 30 (September 1994): 48–73.

have been key partnership founders in places like Atlanta, Baltimore, and Pittsburgh; even in the area of downtown urban development, the federal government has often taken the lead.

The formation of the D.C. Committee on Public Education (COPE) in 1989 marked a new stage in the nature of the relationship between local business and the public schools. Organized by the Federal City Council, a select group of civic and corporate leaders, COPE had more than sixty members drawn from business, government, universities, and community groups.[67] COPE has served primarily as a watchdog, issuing a series of reports that measure the district's progress (and lack thereof) on a number of quantifiable dimensions of management efficiency and academic performance. But it has linked those reports to a structural reform agenda, including support for school-based decision making, public school choice, and contracting out the management of individual schools to private firms. The latter proved highly controversial, and the ensuing racially charged battle (discussed below) may have contributed to a discreet withdrawal by COPE into a less visible role.

Business As an Education Player in Black-Led Cities

As we showed in chapter 2, business is widely regarded to be a major stakeholder in general decision making and an important player in education-specific decision making in black-led cities. But business involvement is just as high in the seven comparison cities. In both types of cities, only elected leaders in the general city government or school board are anywhere nearly as likely to be mentioned as key actors in education policy. In black-led cities, business is more likely, than in the comparison cities, to share the stage with foundations and nonprofits, teacher's unions, religious leaders, and the federal government, while in the comparison cities education professionals are the major voices.

Figure 6.1 indicates that the degree of business involvement in education is generally similar across the four black-led cities; about half of all respondents mentioned business in the education arena. In Atlanta, Baltimore, and Detroit (as in the eleven cities in general) business is less likely to be men-

---

[67] Private-sector members included presidents, vice presidents, or other top level executives from the local telephone company, the *Washington Post*, one of the largest local banks, one of the largest retailers, several major real estate and law firms, and most major local universities. Public-sector members included the general manager of the local transit authority, a representative from the National Oceanic and Atmospheric Administration and NASA, and the acting assistant secretary for civil rights within the U.S. Department of Education. Community-based members included several religious leaders, and the presidents of the D.C. Congress of Parents and Teachers, the Washington Parent Group Fund, and the Washington Urban League.

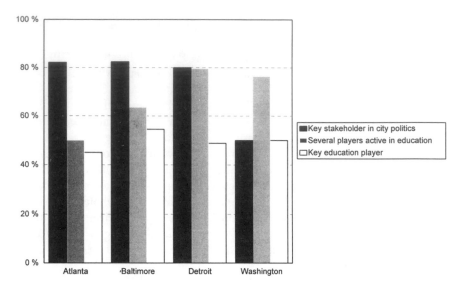

Figure 6.1 Role of business in city/education politics. Percentage of respondents identifying business as key stakeholder in city politics, agreeing that education politics has several key players, and, if they agree that education politics has several key players, seeing business as key players.

tioned relative to education decision making than it is as a general stakeholder in local politics. Because the politics and policy of human capital investment are more complex and problematic as arenas for business involvement, lower levels of involvement followed, even during this period when calls for business involvement in education neared their peak.

D.C. respondents were as likely to mention business as an education player as they were to mention business as a general stakeholder. This anomalous finding probably reflects two idiosyncracies of the D.C. case. First, as can be seen, D.C. respondents were considerably less likely to mention business as a general stakeholder, than were the respondents from the other black-led cities. Lacking a traditional manufacturing base and granting government as the "real" local industry, D.C. simply has not developed as visible and consistent a brand of local corporate leadership as can be found elsewhere. Second, this traditional thinness of local business leadership in general local politics, combines with the fact that business involvement in the schools, through COPE, was at its highest during the time the interviews were conducted. We expect that we would find business less often mentioned as an education player if we were to carry out interviews again today.

Differing Problem Definitions?

How does business involvement in educational decision making affect the prospects for coalition versus conflict? One potentially relevant factor involves the particular problem definitions that business leaders may carry with them. A growing literature within political science and public policy emphasizes that the way individuals think about the sources and mechanisms behind social problems influences the priority they put upon public action and the types of policies they are likely to favor.[68] Business leaders and locally elected leaders may agree that "an education problem" exists but disagree fundamentally about determining the seriousness of the problem or even more fundamentally identifying the problem itself.

Respondents were asked the following: "Recognizing that no city can do everything that it would like to do in education, how would you generally characterize the effort in [this jurisdiction]? Is it: (a) Doing everything that can be done, (b) Doing fairly well, (c) Falling short of what we could be doing, or (d) Not doing well at all." Figure 6.2 summarizes the responses to this question, comparing the responses of business and economic development actors to those of others.[69] Most respondents in black-led cities, despite their position, expressed dissatisfaction with the schools. There is little evidence that business leaders see the problem as more critical than do other knowledgeable and involved actors. The pattern differs slightly in the seven other cities in the Civic Capacity project: those business leaders, generally more critical than nonbusiness respondents, were roughly half as likely as others to say that the schools were doing fairly well or better.

Table 6.1, however, both suggests that business interests and other respondents do characterize education problems differently and allows that these differences in problem definition may be more sharply etched in black-led cities than others. When asked "What do you see as the major challenges in the area of children and youth, especially in education?" business respondents in black-led cities were much more likely than others to mention workforce preparation and crime as their first concerns, while nonbusiness respondents were somewhat more likely to mention students' low self-esteem, health and social problems, finances (in this case, usually referring to

[68] For example, Frank R. Baumgartner and Bryan D. Jones, *Agendas and Instability in American Politics* (Chicago: University of Chicago Press, 1993); David A. Rochefort and Roger W. Cobb, *The Politics of Problem Definition: Shaping the Policy Agenda* (Lawrence: University Press of Kansas, 1994); Bryan D. Jones, *Reconceiving Decision-Making in Democratic Politics: Attention, Choice, and Public Policy* (Chicago: University of Chicago Press, 1994).

[69] In addition to corporate officials, we coded as "business" interests members of the Chamber of Commerce, Minority Chamber of Commerce, Private Industry Council, Community Development, or Economic Development agencies or planning bodies.

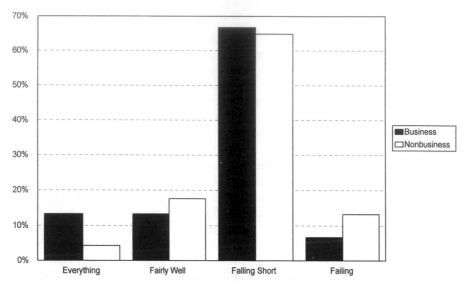

Figure 6.2 Business respondents' view of education efforts. Respondents were asked, "Recognizing that no city can do everything that it would like to do in education, how would you generally characterize the effort in City X?"

insufficient funds), and teacher quality. In the comparison cities in the Civic Capacity project, differences in the way business respondents and others characterized education problems were generally less sharply defined, although those business respondents appeared especially likely to see minority relations as a problem.

In black-led cities there appears to be a potential conflict between business and nonbusiness actors over the priority given to the schools' role as provider of basic work-related skills versus an expanded version as provider of social services and nurturer of fragile psyches. Significantly, as columns 3 and 4 indicate, the division between business members and others does *not* simply reflect a general difference between whites and blacks. Indeed, the respondent's race appears to be a nonissue in determining problem definition.

Normative Evaluations of the Role of Business

In spite of the facts that business is seen as a major player and that business respondents in black-led cities appear to carry a somewhat different view of the education problems than do nonbusiness respondents, our interviews uncovered relatively little resentment of business's substantial role. Figure 6.3 presents some illustrative comments by black nonbusiness-sector respon-

TABLE 6.1
Reported Child and Education Problems (percent)

	Black-Led Cities	Other Cities	Black-Led Cities Respondent Race		Other Cities Respondent Race		Black-Led Cities Respondent Position		Other Cities Respondent Position	
			Black	Not Black	Black	Not Black	Business	Other	Business	Other
Workforce preparation	23.9	9.6	26.4	20.8	10.1	10.6	38.9	22.4	12.1	9.1
Low self-esteem	17.4	13.9	13.6	22.2	13.0	14.0	11.1	18.2	12.1	14.4
Health and social	34.8	29.4	34.5	36.1	36.2	27.4	44.1	33.9	24.2	29.9
Crime and drugs	20.1	22.4	20.9	18.1	21.7	22.9	22.2	20.0	24.2	22.3
School board	4.9	8.9	4.5	5.6	5.8	10.6	5.6	4.8	12.1	8.7
City government	9.8	12.9	7.3	13.9	8.7	14.0	11.1	9.7	15.2	12.9
Public social services	4.9	5.9	7.3	1.4	4.3	6.1	5.6	4.8	6.1	5.7
Child care	1.1	1.7	1.8	—	1.4	2.2	—	1.2	—	1.9
Finances	34.8	36.6	35.5	33.3	29.0	38	27.8	35.2	36.4	35.6
Minority relations	8.7	18.8	9.1	8.3	20.3	17.3	5.6	9.1	27.3	17.8
Union conflict	1.1	0.7	1.8	—	2.9	—	—	1.2	3.0	0.4
School resources	10.3	6.6	13.6	5.6	14.5	5.0	—	11.5	—	7.6
Teaching quality	33.2	43.9	33.6	31.9	43.5	40.8	27.8	33.3	54.5	42.4
No problems										
Number of respondents	184	303	110	72	69	179	18	165	33	264

Source: Respondents were asked, "What do you see as the major challenges in the area of children and youth, especially in education?" The entry refers to the percentage of those interviewed who mentioned the given challenges. Because each respondent was allowed to name three challenges, column percentages add to more than 100 percent.

Positive Assessments	Critical Assessments
I think the interest of the BUSINESS community to become involved is real. I think it is deep. I think it is meaningful. I don't think it's half-hearted. (Washington: General Influential)	Where I would see negative aspects is when business and industry try behind the scenes to influence decisions so they go in their direction and that's where it would be negative. (Baltimore: General Influential)
And there is a lot of integration of leadership tasks in Atlanta. That is business people might meet and be involved with poor people, more in Atlanta, than any other city I know of. (Atlanta: General Influential)	I'm not blaming the BUSINESS community, because I'm not sure if the school system has been receptive to the business communities being taking a very strong role. So I just don't think we've found out how we need to mesh yet. That's not a damnation of either side. I guess is what I'm trying to say. It's just, we just haven't found a way to mesh. Folks are working on it, and working toward it. (Baltimore: General Influential)
I think within probably the last decade they have realized that if their businesses are going to continue and Baltimore City is going to continue, they had to give a damn and so in fact they have become significantly more involved and supportive of the school system then they had for a long time. (Baltimore: Community Activist)	Well I think it's in both the public and the private sector. You know, I don't see the BUSINESS community exercising the kind of leadership that I think is required for these times as well. It's very frightening. It's changed a great deal, and I think that there has been a lot of restructuring and changing in the business community and so you don't have you know the kind of I think coherent and you know cohesive business groups and leadership as we once had in this town. (Washington: Community Activist)
Now, when you have to get down to the nitty gritty and beyond just the top policy makers to try and implement these things, historically we don't know how to do this. I mean, our government agencies don't know how to be partners. The schools don't know how to be partners. I believe that the BUSINESS community in the past have tried pretty hard to try to partner with us. They've been successful in individuals programs and projects. I think they've found both of our systems, neither one of us know how to do this very well. So we're learning. (Washington: General Influential)	I think BUSINESS people always think they can run anything better than anybody else can. And, so, no matter what, they think that management is just this generic function ... And so they are never reluctant to kind of sort of move in and take over. (Atlanta: Community Activist)
There is the Detroit Compact, it is a wonderful program initiative that has given BUSINESS and schools that necessary link. So that kind of program I think is a wonderful example of what can be done. (Detroit: Program Specialist)	I think over the last 10 years, the studies have shown that the CHAMBER OF COMMERCE is the least involved of any chamber of any major city, that the polarization between the city and suburbs is more stringent here than any place else in the country. Clearly, something is amiss. (Detroit: General Influential)

Figure 6.3 How Black Nonbusiness Respondents View Business Involvement in Education Reform

dents in the four cities. The racial cleavage model would lead one to expect that black residents in black-led cities would exhibit sharp antagonism toward perceived "meddling" by the predominantly white business community. Some community advocates and local politicians with whom we spoke expressed deep resentment of business intervention, and in racial terms, but these were decidedly in the minority.[70] Yet among these key actors in local decision making, it was more common to encounter spontaneous assertions about the desirability and legitimacy of an active business role.

As noted in chapter 2, respondents in both black-led and comparison cities rarely mentioned city government versus business as a primary line of cleavage in education politics when asked "When there is conflict, what is its source? What groups are involved?" Table 6.2 provides a further breakdown by respondent's race and position. Business respondents are somewhat more likely than others to see a cleavage between business and local officials, but this view is no more likely in the black-led cities than in the comparison cities. That black respondents in black-led cities are somewhat more likely than white respondents to report such a cleavage might indicate resentment about the economic power and privilege that the predominantly white business elite still enjoys, but this pattern is not strong, and most black respondents see other cleavages as more central to political dynamics in Atlanta, Baltimore, Detroit, and D.C.

Across the four black-led cities, the business/local government cleavage was mentioned most frequently in Atlanta and least in Detroit (Figure 6.4). But, in all those cities, other cleavages—particularly intramural battles within local government and squabbles between interest groups—loomed much larger.

Overall, then, we find relatively little evidence of a sharp, race-related cleavage between business and local officials and relatively little resentment of business involvement among the other active groups from which we drew our respondents. This is not to say, however, that race is inconsequential to understanding the obstacles to stronger public-private education partnerships in black-led cities. Indeed, as we argue in the next section, race is an important background factor; race influences actors' comfort with various potential allies and the calculus of costs and benefits they consider when choosing between inaction and action, exit and voice.

---

[70] To be sure, respondents may have been cautious about how they expressed themselves to our interviewers, and this may mask some resentments that are deeply, but quietly, held. As we argue later, we are convinced that race plays a deeper role in structuring some perceptions and responses than many of our interviewees might want to admit. Although there may have been a reticence to openly express racially tinged resentments of business involvement, however, it does not seem likely that those harboring such resentments would mask them with the kinds of spontaneous assertions of the legitimacy and desirability of business intervention that are illustrated in the table, and that occurred with some frequency.

TABLE 6.2

Perceptions of Cleavages in Education Politics by Race and Position of Respondents (percent)

	Black-Led Cities		Other Cities		Black-Led Cities		Other Cities	
	Black Respondents	Nonblack Respondents	Black Respondents	Nonblack Respondents	Business Respondents	Nonbusiness Respondents	Business Respondents	Nonbusiness Respondents
Local government vs. business	10.9	1.9	4.3	8.0	14.3	5.8	13.3	5.2
State/federal government vs. local government/school board	12.5	20.4	8.7	6.3	7.1	17.3	6.7	6.5
Citizens vs. local government/school board	35.9	20.4	37.0	27.7	28.6	28.8	33.3	30.3
Intra-city: council/mayor vs. school board	56.3	55.6	54.3	67.9	28.6	59.6	60.0	63.9
Citizens versus Business	1.6	1.9	4.3	4.5		1.9	3.3	4.5
City versus suburbs	7.4	7.4	6.5	4.5	7.1	2.9	10.0	3.9
Ethnic conflicts	21.9	11.1	54.3	25.0	21.4	16.3	33.3	36.1
Inability of government to deal with education issues	4.7	5.6	2.2	4.5		5.8		5.2
Inability of government to deal with social issues								0.6
Lack of leadership	3.1	3.7		1.8		3.8	3.3	0.6
Unions	4.7	5.6		1.8	7.1	4.8	6.7	1.3
Interest group versus interest group	31.3	33.3	23.9	30.4	35.7	31.7	20.0	29.0
Nonrecurring conflict	9.4	11.1	2.2	5.4	21.4	8.7	3.3	3.9

Source: Respondents were asked, "When there is conflict (over education decisions), what is its source?" The entry refers to the personage of those interviewed who mentioned the given challenges. Because each respondent was allowed to name three sources, column percentages add to more than 100 percent.

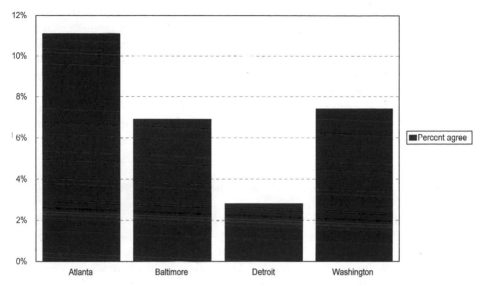

Figure 6.4 Perception that business-local government tension contributes to education conflict. Percentage of respondents claiming that tensions between business and local government caused conflict around education decisions.

RACE AS AN INHIBITING FACTOR TO BUSINESS INVOLVEMENT

Race is a complex, emotion-laden topic about which Americans do not talk easily. As a result, its impact on local politics may be elusive. Some respondents may deliberately mask their views and feelings; some may speak about it in an elliptical manner. In conducting interviews, we observed that respondents often became more wary and guarded when the discussion turned to issues of race. Sometimes we had the impression that our respondents were speaking openly and honestly about issues that they usually did not discuss; other times we suspected that our respondents were less than candid. Occasionally, respondents waited until we had turned off our tape recorders before elaborating on some issue in which race played a significant role. Our coded interviews, and even the extended transcripts themselves, therefore, almost certainly understate the impact of race to some degree.

Based on what we were told, on what was alluded to, and on patterns of interaction that we observed, we are convinced that tensions and uncertainties connected to racial differences do play a significant role in structuring political behavior in Atlanta, Baltimore, Detroit, and Washington, D.C. Their role, however, is more complicated and indirect than one accounted for by the simple racial cleavage model. Although the downtown business sector is predominantly white and the political leadership predominantly black, the active core within each sector is somewhat integrated, and almost all are accustomed to dealing with members of other racial groupings on a fairly regular basis and on fairly equal terms. As indicated in the analysis above, problem definition and orientation toward the schools are not sharply polarized along racial lines. Yet, this relatively elite core of activists—from whom most of our respondents were drawn—sense that race-related anxieties, stereotypes, and hostilities are just below the surface in the broad, usually unmobilized public, and they, therefore, avoid acting so as to trigger an eruption.

Race As a Constraint on White Business Reformers

This racial context complicates efforts to build a governance coalition around school-reform issues. Even racially progressive white business leaders frequently feel they must adopt a low-visibility stance to avoid being labeled as "neo-colonialists." Some continue to be involved in a behind-the-scenes capacity, but others shy away altogether from what they see as volatile and risky.

By anticipating that a group consisting largely of white business leaders could be tagged as narrow and unrepresentative—and therefore vulnerable to strategic attack and political marginalization by forces opposed to education reform—those who established D.C.'s COPE ensured that its membership and leadership included nonbusiness people as well as business representatives, blacks as well as whites. In spite of such self-conscious efforts to present diversity, however, the broad public perceives COPE as representing white, business interests. And sensitivity about racial perceptions frequently has intruded on COPE's strategizing about its agenda and public pronouncements. At least one member of COPE's board considered resigning because he did not like the dynamic of a group always worried that the predominatly black public would view its actions in racial terms. Race, he indicated, is "absolutely" a key dimension. Groups like the Board of Trade and the Federal City Council, he suggested, realize that "to become publicly identified with an issue is to have it defined as a 'white' proposal, and to predetermine that it winds up in the wastebasket."

In light of the racially charged rhetoric that occasionally erupts, it is not difficult to see why white business leaders might be wary about taking a public leadership role. D. F. Glover, a black social scientist, has been a vocal leader of a predominantly black clique on the Atlanta school board; Glover was among the incumbents that the Chamber of Commerce deemed obstructionist and targeted for defeat by EDUPAC. During one televised school board meeting Glover referred to fellow board member Joe Martin as a "buttoned-down racist." Martin, in another forum, observed that just because the system is predominantly black "some people think the leaders in the system should be, therefore, black. . . . That would be another form of segregation."[71]

In Detroit, the informal watchdog group that monitors board meetings occasionally heckles the white board members. During a public hearing about the district's 1994–95 strategic plan, for example, white board member and HOPE sympathizer, Penny Bailer, was called a "blue-eyed devil" for her perceived opposition to the superintendent. One policy leader from Detroit's Chamber of Commerce says the racial situation in the region "is getting worse, more polarized." Jay Silberman, a white D.C. school board member who is generally seen as an ally of COPE, found a phone machine message accusing him of yelling at black women and warning: "The very next time I hear of you hollering at a black woman, I'm going to bust you in your face. Now that's not a threat, that's an actual fact. So, if I hear about it, get ready. You don't know when I'm coming or when it's going to be."[72] Silberman and others were convinced that they recognized the voice as that of a black activist, who had vigorously opposed proposals to both close schools and introduce private management of some poor performing schools. Silberman was so unnerved by the incident that he put a baseball bat near his front door. He brought charges against the activist, but a jury found him not guilty. According to one juror, "We thought it was a personal issue. Maybe Mr. Silberman led [the black activist] to act the way he did."[73]

Although public eruptions of racial confrontation are relatively rare, when they do occur they are often traumatizing, and business reformers and their allies sometimes deliberately steer clear of issues that they expect may be interpreted in racial terms. In D.C., when the racial dimensions of the privatization issue came to the fore, reformers, including the business community, suffered an embarrassing defeat.

Smith's willingness to embrace Baltimore's model for contracting out was a response to the business community's impatience with the slow pace of change. In late 1993, more than a month before Smith announced his own proposal, a business representative indicated in an interview that several of his colleagues—looking for more extreme measures that could be pursued if the superintendent's other initiatives did not soon bear fruit—were monitoring the Baltimore situation closely.

Smith's proposal to experiment with privatization in fifteen schools was cast in racial terms by community advocates opposing the plan. They played upon grassroots resentment of the notion that "outsiders" had more knowledge or expertise than locals did; the opponents baldly linked the outsider

[71] JoAnne Donner, "We're Sitting on a Time Bomb," *Business Atlanta* 2 (March 1991), 24.
[72] Phong Ly, "D.C. Activist Cleared in Threat Case," *Washington Post*, 17 July 1996.
[73] Ibid.

vs. insider issue to the issue of white vs. black. Angry protesters disrupted several community meetings. "With 89.9 percent of the school student body African American, why should we bring in rich, white folks who don't have any credentials of education from anybody to run our schools?" one protesting parent asked.[74] A March 1994 meeting of the board turned nasty when protesters against the contracting out plan were asked to leave. "A protester pulled the tie of a school security guard, who then hit him. Other protesters quickly joined in the brawl at the back of the D.C. Board of Education boardroom."[75] At one meeting, a member of the Save Our Schools group called EAI chairman John Golle a "rich white boy."[76] Allegations were made that contracting out would allow a predominantly white business to "experiment" on predominantly black schoolchildren.

Smith's rapid retreat from a proposal that had broad support from COPE, the business community, several key council members, and at least some leadership within the leading parents' organization probably is partially attributable to his personal preference for consensus-style decision making, but it also seems to reflect a case of severe jitters brought on by the prospect of an issue that could rip away the somewhat fragile veneer of racial harmony. In the aftermath of the privatization debacle, the business community adopted an even lower profile in the local school politics arena. This experience, too, may have made the business community more inclined to work with Newt Gingrich and other conservatives in Congress, who subsequently launched their own program to impose vouchers, charters, and contracting out on the District, through the budget appropriations process.

Race is sometimes used as a political tool in Atlanta, too. Asked about which groups are particularly successful, one Atlanta respondent mentioned the teachers "because they can close votes." Teachers, who resist particular reform proposals, he continued, can deliberately play upon racial identities to broaden their support: "And there is racial convention to all of this too. And in a lot of schools their leadership is African-American and that has more of an impact. You know the business groups, and Apple Corp [a school reform group] for that matter are hindered by the sense that they are a lot of white do-gooders or else in the business establishment there are rich people who don't care about the needs of the parts of town where there are rich people." Erase the Board, a fairly broad-based Atlanta school reform group, has worked on largely parallel tracks with the Chamber of Commerce. But despite its multiracial identity, explained in chapter 3, it opted to run a broad anti-incumbent theme rather than risk racial backlash by supporting some white school board incumbents while targeting black incumbents for defeat.

[74] Sari Horwitz, "School Privatization Shelved," *Washington Post*, 4 March 1993, A1.
[75] Sari Horwitz, "D.C. School Board Meeting Is Disrupted by a Scuffle," *Washington Post*, 17 March 1993, C1.
[76] David Plotz, "School-house Rock," *Washington City Paper*, 1 November 1994, 22.

Business, which was not ready to "throw the baby out with the bath water," coupled its endorsement of a reform slate of newcomers with the selective endorsement of some incumbents, including Joe Martin, the white business-man. But, while EDUPAC did not back away from endorsing incumbents, it *did* fret that its endorsement might send a racial signal that would backfire against them in parts of the black community. As one Chamber representa-tive put it, EDUPAC did not want to be seen as a "white boys' club" trying to run the predominantly black school system, and some in the business community warned that a business endorsement could be a "kiss of death" for their candidate.[77]

In Detroit, a top business civic leader indicated frustration that race con-tinues to create what he refers to as "a dysfunctional civic infrastructure." Even in New Detroit, an organization established almost thirty years ago, after the city's riots, with the specific purpose of bridging racial divisions, blacks and whites "don't even know how to talk to one another yet, they really don't. . . . I mean, people want to collaborate but . . . under pressure we all tend to revert to the behavior we know. . . . Talking about golf, you know, if your game is under pressure, you drop back to all your old bad habits. . . . Batters do that and cooks do that actually, and my experience is that very quickly, when it gets down to the nub, people revert to their old behaviors in this community and that's a very natural struggle."

A white Detroit reformer believes that labor opponents convinced black ministers to turn against the HOPE candidates, which led in part to their subsequent defeat. "I think [for] anybody [who] really wants . . . to get a message across, really win an election . . . the ministers are a key. . . . Labor can impact the black ministers [and] that can have a powerful impact. That's, for example, when I knew we . . . going to lose the election in 1992. . . . We were not allowed to come into the churches to campaign. There is a, there is a lot of black separateness, sentiment in Detroit, you know, through what is called the Black Slate."

HOPE, he also suggests, had become too closely identified with the pre-dominantly white business community. When the Chamber of Commerce threatened to reduce its commitment to the Detroit Compact if the HOPE team was not reelected, the strategy backfired, as opponents were able to play on the racial issue to rally their troops. "Detroit Chamber a week before the election said, if the whole team is not reelected we're going to reevaluate our [support] to the school system, so the opposition immediately cried plantation politics and cut deeply into the black vote. It's hard enough when everybody is saying the same thing, but when the distortions came up and some, the unions about education it was though we were trying to do, that this was elitist, it was anti-union and it was favoring the white people, middle

---

[77] Maria Saporta, "Atlanta Chamber May Weigh in on School Elections," *Atlanta Journal and Constitution*, 24 June 1993.

class people, and you just can't be able to spend a lot of time politically to do that."

At least two strategies might mitigate the racial constraints on the business sector's involvement. First, reformers might attempt to dispell the impression that the business sector is overwhelmingly white. In all major cities there are black-owned businesses, and within the larger white-owned firms black officials are increasingly likely to hold some high-level administrative positions. Business organizations in black-led cities clearly have made efforts to recruit black members, and those black members they do have are often put (cynically, some would suggest) in particularly visible positions. In our interviews, respondents sometimes spontaneously mentioned efforts to more aggressively recruit black-owned businesses into education partnerships. But such efforts were often characterized as frustrating. Black-owned businesses tend to be much smaller and more financially marginal; their owners appear far less able to divert time and resources from the challenge of economic survival. Asked why he is not a member of the Greater Baltimore Committee, one black businessman who has been involved in partnerships with local schools, says: "Really, I don't have time. It's a very time consuming and I won't say stressful but it's a very dedicated situation that we're in trying to make these seven stores the best they can be. . . . That's what I do. . . . It takes a lot of time, a lot of dedication, a lot of effort on somebody's part to keep these seven stores running and looking the way they look on a day to day basis. So I don't really have a whole lot of time to get into that." As Table 6.3 indicates, while the total number of black-owned firms may appear large, and increasing, the proportion with paid employees is very low; about 90 percent of black-owned firms in Atlanta, Baltimore, Detroit, and the District do not have *any* paid employees, and those that do have paid employees are still very small operations.

Second, the racial constraints felt by business could be mitigated through a forceful effort by black public leaders to visibly align themselves with business and explicitly as well as implicitly to challenge the impression that education reform is a racially defined issue. Yet this appears to be less common in practice than much of the existing literature might lead us to expect.

Race As a Constraint on Black Public Leaders

The conventional literature on school-business partnerships presumes that the bond of common interest in economic growth supplants any vestigial traces of racial antagonism that might otherwise prevent black leaders from forcefully and openly allying with the white business community. This view gets additional support from the literature on black mayoral elections, some of which concludes that there is a general trend toward "deracialization" in urban politics, wherein black candidates find themselves compelled to de-

TABLE 6.3
Characteristics of Black-Owned Firms, 1987 and 1992

	Number and Character of Black-Owned Firms, 1987			
	Number	*With Paid Employees*	*Percent with Paid Employees*	*Average Number of Employees*[a]
Atlanta	3,869	672	17.4	4.8
Baltimore	5,044	666	13.2	2.8
Detroit	7,116	1,091	15.3	3.5
Washington	8,275	956	11.6	4.3

	Number and Character of Black-Owned Firms, 1992			
	Number	*With Paid Employees*	*Percent with Paid Employees*	*Average Number of Employees*[a]
Atlanta	5,762	671	11.6	4.9
Baltimore	7,542	512	6.8	4.7
Detroit	9,275	880	9.5	5.1
Washington	10,111	787	7.8	5.4

Source: U.S. Department of Commerce, Bureau of the Census, Survey of Minority Owned Business Enterprises, 1992, Table 6. U.S. Department of Commerce, Bureau of the Census, Survey of Minority Owned Business Enterprises, 1992, Table 6.

[a] For all businesses with at least one paid employee.

emphasize race-specific issues if they hope to forge a coalition broad enough to bring victory.[78] And it is also in keeping with Peterson's thesis that local elected officials, no matter their race or ideology, are compelled to focus energy and attention on policies—including education—that further the city's unitary interest in economic vitality and growth.[79]

Our own analysis, above, also provides some support for the notion that the perceptions of educational problems and priorities held by business leaders and public officials are not sharply polarized along racial lines. And our four cities provide numerous examples of black officials joining with white business leaders to work together for education reform. Why, then, do business leaders in black-led cities appear to be concerned that their efforts—if too assertive and too visible—will be labeled in racial terms? While black public officials share some common interests and perceptions with the business community, it appears that they, too, operate under constraints that limit their willingness to commit themselves fully and completely to a reform alliance with the business community.

Black officials may resist casting their lot with the business community because—in spite of the existence of some shared perceptions, some com-

[78] Huey L. Perry, "Deracialization as an Analytical Construct in American Politics," *Urban Affairs Quarterly* 27 (December 1991): 181–91.
[79] Peterson, *City Limits*.

mon stakes, and a relative comfort level in interracial endeavors—they may harbor fears that white business interests are unreliable allies. There are at least two reasons why this fear prevails. First, black leaders, having attained some power and economic success, have not left behind their fears and suspicions about white racism. To the contrary, Hochschild reports that "well-off African Americans see *more* racial discrimination than do poor blacks, see less decline in discrimination, expect less improvement in the future, and claim to have experienced more in their own lives."[80] If public officials in black-led cities harbor suspicions that white business leaders look down on them and might turn against them, they were wary about expressing it to our interviewers. What *does* sometimes emerge is a concern—not expressed in explicitly racial terms—that business will prove to be unreliable because business interest is neither deep enough nor broad enough to sustain a cooperative endeavor over the long haul, especially if collaboration requires a financial commitment or possible public political confrontation.

Even if black leaders felt confident that business reformers would make reliable allies, they might hesitate to be too closely identified out of concern that such a link could hurt them politically. Although this is a difficult matter to pin down empirically, we found some indications that the racial dimension occasionally can so dominate the definition of the school-reform issue that black elected officials worry that their alliance with corporate leaders might be used by more militant challengers to undermine their legitimacy within the African-American community. When two black members of Atlanta's school board allied with three white members to elect Joe Martin as president, for example, the (black) defeated opponent publicly charged them with believing "society's message about the inferiority of blacks and believe whites make superior leaders."

Some black politicians are better able than others to bridge the class gap within the black community. In D.C., Marion Barry can; Sharon Pratt Kelly could not. In Detroit, Coleman Young could; the book is still out on Dennis Archer. As a black former school board reformer says of Archer:

> If you've never interacted with people on the lower east side or if what I call the inner-city of the west side of Detroit you haven't touched that diversity yet and that's an area that he needs. . . . That doesn't mean he needs to go get some Joe Blow who happens to live on that part of town to be able to interact, but he's got to have somebody who has the ability to cross that line and people have respect for and people are going to be willing to set down and interact with.
> Q: Can he do that?
> A: Dennis can't do it, no.
> Q: Coleman [Young] could?
> A: Coleman could, Coleman came from here.

[80] Jennifer Hochschild, *Facing Up to the American Dream: Race, Class, and the Soul of the Nation* (Princeton: Princeton University Press, 1995), 73.

Black politicians who are perceived as too distant, too educated, too aristo-cratic, are sometimes explicitly characterized within the black community as also being too "white." In racially changing cities, such politicians fre-quently are facing white incumbents; in that context, they may be able to count on support in the broad black community based on the race alone. But, as the black majority in the electorate becomes larger, the pool of potential challengers is more likely to consist of other black politicians, some of whom may have deeper ties at the grassroots level. In that context, an incumbent who has never been able to "cross that line" may have to be concerned that efforts to build common ground with the business community (or a predomi-nantly white state legislature) might hand a weapon to an opponent.

The relevant point involves the distinction between the *electoral coalition* that a politician needs to earn and retain office and the *governance coalition* needed to get things done. Even in overwhelmingly black cities, where they do not need white votes in order to gain office, local officials who hope to marshal local resources and retain support from state and federal govern-ments face clear pressures to avoid basing their political appeals on racial grounds. But others in the black community may be less constrained about the viability of this governance coalition. Racial appeals have the potential to mobilize a normally disengaged constituency and to enable challengers to cobble together an alternative electoral coalition, sufficient to embarrass and potentially unseat an incumbent.

PARTNERSHIPS AND RACIAL POLITICS IN BLACK-LED CITIES

Much of the literature on school-business partnerships presumes that shared interests in local economic development and reputation are sufficient incen-tives to entice business to join local elected leaders and educators in a part-nership similar to the urban development regimes that have been key to downtown reinvestment in a number of major cities. This vision comports with the "deracialized development regime" perspective that we introduced in chapter 1. In contrast, the "racial cleavage model" posits that race-based loyalties and perceptions are divisive and dominant; coalitions between white business interests and black leaders are superficial and short-lived.

Some evidence presented in chapter 6 is quite compatible with the con-ventional literature. Business does appear to be a major actor in the educa-tional decision making arena in all four cities. Although some differences in problem perception distinguish business respondents from others we interviewed, these do not appear to be sharp, and there are some indications that the differences that do exist are not driven by racial differences between business "players" and others. In response to an open-ended question about underlying lines of conflict in education politics, few respondents mentioned business vs. city cleavages; in all cities, respondents were much more likely to mention intramural—and often personalized—conflicts across agencies and branches of the local government. Black respondents—community advocates, educators, and elected officials—had many positive things to say about the business role. Some expressed frustration that the business commitment was too limited or that business participants occasionally come in with a bit too much self-confidence and impatience, but relatively few either directly challenged the legitimacy of business involvement or expressed criticisms in openly racial terms.

This, however, leaves a paradox. Despite the seeming absence of openly race-based issue alignments and confrontation, the partnerships that have emerged in Atlanta, Baltimore, Detroit, and D.C. are limited in a number of respects. Business participation in anything beyond the conventional adopt-a-school mode is limited to a small proportion of unrepresentative firms; bold statements about the need for radical reform typically are followed by much more incrementalist agendas; early enthusiasms wane as progress proves slow and potential costs high.

Why—if racial cleavages in perceptions are not so sharp or openly contested as the racial cleavage model predicts—does it appear so difficult to build a sustainable and forceful education reform regime incorporating black officials and white businesses. It appears that the deracialized development regime model fails to take fully into account a number of obstacles. Some are directly related to racial tensions; probably most are not. But even those that are not directly tied to racial tensions may manifest themselves differently in black-led cities because they both weaken the incentives to overcome surmountable racial tensions and make the potential costs of trying to do so more palpable and immediate.

In many respects the partnership efforts in the four black-led cities encounter similar obstacles to those likely to be encountered in all central-city schools districts, regardless of racial and ethnic configurations. These obstacles have not, for the most part, been anticipated by the existing literature on education partnerships, which adopts a celebratory and naively optimistic tone. The selective material incentives for business to undertake broad education partnerships appear smaller and far less certain than in economic development initiatives. Many larger corporations located in the central city do not depend on graduates of the city's public schools; for administrative positions they can recruit nationally, and even for entry-level positions they increasingly attract workers from the surrounding suburbs. This is a reminder that some businesses physically located within the central cities nonetheless may psychologically have exited, as far as support of some local institutions is concerned.

Even if successfully implemented, systemic school reform is most likely to show pay-offs among younger children, who will benefit from improved education for a sustained period and who have not already been alienated by their school experience; it may take years for the benefits to be realized among high school graduates. Moreover, corporations that contribute to the reform effort are not guaranteed that they will capture benefits that do accrue. If students are turned on to education, perform well, and go off to college, they are free to take advantage of a wider, more open job market.[81] These uncertain benefits need to be judged against the direct return a firm could anticipate by devoting its resources, instead, to its own recruitment and training programs.

The observation that benefits are less clear and sure than the partnership literature implies may help to account for three otherwise puzzling findings. First, as we have noted, business leaders who are actively involved frequently complain that their fellow corporate leaders are slow to follow their lead; rather than bone-headedness, short-sightedness, or racial biases on the part of the foot-draggers, perhaps this reluctance represents a rational calculation on their part. Second, we were surprised to discover that some of the most earnest assertions that business has a stake in the cities' schools come not from white business leaders, but from black, nonbusiness respondents; it is possible that the presumed economic stake of business in the cities' public schools is at least somewhat the product of wishful thinking on the part of those who feel trapped in a deteriorating situation with a dwindling number of powerful allies.

Moreover, while the benefits may be more uncertain than acknowledged, the costs of engaging in broad education-reform partnerships may be substantially greater than those involved in development-oriented regimes. Business already has an expertise in development, but preparing itself to deal on an informed basis with education issues requires an up-front investment in learning more about the sector. Even though systemic school-reform initiatives often begin with the premise that schools currently are wasteful and inefficient, business partners often discover quickly that short-term needs for capital investment, information systems technology, teacher retraining, and severance packages imply an up-front bill that may require new taxes. Furthermore, the political costs and risks to the corporate image can be high if school reform stirs up controversial issues such as values-education, church-state separation, sex education, or other potent social issues that are frequently tied to school policies and only rarely linked to economic development concerns.

Against this backdrop, the racial dimension comes into clearer focus. The partnership issue has to be looked at from three perspectives: (1) business;

---

[81] Concern about this ability to recapture the benefits may help to explain why business— when it does participate—tends to prefer direct partnerships with individual schools and compact-type initiatives to broader systemic reform undertakings; those types of arrangements give the businesses both a direct pipeline to the most promising students and a chance to earn those students' attention and loyalty through summer jobs, apprenticeships, and the like.

(2) public leaders; and (3) potential reform opponents. For business, concerns about getting enmeshed in racial conflicts, fear of being cast as white colonialists, reservations about whether public allies will stand with them if opposition is strong might be pushed aside *if* the benefits of collaboration were clear and sure; given uncertain benefits, and other likely costs, these concerns carry greater weight. Similarly, black public officials' concern about being tagged as elitist by grassroots opponents in the African-American community—and uncertainty about the reliability of business partners whose shared-interests in helping them improve schools might be in tension with their fiscal conservatism, Republican leanings, corporate bottom line, and wariness of bad publicity—might not prove decisive *if* they were confident that improved schools would generate a stronger local economy and bolster their electoral support. But those uncertain benefits may look very speculative, especially since education reform in black-led cities—where declining enrollments and a political culture that endorses a beefy public sector have produced high ratios of administrators and teachers to pupils—usually has meant challenging public employee organizations that have been critical components of those elected officials' original constituencies.

Finally, from the standpoint of potential opponents of school reform and potential competitors for public office, exploiting the latent racial dimension of partnership efforts may be an attractive political strategy. Perry and others have explained the forces that tend to lead to a "deracialized" campaign environment in newly "minority majority" central cities where black politicians are struggling to establish viable citywide coalitions. But these forces may be less relevant in black-led cities where the momentum of demographic change makes it more conceivable that a black candidate could mount a strong challenge by emphasizing race as a defining issue. This is especially the case if lower-income residents, traditionally undermobilized, prove responsive to such campaigns; many of our respondents, believing this is likely, plan their actions accordingly.

CHAPTER SEVEN

The Role of External Actors

LOCAL DECISIONS ABOUT schools are rarely made in a vacuum, yet many analyses of school politics focus on local stakeholder groups, as if their interests, resources, and the relative balance of power among them are the sole determinants of policy. It is understandable why this tendency to think of education policy as a product of local forces emerged. Few political symbols in the United States carry the power associated with the local control of education. Schools are closely identified with the character of their local communities. Indeed, schools are sometimes taken as defining that character. Moreover, many structural reforms introduced by the early twentieth-century Progressives effectively vested authority to set school policies in the hands of education professionals and a relatively homogenous, formally nonpartisan elite, with strong interest in the local schools. Both tradition and institutions, then, historically have insulated school decision making from a wide range of influences external to the local education community. Throughout this book we have emphasized ways in which the horizontal isolation of the education community from other local stakeholders has broken down or, where it remains, become dysfunctional. In chapter 7 we focus on the vertical dimension within the federal system and consider the role of state and national politics in shaping the local school reform agenda.

In spite of traditions of local control, the ultimate formal responsibility for education rests not with local authorities at all, but with the state and, in the case of Washington, D.C., the federal government. These external authorities define the basic structure of local districts, set the limits of their authority, and provide a significant proportion of the resources used to operate schools. Important variations in the formal autonomy granted to school districts exist, as does a varying willingness of state and federal actors to directly intervene in local education appears. Of course, Washington, D.C., as a federal district, is unique. Some traditional roles of state government have been granted by Congress to Washington's city government with others exercised by the Congress itself.[1] As a result, a complex, atypical administrative struc-

---

[1] After establishing a locally elected school board in 1968, Congress generally kept an arm's length from D.C. education policy until the mid-1990s. That was still the case at the time most of the original field research for this book was carried out. Since the establishment of the financial control board in 1995, Congress has found itself drawn deeper into local school policy, including the establishment of an alternative governance structure (the appointed chief execu-

ture emerges. For each city, however, external agents are often key players in education reform.

In addition to varying from city to city, the web of federalism has taken different shapes over time. Part of the story that we tell in this chapter relates to historical changes in the sources of revenue; the local property tax, once the mainstay for funding schools, has become a more constrained and problematic source of revenue, and as state, and to a lesser degree, national funds have become more prominent parts of the funding mix, the officials allocating those funds have become more prominent players as well. More recently, however, states have become more aggressive in their mode and manner of involvement, even as their fiscal contribution to the enterprise has leveled off.

State and national initiatives in such areas as public school choice, charter schools, performance assessment, and takeovers of failing districts should not be thought of simply as autonomous, external interventions. Just as local decisions are not the product of purely local forces, we argue here that state and national programs and policies often depend upon political relationships with local actors, for both their initial impetus and their eventual implementation. Local stakeholders, particularly those who find that they lack the clout to win their battles at the school-district level, may seek to "expand the scope of conflict" by seeking external allies and moving the decision into the state or federal realm where they think they might have a better chance of success,[2] a phenomenon that Baumgartner and Jones refer to as "venue-shopping."[3] Similarly, while the dictum that "all politics is local" may be overstated, state or national officials often do need local constituencies, especially when they are undertaking visible and potentially risky initiatives. And the literature on implementing federal programs makes it very clear that local allies can be critical if top-down programs are to have any chance of success.[4] Coalition-building, in other words, does not stop at the local district line.

The challenge facing education reformers is how to restructure the local policy subsystem that sets education policy. In spite of a broad commitment to strong local control of education, some local actors in Atlanta, Baltimore, Detroit, and Washington have been willing to ally with state or federal officials to impose change. This pattern has become even more evident as the

tive officer and emergency school trustees) and the passage of legislation that initiated charter schools in the District. Because these changes are so significant, we have updated our research and discussion to include this period of intense congressional involvement.

[2] E. E. Schattschneider, *The Semisovereign People* (Hillsdale, IL: Dryden Press, 1975).

[3] See Frank R. Baumgartner and Bryan D. Jones, *Agendas and Instability in American Politics* (Chicago: University of Chicago Press, 1993), 36.

[4] Jeffrey Pressman and Aaron Wildavsky, *Implementation* (Berkeley: University of California Press, 1984).

perception grows that schools are failing in their basic mission of adequately educating children in each city.[5]

The increasingly important role of external actors is not restricted to black-led cities. As we outline in chapter 7, the growing role of the states in local school decision making has been too broad and long lasting for racial politics to suffice as an explanation. Yet, as we have seen throughout this book, race can be, and often is, an important factor even when it is not the only factor. Efforts to engage external actors in local education politics in urban areas often become entangled with issues of race, and in the case of black-led cities such entanglement is almost inevitable. Perhaps the most obvious cases of entanglement between race and external intervention involve the long-term efforts of the federal courts to dismantle the racially separate school systems that once operated in all four cities. Here race is the central issue driving an external intervention. The racial dynamics of more recent external interventions are more complex though just as real. Whenever regional, state, or federal authorities act to impose policy on local actors in black-led cities, it inevitably means that an external white elite is imposing its preference on local minority policymakers. Not surprisingly efforts of local actors to reach out to such external authorities are often perceived as an attack on local leadership. Although the political debate on education policy is almost never framed explicitly in racial terms, the fundamental role of race in structuring patterns of conflict and cooperation is seldom disregarded by any of the principals involved.

TRADITIONAL ROLES OF EXTERNAL ACTORS

The shape and dynamics of intergovernmental relations in education policy in many ways reflect the shape and dynamics of federalism itself. As with federalism more generally, relations among local school districts, states, and the national government have constitutional, fiscal, and regulatory dimensions. The twentieth century has witnessed a secular trend toward greater centralization of authority punctuated by frequent calls for decentralization; constitutional issues frame early battles, and fiscal and regulatory ties become subsequently more important.

Federal and state courts were the dominant external actors from the mid-1950s into the 1980s. In the 1950s, civil rights and other advocacy groups appealed to the federal courts to force the desegregation of the schools based

[5] Interview data gives dramatic evidence of dissatisfaction with local schools. When asked to identify major local problems, a majority of respondents in each city indicated that education was major problem. Specific percentages of respondents citing education as a major problem in their city include Atlanta 54 percent, Baltimore 64 percent, Detroit 55 percent, and Washington 55 percent.

on constitutional arguments. When black parents began to perceive schools as responsible for the educational failures of their children, they also demanded more black teachers and principals. Often their demands met strong resistance from individuals who wanted to maintain the traditional segregated system. Chapter 2 described how education politics in each city has been shaped in part by the history of judicial challenges to segregated dual school systems.

These dramatic legal battles took place against a backdrop of shifting fiscal relationships. As indicated in Figure 7.1, responsibility for raising revenue to fund elementary and secondary education shifted, in fits and starts, away from the local level to the state and national level. The most rapid increase in the state role occurred during the 1930s, a time when many local jurisdictions were beset by fiscal crisis. The national government role increased more slowly and steadily until the rapid increase associated with the "Great Society" initiatives of the mid-1960s. Federal spending for education, growing through much of the 1970s, reached 12 percent of all expenditures for elementary and secondary education in 1980. Spending was dramatically reduced through the Reagan-Bush administrations so that by fiscal year 1990 the federal share of total elementary and secondary education spending had fallen to 7 percent. A modest increase in federal spending since 1990 has increased the proportion of federal funds to 9 percent of total spending.[6]

As a result many local observers feel that the federal government has become largely irrelevant to educational decision making in their communities. Rather than a source of possible local reform, federal policy is seen as creating more problems for local districts: "We virtually, we have very little federal money coming in anymore. We've been cut back, I mean, you know, the federal government has reduced the money it makes available to the schools systems, so and some of that money, for example, had been targeted for handicap children, etc., and when that's reduced it creates more problems." A Baltimore educator reinforces this view: "When Schaefer was mayor and there was still a lot of federal money coming into the city, he did wonderful things with it. When Schmoke became mayor, the money dried up. It's not that he's black that the money dried up. It's just that we had Reagan and Bush. It's just like the money dried up. It's very difficult. It's hard." Only in D.C., unique among our four cases and the nation as well, does the role of federal involvement currently loom large.

In contrast to the relative decline in federal spending, states have become increasingly important sources of education revenue. A combination of anti-tax fervor at the local level and legal challenges to the fiscal inequities associ-

---

[6] National Center for Educational Statistics (1997). Federal Support for Education, Washington D.C.: U.S. Department of Education, National Center for Educational Statistics, fiscal years 1980–1996.

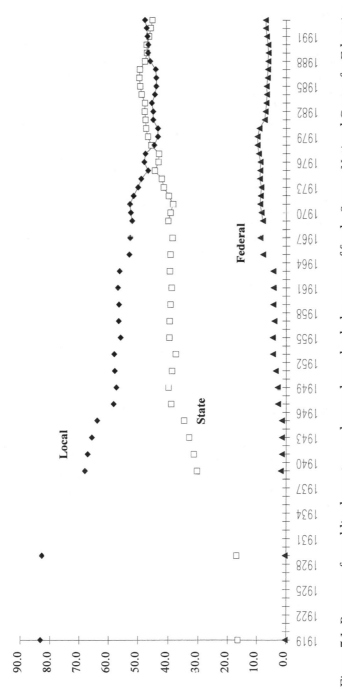

Figure 7.1 Revenues for public elementary and secondary schools, by source of funds. *Source:* National Center for Education Statistics, *Digest of Education Statistics 1997* (Washington, D.C.: U.S. Department of Education, 1997), table 158.

ated with property tax–based funding helped to fuel a shift from local to state revenue sources. Growing reliance on external sources of funding, evident in our four cities, creates a form of dependence that local stakeholders recognize. This fiscal dependence is highest in Detroit and Baltimore where the state provides more than 60 percent of the district's budget.[7] Atlanta obtains 40 percent of its operating budget from the state. The picture is less clear for Washington. Although federal support is higher for Washington than for the other cities, it does not approach the typical level of state investment. This dependence on external funds may have helped to break through some walls that previously had allowed local education to monopolize the decision-making process. As we noted earlier, those interviewed generally support the view that education decision making in their community is a pluralistic enterprise involving multiple actors in a visible arena.

This view is particularly strong in Detroit (80 percent agreement) and Washington (76 percent). Actors in Baltimore (64 percent agreement) and Atlanta (50 percent) are somewhat more likely to see education as a specialized arena. In the mix of relevant actors, a number external to the local arena are seen as important players. For state districts, 10 percent to 20 percent of those interviewed indicated that state government is a key player in education policy. Our interviewing in Washington took place before Congress and the control board aggressively intervened in the schools, but even then almost 30 percent of the Washington respondents mentioned the federal government as an important player.

GROWING REGULATORY ASSERTIVENESS OF EXTERNAL ACTORS

The 1980s and 1990s saw many states pull tighter on the regulatory reins they held in their hands. Given their constitutional responsibility and financial commitment, it is hardly surprising that state and federal governments impose a wide range of regulations on local school districts. Often such regulations are seen as a price of receiving external aid: "We're talking about the politics of education comes with strings attached and also the federal money it comes . . . there's books of strings. Let's face it. Most groups just don't throw the dollars out there and say, 'Do whatever the hell you feel like doing with it.' There's some accountability and there's sometimes, often times some results that they want to see, what they wanted."

States in particular impose a detailed regulatory network on local districts. Mandates define numerous elements of local school policy ranging from the qualification of teachers, the number of hours of instruction to be provided

---

[7] Actually the importance of the state is even higher for Detroit than these data would suggest given the increased role of the state in school finance in 1994.

to students each year, to the rules of engagement between school authorities and unionized employees. Within state systems these regulations are implemented by a state board of education directed by a state superintendent. In Maryland and Michigan this superintendent is appointed by the governor; in Georgia it is an independently elected position. Historically state education units acted as sources of technical and financial support to local districts with relations largely professional and cordial.[8]

State legislatures and governors that historically had been willing to defer to local practice began to demand accountability in a number of ways. Recently states have become much more willing to impose various education reforms on reluctant districts. Spurred in part by the highly critical assessment of American education contained in the influential *A Nation At Risk*, many states passed minimum competency requirements for students and teachers, instituted new testing and assessment procedures, and mandated curriculum reform. Indeed, many current reforms in each of the case cities feature state-level programs and policies. For example, each of our four school systems has been subjected to external pressure to decentralize its administrative structure and grant significant autonomy to individual schools. With New Jersey in the lead, some states enacted legislation specifying conditions under which state officials might take over districts that fail to perform adequately, by dissolving the local school boards and instituting state-appointed overseers in their place. Short of full-scale takeovers, many states are devising new "accountability" systems that involve systematic assessment of local district performance and an array of rewards and sanctions triggered by these performance measures.[9]

Although the relationship between the Washington school district and Congress is in principle similar to that of the other cities and their state government, in practice federal oversight had until recently been much less comprehensive. The degree of attention that Congress devotes to D.C. schools, while waxing and waning, is typically driven by the interests of a small number of members.

With home rule came a period of relative benign neglect. For the most part, Congress restrained itself from interfering with the policy directions

---

[8] Numerous other state agencies are also engaged in state education systems. For example, state units interested in training, labor, and employment issues are often deeply engaged in local education programs. For example, in Michigan the Department of Labor played an important role in the development of the Detroit Compact.

[9] For an overview, see Helen Ladd, ed., *Holding Schools Accountable: Performance-Based Reform in Education* (Washington, D.C.: Brookings Institution, 1996). This movement toward state intervention is still in its early stages, and it is worth noting that states generally are finding it easier to pronounce their *intention* to enact rewards and punishments than to institutionalize such arrangements in the face of political and logistical obstacles. See especially Richard F. Elmore, Charles H. Abelmann, and Susan H. Fuhrman, "The New Accountability in State Education Reform: From Process to Performance," in *Holding Schools Accountable*, 65–98.

set by the new locally elected government; the shift was attributable to two main factors: more sympathetic members sat on the key committee, and Congress was wary of the negative image that could be presented by white officials imposing their priorities on a predominantly black population without voice in electing them. When Congress did exert itself, its focus was much more likely to be related to law enforcement, transportation, or planning and development than education. However, the election of a Republican Congress in 1994 brought into positions of power a cadre of activist conservatives who saw an opportunity to use the city as a showcase to test some of their policy ideas. The District's budgetary collapse and impending default provided the opportunity to reassert congressional authority in the name of fiscal responsibility. House Republicans expressed an interest in radically restructuring Washington schools by contracting with private firms to manage some schools, introducing strong charter legislation, and promoting an experimental voucher program.

During the mid-1990s, local schools districts in Washington and Baltimore were extensively redesigned to permit state and federal authorities to exert more direct authority. The most radical changes occurred in Washington, D.C. There, federal authorities essentially replaced local institutions. The financial control board, created by Congress to bring some financial order to the District, dismissed Superintendent Smith and replaced him with Julius Becton as the chief administrative officer of the district. Becton was to report to a board of trustees appointed by the financial control board.[10] Reflecting his military background, Becton made clear the new and clear line of authority: "The board of education, the city council, the mayor . . . they are just advisors to us and our budget process. We are going to bring some order to this system."[11] When charged with being undemocratic Becton was unapologetic: "I respect democracy. I fought in three wars to protect democracy. I bled. But let me tell you this: Something had to be done. The only aspect of, quote, democracy not working is the fact that the elected school board has been removed from power. If we can help save a generation of kids, I think it is worth it."[12]

Baltimore City School District also underwent important restructuring. In 1997 the Maryland legislature passed a substantial increase in funds targeted to Baltimore schools. However, the plan also called for a significant expansion of state authority in the Baltimore's schools. The existing school board was disbanded and replaced by a new board, jointly appointed by the

[10] A subsequent legal challenge limited the control board's authority to delegate such powers to the appointed board of trustees.

[11] Lori Montgomery "Retired Army General Command of the Public Schools Has Put Kids First and Is Helping Fix the System," *Washington Post*, 10 February 1997, A.1.

[12] Ibid.

governor and the mayor; this new board, in turn, was charged with appointing a new chief administrator for the district.[13]

In 1996, Michigan's Governor John Engler proposed that the state directly take over districts that were failing in their educational mission. When asked to explain this proposal in light of a conservative philosophy of local control of education, Engler was quite emphatic:

> Local control cannot be used as justification for failure. There is a state constitutional authority for public education. We have historically— with my very strong support— delegated that to locally elected school boards. But if the consequence of local decisions is the Benton Harbor example, or Detroit. . . . I just don't think we can stand back. I'm for city "home rule" too, but we wouldn't for a moment suggest that a city could pollute general town water or release toxins into the air.[14]

THE CHANGING ROLE OF THE COURTS

One might argue that the courts' overall impact on education policy has been modest. Although legal restraints to integrated education no longer exist, each of these districts remains highly segregated. In these cities truly integrated education is simply not a viable possibility for most students. However, long-term effects of the desegregation legal battles remain. The racial dynamics imparted to other elements of educational decision making offer a view of the largely unexplored impact of these desegregation cases. This legacy is seen most clearly in the cases of Detroit and Atlanta. The bitter and racially divisive political debate in Detroit has set a tone of mistrust and hostility that continues to be reflected in a wide variety of policy areas. Although the Atlanta Compromise generated less overt racial hostility, it also effectively alienated the local white elite from participating in the schools. Only very recently have white economic leaders shown much interest in re-engaging with either the Atlanta or the Detroit school systems. Baltimore and Washington, which largely escaped hostile court action, seem to have less residual impact from the desegregation process.

Growing conservativism in the Supreme Court and the federal court system generally has meant that a traditional external ally of minority interests is less available than in the past.[15] As a result, central-city school districts

---

[13] There was no formal requirement that the current superintendent could not apply for the new CEO position, however, it was clear to almost everyone involved in the proposal that the new board would seek a new superintendent.

[14] John Engler, "Local Control Can't be Used to Justify School Failure," *Washington Post*, 2 February 1997, C1.

[15] For an overview of changes in the courts' approach to racial issues in education, see Gary Orfield, Susan Eaton, and the Harvard Project on School Desegregation, *Dismantling Desegregation: The Quiet Reversal of Brown v. Board of Education* (New York: The New Press, 1996).

have one less channel for leveraging additional funding. For example, in its 1977 Milliken II decision, the Supreme Court indicated that under certain circumstances states might be required to fund compensatory education programs for minority children in racially isolated schools. In Detroit, this led to a series of programs. In spite of the fact that the remedies proved unable to solve the problem, during the 1980s the courts relinquished oversight, and the programs were scaled back.[16] Furthermore, state courts have become relatively more significant actors as the federal courts have become relatively less willing to play an activist role, a shift especially evident in areas of school finance.

Long after desegregation cases were dismissed, the courts continue to play a significant role in education politics. Judicial action has forced state legislators, governors, and local school authorities to take a number of specific actions. In Michigan, simply the threat of judicial action was an important force in convincing the legislature to fundamentally revise the state's education funding system.[17] The Maryland legislature took up the issue of reorganizing the Baltimore School District and providing additional funding to the district as a means of settling a series of lawsuits claiming that Baltimore was receiving insufficient state funds to provide a state-mandated education. In Washington D.C., the courts have forced administrators to begin to address serious infrastructure problems by closing schools until minimum physical repairs are made.

Clearly, the courts have played an important role in setting the agenda for both internal and external policymakers in each city. Unlike the desegregation cases, however, the courts have been reluctant to impose solutions. Rather, the courts have deferred to the executive and legislative branches to craft remedies to identified problems. Often these remedies are embedded in broader state-level reform efforts. Elected bodies—governors and legislators—are typically more responsive to public opinion than are courts; thus, courts have historically proven more attractive venues to minority groups that lack the voting power to assert their interests through the other branches. As central-city populations have fallen, moreover, state elected bodies have become somewhat less sensitive to their needs when they are perceived to be in conflict with the expressed interests of rural and suburban voters. Thus, the fact that remedies increasingly are being shaped by governors and legislatures presents an additional challenge to black-led cities. It is to such issues we now turn.

[16] Susan E. Eaton, Joseph Feldman, and Edward Kirby, "Still Separate/Still Unequal: The Limits of *Milliken II*'s Monetary Compensation to Segregated Schools," in *Dismantling Desegregation*.

[17] There was serious concern among the state policymakers that the state's finance system might be found unconstitutional by state courts due to large variations in district spending for education.

TABLE 7.1

Factors That Would Allow Cities to Make a Greater Effort in Education (percent)

	Black-led Cities	Other Cities
Improved school bureaucracy	30.6	44.9
More involved mayor or city council	8.1	3.3
Stronger superintendent	1.9	2.5
Reduced central bureaucracy	3.8	8.0
Redistribution of resources	52.5	46.4
More capable school board	6.9	7.2
More control to school board	1.3	3.3
More control to individual schools	18.1	9.4
More control to parents	21.3	14.5
More union involvement	1.3	1.1
Increased political support	10.0	15.9
Design of government agenda	8.1	12.3

Source: Respondents were asked, "What would enable City X to make a greater effort in the area of education?" The entry refers to the personage of those interviewed who mentioned the given response. Because each respondent was allowed to name three factors, column percentages add to more that 100 percent.

CURRENT ISSUES AND INTERVENTIONS

Each city school system has faced repeated externally driven reform efforts. Much of this pressure for change has come from state authorities, sometimes through the prompting of judicial decisions. Three areas of policy are particularly important: funding, accountability, and institutional structure. Funding issues include the appropriate minimum spending level, the degree of spending inequality across school districts, and the specific taxes used in financing education. Tied to the issue of finance is that of public accountability. States are increasingly interested in imposing measurable standards by which school outcomes can be evaluated. Such standards almost inevitably indicate that large urban districts such as those in this study are doing a relatively poor job in educating their youth. Finally, there are a number of efforts to impose new organizational structures on schools. These reforms often contain what seem to be contradictory demands for increased districtwide fiscal and management accountability, on the one hand, and greater school-level autonomy on the other. Reforms often include some support for charter and other independent schools.

The local salience of these issues is revealed in Table 7.1, which reports the set of factors identified by respondents as those most likely to enable a city to make a greater effort in the area of education. Note that the most important set of responses centers exactly on those issues most directly the responsibility of state actors. Particularly salient are issues of resources and administrative structure. While it is possible to discuss these issues separately, it should be understood that they are almost always intertwined, both conceptually and politically.

School Finance

In all four cities school finance is a contentious public issue. The debate has focused on two dimensions: overall funding levels and the particular mix of taxes used. Actors in large urban school districts tend to focus on the level of funding. Without exception, each of our school districts has long complained that it is underfunded. Each points to wide disparities between itself and more affluent districts in the state or surrounding region. Although federal courts have ruled that such variations do not violate the U.S. constitution, school districts across the country have had some success in claiming that these disparities do violate state constitutions. Such claims are based on the assertion that large spending differentials put children living in less affluent communities at a disadvantage.[18] Even where there is no obvious constitutional requirement for more equal spending, district representatives often argue that it is simply good public policy to constrain spending disparities.

State and federal authorities have in fact been sympathetic to demands of these large districts for more financial support. However, support for an increase in funding is often tied to expanding the substantive role of the state in education policy. Typically, the external authorities justify this expanded role by citing a history of poor performance, management failures, and abuse of power by local officials. In both Detroit and Baltimore, a case can be made that statewide pressure to address funding inequities was the driving force behind the subsequent expansion of state involvement. In both cases, too, state officials insisted on local management and governance reform as part of a political settlement with suburban and rural officials; the *quid pro quo* was designed to reassure constituents that added investment in the central-city schools was not a simple "give-away." In D.C., the evidence suggests that Congress placed higher priority on instituting governance and management reform than it did on addressing fiscal needs. In general, Georgia's intervention in Atlanta's educational decision making has not been as aggressive as in the other three cases.

Michigan's implementation of extensive school finance reform was dramatic, but discussions about the need for such action had taken place frequently in the state legislature during the previous twenty years. The legisla-

---

[18] Not surprisingly the power of this claim varies from state to state. The argument would seem to be strongest in those states having specific constitutional requirements for public education.

ture emphasized two specific issues. First, they sought to reduce the enormous funding gap between the state's poorest and wealthiest school districts. Second, legislators had a long-standing commitment to reduce dependence of school financing on local property taxes. In 1993 school reform rose to a particularly prominent role in state politics: Governor John Engler proposed a school reform plan featuring a school financing formula that shifted the burden from property taxes to sales taxes and guaranteed a minimum per pupil expenditure of $4,800 for all Michigan public schools. Engler's school reform measures were approved by the legislature, despite opposition from the Michigan Education Association (the state's largest teachers union) and Democrat legislators. The sales tax element of the plan required a constitutional amendment, which was put to a vote 2 June 1993. The ballot proposition was roundly defeated by the voters, despite strong support from the business community, the MEA, the Michigan Federation of Teachers (MFT), and a $1.5 million media and grassroots campaign launched by Governor Engler to win its passage. The only organizational opposition was mounted by the UAW and AFL-CIO, which argued that the plan would hurt the state's poorest districts.

A second round in the fight to reform the state's school system commenced in July 1993, when the Michigan Legislature shocked most observers by voting to simply abolish the property tax that funded school districts in the state without replacing it with another revenue source. In the aftermath of this rather radical fiscal surgery, Governor Engler proposed a second school reform proposal to the legislature in October 1993. After two months of bruising legislative fights, the compromise school reform plan that was hammered out included most of the Engler proposal's principal recommendations. Proposed reforms were expanded from simply financing to increasing the role of the state in providing a quality education. The major elements of the final school reform proposal included state regulation of total school expenditures, a specification of the taxes to be used to finance the schools, and a state-level program to improve educational quality. The tax plan guaranteed minimum expenditure of $4,200 per pupil and imposed an expenditure ceiling of $6,500.[19] The state's poorest school districts would receive 10 percent more than the minimum grant for each student who qualifies for federal hot lunch assistance. The proposal also significantly altered the taxes used to finance schools. The significant reduction in local property taxes was replaced by an increase in the state sales tax. Finally, the reform plan outlined several state actions to improve education: mandating a statewide core

[19] To obtain support in some of the state's richest districts the law permitted the Michigan's thirty-five highest spending districts to levy local property taxes to raise per pupil expenditures above $6,500.

curriculum as a prerequisite for school accreditation, lengthening the school day, and introducing charter schools.

The ballot proposal necessary to implement this plan received overwhelming support in March 1994.[20] The impact of the financing reform on the Detroit school system is considered to be generally favorable in the short term. The large portion of "at-risk" students in the Detroit school system generated an additional $65 million in revenue. The per pupil expenditure for Detroit was projected to increase from $5,295 in 1993–94 to $5,887 in 1994–95.[21] Nevertheless, Detroit school officials expressed concern that the additional funding would still be insufficient to cope with the serious drug and social problems that plague the district.

The overall impact of this school reform package is likely to be profound. At least from a tax-and-revenue perspective, education became essentially a unitary state system. Local school authorities were left with little discretion in levels of education spending because the state constitution imposes strict taxing limits. Although the variation between districts was significantly reduced, many feared that specified levels would prove insufficient, particularly for urban districts, and that long-term reforms would be unstable, given the relative volatility of revenue derived from sales tax compared to that based on property.

School finance also generated a spirited public debate in Maryland. In contrast to Michigan, however, the issue focused much more narrowly on the city of Baltimore and its schools. City leaders were very aggressive in framing the finance issue in terms of funding disparities in the state. In 1994 the state of Maryland was sued by the American Civil Liberties Union, which charged the state with failure to meet its constitutional responsibility to fund the Baltimore schools at levels necessary for students to receive an adequate education. Several months later the city, making a similar claim, filed its own lawsuit against the state. Not surprisingly, the city's lawsuit created a good deal of hostility in the legislature. For example, during its 1994–95 session, the Maryland Legislature was prepared to implement a number of punitive actions to force a change in Baltimore management practices. The legislature voted to withhold more than 10 million from the city's schools if administrative reforms were not implemented. At the urging of Mayor Schmoke, Governor Glendening vetoed the measure. However, Glendening did commit the state to withhold these funds in the coming year if reforms were not forthcoming. Meanwhile an ongoing set of negotiations between the governor and the mayor sought an agreement that would link increased state aid

---

[20] Important elements of the nonfinancial portions of this plan were never implemented. Of particular interest was the later rejection by the legislature of the notion of a state-mandated curriculum.

[21] Mark Hornbeck, "City Districts to See More Cash," *Detroit News*, 9 January 1994, 1C.

to an expanded state oversight role in the city's school. The governor suggested a $140 million increase in school aid over the next four years if the city was willing to enter a "partnership" with the state. This "partnership" involved a significant increase in the direct authority of the state in the Baltimore school system. For example, as noted earlier, it replaced the current school board of education with a new school governing board jointly appointed by the governor and the mayor; the current school superintendent was to be replaced by a CEO appointed by the new governing board.

Not surprisingly the proposal set off a political firestorm. Mayor Schmoke, reluctant to support the plan, was subjected to considerable pressure to oppose it. A number of prominent community leaders, seeing the proposal as an attack on local autonomy, vigorously opposed it. The plan also faced vociferous opposition from Washington area counties, which claimed that such investment in Baltimore ignored the demands placed on their school systems by low-income students. In the end, however, the plan was endorsed by the mayor and narrowly adopted by the legislature.

The politics of school finance in Washington has become entwined in a broader political debate on the fiscal health of the entire city. Although there had been a tendency to grant the District relatively greater autonomy during the past two decades, a serious financial crisis in the early 1990s prompted Congress to reverse this trend. In return for an increase in federal support for the city, Congress imposed on the city in 1995 a financial control board. This board was charged with reestablishing the city's financial stability. Although the board demanded the city implement a series of budget reductions, it actually sought to protect and even expand the level of financial investment in the school system.[22] However, as noted above, the control board coupled its investment of new resources with the virtual ouster of the existing local authorities.

Impatient with the slow pace of progress and spurred into action by revelations involving sloppy contracting procedures by the superintendent's office, the control board attempted to put rigorous financial controls on the system by replacing the sitting superintendent with a chief operating officer and creating an appointed board of trustees to which it assigned most responsibilities previously handled by the elected board. Both the chief executive officer, General Julius Becton, and the appointed trustees quickly indicated that they felt the system would require a substantial infusion of funds to bring about needed changes. In April 1997, for example, Bruce K. MacLaury, former president of the Brookings Institution and chair of the

[22] The control board has sought a reallocation of District resources to school and education, fire, and police budgets. The Congress has been reluctant to provide new funds for the school system. Overall the federal contribution for schools actually declined under the Republican Congress, with a $28 million cut in 1995.

appointed trustees, indicated that they would need $200 million per year for ten years. But Congress made it clear that it was not willing to invest until it was convinced that inefficiencies and waste had been wrung from the system. "I believe Congress will want to know if we have done everything in our power to maximize money savings before coming to the taxpayer," MacLaury indicated.[23] As a result of this pressure, the trustees made a series of school closings one of the first items on their agenda. Reflecting the emphasis on efficiency, the criteria employed to select sixteen schools for closure included enrollment, estimated cost for needed physical rehabilitation, and potential income from sale or lease of the building—not academic performance.

The terms of the political debate in Georgia were quite different. Here the emphasis was on a broad-based state effort to increase overall investment in local education. In 1994 Governor Miller proposed a series of eleven initiatives including a 5 percent pay increase for teachers, expanded prekindergarten programs, an in-state college scholarship guarantee (HOPE scholarships), and increased investment in school-based technology. Buoyed by a booming economy and expanding lottery proceeds, the legislature was receptive to these proposals.[24] In 1997 Governor Miller proposed a state budget which in his words "lavished money on education." His program included an expansion of the HOPE scholarship program, guaranteed internet access for all school buildings, and reduced class size across the state.

Accountability

Closely associated with issues of school finance is that of accountability. Legislators at both the federal and state level are becoming more insistent that school districts provide concrete evidence that the large sums of money being invested in local education are actually paying off. Each of our cities has been subject to increased state review. Often this review involves performance indicators based on standardized testing. These tests sometimes invoke punitive state action if minimum standards are not met. Without question the consistently poor performance of each city on these standardized tests generated significant public support for fundamental change in each local system.

Of our four cities, Baltimore and D.C. have been singled out for direct intervention. In D.C., the momentum behind intervention grew out of con-

    [23] Michael Powell, "Good D.C. Schools Would Go With Bad," *Washington Post*, 11 April 1997, DO1.
    [24] Betsy White, "School's Fiscal Drought Ends," *Atlanta Journal and Constitution*, 30 January 1994, C4.

gressional concern over fiscal and management issues. The perception that the schools also were doing a poor job of educating the students added credibility to the intervention, but Congress acted well before a process for reliably assessing performance was in place, and performance issues were not the motivating force. Statewide-test performance, in contrast, played a more integral role in Baltimore. In 1992 the legislature created the Maryland School Performance Assessment Program, a testing program for all students in the state. Predictably, Baltimore did not fare well in the testing program: only 14.3 percent of tested students reached minimum state standards, compared with 43 percent for the entire state; in 70 of 116 elementary schools, fewer than 10 percent of tested fifth graders reached minimum state standards. These very low scores brought a strong public reaction that significant changes were needed in the Baltimore system. In 1993 the legislature passed the Public School Standards Act, which allowed state intervention at the school level if the performance of that school was declining. In 1995 the only three schools targeted for state restructuring were located in Baltimore. The next year, an additional thirty-five city schools were targeted for possible restructuring. Through 1997, the state had not actually assumed control of any Baltimore schools. However, it did invoke the Public School Standards Act to force changes at a number of schools. Targeted schools were required to develop a concrete and achievable improvement plan. State authorities rejected some early drafts of plans on the grounds that stated goals were not in fact achievable. Specific personnel changes also were required, including in one case the dismissal of a principal.

The Michigan Education Assessment Program likewise used statewide testing to assess school-level performance. The legislature declared that schools showing consistently low performance might be subject to a reduction in their state aid. The legislature also attempted to impose some measure of quality control of high school education by requiring the State Board of Education to establish minimum scores on a high school proficiency test for a "state endorsed" high school diploma.[25] Detroit schools did quite poorly on these exams. In the 1994–95 school year Detroit reported only 10 percent of its tenth graders received satisfactory scores on the math MEAP (compared to a 36 percent state average), and only 34 percent scored acceptably on the science MEAP (compared to a 52 percent average across the state). Interestingly, the low test scores in Detroit did not lead to calls for the sort of direct school-level intervention targeted to Baltimore. Governor Engler did suggest the possibility of a direct state takeover of low achieving districts.

[25] The designation of state-endorsed diploma was implemented with the class of 1997. Students who do not meet the minimum standards will still be allowed to graduate without the endorsement. The impact of not having the endorsement program is quite unclear.

However, when enabling legislation was introduced in the legislature, it become immediately clear that the governor had little support for such a policy.

State authorities in Georgia also moved toward imposing much more rigorous accountability standards on all districts in the state. The legislature developed a broad school performance review based on standardized testing and mandated the publication of both system and individual school testing results. In 1995 the state sought to force greater accountability through a "guarantee" that a high school diploma would indicate proficiency of specific skills. The state guarantee meant that any employer not satisfied with the reading and math skills of any employee could send the employee back to the nearest state school for adult education to improve those skills at no cost to either party. Zell Miller, Georgia's governor, argued that such a guarantee was an important mechanism to force local education system to increase educational quality.[26] The scope of evaluation expanded in 1996 when the state began to grade individual schools in eight performance areas: school readiness, dropout rates, core academic knowledge, teacher training, math and science, adult literacy, safety, and parental involvement. Not surprisingly the Atlanta school district did not fare well in these early evaluation efforts. Although there appeared to be support in the legislature for direct state intervention in those schools with poor evaluations, at the end of 1997 Georgia still had not taken this stronger step.

Structural Reform

In addition to financial and accountability reforms, a significant effort has been directed to redesigning the structure of local educational systems. Such reforms differ in formats, but they almost always seek to restructure the way educational policy is determined within the local community. Specific restructuring proposals are often justified in the language of the economic market by emphasizing competition and consumer choice. Each city, subjected to external efforts to decentralize school systems, placed relatively greater freedom of action at the building level. More radical proposals include expanding parental choice through school and district transfers and creating publicly supported charter schools.

Once again, Michigan has engaged in the most systematic reform efforts. During the first several years after Michigan passed enabling legislation in 1993, more than eighty charter schools were created across the state. Eleven of these, operating in Wayne County, thus might draw on students in the

---

[26] Julia Hariston, "Miller Proposes to Guarantee Quality of School's Diplomas," *Atlanta Business Chronicle*, 17–23 February 1995, 2B.

Detroit Public Schools.[27] These schools receive the per capita state support that would normally be sent to the local public school system. Although the number of schools actually operating in Detroit is small, the number seemed likely to increase. Parents and faculty in a number of "empowerment schools" have expressed strong interest in applying for charter status. In March 1997, Superintendent Snead called for the Board of Education to sanction up to ten new charter schools in the city by the following fall. "I know there is no best way to educate children," Snead declared. "It is for this reason that we have embraced the charter school concept."[28]

Although Snead was supportive of charter schools in the abstract, the district proved quite wary about specific proposals to open charter schools in the city. In particular, district representatives complained that a school established by a neighboring school district to serve Detroit high school dropouts was little more than a cash cow for the academy and the chartering district.[29]

In 1995 the Michigan Legislature sought to create competition between public school districts by permitting student initiated cross-district transfers. The legislation did not require districts to accept transfer students; rather, districts were permitted to decide whether and how many students they would accept. However, if the district received more applications than seats available, applications were to be accepted by random lot. Districts were not permitted make admissions decisions. As a result of these restrictions the interdistrict transfers have had only a modest impact on Detroit schools. Only a few neighboring districts have agreed to such transfers. Finally, Michigan has attempted to directly reorder the local educational regime by dramatically reducing the authority of the teachers unions. Restrictions included outlawing strikes and forbidding school districts to enter collective bargaining on a number of issues such as distance education and privatization of nonteaching services.

Georgia also sought to impose a measure of local restructuring. Based on a belief that local school districts were committing too many resources to central administration, Governor Miller called on the legislature to force districts to redirect $30 million from central staff to school-based counselors and technology specialists. This reallocation was to be accomplished by simply capping the number of permissible central staff members at twelve.

[27] Michigan Resource Center for Charter Schools, *Michigan's Charter School Initiative* (Mt. Pleasant, MI: Central Michigan University Press, 1996).

[28] Charles Hurt, "Snead Backs 10 Charter Schools," *Detroit News*, 6 March 1997, 3C.

[29] Many are particularly critical of the schools' practice of paying students to attend on state census days. Although the "official" count suggested the school has over 1,200 students, the facilities actually had space for only 500. Opponents of charter schools pointed to the problems of this school as showing a need for greater regulation of charter schools. Gonwar News Service Inc., "Schools of Choice Under Fire for Alleged Fraud," 18 March 1997, 1.

Miller argued, "We need to focus our resources on children and teachers, not central office bureaucrats."[30] A compromise, enacted by the legislature, cut 16.9 million dollars from central office across the state. Rather than imposing a universal cap on central administration staff, local school districts were permitted to fund positions on a formula based on student population.[31] The Georgia Superintendent of Schools proposed a broad decentralization of authority to local districts through the creation of a state block grant program. However, the proposal was rejected, largely on the basis of opposition from the school districts themselves.

Issues of choice and chartering have also become important symbolic issues in Washington and Baltimore. The Republican-dominated Congress has expressed some interest in using Washington as a laboratory for several of their ideas about education. In 1996 the Congress gave the District's Board of Education and newly formed Public School Charter Board authority to charter schools outside the school district administrative structure. By September 1998, eighteen charter schools were operating and more were authorized to open later that year. However, during 1996–97 only two of these schools were actually operating.[32] There was also strong congressional support for some sort of education voucher program. Strong resistance by congressional Democrats so far has stymied such voucher proposals for the District, but the notion seems destined to keep reemerging. Although there has been some interest expressed in similar programs in the Maryland legislature, no enabling legislation has actually been implemented.

VARIATIONS IN STATE POLICY

State Intervention and the Politics of Race

We have seen that over the past decade external policy actors have become more willing to intervene in each of our four school systems. This process has been most complete, at least in the short run, in Washington with the virtual suspension of the elected school board. In Michigan all districts have lost the capacity to independently determine spending levels. The Baltimore school board is now appointed jointly by the governor and the mayor. Interventions have been less dramatic and largely symbolic in Atlanta. However, given the experience of the other three cities, such symbolic politics could have a more substantive future.

[30] Betsy White, "Graduation Would Get Tougher If State School Board Wins Push," *Atlanta Journal and Constitution*, 14 November 1996, D2.

[31] "Legislative Status Report," *Atlanta Journal and Constitution*, 19 March 1995, C4.

[32] The entire school charter movement in Washington was subject to a good deal of intense scrutiny following an alleged assault on a reporter by the director of the Marcus Garvey Public

TABLE 7.2

Black Representation in State and Federal Legislatures

	Number of Blacks	Percentage Black of Total Membership	Percentage of Democratic Members Who Are Black	Percentage of Population Who Are Black
Georgia				
Upper Chamber	9	16.1	20.0	27.0
Lower Chamber	27	15.0	18.4	
Maryland				
Upper Chamber	7	16.1	20.0	24.9
Lower Chamber	24	17.0	20.7	
Michigan				
Upper Chamber	3	7.9	16.7	16.7
Lower Chamber	12	10.9	19.7	
District of Columbia				
U.S. House	38	8.8	17.0	65.8
U.S. Senate	1	1.0	1.9	

Source: David Bositis, Black State Legislators: A Survey and Analysis of Black Leadership in State Capitals (Joint Center for Political and Economic Studies, 1992). 1990 United States Census, Database: C90STF1A.

Black students make up between 70 percent and 85 percent of the children enrolled in the public schools of Atlanta, Baltimore, Detroit, and D.C. Yet, as indicated in Table 7.2, the external legislative bodies that are becoming increasingly involved in those cities' school policies are from 83 percent to 99 percent nonblack.

The racial implications of white-dominated legislatures and appointed boards making decisions about minority school districts such as Atlanta, Baltimore, Detroit, and Washington are widely understood by those involved in the process. To be sure, external state actors almost never use racial language to justify their intervention.[33] Asked to respond to the charge that his

---

Charter School. See Debbi Wilgoren, "Charter Schools in Limbo Under New D.C. Board: Officials Are Renegotiating Previous Regime Agreements," *Washington Post*, 3 March 1997, D01.

[33] This is not to say, however, that such references have always been absent. For example, historically race has been an important factor for congressional leaders in their treatment of Washington schools. In the years before home rule, the District was under the direct control of congressional committees that were dominated by Southern segregationists who had little tolerance for the emerging black majority. During the 1940s, the chair of the Senate committee overseeing the District was Theodore Bilbo, who reportedly commented about the local bureaucracy that "if you go through the government departments, there are so many niggers it's like a black cloud all around you." On the House side, the chair of the District Committee, from 1948 to 1972 was John Macmillian. Macmillian, from a small town in South Carolina, was

threat to take-over the Detroit school system was racist, Governor Engler claimed, "What's racist is those who ignore the problem and deny those kids a decent education."[34] Yet the targets of such efforts often see the reforms as assertions that African Americans are unable to manage their own affairs. Such top-down reform is seen in these communities as consistent with a general mistrust and suspicion of minority-dominated political units.

Mistrust of external actors is rooted in a widespread belief that their decisions work against the interests of local political and education elites. For example, in Washington the appointed school administrator and board of trustees embarked on an aggressive campaign to close underutilized schools. Although there was broad agreement that some schools did need to be closed, opposition to specific decisions was sometimes expressed in starkly racial terms. At one public hearing, an African-American mother expressed a common perception that minority children were relatively more likely to be subject to closings. In objecting to having her neighborhood school closed she exclaimed: "They wouldn't move the kids in white neighborhoods. The kids should not have to move."[35] This occurred against a backdrop of general racial suspicion about the biases of the control board. A poll reported by *The Washington Post* revealed systematic differences in how white and African-American residents perceived the work of the congressionally imposed control board: "Opinions were split sharply along racial lines. Nearly two out of three white residents said they approved of the control board's work, while one in five respondents disapproved. Black residents were far more critical and far more divided. Nearly half said they disapproved of the board, while 40 percent expressed support."[36]

The shift toward state authority facing Atlanta, Baltimore, and Detroit mirrors a long-term decline in the influence these cities have on state political institutions. This decline is in part a function of simple demographics. As the relative population of the city declines, the influence of the city in the state legislature will also decline. As we saw in chapter 2 this decline has been quite dramatic. Figure 7.2 documents the decline in the relative proportion of the state vote represented by Atlanta, Baltimore, and Detroit.

---

considered by many to be the equivalent of a "mayor" of the District; he used his clout to keep the city's social service budget low, to provide access and responsiveness to the white business community, and to block any efforts to provide the citizens of the District with power to govern themselves. Macmillian's defeat in 1972 opened the door to the pro–home rule forces within the national government.

[34] John Engler, "Local Control Can't be Used to Justify School Failure," *Washington Post*, 2 February 1997, C1.

[35] Debbi Wilgoren and Maryann Haggerty, "Proposed D.C. Closures Spur Community Action," *Washington Post*, 20 March 1997, D01.

[36] David A. Vise and Richard Morin, "Control Board Can Do Better Residents Say; Poll Finds Discontent on Schools, Services," *Washington Post*, 12 May 1997, A01.

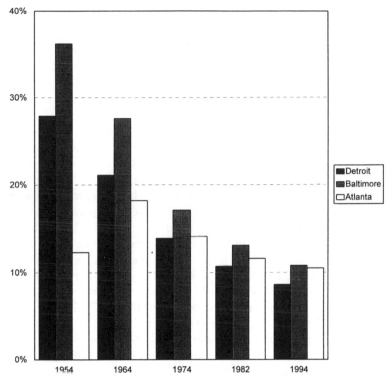

Figure 7.2 Proportion of state vote found in cities. *Source*: Richard M. Scammon, *American Votes: Handbook of Contemporary American Elections Statistics* (Washington, D.C.: Congressional Quarterly, 1954, 1962, 1964, 1974, 1982, 1994).

Beyond simple numbers, however, there is a strong sense that state-level institutions have often explicitly embraced an explicitly anti-urban ideology. Large cities are seen as costly liabilities, rather than centers of wealth and opportunity. An educational leader in Detroit remarked:

> The opposition in the state legislature against the city of Detroit is absolutely almost incredible. Just put Detroit's name on it, and you provoke something. I recall that a candidate running for office in Holland ran against Detroit. That is a very serious and incredible kind of political problem we have here involving race and nothing that Mayor Coleman Young has ever done has ever justified this. . . . That kind of treatment of Detroit continues to provoke conflict between the city and suburban communities, between blacks and whites.

Embedded in this distrust of large cities is the sense that local authorities, simply incompetent to make educational policy decisions, need to be replaced. Resentment by urban legislators occasionally is expressed in explicitly racial terms. During the debate in the Maryland legislature over the plan to reorganize and increase funding to the Baltimore schools, Senator Barbara Hoffman rose to express her opinion of the opposition to the plan: "You want to know how it comes across? It comes across as racist. The undercurrent I see is, 'These black people can't learn, so why spend money on them?' I don't think that's what is said or what is thought, perhaps. But it certainly comes across that way."[37]

Although the institutional context is quite different, a similar sentiment drives a good deal of congressional policy toward the District of Columbia. Indeed, current congressional leadership points to a perceived overall failure of home rule and cites the need for congressional action to restore needed "order." The imposition of the financial control board represented a sharp intervention; to all intents and purposes, Congress temporarily eliminated home rule in the arena of education policy.

Local suspicion of state-mandated reform is greatest when that reform is most targeted. It is interesting, for example, to contrast local responses to state action in Detroit and Baltimore. In spite of some misgivings, Detroit's Mayor Archer was persuaded to publicly support the ballot measure that implemented the education reform in the state. However, Baltimore's Mayor Kurt Schmoke strongly rejected the very targeted legislative criticism of the administrative capacity of the Baltimore schools. Schmoke, normally reticent about invoking race as an issue, was uncharacteristically willing to point to the racial implications of this state action. "The idea that management is the primary problem is insulting and paternalistic," he indicated, "and to my mind gains currency, in certain circles, because it is politically expedient and appeals to popular stereotypes."[38]

This shift toward state authority also has an important if indirect effect on local school districts. Shifting the decision-making venue sometimes destabilizes local-level coalitions. Local economic elites may find it more comfortable not to engage local minority political decision makers but may instead seek out coalition partners at the state level. At times this may reinforce the distance between the political and economic elites of the city. A good example of this occurred in the debate on school finance reform in Michigan. The Detroit Renaissance, an organization of Detroit's leading CEOs, was active in creating the Detroit Compact and several other education initiatives; however, when the arena shifted to the state level to discuss taxes, Renaissance actively tried to reduce the overall level of expenditure to schools in the state. It is difficult to imagine Renaissance leaders calling for reduced school

[37] Terry M. Neal and Richard Morin, "Heated Rhetoric Roils Md. Assembly Tensions Over Race, Class Surface in Rift Over Baltimore School Funding," *Washington Post*, 12 January 1997, B01.

[38] Jean Thompson, "Schmoke Says School Aid Offer Falls Short," *Baltimore Sun*, 21 June 1996, A1.

funding within the local political arena, but shifting the political venue to the state level effectively removed such constraints.

A shift of political venue may dramatically alter policy goals. As reported above, Washington's control board demanded that the appointed school trustees seek to maximize efficiency and cost reductions by closing schools. Consistent with this charge, the trustees explicitly rejected educational excellence as a criterion to be considered in school closing decisions. Thus, parents and teachers, who opposed specific closings on the ground that closure targets were in fact doing a good job of educating students, were not challenged on their facts but merely told that their argument was irrelevant. It seems unlikely that an elected school board, responsible to a local electorate, could make the political decision to dismiss educational quality in closing decisions.

LOCAL CAPACITY AND EXTERNAL ACTORS

Education reform in Atlanta, Baltimore, Detroit, and Washington illustrates the importance of external actors in education reform efforts. Certainly it is impossible to understand current reform efforts in these cities without understanding the important role often played by state and federal actors. Note, however, that external actors seldom act in total isolation from the local political system. The process that we have described is not one of external agents imposing their will on a uniformly resisting or even indifferent population. Rather, external policy coalitions often cooperate closely with local partners in efforts to restructure the local education system. Indeed, these coalitions are often actively sought by some local actors who are dissatisfied with the local political outcomes. Just as minority groups looked to the courts, other groups now seek external intervention to obtain goals they are unable to achieve in the local political area. Examples range from taxpayers seeking property tax relief to parents who see external actors as more sympathetic to their desire to institute charter schools or voucher programs.

Business interests in particular are often available to join in coalitions with outside actors. In one sense this may seem surprising. After all, a large literature has convincingly documented the privileged position of economic interests in local politics.[39] Business elites often get their way, either because of the financial resources they control, their general attractiveness as coalition partners, or the widely accepted notion that what is "good for business" is good for the city. Why, then, should business find it necessary, or even desirable, to broaden the scope of educational decision making by engaging

[39] E.g., Peterson, *City Limits*; Clarence F. Stone, "Systemic Power in Community Decision Making: A Restatement of Stratification Theory," *American Political Science Review*, 74 (1980): 978.

in alliances with state or federal actors in the name of school reform? The answer may involve both push and pull factors more evident in the education policy arena than in the developmental and service distribution issues that typify much of the rest of the urban political agenda.

Various factors interwoven with race make the local political environment less amenable to business influence. As we noted in chapters 4 and 5, a legacy of shared interests, experiences, and perceptions gives public education special potency as a mobilizing force within the black community. Black political and educational leaders are simply less willing to assume the secondary role that they are often assigned in economic policy, and they are more able to count on grassroots support to back them up if they take an assertive stand. As we noted in chapter 6, the informal social and cultural factors that in other cities make it easier for political and economic elites to find common ground, can play out differently in black-led cities, where race-based loyalties and suspicions make public-private partnerships more politically volatile. By constraining their influence in the local educational arena, such factors may serve to push business leaders in the direction of external alliances.

Economic elites also may be attracted to external partners because such linkages expand their potential range of action and influence in education and more generally. State and federal authorities are correctly seen as having access to significant resources, including not only material resources but also the political capacity and legitimacy to frame public policy in desired ways. In an era in which cities themselves are seen as increasingly limited in the range of things they can accomplish, state and federal allies are relatively more valuable. Helping a governor deliver on a campaign promise to improve the schools, for example, may seem to local business leaders like a tactically astute means of garnering support for other issues that concern them, such as tax relief, transportation investments, or regulatory reform.

The strong relationship between external actors and key local stakeholders points to one explanation of why it is so difficult to sustain educational reform in these cities. Successful policy implementation demands a strong and stable coalition of public and private actors. For the most part, minority leaders now have firm control of the formal institutions of local governmental power in these cities, but their capacity to draw on private resources remains elusive. According to the development regime perspective, local public and private actors share a common economic stake in the state of public schools that should be sufficiently powerful to draw them together in a race-neutral coalition to bring about significant and sustained reform. Much as the politics of patronage and racial identity pull some local political leaders away from such alignments, the option of shifting responsibility for education decision making up the ladder of federalism can exert a force on local economic elites that makes them less available for locally based coalitions for school reform.

School Reform As If Politics and Race Matter

STUDENTS OF AMERICAN education have long recognized the various roles played by schools in serving the national interest. They act as venues for socializing our youth into dominant norms, preparing future citizens to serve as informed voters and political actors, and training future workers in the skills and habits that our economy requires. However, schools are most often seen as vehicles of individual advancement. Few symbols are quite as powerful as education's potential role in promoting social and economic mobility. Indeed, this prescription is often offered as a broad strategy for disadvantaged populations. Minority communities are routinely advised to invest in education as a means to improve their status. In all social classes parents admonish their children to work hard in school so that they might be more successful in later life.

Given this widespread belief in the power of education, it is hardly surprising that many in the African-American community were eager first for meaningful participation and then control over urban schools. Within the African-American community there was a general sense that white-dominated school systems were inattentive and poorly equipped to deal with the needs of minority youth. There was an almost naive faith that if African Americans could assume positions of authority within and outside the classrooms, then what had often been a hostile environment for minority children would now be restructured to better meet their needs. Underlying this anticipation was continued belief in the central role of schools. At issue was not so much the potential value of education—which was taken for granted among both blacks and whites—but rather how schooling was actually being provided to African-American children under the existing regime.

Atlanta, Baltimore, Detroit, and Washington provide dramatic illustrations of the disappointment that followed the assumption of power by African Americans in local education. Inconsistencies and inadequacies among the available measures of educational performance make it impossible to offer precise comparisons across school districts. And, it is especially difficult to make clear-headed assessments of school performance that take into account the known fact that it is much more difficult to succeed when children come to school already depleted in many ways due to the socioeconomic conditions in their families and communities. Although some might wish to argue that these schools are doing as well as they can *under the circumstances*, it is clear that they are not doing anywhere nearly as well as was either hoped for or expected by those who fought the hard battles to bring about the shift in racial control. Not only do these districts do poorly on conventional measures of academic success, but they also suffer a crumbling physical plant, administrative weakness, and widespread violence. It is a sad commentary on shrinking expectations to note that the benchmark of success in inner-city education policy is often framed in terms of the physical safety of students and staff rather than learning and pedagogy.

Although this part of our story is consistent with a large academic and popular literature that documents widespread shortcomings in urban education, we have argued that the conventional explanations for this low level of performance are at best inadequate and sometimes misleading. Much literature on education reforms suffers from one or more of four major faults. First, there is a tendency to overstate the importance of getting school reform on the public agenda. Acknowledging that the problem exists is more than half the battle, some accounts suggest. Implicitly, this view rests on the premise that inner-city parents and officials simply have not tried—or not tried hard enough—to do something about school reform. In contrast, we have argued that recognizing the need for reform is far less than half the battle. In each city there have been serious efforts to reform schools. Districts move from one reform to another, often with what seems to be remarkable speed. Over the period of just a few years districts have experimented with site-management, local empowerment, choice schools, experimental curriculums, and various partnership arrangements with nonschool actors. The problem appears to be not in initiating reform but rather in sustaining it.

A second fault of much reform literature is a tendency to provide one-dimensional accounts of the cause of poor performance: they read as if the problem is *simply* a matter of mismanagement, or bureaucratic imperialism, or unstructured curriculum, or insufficient resources, or lack of parental involvement. Such simplistic explanations of the source of the problems in urban education tend give birth to equally simplistic proposals for solving those problems. The promotion of various "silver bullet" reforms is more than a distraction; it is corrosive and counterproductive. Indeed, in large measure the helter-skelter pursuit of the simple solution accounts for the pattern of ephemeral and undigested reform initiatives that we document.

A third fault is a tendency to ignore politics—or, just as bad, to portray politics only in negative terms, as part of the problem rather than an avenue to a solution. Education reform is fundamentally a political process. Instituting reform cannot be analyzed simply as a problem of program design because program designs mean little if they cannot be actualized. Rather, proposals for reform must be considered in the context of the political environment in which they will either wither or take root. We have argued that the failure of education reform should be understood as a failure of political leadership to generate a sustainable coalition to bring together the political and social resources necessary to implement real change in city schools.

Finally, the existing literature on school reform fails because it succumbs to the temptation to treat issues of race as if they are best left unspoken. We are not among those who argue that race is *the* story, or the *real* story, behind urban school reform or its absence in black-led cities. Racial transition in control over the local levers of political control has not generated its own solution to the challenge of building a sustainable coalition for improving inner-city schools. Moreover, racial identity or racial antagonism do not make the challenge of education reform in black-led cities fundamentally different from the challenge faced in many other struggling school districts with differing racial characteristics. But attitudes, orientations, and allegiances that are tinged by race make an already difficult challenge even more formidable. Acknowledging the complicating factor of race does not, by itself, make the problem go away. Indeed, for some, acknowledging the role of so potent and unpredictable a phenomenon as race may reinforce a sense of fatalism, a sense that the problems of inner-city schools may be simply too hot to handle. As we elaborate, we believe it is possible to confront the role of race and yet still keep it in perspective, and we suggest that such a confrontation may help to redirect the substantial energies already invested in urban school reform into channels that will ultimately prove more successful.

RACE AS A COMPLICATING FACTOR IN THE POLITICS OF SCHOOL REFORM

In chapter 1 we suggested that the politics of educational reform in black-led cities might take different forms depending on the salience of race and the degree to which education interests are able to coalesce around concrete reform efforts. Much of the literature on education reform posits an environment in which race is decreasingly salient. This helps to buttress an optimistic vision of the prospects of reform. Freed from the emotion-laden politics of race, black and white local stakeholders should be quicker to recognize their shared interest in improving school performance. The same kinds of informal cooperation that have allowed black officials and white business leaders to cooperate on economic development projects could be transferred to the next logical target—a deracialized coalition to support investment in human capital. A second perspective, however, suggests that education reform may be more problematic than this, even in the absence of sharp racial divisions. Politics as usual frequently prevails: local officials favor initiatives with short-term and certain electoral pay-offs; education professionals use their control over information and implementation to blunt changes that threaten their material interests; business leaders meet their labor needs through relocation or in-house training; and business focuses its involvement in collective politics on more conventional initiatives to limit taxation and regulation and procure government contracts. Such politics can produce a fragmented form of hyperpluralism that is fundamentally inhospitable to the kind of broad-based, long-term alliance that is necessary if school reform is to graduate from episodic eruption to genuine systemic change.

A continued high salience of race, we suggested, could also be compatible with either an optimistic or a pessimistic prediction. Shared racial identity among major stakeholders in black-led cities could become a unifying force by building bridges of loyalty and trust between officials and the community and infusing the goal of education reform with some of the fervor that characterized the civil rights movements and the effort to desegregate public schools. Alternatively, racial identity might be a source of polarization, exacerbating rifts between public officials and key stakeholders in the business community and between the city and important external actors.

Not surprisingly the empirical reality of school reform we found through our research was more complex than suggested in the simple two-by-two typology offered in chapter 1. In many important respects, the politics of education reform in Atlanta, Baltimore, Detroit, and D.C. resembles that in other central-city school districts. Fragmented interests provide the general challenge that confronts school districts regardless of their racial composition. Racial transition does not provide a natural solution. Black mayors seem no less likely than white mayors to squabble with black school boards; black educators seem no less likely than white ones to use their positions of authority to co-opt parental initiatives. Furthermore, race does not become the defining cleavage in school politics in black-led cities. Black stakeholders seem no less likely than white ones to see education problems as severe; black officials and white business leaders join in partnership arrangements intended to bring about systemic change.

Although the picture is not as neat and tidy as would be the case if any one of the ideal types was found consistently to apply, we believe that the patterns we have uncovered support two strong conclusions. First, race remains an important variable in educational politics. To be sure, the way in which race expresses itself has changed since desegregation defined local school politics. Often indirect, race may express itself in surprising ways. Nevertheless, race is a critical social and political variable that constrains both how internal elites interact with each other and how they deal with external actors. We argue that any effort to explain urban education politics on the basis of a deracialized model misses half the story.

Race remains a critical issue in educational politics in at least three different ways. First, race is important within the African-American community itself. Ties of race and culture are important in all four cities. In each city black political and community leaders, as well as average citizens, are reluctant to criticize educational leaders who are also black, lest these criticisms be used to attack local black-dominated institutions.[1] Black community leaders are especially leery of any proposed reforms that seem to undercut the financial stability of black professionals employed by the school system. We have argued, though, that this widespread concern about jobs and economic issues around reform is not simply an expression of personal self-interest. Although self-interest is certainly very important here, it must be understood that we are observing more than a small selfish elite trying to protect its privileged status. The bonds that link minority teachers and administrators to the larger African-American community have been forged by shared experiences, expectations, and concerns. In addition to these powerful psychological links, there is a broad sense within much of the African-American community that black educators (and other local public employees) play a critical role in the economic health of the local community. Thus, reforms that threaten existing educational institutions are seen as carrying real risk to the community. Calls for Draconian reforms based on claims that "nothing could make the schools worse" are simply unconvincing in such an environment. Predictions about political behavior based on assumptions about deracialized personal interest fail to take into account the way communal identities and interests shape responses. Reform efforts that rely on such one-dimensional predictions are likely to continue to underestimate city residents' wariness toward systemic changes, especially when the most visible sponsors of those changes include corporate and external actors.

The high salience of race also imposes important constraints on white actors in local education. It is problematic for whites in black-led cities to assume a visible role in any education reform effort. It is problematic in part because their participation makes it more likely that the reform initiative will be framed in racial terms; such a framing of the issue increases the risk of polarization and sharp resistance. It is problematic also because potential leaders feel or anticipate personal stress when and if they find themselves embroiled in racially tinged conflicts. As a result many white parents have essentially retreated from systemwide politics to focus on support efforts toward individual schools. This local focus has the ironic effect of reinforcing racial mistrust since the larger black community often resents these school-level efforts as parochial and "elitist." It is interesting that middle-class black parents feel some of these same pressures and are very reluctant to openly criticize black leadership in the district.

In addition to reinforcing general tensions between racial communities, the symbolic importance of race has a specific negative impact on efforts by

---

[1] Note that such a concern is by no means without some foundation. Over the period of our study local authority was substantially reduced in Washington and Baltimore. School finance

the African-American community to build linkages to local economic elites. In each city there is a clear racial dimension to efforts to recruit business elites to support the city schools. Such efforts, popular in all cities, have been vigorously pursued by school officials. There has been some success in recruiting these elites to become active in the schools. School-level business relationships are common. In Detroit, Atlanta, and Baltimore business interests have supported a formal compact that provides resources to students adhering to a particular academic standard. Although these efforts meet with widespread support and approval, clearly these largely white economic elites are quite constrained in terms of what they can actually do. When business leaders try to move beyond simply providing resources, much more resistance and often resentment follow. Such resistance and resentment might be insufficient to scuttle reform *if* business leaders were convinced that such efforts are critical to the long-term viability of their investments. We have suggested, however, that the economic stake of many businesses in the central city may be less direct and certain than reform proponents prefer to assume. In that context, the prospect of getting mired in ongoing battles in a racially polarized setting may be all that is needed to convince business leaders that their energies and resources would be better spent in other ways.

Finally, race affects education politics through the relationship between local African-American elites and largely white external political and economic elites. State-level politicians seldom mention race as they move to impose various reforms on local government. Yet the study of local districts shows that racial tensions, never far from the surface, can spill out in a very public and powerful way. For example, some local opponents framed the resistance to plans of the state of Maryland to assume a more direct authority in Baltimore City in explicitly racial terms. Just as race makes coalitions between black and white actors more difficult to sustain, it can also make it more likely that external actors and city economic elites will find common ground. External actors, anxious to find some allies at the city level, may see business leaders as appealing coalition partners. Compared to local elected officials, business interests are seen as reliable and prestigious allies who bring resources to bear and are unlikely to present potential political threats to state politicians. Local economic elites, frustrated by the slow pace of reform and the use of the racial issue to challenge their right to take a public stance, are more readily drawn into alliances with external actors who share their impatience and have formal authority to overcome local veto. Such coalitions may pursue agendas quite different from those that would be developed at the local level. This tendency was revealed during the debate on

---

reform in Michigan essentially removed local flexibility in funding levels. The state of Michigan has also been quite active in supporting charter schools as alternative to local public education.

school finance in Michigan. Many business groups in Detroit, which had been active at the city level to expand educational opportunities, were active with legislative allies to reduce funding for all Michigan schools.

The fact that these manifestations of racial divisions are subtle and indirect is important. There is a qualitative difference between racial tensions of this kind and the open, inflexible, unbridgeable cleavages that characterized battles over school desegregation in other settings at other times. That these relatively shallower and less direct forms of racial tension are nonetheless sufficient to present real obstacles to school reform partially reflects the depth of historical racial cleavages. It also reflects, however, our second strong conclusion: the challenge of putting together and holding together a coalition for systemic school is formidable.

The pattern of energetic and yet unsuccessful efforts to bringing school reform that we find in each of the cities suggests to us that the job is simply much tougher than proponents of reform have been willing to acknowledge. Rather than a simple extension of the kinds of informal public-private cooperation that has characterized attempts to bring about the physical redevelopment of the urban core, building a local regime supportive of investment in human capital requires a much higher level of civic capacity. Building sustainable coalitions for systemic school reform is much harder than building partnerships for downtown development partly because the pay-offs are less immediate, tangible, divisible, and assured. It is harder, too, because the alternatives to working collectively to solve the problem are well-established and well-known: personal exit to suburbs, private schools, or school-specific solutions; corporate exit to suburbs, in house training, or personnel recruitment from other areas; political leaders' option to focus on other issues.

In this context—where the prospects for long-term success are uncertain and the likelihood for immediate success negligible—the added doses of mistrust, suspicion, wariness, and volatility associated with racial politics can have substantial consequences. To acknowledge the difficulty of the challenge, however, need not lead us to despair about its prospect for progress. In the next, and final, section, we consider what positive steps might be taken to make it more likely that school reform can be sustained.

EDUCATION POLICY AS IF POLITICS AND RACE MATTER

What should policy makers and concerned citizens do if they take seriously the evidence and interpretations that we have offered? We offer no quick fixes. In fact, we believe that the temptation to look for quick fixes is part of the problem. Nor do we take an emphatic stand on any of the raging debates about this or that pedagogical innovation or strategy for restructuring the organization of schools. We do not believe that the future of urban education in the United States hinges on whether or not school districts adopt or reject vouchers, or Afrocentrism, or single-sex education, or whole-language instruction, or child-centered education, or ebonics. We think it depends on such things as whether they can organize themselves to define clear goals, enlist the support of diverse stakeholders, maintain commitment even in the face of competing demands for public attention, monitor progress, reward success. Our recommendations reflect these beliefs.

Playing for the Long Term:
De-Emphasizing Agenda-Setting in Favor of Implementation

In the mistaken belief that urban residents and policy makers have been indifferent to education problems, many reformers have adopted tactics designed to push school reform to the top of the public agenda. But the very tactics that help to build attention and enthusiasm can set the stage for disillusionment and resignation when it becomes apparent that a short burst of effort will not suffice. Anthony Downs has noted the tendency of the American political process to cycle issues up and down the public's attention span.[2] Although he suggests that the problem may be endemic, we believe the problem is exacerbated by political strategies that can be altered to good effect.

To broaden attention and build enthusiasm, proponents of reform have promised more rapid and more substantial gains than they can deliver, overemphasized the importance of individual leaders and educational techniques, attempted to work around existing institutions rather than through them, and deemphasized unresolved value conflicts and competing visions about what schools should do. Individuals and groups that "sign on" to a reform initiative in the expectation that their commitment need not be long can quickly grow impatient. This accounts in part for the tendency of reform movements to wax and then wane. It also helps to explain the tendency for some of the original reform partners to become disenchanted with newly hired superintendents or newly elected school boards before they have had much of an opportunity to get things underway. Without shaving down long-term goals for excellence and equity, it is advisable for school reforms to *identify interim, nearer-term objectives that can serve as benchmarks and to acknowledge from the first that the local commitment must be measured in decades not years.* Specific objectives must be identified by stakeholder groups. However, examples of achievable goals can be cited from reform

---

[2] Anthony Downs, "Up and Down with Ecology: The Issue Attention Cycle," *Public Interest* 28 (1972): 28–50.

efforts in Atlanta, Baltimore, Detroit, and Washington. For example, school-business compacts that guarantee college support seem to be associated with increased student attendance and classroom achievement. Parent involvement in school affairs, either as volunteers or in parent organizations, can be increased when such participation is sought.

Too great a focus on individuals—that is, superintendents as super-heroes—or specific techniques as a panacea creates the false impression that the basic ingredients for reform are already present, with only a missing catalyst needed to stimulate the desired reaction. The continual evidence that individuals and techniques that have worked in one venue do not necessarily work in others highlights the senses in which reform requires a network of interacting and mutually supporting factors. Instead of suggesting that key individuals or techniques will suffice, serious efforts at school reform should *focus on building working relationships among a wide range of stakeholders inside and outside of government and inside and outside of the education community.*

Part of this may mean making a deliberate effort to incorporate the existing school bureaucracy rather than attempting to work around it, as has more commonly been tried. In their classic analysis of implementation failures, Pressman and Wildavsky acknowledge that it is tempting to try to bypass bureaucracy: "The first temptation is to establish a new organization. This way you can hire new people, establish your own rules, and work out patterns of operation you believe will facilitate the new activities."[3] But those advantages are usually transitory. "Little by little the regulations that apply to everyone else also apply to it. Accommodations are made with the other organizations in its environment. Territory is divided, divisions of labor are established, favors are traded, agreements are reached."[4] Efforts to circumvent the bureaucracy, in other words, usually wind up creating a new bureaucracy. And, to the extent that fragmentation and unclear allocation of responsibility were part of the original problem, this can leave things worse off than they were before. Moreover, as Pressman and Wildavsky also note, the reason why bureaucracy reemerges has a lot to do with the fact that—in spite of its often frustrating elements—bureaucracy serves a critical function in getting things done.

If one wishes to assure a reasonable prospect of program implementation, he had better begin with a high probability that each and every actor will cooperate. The purpose of bureaucracy is precisely to secure this degree of predictability. Many of its most criticized features, such as the requirement for multiple and

---

[3] Jeffrey L. Pressman and Aaron Wildavsky, *Implementation* (Berkeley: University of California Press, 1973), 128.
[4] Ibid., 130.

advance clearances and standard operating procedures, serve to increase the ability of each participant to predict what the others will do and to smooth over differences. The costs of bureaucracy—a preference for procedure over purpose or seeking the lowest common denominator—may emerge in a different light when they are viewed as part of the price paid for predictability of agreement over time among diverse participants.[5]

One reason that reformers may have failed to build broader networks and incorporate existing institutions is their reticence to acknowledge latent disagreements about what constitutes "good" education. Calls to make the school system more efficient imply that the key unresolved issues have to do with selecting *means* rather than setting *goals*. When that is really the case— when goals are clear and shared, but the best means to maximize those goals is uncertain—it makes sense to grant discretion to those with a claim to technical expertise or proven success in other venues. When it comes to choosing how to fix a car's sputtering engine, for example, we may have little compunction about handing the keys to a mechanic and following his or her advice about what needs to be done. But when goals are unclear or potentially in conflict, we need alternative mechanisms for making decisions, and one of the most important such mechanisms is public deliberation and voting through democratic channels. *Instead of a "full speed ahead" approach that assumes that the public already knows what is wrong with its schools and knows what it wants from them, efforts to jump-start reform ought to begin with a period of broad public dialogue about what schools can and should be expected to do.* Although it undoubtedly is true that all (or at least nearly all) residents in Atlanta, Baltimore, Detroit, and D.C. share a desire for "better education," it is far from clear (and indeed doubtful) that they share a vision of what that education should entail. For example, where should the balance be drawn, among college preparation versus entry-level job skills, nurturing curiosity and innovation versus enforcing discipline and authority, building children's self-confidence versus preparing them for a harsh and competitive environment, encouraging critical analysis versus respecting and rewarding faith in a higher order, emphasizing academics versus emphasizing physical and cultural well-roundedness? Or where we should draw the line between making the educational system the best it can possibly be versus balancing the expense of schools against other legitimate demands on the budget or the need for tax relief? A deep and sound tradition in democratic thought holds that questions such as these should be subject to public deliberation and collective decision making. That is *not* because that process is guaranteed to produce the best or even a good solution in each instance but because

---

[5] Ibid., 133.

the experience of engaging in that process is the best preparation for citizens to learn how to make responsible decisions over the long run.

Formal Power to Succeed

Partly due to frustration and impatience, many school reformers have been attracted to initiatives that bypass or overrule local authorities. These include external interventions by Congress or the states. They also include various strategies to invoke markets or civil society, in place of governments, as the venue in which key decisions should be made.

We, too, have stressed the importance of multiple actors coming together to create public policy. Drawing on the concept of civic capacity (chapter 1), we began with the premise that public officials cannot do it alone. But to say that local authorities cannot do it alone is not the same thing as to say that the authoritative use of local power is not a necessary component of any long-term enterprise. Effective public policy is ultimately centered in formal political institutions. Only such policy centers provide legitimacy for collective action and the opportunity for the public to hold someone accountable. Thus, effective local political institutions become an essential element of reform effort.

Education policy authorities must meet at least three conditions if they are to spur true educational reform. First, *education policy centers must have substantial policy autonomy.* Collective political action requires a minimum capacity to organize and to act. Although both our conceptual framework and empirical analysis reject the notion of a direct command control model for policy making, it remains important that political actors have formal authority within a policy arena. For example, when Michigan assumed the responsibility for setting the spending levels for the state's public schools, one result was to shift future political debate about school funding levels to the state. Washington, D.C., provides an even more dramatic example. Here the board of education has been rendered nearly irrelevant to local educational decisions. Not surprisingly the board has largely lost the attention of the community in educational matters. When local authorities are seen as having little or no authority, these authorities are unlikely to be successful in mobilizing other community actors around such issues.

Second, *education policy centers must have political resources.* Whether they like it or not, education leaders operate in a political environment. To exercise effective leadership, they must have a minimum of effective resources; moreover, they must have the willingness and the skill to use such resources. Too often education reform is framed in largely nonpolitical terms. Rather than seeing reform as a political process, education leaders frame such issues as curricular or technological. As a result reform debates are portrayed as requiring "expert" analysis and kept internal to the education community. As we have seen, the results of such a process are almost always ineffective policy.

Obviously one set of necessary resources is material. Potential coalition partners must be persuaded that education leaders control sufficient resources to actually implement agreements. Equally important, however, are more symbolic resources. This includes, for example, a degree of legitimacy within the community. Education leaders are unlikely to be attractive coalition partners if they are viewed as without standing in the larger community. We have noticed that this symbolic power is sometimes lacking in each of our cities.

Third, *education policy centers must have leadership.* Current social science often understates the direct role of leadership by stressing instead a variety of structural and situation explanations for political outcomes. Certainly such aggregate variables are important. Indeed, in highlighting the failures of superintendents who were brought in with reputations as "proven" leaders, we have argued that leadership is insufficient, especially when leadership is thought of as a personal quality readily transferred from situation to situation. However, in each of these cities, individual leaders have made significant contributions to reform efforts by taking personal risks, by working to reframe public discussion, by reaching out to new allies, by drawing in old allies from other issue areas. Leadership, conceived as a relationship between individuals and others within the community, is important because the power of the idea of reform in itself is insufficient to draw partners together and hold them together in the face of competing demands on their energy and time.

Building Confidence and Trust

Saul Alinsky, whom many consider to have been this nation's preeminent political organizer and tactician, emphasized that mobilizing people who have grown used to political and policy disappointments requires insuring early successes, lest the participants fall back quickly into habits of resignation and despair.

> The organizer's job is to begin to build confidence and hope in the idea of the organization and thus in the people themselves: to win limited victories, each of which will build confidence and the feeling that "if we can do so much with what we have now just think what we will be able to do when we get big and strong." It is almost like taking a prizefighter up the road to the championship—you have to very carefully and selectively pick his opponents, knowing full well that certain defeats would be demoralizing and end his career.[6]

[6] Saul D. Alinsky, *Rules for Radicals* (New York: Vintage, 1971), 114.

Parents and policy makers interested in building a sustainable coalition for school reform—and in bridging the chasms of suspicion rooted in race—according to this reasoning should *focus initially on winnable victories*. Residents of Atlanta, Baltimore, Detroit, and D.C. have rich experience with failure. Failed collaborations breed fatalism and lack of confidence in one's partners. Yet small successes can and do occur. Reading levels can increase, school grounds can be improved, and parent participation can grow. This is the basis for more fundamental reform and improvement.

Pursuing winnable victories does not necessarily mean settling for trivial or symbolic gains. Although trite, the expression that "every journey begins with a step" is undoubtedly true. That does not mean that a tiny step is as good as a large one, nor is buying a map. Part of the problem is that we typically analyze progress in measurements far too gross to register small gains—a point on which we elaborate. Even absent precise measurement of educational gains, however, it is possible for reformers to tactically emphasize winnable goals. That may mean focusing first on schools where principals and teachers are receptive, for example. Battling to impose reform on reluctant targets ultimately will be necessary, but such battles should come easier after early victories have been gained.

A second strategy for building confidence and trust is to *take advantage of individuals and groups that have already established reputations for reliability and loyalty*. Here, too, Alinsky has insights to offer. He emphasized the importance of "indigenous leaders" and warned against the tendency to build superficial partnerships among formal agencies that are, themselves, simply "superimposed upon the community."[7] While this may seem self-evident, it actually runs counter to some reform strategies that have been most aggressively pursued. Instead, as we saw most clearly in Detroit and D.C., there is a tendency for reformers to seek outsiders as superintendents. One assumes that the ideas and personal skills of the superintendent generate success; thus, a superintendent who has proven successful elsewhere should be able to replicate that success again and again. We have argued, instead, that the success of reform leaders depends upon the network of relationships from which they can draw. Outsiders have difficulty constructing such networks from scratch, and the districts most in need of reform are unlikely to have such networks ready and available for the newcomer to exploit. Similarly, external interventions, such as the congressionally mandated chief executive officer and board of trustees in D.C., violate this principle. The difficulties with school openings that tainted General Julius Becton's administration of the D.C. schools were not very different from similar problems experienced under his predecessor. Becton's complaint that the federal court was primarily responsible had considerable

---

[7] Saul Alinsky, *Reveille for Radicals* (New York: Vintage, 1969), 64–65.

face validity, but Becton, lacking a reservoir of trust and support upon which to draw, was left vulnerable and somewhat isolated.

A third strategy for building confidence and trust involves *defanging the cutback threat*. School reformers often emphasize the potential for savings through greater efficiency. This is seen as a way to broaden their constituency; the prospect of lower taxes for comparable outputs presumably appeals to business groups and residents who do not have children in public schools. But the price of appealing to these groups is not just the fervent opposition of educators who fear that their jobs are at stake. It includes the heightened suspicion of the broad African-American community that, for both historical political and contemporary economic reasons, is reticent to endorse assaults on the public sector. We believe that there is a constituency for reform even among teachers themselves *if* they can be reassured that reform will bring them the resources and support they need to do their jobs better. Their fears to the contrary are not unrealistic, given the tendency of some elements of the reform coalition to place heavy emphasis on the high per pupil costs in some central cities, the need to close buildings, and the "overmanning" attributable to the decline in the number of pupils in some central-city systems. It may even be worthwhile for reform advocates to adopt a pledge of no net-loss of jobs to quell such fears. Such a pledge need not, and should not, mean a promise that all current teachers and staff members will be protected. Selective firings, for continually poor performance, are highly appropriate. The goals should be to build a common cause between parents, community, and those educators who want to educate and to drive a wedge between these stakeholders and those educators who are truly incompetent or corrupt.

Evaluation for Mobilization, Not Intervention

Additional difficulties for reformers are rooted in the process by which proposed changes are typically monitored and evaluated. School districts put relatively little effort into the evaluation of reform efforts. As a result, debate on policy impacts is often based on impression and faith rather than any rigorous empirical evidence. Note, however, the issue here is much more complex than simply calling for larger evaluation budgets and staff. Before useful evaluation can be done, the logic of that evaluation must be rethought.

All too often, contemporary evaluation efforts rely on indicators that almost assure failure. In particular, the near-universal reliance by school districts on standardized test scores as measures of educational outcome makes it highly unlikely that innovative programs will be judged successful. The evidence is clear that such scores are difficult to raise and are nearly impossible to do so in the short term. We argue that an evaluation almost certain to show failure is self-defeating. Rather, standards must incorporate the possibility of success. Indeed, borrowing again from Alinsky's maxim of community organization, goals (particularly initial goals) ought to be chosen with an eye to making sure that goals can be reached. Note, this does not mean that program evaluation should lack standards or be trivial. But policy makers must directly confront the issue of what can actually be accomplished in both the short term and the long term.

The nearly exclusive focusing on test scores not only creates impossible near-term standards for reform to meet but also promotes a mechanical and centralized approach to education policy. Scores are often used in a mechanical way to identify successful and unsuccessful schools. These designations often trigger automatic responses, very often sanctions. This approach encourages central authorities to design and implement reforms but provides them little capacity to make them work.

As alternative to this central command and control model, we would propose an evaluation framework that stresses community mobilization rather than sanction and school-level remediation. In such a model a variety of performance measures would be aggressively circulated to allow community members to have some sense of the relative performance of their schools and permits the identification of marginal improvements. Moreover, it is possible that such a strategy will promote community mobilization for reform efforts.

Performance data can help to create conditions conducive to sustained reform by extending to parents and community groups information they need to identify problems in their neighborhood schools and to respond appropriately. Literature in the education field emphasizes the importance of parent involvement as an important resource in the battle for school improvement, but studies also show that many parents seem satisfied with the way things are. Proponents of school choice as a vehicle for education reform also stress the need for informed parents, but options for choice frequently are underenrolled. There is evidence that lower-income parents may lack access to the kinds of information they need to exercise choice effectively.[8]

Low levels of parent participation may reflect not only insufficient or inaccurate information about school performance but also a fatalistic conclusion that schools cannot make much of a difference in their children's lives. Parents who see that their children are earning decent grades and are being promoted on schedule may be too quick to assume that things are going fine. An independent source of information about school performance might challenge complacency, where it is unwarranted. By the same token, in some

[8] Bruce Fuller and Richard F. Elmore, with Gary Orfield, *Who Chooses? Who Loses?: Culture, Institutions, and the Unequal Effects of School Choice* (New York: Teachers College Press, 1996).

cases solid performance data may reveal that some schools *are* doing better than realized, and this may build community confidence in institutions capable of succeeding in spite of substantial obstacles.

There is little doubt that local institution building is difficult. Yet there is also evidence that such efforts can succeed. Cities have been able to incorporate low-income residents in planning and development decisions. Some public housing authorities have been able to incorporate residents in the management of their own housing. Indeed, the city of Detroit was been able to generate considerable parental engagement in their empowerment schools. However, such lessons underscore the fact that such efforts are often very slow and often expensive.

Foreign Relations

We have argued that effective school reform requires an anchor in local political institutions that serve as policy centers for decision making, implementation, and accountability. However, such policy centers must be linked to a variety of external actors, including private business, community-based organizations, and important decision-making arenas at both state and national levels. The probability that such linkages will develop depends on not only the character of the policy center but also a number of broader conditions. We can suggest four.

First, *groups must share sufficient common interest for joint action.* It is perhaps obvious that there needs to be some common interest for groups to cooperate within a particular policy sphere. Less obvious, however, is the possible variation in the ways in which issues can be framed and the impact that may have on possible coalition partners. For example, in several cities there have been efforts to define education in terms of economic development. Such a redefinition has at its base a strong desire on the part of educational leaders to recruit business to join efforts to restructure local schools. What is less recognized is the fact that such efforts can sometimes act to reduce access to other community partners who see their interest in educational reform in very different ways. Moreover, economic development can take different forms. In some guises, for example, it may be interpreted as coincident with the interests of large corporate employers; in others, it might be thought of as community-level economic development or increased entrepreneurialism and small-business growth. Although one school of thought holds that all cities and residents within them hold a unitary interest in undifferentiated economic development,[9] it is naïve to expect that individuals and

---

[9] Paul Peterson, *City Limits* (Chicago: University of Chicago Press, 1981).

groups with sharply different experiences will spontaneously define their interests in overlapping terms. Shared interests are necessary for sustained collaboration, but such interests in diverse urban settings must be proactively shaped, through open discussion, negotiation, and compromise.

Second, *groups must share sufficient mutual trust for joint action.* In each city we noted an interesting puzzle. Education reform failed even in the face of a wide consensus that such reform was badly needed. Some of that surprise is based on an overly simplistic view of joint political action. Political cooperation does not follow directly from a shared set of abstract political goals. Of the other conditions that must be met, one of the most important is trust. Political action always involves some opportunity costs because other objectives must be deemphasized. There are also direct risks as well. If a political coalition fails to achieve desired outcomes, then limited political resources have been used and may be permanently lost.

Trust is often missing in each of our cities. In part this represents a lack of strong working relationships among key players in the community. Indeed, the local history is often quite the opposite. Local hostility and mistrust rule. The long history of strained racial relations has left a legacy that exacerbates and gives greater focus to the kinds of intergroup suspicions that would be typical even in a racially homogenous setting. In this environment leaders and groups are unwilling to commit to joint action, even as they endorse the goals of the reform movement.

Third, *groups must be confident about their partner's long-term commitment to a mutual agenda for joint action.* Many commentators have observed the importance of a long-range view in public policy. Policy impacts are likely to be indirect, difficult to measure, and will certainly occur only after a significant lag. This would almost certainly seem relevant for educational reform. Therefore, the short-term support for education reform is insufficient to ensure its successful implementation. This need for a long-term commitment has sometimes acted as a limiting force on support for reform movement. For example, business interests often demand evidence that programs, such as compacts, improve school performance in a relatively short period of time.

Finally, *contradictory crosspressures may preclude joint action.* Students of public policy often make the error of examining the dynamics around a single issue and ignore the broader political context in which such decisions are made. This ignores the significant crosspressures to which political actors are subjected. We have noted that many local actors in education reform have a variety of constituencies, which may have inhibited full cooperation with a school-reform movement. For example, nascent public-private partnerships to bring about education reform can be "infected" by public-private conflicts in other issue areas. Business leaders may sour on school-

reform coalitions if they perceive local public officials as unresponsive in
other areas like tax reduction or regulatory reform. Similarly, local officials
may sour on school-reform partnerships if they believe business and wealthier white residents are supporting state government initiatives that undermine home rule.

PROSPECTS FOR A HUMAN CAPITAL REGIME

The story of education reform in Atlanta, Baltimore, Detroit, and Washington does not lead us to be optimistic about the future of urban reform in
large American cities. School districts face the tremendous challenge of educating an at-risk population with, at best, modest resources. In addition, each
school district suffers from a significant deficit in civic capacity. Fragmented
links to the external community often feature significant hostility and mutual
mistrust. Increasingly local educational and political elites feel that they are
under attack as external actors move to enforce some measure of reform in
their system.

Central cities are desperately in need of the will and the ways to broaden
their capacity to develop human capital as aggressively as they occasionally
manage to develop their physical capital. Often, urban school-reform initiatives have self-consciously attempted to imitate the structure and style of
public-private partnerships that have succeeded in carrying through downtown development initiatives. Often, too, the corporate- and public-sector
participants in school reform include some of the very same actors who have
succeeded in these other endeavors, but clearly they find the road much
rockier when they turn to school reform. To urbanists who have found the
concept of "regime" useful, this points to an important question: What range
of issues can be the focus of a functional political regime? There is little direct
evidence as to whether the lessons learned from economic development can
be applied to other policy domains. This research has explored whether education or human capital can serve as a regime platform. In spite of the general
failure of reform in all four cities, we would not go so far as to conclude that
the construction and sustenance of human capital regimes is impossible in a
diverse central city. Clearly, however, calls to action based on a simple abstract call for "quality education" are insufficient.

Education leaders have shown interest in linking education reform efforts
to more successful efforts of economic revitalization. They have done this in
two ways. First, all cities have made an effort to recruit economic elites
into an education-reform coalition. Even more interesting, education leaders
have attempted to define reform in explicitly economic development terms.
Educators' appeals to economic leaders focus on their direct stake in local
schools by citing the schools' role as the source of skilled labor in the coming

decades; without such a skilled labor force, they predict a bleak economic future.

There is little doubt that the economic implications of education seem valid and provide powerful support for education reform. However, it is equally clear that the tie to local economic interests is long term in nature and much less direct than traditional redevelopment strategy. There are also some significant political dangers to tying education to a narrow vision of economic development. A number of benefits of good education are more apparent and more immediate at the individual level than are those that accrue to the aggregate economic system, and the capacity of a local jurisdiction to capture aggregate economic benefits also is uncertain. If linking education reform to economic revitalization means that job growth and fiscal surpluses will be taken as the measure of success, school-reform efforts might be declared failures even if they are succeeding in giving individual inner-city children the tools they need to succeed. By the same token, the linkage could lead to false or premature declarations of success—for example, if national economic policies spur inner-city investment—with a consequent loss of urgency.

A related question about education is the appropriate role for economic elites. Much empirical research on regime formation supports the view that economic elites have a privileged position in the policy process. In the case of economic development, this privileged position follows from both a control over significant social resources and the central interest of economic elites in such efforts. It is much less clear whether coalition efforts on human capital investment can be expected to sustain the same kind of long-term commitment by economic elites. This poses the general question: Can a policy regime be established without economic elites in a central role. Again no unambiguous answers are provided by these cases. But they do certainly suggest that, absent such economic elite engagement, the prospects for sustained reform are greatly reduced. Whether it is possible to craft alternative institutional structures, which would moderate the impact of their absence, is a question that remains, in our minds, unresolved.

Finally, our cases provide evidence about the confounding influence of race in civic capacity. Here our conclusions are clear. Race matters. Although each city has made a significant effort to downplay the direct importance of race, its impact is pervasive. In each city racial factors have made long-term collaboration on school reform more difficult. The impact of race is both direct and indirect. Most obvious are explicit racial distrust and struggle; obviously tradition makes it difficult to develop and sustain relationships. Cooperation is problematic even when issues are framed in a race-neutral manner because the potential of race being used as an overt symbol remains. When race is used as an overt political symbol, it is nearly impossible for African-American political leadership not to respond in some way. On-going political coalitions effectively become much less stable than they might seem. Race also sets barriers to white economic elites, parents, and other community actors who might otherwise want to engage in school-reform efforts.

The issue of how best to encourage widespread citizen participation around the issue of public education leaves us with a fundamental question in democratic theory. The need to confront the role of race does little, in and of itself, to help us see how this goal can be reached. Once again we need to stress that there is no simple or universal strategy. At a minimum, however, citizens must perceive that a platform for their participation exists, one on which their concerns and views are taken seriously. It also seems clear that meaningful participation must be more active than simple electoral politics. Political and community leaders must invest in an institutional framework that promotes a deeper level of engagement. Useful options range from traditional school-community organizations to nonprofit organizations created to promote citizen incorporation in local politics.[10]

It is important to recognize, however, that the future is far from hopeless. In each city we spoke with tireless workers and leaders, in and out of the classroom, who are committed to improving the quality of local education. In each city teachers, administrators, parents, community leaders, and business leaders have come together to support local education. Goodwill and dedication is not enough to guarantee a successful reform effort, but, absent such a commitment, success is quite unlikely. Moreover, we have seen examples of where policy change once enacted can have a positive impact. The task is clearly difficult, and whether local leaders can overcome the obstacles to such reform is certainly an open question. We wish them well.

[10] See Richard C. Hula, Cynthia Y. Jackson, and Marion Orr, "Urban Politics, Governing Nonprofits and Community Revitalization," *Urban Affairs Review* 32, no. 4 (1997): 459–89.

Tabb, David H., 6

Tate, Katherine, 144

teachers, Atlanta: absenteeism of, 136–37; pay levels for, 135–36

teachers' unions: as barriers to education reform, 116- 17, 152–53; demands of Atlanta's, 136; Michigan's attempt to reduce authority of, 265; power and influence of, 152; role in school politics, 127–37. *See also* Baltimore Teachers' Union (BTU); Detroit Federation of Teachers (DFT); Washington, D.C.

Toch, Thomas, 215–16

Toomey, D., 199

Trade Union Leadership Conference (TULC), Detroit, 38

Tucker, Cynthia, 116

Tyack, David, 152

University of Wisconsin, Madison, School Community Relations Group, 161

voucher program: support in Washington, D.C. for, 26, 254, 266

Washington, D.C.: black control of key positions in, 6, 35–36, 55–62; black ministers' role in school politics, 146–49; blacks in federal legislature, 267; business response to education problems, 226- 28; charter school legislation, 254; charter schools in, 266; congressional support for voucher program, 26; Council of School Officers (CSO) opposition to school reform, 133; education reforms (1988–1997), 74–82; effect of desegregation in, 42–44, 47–49; electing school board representatives (1968), 35; enclave schools, 198–201; Fannie Mae employee mentoring at Woodson High, 215, 220; financial mismanagement of school system, 69; Lawyers' Committee for Civil Rights Under law, 184–85; League for Universal Justice and Goodwill, 138; parent fund raising at school level, 199–200; parent organizations and community participation, 183–89; physical condition of schools, 67–68; proposed Center for Educational Change (CEC), 110; Public School Charter Board, 266; race as determinant of education quality, 42; racial transition in school system hierarchy, 52; rate of population loss among children (1960- 1990), 196; recent reform in education politics, 84; school board role in personnel hiring, 125; school desegregation, 47–50; school system patronage politics, 124; school system reform initiatives, 12–13; students' scholastic performance, 66–67, 70–71; transition to black political control, 35–36; voucher program, 26, 254, 266; Washington Teachers' Union (WTU), 133- 34; work of WPGF with PTAs, 201–2. *See also* Barry, Marion S.; Committee on Political Education (COPE); Congress; financial control board, Washington, D.C.; home rule, Washington, D.C.; school board, Washington, D.C.

Washington, Walter: as mayor of D.C., 33, 35

Washington (D.C.) Parent Group fund (WPGF), 201–2

Welch, Susan, 4

white flight: from D.C. (1970s), 53, 200; from Detroit, 54; effect of, 46

whites: control of levers of power in Baltimore, 39; decreased involvement in D.C. public schools (1970s), 53; economic power in Detroit, 39; public school attendance in black-led cities, 197

whites, Washington, D.C.: attention to local issues, 54; continued commitment to public schools, 53–54; perception of Barry, 36

Widick, B. J., 39

Wilcox, Preston, 156

Wildavsky, Aaron, 281–82

Williams, Gertrude, 94

Wilson, Willie, 148

Wong, Kenneth, 124

Yates, Douglas, 15

Young, Andrew: creates Task Force on Public Education, 168; as mayor of Atlanta, 37

Young, Coleman: actions as state senator in Detroit school system, 176; as mayor of Detroit, 38–39, 41, 54, 242

Young, Jean, 168